Matters of the Heart

TWO BOOKS IN ONE VOLUME

My Spiritual Inheritance

Juanita Bynum

Charisma
HOUSE
A STRANG COMPANY

Most Strang Communications/Charisma House/Siloam/Realms products are available at special quantity discounts for bulk purchase for sales promotions, premiums, fund-raising, and educational needs. For details, write Strang Communications/Charisma House/Siloam/Realms, 600 Rinehart Road, Lake Mary, Florida 32746, or telephone (407) 333-0600.

MATTERS OF THE HEART/MY SPIRITUAL INHERITANCE by Juanita Bynum
Published by Charisma House
A Strang Company
600 Rinehart Road
Lake Mary, Florida 32746
www.charismahouse.com

Unless otherwise noted, all Scripture quotations are from the Amplified Bible. Old Testament copyright © 1965, 1987 by the Zondervan Corporation. The Amplified New Testament copyright © 1954, 1958, 1987 by the Lockman Foundation. Used by permission.

Scripture quotations marked KJV are from the King James Version of the Bible.

Scripture quotations marked NIV are from the Holy Bible, New International Version. Copyright © 1973, 1978, 1984, International Bible Society. Used by permission.

Scripture quotations marked THE MESSAGE are from *The Message: The Bible in Contemporary English*, copyright © 1993, 1994, 1995, 1996, 2000, 2001, 2002. Used by permission of NavPress Publishing Group.

Cover design by Rachel Campbell

International Standard Book Number: 1-59185-923-9

Matters of the Heart previously published separately by Charisma House, ISBN 0-88419-832-4, copyright © 2002.

My Spiritual Inheritance previously published separately by Charisma House, ISBN 1-59185-412-1, copyright © 2004.

05 06 07 08 09 — 987654321

Printed in the United States of America

Book I

Matters of the Heart

of the

Heart

Juanita Bynum

Charisma
HOUSE
A STRANG COMPANY

To Mother Estella Boyd:

*Thank you for the impartation
of the new heart message.*

Contents
Matters of the *Heart*

Preface

If you believe in God, you already know that we are entering a new era. Things have stepped up in the third realm, and they are rapidly changing on earth. If you listen to God and have felt the "temperature" of the spirit realm steadily rise, this book will confirm to you what He has already spoken.

> O Judah, and ye inhabitants of Jerusalem; Believe in the LORD your God, so shall ye be established; believe his prophets, so shall ye prosper.
>
> —2 CHRONICLES 20:20, KJV

Hear me. It is time to seek God like never before. It is time to fall down at the altar and ask Him to renew your heart. It is time to become more like Jesus, *for real.* "Church as usual" is over. It is time to take off the "old wineskin" and put on the "new man." (See Matthew 9:16–17; Colossians 3:9–10.) God has been walking me through this process for several years.

As I began to write this book, I realized that I could only "birth" chapters as the Holy Spirit moved me—and say only what He had given me to say. So as you read on, understand that this is a work of the Spirit. God wants you to know that He is breathing a message through His prophet for this hour.

This birthing has been difficult, sometimes painful,

so I know it will not be easy for you to read or to digest. Why? It is spiritual "meat." It takes more "energy" to digest meat in the natural, and it is no different in the realm of the Spirit. You will have to work through the revelation, just as God led me to do. So take your time, chew every piece, and let it go down deep—because by the time you finish, a "new" work will have begun inside of you.

A Work of Obedience

In Acts 5:29 we read: "We must obey God rather than men."

Peter and the other apostles said this to the high priest after being arrested for preaching the gospel in Jerusalem and then being supernaturally set free by the angel of God. The religious leaders were perplexed, and they commanded the apostles never again to preach in Jesus' name. The apostles stood their ground. God had prepared them for that day. They had learned from walking with Jesus and were empowered by the Holy Spirit. Under intense persecution, they boldly stood for what God had called them to do. I have come to this same realization. If you let this Word go deep, so will you.

The prophetic call in this book will not "tickle" your ears. As a matter of fact, your flesh could become uncomfortable or even flare up before you discover the Truth that will set you free (John 8:32). Watch out! This Word is not meant to please the status quo or the religious elite. It is a Word for this hour, for those who are ready to *get real* with God—

and themselves. If your heart has been crying out for more, then get ready to move to the next level.

It takes more "energy" to digest meat in the natural, and it is no different in the realm of the Spirit.

Church, as we have known it, is over. Without realizing it, we have fallen into error—even while we have continued to do "good" things for God. We have tripped, stumbled and fallen in doing what He requires. Now God is sounding the charge. He is calling us to get back up:

> For a righteous man falls seven times and rises again, but the wicked are overthrown by calamity.
>
> —PROVERBS 24:16

God is crying out:

> Remember then from what heights you have fallen. Repent (change the inner man to meet God's will) and do the works you did previously [when you first knew the Lord], or else I will visit you and remove your lampstand from its place, unless you change your mind and repent.
>
> —REVELATION 2:5

Righteous one, God is calling you to turn! Get up, turn around and start walking in a new direction. God is calling for change from the inside out, whether you minister from the church platform, work in the nursery or sit in the pew. Change is necessary for all of God's people. Whether you are a pastor, lay minister, church member or missionary, God wants you to "divide" this Word, first to yourself, and then to others.

I have come to this same realization. If you let this Word go deep, so will you.

This book will give you revelation, information and inspiration to do just that. When you get to the scientific chapter on the heart, for example, you are going to be amazed at what God has already done inside of you! You will either shout "Hallelujah!" or fall to your knees. One way or the other, you are going to learn a few things that even I have never heard taught *anywhere* before. Then you will know exactly where you stand with God and how you have been built to walk in His ways. The choice is yours.

As you read, God will deposit something "new" inside of you if you ask for it. Receive and embrace this Word. Receive this prophetic call, and God will bless, strengthen and guide you in the days to come. Your heart will begin to turn in a new direction… and, like me, you will know that you can never turn back.

> Therefore if any person is [ingrafted] in Christ (the Messiah) he is a new creation (a new creature altogether); the old [previous moral and

spiritual condition] has passed away. Behold,
the fresh and new has come!

—2 CORINTHIANS 5:17

It is time to let go of the past. Let go of religion. Let
go of sin and anything that keeps you from drawing
close to God and obeying His prophetic cry for this
final hour.

Read on, and enter the new day.

Introduction

How It **All Began**

It happened unexpectedly. I knew that I was saved—born and raised in the church for that matter—so why was God birthing this "new heart" message in me? Didn't He know to whom He was talking? I had grown up in the ministry and then moved on into my own full-time ministry, so I was used to the routine. Certain things were just part of my personality...had been for many years. I didn't realize it at that moment, but it was time for a change.

Many of God's people think the way I thought. We assume that we operate from our personalities, that we have a certain style—a *modus operandi*—when really, it is a much deeper matter. In actuality, our preconceived thought patterns move us far away from God's character and from what He expects from us as His children.

It was difficult for me to receive this message about a new heart. I already had a major "platform" and was in the public eye. But that did not matter to God. Though it was painful and slow, I had to begin taking that deep, inner look. I needed to "internalize" my walk with God.

So many of us want to concentrate our efforts on our "overt" walk with the Lord, one where we are more interested in what others think than we are with what God thinks about us. We constantly try to "fix up" what people see about us.

Right before we held the Chicago Summit in May of 2000, God confronted me with this "new heart" message, and I ended up preaching it then—and since. Before the Chicago conference, we had held a summit in Pensacola, Florida—which did not turn out the way that I thought it should have. We had rented a ten-thousand-seat auditorium, and only about six to seven thousand attendees showed up. But it wasn't just the attendance; across the board the conference did not turn out the way that I had hoped. Immediately after that conference, I started carrying a burden—Pensacola had been unsuccessful.

As the date approached for the Chicago Summit, the Lord began to get my attention. We were planning to have the event in a beautiful church that seated forty-five hundred people. It was going to be impressive. You see, I was determined, because of what had "happened" in Pensacola, that I was going to make the Chicago Summit go over the top—everything was going to be just right.

Then I was hit with the unexpected. A couple of days before the conference, we ran into difficulties with the building and had to switch to another facility. It was not as big and was more difficult for the people to get to. As we made the last-minute switch, I found myself, again, going into turmoil. How could this happen? We had been fasting and praying for this meeting!

God began to deal with me. He started showing me that my "burden" was not for the people and what I felt they would receive. I was more concerned for *my image*, what I would project and what others were going to "read it" to be. I shut down. As I prayed, I remembered the day that my assistant, Tonya, had called me. Just as I pulled up to my garage, the phone rang and she explained why we were not going to be able to use the "beautiful" facility. When she was finished I hung up and began to weep.

As the tears rolled down my face, God said, "You are thinking like man. You are always concerned about the outward appearance. You are always trying to make that outward image look acceptable." He continued, "Jesus made Himself of no reputation... yet it is your reputation that has become most important to you. You are thinking about all that you are doing, the major platforms where you are able to speak and all the exposure that you are getting. But what is the condition of your heart toward Me and toward My people?"

I sat there in my driveway, confused, and said to the Lord, "My heart...? You know that everything I am doing, I am doing to please You."

He responded, "You are not doing what you can to please Me. You are doing what you can to please people. You are doing what you can to be accepted by people, so they can say, 'Oh, Juanita Bynum is really successful. Oh, she did a conference...'"

Then He began to show me how my burden for the Pensacola Summit was not really about whether the people had or had not been blessed. They were blessed. But the truth was that I had left that conference wondering, *What are people going to say because the auditorium was not filled? What are people going to say because this or that thing was not right? What are people going to say because the flyers looked homemade?*

God said, "Let Me show you some little things...," and He started surfacing things about my personality, things I had reasoned were "just me"—but really, they were errors in my heart. He said, "The sad thing is, you are so far away from Me. You are nowhere near Me, though you think that you are."

He took me to Ephesians 2:8, which says that we are not saved "by works." Then He continued, "You need to accept the fact that I am making you the 'righteousness of God.' You have been working under the assumption that all of your works have impressed Me, and *I am not impressed by any of it.*"

Finally He said, "The reason that I am not impressed is because you are so far away from the goal that I have set for you. You are racing, trying to 'make it happen' on a big scale in auditoriums and all of that. But what about the little, everyday people whom I put on your heart to be a blessing to? You have ignored *that* because you think nobody can see it."

God dealt with me as I sat there in my driveway. He said, "I want to give you a new heart."

"A new heart?" I asked. "But I already feel like I am saved."

"Your salvation is according to the salvation of the traditional church," He responded. "Now, I want to save you *for real.*"

A Real Conversion? A True Salvation?

~~❧~~

I was not expecting to receive a "new heart" message. I felt that I had given my heart to God when I was converted, but somewhere along the way it had gone into a dormant state. I began to operate from my "works," not from my heart. I am not even sure that I can explain or make sense of it, but I will try.

God saves and converts your spirit, which is where your heart is. Your mind, on the other hand, resists being transformed. If your mind is not transformed, then the miracle "heart" that God has placed in you will never be able to manifest in your lifestyle. This is because your mind, which is comprised of your soulish emotions and intellect, wants to run and rule. When the new heart is neglected, the mind assumes control through the old, carnal nature. That is what happened to me.

I knew that I had accepted Christ as my personal Savior. My spirit man, or my heart, was converted, and I began to get into the Word. You see, I wanted to transform my mind so that my life could begin to experience what had happened in my heart. Then somewhere along the line, I started reading the Word of God to prepare me to preach the gospel—not to convert my own mind.

When I began doing this, even though I was preaching a powerful gospel, I was having difficulties and struggles in my personal life, constantly warring against the flesh. My mind warred against my heart, and my heart warred against my mind. I could never seem to bring my thoughts and emotions under subjection to my converted heart.

My ministry became my career, and even though I knew that I had been called to preach, I believe it was God's compassion for His people that kept me there. Hear me. When God's people cried out in the Old Testament, He would supply what they needed because He had heard their cry. His heart is tender toward His people. So when I said to Him that I was willing to "go," and there was a cry from His people, He anointed me and used me in His work.

Yet God loved me so much that He said, "While you are preaching to others, I do not want to forget about you."

The True Heart Revealed

The Lord took me to Jeremiah 17:9–10, where He said:

> The heart is deceitful above all things, and it is exceedingly perverse and corrupt and severely, mortally sick! Who can know it [perceive, understand, be acquainted with his own heart and mind]? I the Lord search the mind, I try the heart, even to give to every man according to his ways, according to the fruit of his doings.

God had tried my heart, and I had failed the test. As a result, in all the good that I was doing, my heart still wore the core of wickedness.

If we are not careful, we can be doing a religious work and still be backslidden in our hearts. We can do this without realizing it, either because our works are so *wonderful* or because the responses our works are getting are so *wonderful*. We may even feel God's anointing and presence upon our works, which can, in itself, become a deception. How? Our works can be so "good" that we never stop to recheck our heart to see if it is found in right standing with God.

Regardless of everything I do—the preaching, the singing and all of the ministering—I am still human just like anyone else. Recently God told me, "I want you to turn off the music...turn off all the preaching tapes...be alone with yourself and see what comes out of your mind. Then you will know what state you are in. If you do this, you will be surprised what you hear yourself saying."

I had to be honest with myself and realize that my heart was not right. What I really said to myself, and what is hard for me to say even now, is, "Am I really saved?" I am not talking about a "hallelujah" experience. I had to ask, "*Am I really saved?* Does Jesus really live here? Am I sure, beyond the shadow of a doubt, that He lives in me? I do not have any doubt that He uses me...but does Jesus live here? Am I His?"

As God began to minister to me about a new heart, He took me to John 10:24–26, which says:

> So the Jews surrounded Him and began asking Him, How long are You going to keep us in doubt and suspense? If You are really the Christ (the Messiah), tell us so plainly and openly. Jesus answered them, I have told you so, yet you do not believe Me [you do not trust Me and rely on Me]. The very works that I do by the power of My Father and in My Father's name bear witness concerning Me [they are My

credentials and evidence in support of Me]. But
you do not believe and trust and rely on Me
because you do not belong to My fold [you are
no sheep of Mine].

It was like I experienced an awakening. The Lord
said, "Do you not know that when you constantly
walk in rebellion to the things that I tell you to do…
and the things that I say *no* to…and things you know
I am displeased with…and you keep doing it, contin-
uing in that way, that is when you have to ask yourself, 'Am I really His?'"

When I heard God tell me that, I remembered
John 10:4–5, which, in essence says, "My sheep
know My voice, and a stranger they will not follow."

The Lord continued speaking to me, saying, "If you
continue to go in this direction and to think that way,
then I cannot be there. I can't be there if you continue to think that everybody owes you something. If
you respond to others by thinking, *Oh, these people
offended me. I can't stand that one. I do not like her.
I am not speaking to this one over here,* I cannot be
there. If you travel all over the country, yet continue
to feel that way, I won't be there. I am not talking
about a sporadic thought pattern—I am talking about
that constant discord in your heart. If you continue
in that discord, then I cannot be there."

Hear this message that God gave to me. Sin and
God cannot dwell in the same heart at the same time.
Righteousness and unrighteousness cannot dwell in
the same temple. I am talking about your heart.
Thought patterns can emerge in your mind because
it has to be transformed. But when all the stuff that
goes on in your mind becomes a continuous rotation,

and it comes out in your behavior, then *are you really saved?*

We Must Receive a New Heart

~~~

You may wonder what happened at the point of conversion when you came up to the altar to be saved from your sinful nature. Was your heart truly converted? What happens to your heart at the moment of repentance?

We can look at the example of King David, a man after God's own heart. When he reached his moment of repentance and asked God to forgive him for his sins, he said, "Create in me a clean heart, O God, and renew a right, persevering, and steadfast spirit within me" (Ps. 51:10). That is exactly what took place right at that moment you asked Him to forgive you of your sins. He created a clean heart in you and renewed a right spirit within you. Within your heart your spirit *sits*.

It is your "old mind" that keeps you functioning outside of the will of God. Your mind needs to be transformed constantly by a process of renewing. (I will go into more detail about the renewing of your mind in chapter nine.)

In Romans 12:2 we read, "Do not be conformed to this world…" Whatever you do now, it should not conform to this world's way of thinking. In order to be transformed, you must renew your mind *every day*. When the renewed mind lines up with the conversion that is in your heart, you are a new creature—completely inside and out.

The only way your renewed mind can fail to come into harmony with your new heart is by your choice. You must choose whether to follow the stubborn habits that are stored in your memories or to submit to the wisdom that flows out of your new heart.

The most important thing is to have the new heart and to know that you know— *you have it*.

When God gave me that revelation as I sat in my car, I began asking, "God, give me a clean heart. Give me a new heart, right now. Save me all over again, right now. Save me, right here in this car, until I know that I am saved." I cried out, "Save me, Jesus!" just as I did when I first got saved.

Immediately, an old hymn came up in my spirit:

> Give me a clean heart, so I may serve Thee, Lord.
> Cleanse my heart, so that I may be used by Thee.
> Lord, I am not worthy of all these blessings,
> But give me a clean heart…[1]

A New Heart…a New Life

By the time I arrived in Chicago, everybody saw it— I was renewed. I was a new person. *Brand-new*. It was an experience that I had never had before in my Christian walk. I cannot put words to it. Suddenly, preaching, television, major platforms and all those wonderful things became secondary. Since May 2000, the first thing on my list has been making sure that everything I do pleases God. Now, for every thought pattern I ask, "Where did that thought come from?" If it is not a thought from my renewed mind, I say, "No! I rebuke that right now."

Since that life-changing encounter with God, I became the custodian of my own heart. Caring for my new heart is my major job right now.

Don't Be Lost in the Church

Since that time, I have also been compelled to give someone else the same opportunity—the opportunity to get saved *for real*. Yes, I mean it. God has birthed a "new heart" message in me!

Since it became my own experience, I have felt like I need to tell the world! I have to tell the nations what I found out. I have to tell the world about this new heart. I have to tell them that they must make sure they get it…that, above all—*everything*—it is vital to have this new heart. The most important thing is to have the new heart—and to know that *you have it*.

The scary thing is, I had gone a long time not knowing the state that I was in because my works were so wonderful. Every time I think about it, I am amazed how I could help others find the way to Christ while I was lost in the church! I shake when I think that I could have gone to hell from major platforms.

I want to make this clear. We must all come to a

place where we either admit that we do not have a new heart or that we have mastered the *act* of salvation and become the *great pretenders*. Let me give you an example. Suppose someone tells you, "When you are saved, you are supposed to love Sister Watermelon." So you speak to Sister Watermelon and hug her; you do the saved "act," but in your heart, you cannot stand her.

What has happened to the church across the board is that we have become men pleasers. We have taught each other to master the church "act." Everybody looks saved; we know how to act saved; we know how to do saved stuff; and we know how to project saved. But our hearts are far from it—we are not even close.

We think, *Now that I am sanctified, I do not want to be "looked down upon" or "scorned." I do not want to be out of relationship with my pastor, so I am going to come to church, "like he said."* But in reality, our hearts are far from the church—we are not even there.

A person who maintains the reins of his heart and controls the patterns of his mind impresses God.

We are the great pretenders. To all who fit into that category, one day Jesus will say: "You say you have cast out devils in My name and have healed the sick in My name—but begone from Me; I never knew you." (See Matthew 25:41.) *Don't let Him say that to you!*

What Jesus means is this: "I never had a relation-ship with YOU. You worked for Me, but I did not have a relationship with you."

One day Jesus' disciples came running back to Him, saying, "Lord, even the devils are subject unto us through thy name" (Luke 10:17, KJV).

Jesus replied:

> Rejoice not, that the spirits are subject unto you; but rather rejoice, *because your names are written in heaven.*
>   —LUKE 10:20, KJV, EMPHASIS ADDED

Right from the beginning, Jesus was letting them know: "Do not get high about what happens in My name. You had better be high about the fact that your name is written in the Lamb's Book of Life." Right there, He set the priority. He said, "I am not impressed with spirits that are subject to you. All that you say you just did—great, but be impressed that you are saved. Then I am impressed." A person who maintains the reins of his heart and controls the patterns of his mind impresses God.

A New Birth…a New Mandate

God birthed the "new heart" message in me, and since that time, everything that I have preached on major platforms—anywhere that I have preached—I have *experienced* it. I have not experienced any-thing greater.

Everybody thought my book *No More Sheets* was an awesome message. It went to thousands, yes millions, of people. I preached that message because I had experienced it, but let me say again, I have not experienced anything greater than when God gave me a "new heart."

I have a mandate from God to preach this message. "A mandate?" you might ask. Yes, because I believe that of all the messages I have ever preached, this will be the greatest—regardless of whether or not it is recognized as such by man. The "new heart" was Jesus' greatest message. It is the Bible's greatest story. In all of Scripture, that with which God is most concerned is this vital truth—*the matters of the heart*.

Chapter 1

We Need a **New Heart**

Yes, we have a problem. Jeremiah 17 says that the heart is desperately wicked and "deceitful above all things...Who can know it" (v. 9). Yet before we can begin to look at this problem of the deceitful heart, we need to address another problem—an issue that has been part of Christendom for generations.

The Impossible Dream

God has brought me into relationship with a few secular people. In other words, they are not saved, and they do not go to church. They were, however, born and raised in the church. In my witnessing to them, one of them said to me, "We look over into Christendom and see either people who are very dogmatic about what they believe or who are so shallow in their beliefs that it is hard to accept that God can stabilize a person's life."

That surprised me. I was amazed, first, that he would even say it, and second, that he had made a valid point. Then this gentleman made a statement

1

that knocked me off my feet: "If you can find a way," he said, "if somebody in Christendom can find a way to make living for God attainable and reachable, then you do not know how many people would come to Christ."

I do not believe his standpoint was that the church should teach mediocrity. It struck a note inside of me concerning the Word that God had spoken to me about the new heart. While we were talking, I began to reflect about this new heart, and I remembered the reason why God had prompted me to write this message.

Take Me Back...

I had first heard about the new heart from Mother Estella Boyd, a powerful woman of God from Detroit. A lot of people know Mother Boyd and how powerful she is in the Spirit. There are times that she would say "deep" things, things that would scare me, because she ministers and speaks revelation from the third realm.

One night I was in a church meeting that Mother Boyd was leading. On this particular night, we were in one of those "afterglow" services (that is what we call it when we have had church and the power of God has fallen, leaving everyone kneeling and prostrate all over the place, praising God and wiped out—lying there in the presence of the Lord or sitting still in His presence), Mother Boyd spoke out, "We gonna be alright when we get that new heart." Half of us were on the floor or resting in the pews, clothing disheveled and hair out of place after persevering in worship during the service that night. It was unsettling to hear Mother Boyd telling us that we needed a "new heart" and that we would be all right when we got it. It was five years ago that Mother Boyd spoke that Word, and it has never left my spirit.

At some point I stored it away in the deep part of my mind, thinking to myself, *You know what? That is deep.* When I was first saved I believed that if I just kept working at it—kept letting God do what He was going to do in me—eventually, He would "fix" my heart. So I had learned to stash away such revelations deep within my mind so God could somehow just use that information to do His "fix" on me.

Mother Boyd's words about the new heart had really stung me, and they were always there in my mind, just deep enough that I never forgot them. Yet I never acted upon them. Then after my experience in Chicago in May of 2000, I started "guarding" my heart. But I did not begin to pursue the "new heart" until almost a year later, sometime around January 2001.

That day when the gentleman suggested to me that people were looking for a God who was attainable and reachable, I asked myself, "Is God attainable?" I realized I could not answer that question. But I stood there trying to figure out how and why the Lord had brought back to my memory His earlier message to me as I sat in my driveway about the "new heart."

Why is this happening? I thought. I did not understand exactly what the Lord was doing.

Time to Walk Out the Problem

I began to question God about this new heart. I felt strange, like some kind of cancer was eating away at me, something that I could not shake off. I knew that I was getting some signals from God. Not only would I preach this message—I was about to learn how to "walk it out."

I realized that since the night I first heard Mother Boyd speak about a new heart, I had felt as if I were falling all over myself trying to understand what she meant. I had to come to terms with God and with myself.

I started to observe people in ministry. I looked at the church—perfectly structured. I saw the choirs dressed in beautiful robes and the praise and worship teams with their matching outfits. One pastor would have on a nice Versace suit and tie, and his wife would be sitting there with a St. John knit on—it all looked so perfect. It oozed "spiritual perfection" to the point that it became a problem for me.

The more I looked at the *problem*, the more I was forced to turn around and look within myself at my own situation. "OK, Juanita," I said to myself, "what is your problem? What is it that bothers you about this *so-called* walk with the Lord?" I began to examine this, and I remembered the lives of people who had stood before me throughout the years. I almost felt like a mouse that was chasing a piece of cheese, one it will never catch because it is tied to a cat's tail. That cat was running me all over the building! I could smell the cheese; I could come near the cheese; but I could never get a grip on the cheese because the cat was always moving.

So I said, "What is *my* problem?" I realized that through the years my problem had been my own feelings of spiritual inadequacy. I would look at my spiritual superiors and think to myself, *I can never become that. I can never be like Mother Boyd. I cannot ever be like Bishop Stacks. I could never be like the many people that God has placed in my life as spiritual examples.* I felt that I could never be like them because they were the epitome of spiritual perfection. Their status, to me, was *unattainable*.

When we pursue the "image" of perfection, we cannot strive to understand the heart of God.

Once I started my ministry, God helped me to realize the error of my heart. People began to come up to me and say, "Prophetess Bynum, you are such a blessing." "Prophetess Bynum, you have really blessed my life. You are such a woman of God."

Yet during that time there were areas in my life where God was still dealing with me. God was breaking some things in me and breaking other things *off* me. In other people's sight, my own image had become *unattainable*, but that was not reality. God began dealing intensely with me about my need to preach the "new heart" message.

If we consistently paint a picture that everything is perfect, beautiful and wonderful—"You know you

have reached God when you look like me...dress like
me...walk and talk like me"—then we have totally
missed God! We have become a group of people who
constantly pursue an image—not God! Is this reality?
When we pursue the "image" of perfection, we cannot
strive to understand the heart of God.

Who is trying to understand what God requires of
us? Who is trying to understand that our life in
Christ, though part of Christendom, is founded on an
individual relationship that each one of us must have
with the Lord...alone?

The Brain Has Assumed Control

When I began to understand the basic truth God was
birthing in me about the new heart, I started to
understand that the heart is "desperately wicked."

We are all struggling in our own way, trying to
make sure that we "do right" from our heart.
Through my study, I discovered that this world has
become a brain world. It functions from the activities of the brain, out of the intellect of our finite
brains. We are consumed with brain knowledge, and
because we are consumed with this knowledge, our
lives are constantly being constructed and operated
by the laws of the intellect. What that means is this:
If you do me wrong, then my intellect (based on the
information that I have gathered from you) reacts
and says, "I am going to do you wrong."

The brain teaches us how to scheme, lie, connive
and manipulate. Here is the truth. God has put a
spirit of conviction in our hearts, which corrects us

when we do something wrong. The world, however, has trained us to bypass our heart's conviction and to operate within the realm of our mind and emotions. For this reason, we have a chaotic world.

This is also the reason why no one is seeking after God for a changed, *new heart*. We do not want to change; we only want to feel better—for the moment. In order to get *eternal* gratification, we have to give up something *right now*.

My mother used to say, "You know that you are growing when you give up your right to 'be right.'" You are maturing when you are the first to apologize, the first to keep the peace, when you are the first to say, "What did I do wrong?" rather than nailing the other person to the wall for what they did to you. You evaluate yourself and say, "What did I do to that person? Was there something that I did to provoke his or her response?" When you look at the issue this way, then you can overcome a situation that has stagnated our society.

In order to get *eternal* gratification, we have to give up something *right now*.

Everybody is moved by their emotions through their *logical* minds, which always look out for "Number 1." Emotions and logic react to the "threats" they perceive around them—everybody else is always wrong. This is how the "old heart" rules. It is the reason power struggles are so prevalent in our world.

What Does the Bible Say About It?

The Bible says that we are born in sin and shaped in iniquity (Ps. 51:5). We are born with an "old heart" nature that is already *coated* with the potential to do wrong. When we come into the world, our hearts are already shaped for this sin.

Iniquity is anything you do that God is not in. It is anything done against the will of God or against the laws or nature of God. If something is contrary to His character, it is iniquity. You have been shaped in that area by what society has taught you.

Because your heart is composed of the potential to sin, your mind is gradually trained to become a professional sinner. When your heart and mind "match up" in the spirit, then you have the heart described in Jeremiah 17:9 as "desperately wicked" (KJV). It is desperately deceitful...who can know it? Who can understand the depths of that heart?

How do I know that what I am saying is correct? In Deuteronomy 8:11–14 we read:

> Beware that you do not forget the Lord your God by not keeping His commandments, His precepts, and His statutes which I command you today, lest when you have eaten and are full, and have built goodly houses and live in them, and when your herds and flocks multiply and your silver and gold is multiplied and all you have is multiplied, then your [minds and] hearts be lifted up and you forget the Lord your God, Who brought you out of the land of Egypt, out of the house of bondage.

When you look at our society, you see that this is true—and I am not just talking about the secular world; I am talking about the church! We are in church, dancing and shouting and speaking in tongues, yet we have hearts of iniquity just like the world. How do I know this? Our barns are filled, our flocks are fed, our herds are gathered, and we have multiplied. We have built houses, and we have multiplied our strength. Our silver has been multiplied, our gold has been multiplied, and now our minds and our hearts are lifted up—against God and against each other—full of pride. We have forgotten the Lord.

It took the disaster of September 11 to bring a "seek" back into this country. It took this attack and the fear of ongoing terrorist attacks from another country to bring us to our knees. It took this incident to help us realize that in spite of all the cars, houses and everything we have, we need the Lord. Before September 11, our hearts and minds had left the Lord. We were not seeking Him. When we walk with hearts that are "shaped in iniquity," hearts that are born into sin, seeking the Lord is not important in them. This kind of heart does not come with a "Yes, Lord," in it.

What Is Our First Priority?

We have a people and a church society that are doing everything they possibly can to walk in the ways of God. But Deuteronomy 10:12 says that there is no way to walk in the ways of God unless you fear the Lord and love Him "with all thy heart and with all thy soul" (KJV).

In this scripture the word *soul* indicates all of your mind and all of your emotions.[1] Thus you cannot walk in God's ways unless you fear Him as God— with a fear unto obedience, not a fear that tries to escape Him—a fear that submits to Him, totally and completely. Above this, you cannot walk in His ways unless, *number one*, you love Him from the center of your being, your heart.

When you say, "I love You, Lord," but still walk in your own ways, then you do not really love the Lord.

So how can this "old heart," which was "born in sin" and "shaped in iniquity," love God? Real love cannot come out of this heart. Only a *phileo* kind of love (which means the natural human affection, with its strong feeling, or sentiment) can come from a wicked heart.[2] *Agape* love (unconditional and eternal) is never found in our "old hearts." The only way that you can truly love God is to love Him with the same love that He has given to you. It has to match in the third realm. You cannot love God from an earthly level, because God is eternal, and it can never work to love Him from an earthly perspective.

Anything that is of the earth is temporal. That is why 2 Corinthians 4:18 says, "...we consider and look not to the things that are seen...for the things that are visible are temporal..." Those things never last. We must look toward the things that are eternal, because only these things will endure throughout eternity. Whether you realize it or not, you have already been "built" to see the eternal—the choice is yours.

Loving God brings about a commitment to Him. When you love somebody, you are committed to him in every way. There is nothing that you will not do for someone you love. You would be willing to lay down your life for your loved one. So when you say, "I love You, Lord," but still walk in your own ways, then you do not really love the Lord. You are still going about in your "religious affairs," and you do not have a real relationship with Him, which will bring about a change of character and a change in the way you walk. A real relationship with Him enables you to walk in His commandments.

If you do not have a real relationship with Him, then you merely "appreciate" Him for the life and breath that He has given you. You are grateful for the way He makes for you out of no way and for all the things He permits you to have. But you are still operating from a materialistic standpoint—and that is not real love. It cannot become real until you become committed and submitted to *His ways*.

The Deception of Prosperity

We must learn to deal with the deception of prosperity. We can find ourselves saying things like this: "I feel so much love for the Lord because of all the things He has blessed me with." Beware of the deception that can come with the prosperity of God's blessing upon our lives. God told the children of Israel:

> And you shall [earnestly] remember all the way which the Lord your God led you these forty years in the wilderness, to humble you and to prove you, to know what was in your [mind and] heart, whether you would keep His commandments or not.
>
> —DEUTERONOMY 8:2

God has allowed us to look upon the example of the children of Israel in the wilderness so that we could learn from their experiences. Just as He needed to humble the Israelites and create a spiritual hunger within them, so too He has "humbled" us and "allowed you to hunger" (v. 3). We see that God:

> ...fed you with manna, which you did not know nor did your fathers know, that He might make you recognize and personally know that man does not live by bread only, but man lives by every word that proceeds out of the mouth of the Lord.

I believe that God has allowed not just the secular world, but also the church, to go the "way" that we have gone to prove to us that we really do not love Him. He has done this to "try" us and to see what is really in our hearts and minds. The problem we face today, which is a huge problem and a mighty task, is that we, God's people, must ask for a new heart.

The problem becomes finding a people willing to do

this. We have to plow deeply into the church system to find people who are crying to God…a remnant sitting in the body of Christ in this hour that is willing to say, "I have to have the heart of God. I have to have a new heart. I have to be able to have a real relationship with God outside of the pews, outside of the choir roll, outside of my favorite preacher or evangelist. How do I get back to God—simply God?" Simply God, without all the props. Simply God, without all the drama. Where does this relationship start? How does it begin? What is the real purpose of your relationship with God?

The problem that we face today, which is a huge problem and a mighty task, is that we, God's people, must ask for a new heart.

Having taken a deep look at the church, the instrument God uses to draw people into His kingdom, I have to ask this question: How can the church do the work of the Spirit—not just the work of Christendom—to the point that she has the power to be as compassionate as Christ Himself? Where will we find the eternal love we need to embrace the kind of sinners who are coming to Christ in this hour? How can we work for God when our hearts are far from Him, when we do not know who He is?

The Deception of Religion

~~~~~~

As a prophet I look at Solomon's example and am concerned about the longevity of the church. If we, the church, do not make this switch—the switch from being a religious organization to having a relationship with our Father—in the twenty-first century, then we are going to fail in our efforts. We will not be able to accomplish what God has given us to do.

King Solomon inherited the kingdom of his father, David, and was handed the plans of the tabernacle that David had earnestly desired to build. Yet in 1 Kings 11:3, we discover that "…his wives turned away his heart from God." Even though he began his reign over Israel by seeking God's wisdom, and even though he built the temple of God, his kingdom became little more than a religious organization—and he lost his relationship with his Father God. We discover that he even followed his foreign, idolatrous wives into the worship of false gods, building temples of worship to these gods (v. 8). As a result:

> The Lord was angry with Solomon because his heart was turned from the Lord, the God of Israel.
>
> —1 Kings 11:9

King Solomon failed to receive his new heart. Just as it was with Solomon, I believe God's anger is kindled against us when He sees the way we are being drawn into worldly change, causing us to turn from Him and to begin walking in the way of the world around us.

Like Solomon we do not even realize that our

hearts are being drawn away. We may even say, "I've been religious all my life. Do I really need a new heart? Why would God be angry with me?" We may have walked closely with God in the past and, like Solomon, may have even prayed for His wisdom to guide our steps. Verse 9 goes on to tell us that God had already appeared to Solomon and commanded him that he should not go after other gods! However, Solomon did not do what the Lord had commanded. His disobedience kindled the anger of God:

> Therefore the Lord said to Solomon, Because you are doing this and have not kept My covenant and My statutes, which I have commanded you, I will surely rend the kingdom from you and will give it to your servant!
>
> —1 KINGS 11:11

This is a powerful revelation—one that carries great significance for us. God has been forewarning the church structure for many years, saying, "Get this thing together; get this thing in order. I want you to provoke My people to come after My heart, to provoke My people unto righteousness."

Even now, God is starting to put His Word into the mouths of people outside the church walls. People outside of the church "organization"—hippies, secular artists and others—are rising up and leading God's people! They were not born and raised in the church; they knew nothing about God, but through divine impartation God is teaching them. God is using these "slaves of this world," people functioning in a "servant's status," instead of the disobedient "sons and daughters" in organized religion.

We in the church have considered ourselves to be "structured" and "mighty." We think that we have all of the answers. We have an appearance of God—but because we have not turned our hearts toward Him, we are leaving Him with no option. We are leaving God with no other choice except to reach out, get the heathen and raise them up. They are the ones who have received the new heart. They are teaching people to come to Him.

This problem affects not only the church, but also the world. Like Solomon, many believers have prosperity in their own eyes. They have built mighty temples to God, just as Solomon had done. They have received the accolades of men. But it is at this very point of "self" success that the heart can be in its greatest form of deception.

Then the world cannot see Jesus, nor can people come to Him.

Why? Because, without realizing it, these leaders have come to expect others to praise their works. They have become people pleasers. They have forgotten that as God's children they have been called to carry the image of Christ—that of a servant to others.

> And whoever desires to be first among you must be your slave—just as the Son of Man came not to be waited on but to serve, and to give His life as a ransom for many [the price paid to set them free].
>
> —MATTHEW 20:27–28

When we forget that we are here to serve, not to be served, the cycle of deception is in full swing. Then the world cannot see Jesus, nor can people come to Him.

Yes, church, we have a problem...and this is just the beginning.

Chapter 2

We Have an
Inside-Out Problem

God continued to unfold His revelation about a new heart as He taught me about the training base for the spirit of iniquity—our brain. The brain is the "computer" that gathers data from the world into this "character training center."

As I examined the role our brain plays in turning our hearts from God, I began to understand why everyone in our society learns to blame his or her shortcomings and lifestyle on somebody else. The easiest thing for the mind to do is to push blame toward another person.

When confronted with our own wickedness, it is so easy for us to say, "Well, I am evil because this or that happened to me," or "I am this way because that thing happened to me." Let's take a closer look at the spiritual side of the brain's training center. Psalm 51:5 records David's words:

> Behold, I was shapen in iniquity; and in sin did my mother conceive me.
>
> —KJV

No matter how a person comes into this world, and even though that person may be "morally good," the nature of sin hovers over that person's heart because it operates within the cold, carnal nature.

The easiest thing for the mind to do is to push blame toward another person.

Sin is manifested and activated as a result of the information that is fed into our sin nature from the world, via the "old heart" and the brain. When that sin information reaches the heart, it connects with the cold, carnal area in the heart. There the brain rationalizes that information as being "acceptable." From this union of our old, carnal heart with our brain, we manifest that information as an act of sin. Thus we become "sinners." From this, we are shaped in iniquity, shaped and raised up to walk in an era of disobedience toward God.

Mark 7:16–18 says:

> If any man has ears to hear, let him be listening [and let him perceive and comprehend by hearing]. And when He had left the crowd and had gone into the house, His disciples began asking Him about the parable. And He said to them, Then are you also unintelligent and dull and without understanding? Do you not discern and see that whatever goes into a man from the outside cannot make him unhallowed or unclean...

What comes into you from the outside is not what makes you unholy! Mark continues his explanation by saying:

> And He said, What comes out of a man is what makes a man unclean and renders [him] unhallowed. For from within, [that is] out of the hearts of men, come base and wicked thoughts, sexual immorality, stealing, murder, adultery, coveting (a greedy desire to have more wealth), dangerous and destructive wickedness, deceit; unrestrained (indecent) conduct; an evil eye (envy), slander (evil speaking, malicious misrepresentation, abusiveness), pride (the sin of an uplifted heart against God and man), foolishness (folly, lack of sense, recklessness, thoughtlessness). All these evil [purposes and desires] come from within, and they make the man unclean and render him unhallowed.
>
> —MARK 7:20–23

Is this God's choice? No! In the Garden of Eden we chose our own destiny. (See Genesis 3:1–24.) The Book of James goes on to explain further.

> Let no one say when he is tempted, I am tempted from God; for God is incapable of being tempted by [what is] evil and He Himself tempts no one. But every person is tempted when he is drawn away, enticed and baited by his own evil desire (lust, passions). Then the evil desire, when it has conceived, gives birth to sin, and sin, when it is fully matured, brings forth death.
>
> —JAMES 1:13–15

Our Problem Is Inside Out

The world—and part of the church—is crying out, but our problem always seems to be someone else's fault. Before you will see your own need, you must be confronted—just as I was—with the reality of what God is saying. The problem is not what is entering your life from external sources. It is not the fault of what is taking place around you. Those things that come "at you" from external sources are merely identifying with something that is already in your heart.

If the outside "problem" finds a place of identification, a familiar spirit, inside of you, then you absolutely, no doubt about it, need to be transformed. You need the "new heart." Jeremiah 17:9 says, "The heart is deceitful above all things, and it is exceedingly perverse and corrupt and severely, mortally sick! Who can know it [perceive, understand, be acquainted with his own heart and mind]?"

The heart determines whether or not you enter the kingdom of God.

Is this verse talking about someone who deals with "little ill feelings" against someone else? What kind of heart is this verse talking about? Why is the church in the position now of not realizing we need a new heart? Why do we feel that by getting our outward appearance "right," we are getting somewhere with God?

It is because man looks outside, but God looks within—at the heart. It is our hearts that God is coming back for—nothing else. The heart—not the mind—determines whether or not you enter the kingdom of God.

We should not be concerned with outer things. We should focus on what is inside. When we get the "inside" to line up with God's Word, we will change! God will give us a new heart, and this heart will begin to manifest on the outer man just as the old heart works from the inside out.

What Is Our Old Heart Like?

What about our old heart? Is it simply a "poor, little, confused, messed-up heart"? We can begin to understand the condition of our old heart by taking a closer look at Jeremiah 17:9.

> The heart is deceitful above all things, and it is exceedingly perverse and corrupt and severely, mortally sick! Who can know it [perceive, understand, be acquainted with his own heart and mind]?

In this verse the word *deceitful* means, "to mislead by a false appearance or statement; to trick." We must recognize, first and foremost, that *God* called the old heart "deceitful above all things." It does not matter how much you try…how many Bible studies you attend…or what Bible classes you take. I do not care how many times you say, "If I can just go to church and sing in the choir, everything will be all right."

No! Remember that this wicked heart not only misleads people, it *misleads YOU*. This heart gives a false appearance, not just to people, but also to YOU. It makes you think, *Because I look right, I am right.*

But there is another definition for the word *deceitful* that startled me—it also means, "to be unfaithful." The saddest fact about this heart—and again, shockingly so—is that it is "unfaithful." It can never be dedicated to God. It can never keep a commitment. Maybe this is the reason why people constantly move in and out of relationships, or why the divorce rate is so high. Perhaps it is the reason why so many children are living in orphanages, or why prostitution is rampant. Maybe it is even why is there such a lack of integrity in the body of Christ. This deceitful heart does not have what it takes to be faithful to anything—God or man.

The word *perverse* means that this heart is "willfully determined *not* to do what is expected or desired." It is "turned away from what is right, good or proper." This heart already has a willful desire built into its mechanism *not* to perform what is expected or desired.

For example, when we teach or minister from the Word of God and expect that, as a result, people will behave in a certain way, we are appalled when they do not walk in this light. We expect them to be different, but if the heart within them is like the heart described in Jeremiah 17, it does not have the capacity to be "penetrated" by the Word! It is already full—of deceit! It comes with a built-in will that says, "I will not yield to God. I will not obey the things of God." Rebellion is already part of the makeup of the old heart. The old heart's nature is to go in the opposite direction of where God has sent it.

So when this heart hears the Word of God, it sits dormant in the sanctuary. The mind may "hear" the Word, yet the heart remains unchanged. Why? You need a "new heart" to receive and walk in the ways of God!

This deceitful heart does not have what it takes to be faithful to anything— God or man.

The verse in Jeremiah also calls the old heart "perverse and corrupt and severely, mortally sick." Not just mortally sick—*severely*, mortally sick. The word *severely* means, "grave, critical or harsh." It is "of extreme, intense violence in character and nature." This heart destroys everything that it touches. It can act "seemingly" for a little while, but this heart eventually tears up relationships. It is harsh, not kind. This heart will lead you to your grave. It is a heart of detriment that will literally steal your life away.

Since its nature and character are violent, you cannot correct it. When confronting people with an "old heart," you can expect rebellion and a harsh and violent reaction—in both attitude and conversation.

The verse says, "Who can know it [perceive, understand, be acquainted with his own heart and mind]?" *Acquainted with his own heart...* When you look up the word *acquainted,* you will discover that this phrase means, "Who is familiar enough with his own heart to furnish it with knowledge?" This is powerful. Who knows the depths of his heart to the degree that he can furnish this heart with the knowledge it will take to walk toward God? No man does. God tells us in Jeremiah 17:10:

> I the Lord search the mind, I try the heart, even to give to every man according to his ways, according to the fruit of his doings.

What are these "doings"? I believe that as God searches the heart and mind, He is going to give us the fruits of the "doings" listed in Mark 7, those unclean things that come out of our old hearts. (See Mark 7:20–23.) Yes, we have a real problem.

The Insensitive Heart of Man

The Bible says in Matthew 13:15:

> For this nation's heart has grown gross (fat and dull), and their ears heavy and difficult of hearing, and their eyes they have tightly closed, lest they see and perceive with their eyes, and hear and comprehend the sense with their ears, and grasp and understand with their heart, and turn and I should heal them.

Ephesians 4:17 adds:

> So this I say and solemnly testify in [the name of] the Lord [as in His presence], that you must

no longer live as the heathen (the Gentiles) do in their perverseness [in the folly, vanity, and emptiness of their souls and the futility] of their minds.

The word *futility* means that worldly minds are "incapable of producing any result...ineffective, useless and unsuccessful." People who operate from their soulish realm, through their minds, are incapable of producing anything of eternal value.

> Their moral understanding is darkened and their reasoning is beclouded. [They are] alienated (estranged, self-banished) from the life of God [with no share in it; this is] because of the ignorance (the want of knowledge and perception, the willful blindness) that is deep-seated in them, due to their hardness of heart [to the insensitiveness of their moral nature].
> —EPHESIANS 4:18

Can you see what this is saying? These ignorant minds want knowledge, but only according to their own perception. They have chosen to be blind; it is deep-seated in them due to their "...hardness of heart [to the insensitiveness of their moral nature]."

The Word cannot penetrate a "hardened," insensitive heart. The only way this heart can live is by the "knowledge" of the mind, which takes us back to the fleshly information center, the brain.

Iniquity constantly feeds the "old heart" information from the earthly realm. This spiritually insensitive heart fails to discern the truth of the Word and sends this "new knowledge" on to the brain. In turn, the brain tries to rationalize, or figure out, the spiritual revelation. When it cannot, it rejects the Word and tosses it to the side. Sadly, nothing that has the "breath of life"—especially the Word of the Lord—is welcome in the hardened heart. In its partnership with the mind, this heart cannot be penetrated.

If we do not ask for and receive a new heart, deception spreads like a virus. What are the telltale signs of a diseased heart? Let us look at a few examples.

Soil Along the Roadside

Listen to the [meaning of the] parable of the sower: While anyone is hearing the Word of the kingdom and does not grasp and comprehend it, the evil one comes and snatches away what was sown in his heart. This is what was sown along the roadside.

—MATTHEW 13:18–19

How is the "evil one" able to snatch a Word that has been sown in someone's heart? He is familiar with the grounds. He (Satan) already knows that the Word is trying to penetrate that heart; he knows the base character of that heart does not have what it takes to absorb and to hold that Word. The enemy knows already that the Word is sitting in a heart that has been consumed by the spirit of perverseness.

Have you ever known somebody who heard the Word of the Lord and then tried to change its meaning in order to justify his sin? This is what happens when the old heart is in operation. Satan, already familiar with the ground within that heart because he lives and rules there, *projects* himself there because he does not have a home. He takes control

of that ground because the heart is filled with all of
the enemy's works. That heart is filled with his
ungodly character, and he will not allow anything
that is righteous and holy to remain there.

At the point the Word of the Lord tries to penetrate
into that heart, holy things are illegally trespassing
on the enemy's ground. He has taken possession of
that old heart. Satan has "grounds" to operate anywhere that he gains a legal precedent. The earth
realm is "legal" ground for Satan. This is why believers must walk in the Spirit.

Satan has authority to do things according to the
flesh because this ground belongs to him! He is "the
"prince of the power of the air" (Eph. 2:2). The
worldly realm is his, but Satan has not been given
authority over the spiritual realm.

If your heart is not "spiritual," God would say to
you:

> For whoever has [spiritual knowledge], to him
> will more be given and he will be furnished
> richly so that he will have abundance; but from
> him who has not, even what he has will be
> taken away.
>
> —MATTHEW 13:12

Are you getting the revelation? God warns that if
you do not walk in the Spirit (and the way to "walk"
in the Spirit is to receive the "new heart" of the
Spirit), then Satan can take anything righteous that
hits those grounds. He has a legal right to cancel it!
You have given the right to him. Your heart has
become foreign ground.

Rocky Soil

> As for what was sown on thin (rocky) soil, this is he who hears the Word and at once welcomes and accepts it with joy.
>
> —MATTHEW 13:20

Emotionalism—are you seeing the revelation? Many people hear the Word and "accept it with joy." You can see it every Sunday in the church. People hollering back at the preacher…shouting, "Amen, preach it" all over the church. "Yet…," the Bible says:

> …it has no real root in him, but is temporary (inconstant, lasts but a little while); and when affliction or trouble or persecution comes on account of the Word, at once he is caused to stumble [he is repelled and begins to distrust and desert Him Whom he ought to trust and obey] and he falls away.
>
> —MATTHEW 13:21

God is describing people who hear the Word, but there is no real heart penetration. There is no depth to where His Word can be planted. It floats around in the "emotional" realm, and when something else "exciting" charges these emotions in a different way and direction, the first Word is canceled out. The emotions, which are fleshly, take precedence at that moment over the Word of God. The Word does not reside in this heart, and it cannot find a resting place.

Thorny Soil

~⌢⌣⌢~

> As for what was sown among thorns, this is he
> who hears the Word, but the cares of the world
> and the pleasure and delight and glamour and
> deceitfulness of riches choke and suffocate the
> Word, and it yields no fruit.
>
> —MATTHEW 13:22

The Word of the Lord cannot be implanted into
the old heart. In order for the Word of the Lord to
penetrate and take root in our lives, we must have a
new heart. We must unseat Satan from his throne in
our lives. James 1:21 tells us how to do that:

> So get rid of all uncleanness and the rampant
> outgrowth of wickedness, and in a humble (gen-
> tle, modest) spirit receive and welcome the
> Word which implanted and rooted [in your
> hearts] contains the power to save your souls.

The Bible tells us that once we have that new
heart, we are to:

> Be doers of the Word [obey the message], and
> not merely listeners to it, betraying yourselves
> [into deception by reasoning contrary to the
> Truth].
>
> —JAMES 1:22

People who do not have the "new heart" hear the
truth and then start "betraying" themselves through
deceit (reasoning). They rationalize that truth and
come up with every reason why "this is not what the
Bible means." Their hearts are so filled with the

world and the things of the world that they are deceived into thinking they have all they need.

Don't allow the "world and the pleasure and delight and glamour and deceitfulness of riches" to "choke and suffocate the Word" when God attempts to penetrate your heart with it. Don't let these "good" things choke the Word out of your heart! That is perversion.

> For if anyone only listens to the Word without obeying it and being a doer of it, he is like a man who looks carefully at his [own] natural face in a mirror; for he thoughtfully observes himself, and then goes off and promptly forgets what he was like.
>
> —JAMES 1:23–24

A pattern repeats throughout the Bible—we need a new heart. Why? Let us look at one example of a "good heart" to see what God desires.

Good Soil

> As for what was sown on good soil, this is he who hears the Word and grasps and comprehends it; he indeed bears fruit and yields in one case a hundred times as much as was sown, in another sixty times as much, and in another thirty.
>
> —MATTHEW 13:23

The person represented in this parable about the good soil has a converted heart. This person, who has received a new heart, has an "active" Word on the inside. God's spoken Word comes alive and produces good fruit. This Word has the power to save and the power to keep. How do I know it is operative? Hebrews 4:12 says:

> For the Word that God speaks is alive and full of power [making it active, operative, energizing, and effective]; it is sharper than any two-edged sword, penetrating to the dividing line of the breath of life (soul) and [the immortal] spirit, and of joints and marrow [of the deepest parts of our nature], exposing and sifting and analyzing and judging the very thoughts and purposes of the heart.

The penetrating Word is filled with power! It energizes your spirit, heart and soul as it accomplishes God's will. This Word can never be stagnated. It goes down into the intricate parts of the inner man and "dissects" everything it finds there. When the enemy comes in "like a flood," that Word knows how to swim. When the fire rages, that Word knows how to hold its breath. When the wind starts blowing, that Word is anchored. When the sun starts to blaze, that Word knows how to get in the shade—regardless of what life's temperature may be.

When the Word takes up residence in this heart, it operates with divine power and produces more fruit. This heart embraces the Word it has received and produces more than it has been given. The Word that goes into a "new heart" is active. It "identifies" with the divine nature of God and multiplies.

Spiritually Lazy "Prey" in the Pews

Let us return to the "old heart" and our text from Ephesians chapter 4. Since it is not made up of "good soil," this heart rejects the Word, and the downward cycle continues:

> In their spiritual apathy they have become callous and past feeling and reckless and have abandoned themselves [a prey] to unbridled sensuality.
>
> —EPHESIANS 4:19

What a horrible situation. The people about which this verse is speaking have fallen prey to everything that is moved by the "prince of the power of the air," everything that swings in society—strange and perverted sensualities that prey upon people who do not have the new heart!

The Word that goes into a "new heart" is active. It "identifies" with the divine nature of God and multiplies.

Spiritual apathy has no built-in defense system; nothing "foreign" can be shielded off. Spiritual laziness leaves no other alternative but to live a reckless existence! These people are "prey" to "unbridled sensuality," eager and greedy to indulge in every form of impurity that their depraved desires suggest and demand.

Lazy people do not digest the Word; they do not have the ability to break it down. They are defenseless against the enemy's thrust into "unbridled sensuality." That is why we are appalled at what we see in this world—cloning of human beings, men changing their sex to become women, women becoming men—all kinds of degradation, because this world has become a prey.

When the church does not step over into the spirit realm and receive this "new heart," then we sit idly by and become prey to the enemy. That is why we see so much degradation in the church! Things that have never happened before in the body of Christ are coming up out of our deceived hearts.

Here is the problem: The church has been preaching the gospel, but we have not been preaching conversion. We have been ministering to people about where they need to be, but we do not have the power to get them to where they should be! We have been telling people what God is saying, but we do not have the anointing upon our lives to destroy the yoke of the devil so that they can be converted—the proper way—to receive a new heart so the Word can penetrate and produce.

People are sitting in churches like "prey" in the pews. We are sitting like rabbits that are waiting for the next lion or tiger to strike. We are like deer prancing in the wilderness, waiting for the next wild animal to attack us, and we have no defense! Though we have spiritual mothers and fathers, and though we have pastors, we still have no defense. Why? Because we have not yet received a new heart.

Therefore, we are open prey to the devil and whatever kind of spiritual sensuality that swings in the
atmosphere. We cannot help but to indulge.

We operate in our soulish realm. When our mind
hears the Word of God, we know that what we are
doing is wrong. We know that God is displeased.
According to the Word of God that we hear, we know
that we are hell bound. But we cannot stop the
downward spiral because the old heart is racing
toward every damnable sin.

The heart races to impurity because that is its
nature. My pastor often told us, "If you take a hog
out of the hog pen, put a white bow on it, get him all
clean and sit him in a white living room on a white
couch, the first time that hog sees slop, he is going to
run out of that house and back to the slop, because
that is his nature."

We try to dress people up in the church. We have
incredible stained-glass windows and the most beautiful churches the world has ever seen. But the
minute the body of Christ, the spiritually lazy people
resting in the pews, sees the devil's slop—sexual
impurities, lies and deceit—they run right back to it
because that is still their nature.

Our loving heavenly Father warned us about this
tendency in Ezekiel 11:14–18:

> And the word of the Lord came to me, saying,
> Son of man, your brethren, even your kindred,
> your fellow exiles, and all the house of Israel, all
> of them, are they of whom the [present] inhab-
> itants of Jerusalem have said, They have gone
> far from the Lord [and from this land]; there-
> fore this land is given to us for a possession.
> Therefore say, Thus says the Lord God:

> Whereas I have removed [Israel] far off among the nations, and whereas I have scattered them among these countries, yet I have been to them a sanctuary for a little while in the countries to which they have come. Therefore say, Thus says the Lord God: I will gather you from the peoples and assemble you out of the countries where you have been scattered, and I will give back to you the land of Israel. And when they return there, they shall take away from it all traces of its detestable things and all its abominations (sex impurities and heathen religious practices).

Listen closely. In this hour God is saying the same thing to us:

> And I will give them one heart [a new heart] and I will put a new spirit within them; and I will take the stony [unnaturally hardened] heart out of their flesh, and will give them a heart of flesh [sensitive and responsive to the touch of their God], that they may walk in My statutes and keep My ordinances, and do them. And they shall be My people, and I will be their God.
>
> —EZEKIEL 11:19–20

What is the answer to the problem? We need a new heart.

Chapter 3

The Prophecy **Begins**

You may wonder why God did not deal with me personally concerning my need for a new heart until this late date in my ministry. God did begin dealing with me long before I really grabbed hold of His Word to me about my need for a new heart.

I remember earlier times when the Lord spoke deep inside of me, sometimes in the middle of the night or during my prayer time, saying, "Juanita, you need a new heart." But I did not understand. I felt that I had it all together. I knew that there were some things I had to deal with because of situations that had been caused by past offenses. But I felt that I had been "working with it."

We all have areas that have become our "strongholds." We consider these areas to be our "weaknesses," a term we have been taught by the preaching in this era and season of life.

The mass majority of teachings that I have heard say, "Be encouraged," "It's OK," "That's your weakness" and "God understands." By all means, the Lord does understand. Yet I believe that when you have been called to the office of a prophet and begin to seek the Lord with intensity, you strive not simply to receive a Word from Him to deliver to people, but to receive a Word from the Lord for *you*.

When you hear a Word from Him, you begin to change "inside." You asked for a Word *for yourself*—one by which you can *live*.

Transforming Prayer

Several years ago, my life began to take a turn when God called me to pray at 5:00 A.M. each morning. I would go into prayer for others, but I found that I began to yearn for another level in God for myself. I began to seek the Lord for a new depth in Him, for the God of Abraham and the God of Jacob. I wanted the God of the Old Testament. During this time, I remember seeing manifestations of the Spirit and character of God in Africa. "God," I prayed, "I want a relationship with You so that I can believe You for anything. I want to know who You are beyond a shadow of a doubt."

As I sought the Lord with intensity, I began to change. One of the first scriptures I heard Him speak to me was Matthew 5:8:

> Blessed are the pure in heart: for they shall see God.
>
> —KJV

I had read this verse from the Beatitudes many times. As a "Sunday school baby," I was raised on the Beatitudes. As far back as I can remember, even when I was three or four years old, my mother took us to Sunday school. The Beatitudes were some of the first Bible truths that I learned.

As I began to seek the Lord, "Blessed are the pure in heart: for they shall see God" came alive in my spirit. How could this happen? Why would God take me back to when I first learned about Him? After years of walking with Him, I had come to understand that there are different levels of revelation. There is the "milk" level of the Word, which leads to learning the "bread" of the Word, and, finally, you are able to move up to the "meat" of the Word.

Though I had heard this scripture many times before, I believe that God was trying to reveal the "meat" of this Word to me, which was the revelation of it from the third realm. From this realm behind the veil, we encounter the divine presence of God. It is where we learn the fullness of His heart and instruction. This is how, I believe, the Lord allows us to know "of" Him. Our spiritual level of understanding is based on the position of our heart "with" Him.

As this Word of the Lord, "Blessed are the pure in heart...," settled in my spirit, I remembered that I had always interpreted it to say, "Blessed are the pure in heart: for one day, when we die and go to heaven, we shall see God." The Lord began to say to me, "I desire that your spiritual eyes see Me now, but the only way that I can reveal My mysteries to you is according to My Word...the mysteries not yet revealed to man."

In Jeremiah 33:3, God said, "Call to Me and I will answer you and show you great and mighty things."

The Lord further said to me, "I will show you secrets that have not yet been revealed to man. I will

not reveal My secrets to those whose hearts and
motives are not pure." Then He added, "If you want
to see Me in a way that you have never seen Me
before, then I am compelling you to get a new heart."

I tried to respond by saying, "Well...I am struggling, and I see some things...I know that everything
in my heart is not right. God, I just want You to fix
it." During this season of early morning prayers, God
revealed to me that He had no desire to reconstruct
and "fix" my old heart. His desire and purpose was
to give me *a new heart*. Deep down, I knew that He
was right. How did I know this? The Lord took me to
Luke 6:45:

> The upright (honorable, intrinsically good)
> man out of the good treasure [stored] in his
> heart produces what is upright (honorable and
> intrinsically good), and the evil man out of the
> evil storehouse brings forth that which is
> depraved (wicked and intrinsically evil); for out
> of the abundance (overflow) of the heart his
> mouth speaks.

When I listened to the language that came out of my
mouth and observed some of my actions, I began to
face what I call "the truth of all truth." Some of those
actions repeated themselves over and over again, even
after much time in prayer about them. The truth I
faced was that, like the apostle Paul said, after I had
preached to others, I had become a castaway (1 Cor.
9:27). I sought the Lord even more intently and said,
"God above everything..." I put my ministry, fame
and television personality on the back burner. I said to
God, "I do not care what comes and what goes. Most of
all, I want to make sure that I am saved *for real*."

A Revelation for the World

As the Lord continued to deal with me about the new heart, I knew that by the time for me to minister that Word, I would already have learned to "walk it out." At that time, I did not understand why I had a problem forgiving people who had offended me. I did not understand why I was praying, "God, You know that I am trying to forgive them, but it just seems like I can't."

He began to reveal to me that the "old heart" does not come with forgiveness in it. The old heart does not come with mercy. The old heart does not come with compassion. This heart is born to be unfaithful to God. It is born without submissiveness. The nature of this heart is to operate from a spirit of rebellion—everything is conditional. You may hear that the unconverted heart has "eternal" qualities, but this contradicts the Word of God.

"You must begin to reveal this Word to the world," He told me. "I am not giving you this truth so that you hide your hands and say to people, 'Everything is going good. Everything is OK.'"

It made me stand back and take a long look at what I thought I had known and understood for so long. On the exterior, you can look at the church and see megachurches springing up everywhere. Christian programs have high ratings on television. Overall, Christendom is beginning to gain a new-found respect in the world.

Even still, I had to stand back and ask, Are we gaining respect because we are preaching an

uncompromising gospel? Are we "crying loud" and
"sparing not"? Or is the respect we are starting to
enjoy coming to us because the church is becoming
very cosmetic? Have we taken on the "cloak" or
appearance of the world to such a degree that the
world feels comfortable coming to the God we preach
about? Are they coming to Him because the God we
preach, after all, does not require us to sell out?

This "relaxed" gospel does not require that we
lament, grab hold of the horns of the altar and travail
for the birthing of souls—the "true" birthing process
that happens when a soul comes through the birth
canal the proper way. Today's "religion" says, "Come
as you are and stay as you are. It is just between you
and God, because God understands." Watch out!
The Bible says that in the last days, the hearts of
men will "wax cold," and they will not "endure
sound doctrine" (Matt. 24:12, KJV; 2 Tim. 4:3, KJV).

What do I mean by sound doctrine? Sound doctrine is the kind of doctrine that converts men's
hearts.

A Sober Realization for Ministers of God

When you understand this Word, then you know
that at some point you are not going to be the most
popular person. You know that you are going to take
a stand that is going to bring you much persecution—as it has me.

I know who I am called to be for God. I know the
kind of prophet He has called me to be. Some prophets
are called to prophesy "good." Some prophets are

called to prophesy prosperity. But I am called to stand on the wall. I am called to cry loud and spare not. I am called to make God's people aware that while they are getting a new house, a new car and a new job, they need to be trying to get a new heart. The new heart causes us to see the things of God.

The new heart brings the understanding that when everything looks chaotic, because your heart is pure you can see above the chaos and the attacks that Satan blows in your direction. Although you are glancing at the debris surrounding the place where you stand, you can still see God. When you have a pure heart, God is not hidden.

The new heart causes us to see the things of God.

The Lord began to speak to me from Matthew 23:23–24:

> Woe to you, scribes and Pharisees, pretenders (hypocrites)! For you give a tenth of your mint and dill and cummin, and have neglected and omitted the weightier (more important) matters of the Law—right and justice and mercy and fidelity. These you ought [particularly] to have done, without neglecting the others. You blind guides, filtering out a gnat and gulping down a camel!

God began to show me that we, my fellow ministers and prophets of this hour, have begun to concentrate on the houses, the cars, the new jobs and the money that is coming. Yet we have failed to focus on what is most important. Due to lack of prayer, our hearts have become insensitive and, thus, impure. We cannot hear the heartbeat of God. We do not understand that God's heart has picked up the pace. In times past, God "tolerated" certain things. Now, the pace has picked up, and things are different.

Why? God said to me, "After I have come to you and forewarned you over and over again…" God help us. His tolerance level is being weighed down, worn thin, because now people are not walking in iniquity because they are ignorant. They are walking in iniquity because they are rebellious. The Bible says that "rebellion is as the sin of witchcraft" (1 Sam. 15:23).

The Lord says that now the "weightier" thing is our need to get a new heart. If we neglect doing this, the Lord would say from Matthew 23:25–28:

> Woe to you, scribes and Pharisees, pretenders (hypocrites)! For you clean the outside of the cup and of the plate, but within they are full of extortion (prey, spoil, plunder) and grasping self-indulgence. You blind Pharisee! First clean the inside of the cup and of the plate, so that the outside may be clean also.
>
> Woe to you, scribes and Pharisees, pretenders (hypocrites)! For you are like tombs that have been whitewashed, which look beautiful on the outside but inside are full of dead men's bones and everything impure. Just so, you also outwardly seem to people to be just and upright but inside you are full of pretense and lawlessness and iniquity.

A Divine Paradigm Shift

God began to say to me, "In this hour I am calling forth my prophets to purify themselves so that they will not prophesy through eyes of deception. Looking at this 'glorious' church and prophesying of her beauty, they have not been able to see on the inside of the church. She is full of lawlessness and iniquity and everything that is impure and unclean."

He told me, "I want you to begin to 'major' in what I am majoring in right now. It is a fact that I am taking My people along a certain route, and I am blessing them. I am allowing them to get the things that their hearts desire, because this will be the catalyst that I will use to prove to them that it was never Me they wanted. They wanted Me for *things*—they wanted Me for a car, they wanted Me for a house, they wanted Me for a job and for a new husband.

"When I give them everything that their heart desires, and when a newfound walk in Me does not come out of that, or a new heart, then I am showing them that they were never after a walk of righteousness when they came to Me." Then He took me to the prayer of Jeremiah:

> O Lord, though our iniquities testify against us [prays Jeremiah], deal and work with us for Your own sake [that the heathen may witness Your might and faithfulness]! For our backslidings are many; we have sinned against You. O Hope of Israel, her Savior in time of trouble, why should You be like a sojourner in the land and like a wayfaring man who turns aside and spreads his tent to tarry [only] for a night? Why

should you be [hesitant and inactive] like a man stunned and confused, like a mighty man who cannot save? Yet You, O Lord, are in the midst of us, and we are called by Your name; do not leave us!

—JEREMIAH 14:7–9

Hear God's reply beginning in verse 10:

[And the Lord replied to Jeremiah] Thus says the Lord to His people [Judah]: In the manner and to the degree already pointed out have they loved to wander..."

As I read this, He told me, "Though prophets are crying out to Me on behalf of the people, I have to allow you, Juanita, to begin to see the nature of the people." We must be careful that we are not crying out for a people, or for individuals, who do not even *want* God! He said to Jeremiah, "These people are wanderers..."

God said to Jeremiah, "'To the degree already pointed out' to you, My people have loved to wander. They have loved to stray away from Me."

They have not restrained their feet. Therefore the Lord does not accept them; He will now [seriously] remember their iniquity and punish them for their sins. The Lord said to me, Do not pray for this people for their good. Though they fast, I will not hear their cry; and though they offer burnt offering and cereal offering [without heartfelt surrender to Me...]

—JEREMIAH 14:11–12

There goes that phrase again, "...without heartfelt surrender..." Even though we are doing many wonderful things in the body of Christ, God said to me, "Though, Juanita, you are going forth and doing this, and doing that, and fasting…it is not a heartfelt surrender to Me. I still do not see in you that your will has been yielded to Me to the point that you want a new heart."

Then God continued speaking to me from Jeremiah 14:12–13:

> …or by offering it too late], I will not accept them. But I will consume them by the sword, by famine, and by pestilence. Then said I, Alas, Lord God! Behold, the [false] prophets say to them, You will not see the sword, nor will you have famine, but I [the Lord] will give you an assured peace (peace that lasts, the peace of truth) in this place.

God is sending us a warning. We must be careful that while we are prophesying prosperity and peace, God is not moving in a whole different vein!

> Then the Lord said to me, The [false] prophets prophesy lies in My name. I sent them not, neither have I commanded them, nor have I spoken to them. They prophesy to you a false or pretended vision, a worthless divination [conjuring or practicing magic, trying to call forth the responses supposed to be given by idols], and the deceit of their own minds. Therefore thus says the Lord concerning the [false] prophets who prophesy in My name—although I did not send them—and who say, Sword and famine shall not be in this land: By sword and famine shall those prophets be consumed.
>
> —JEREMIAH 14:14–15

The Lord began to deal with me and say, "If you are going to walk in this office in this last hour, I am compelling you to cry out to My people. Provoke them to desire a new heart. Though you hear one prophet over here..." (I am not saying that God told me these would be false prophets) "...though you hear one prophet over there saying, 'Blessings,' and another saying, 'Peace,' you had better cry out what I am calling YOU to cry out.

"At this time, as I am calling you to cry out concerning the new heart, there is already a remnant of people that I have prepared, and I have already begun to turn their minds. I have set them in the birth canal to receive this conversion. If you dare not speak what I call you to speak, you will cause a host of men and women to be lost in trespasses and sin because you went with the popular prophecy."

I have been asked on many occasions, "Why do you think God is saying this right now? When you look at it, our churches are bigger now than ever before." Yes, but are the people really being delivered? Are they coming into an understanding of the true plan of salvation? Are they coming into an understanding of "counsel," or are they coming into a true understanding of conversion?

I picked up Jeremiah's burden from what he saw, according to his words in chapter 9:

> Oh, that my head were waters and my eyes a reservoir of tears, that I might weep day and night for the slain of the daughter of My people! Oh, that I had in the wilderness a lodging place (a mere shelter) for wayfaring men, that I might leave my people and go away from

them! For they are all adulterers [rendering worship to idols instead of the Lord...]

—Jeremiah 9:1–2

People are rendering more worship to their pastors, to the beauty of their churches, to the worship songs than to God, "Who has espoused the people to Himself" (v. 2). Idols have espoused the people to themselves!

They are a gang of treacherous men [faithless even to each other]. And they bend their tongue, [which is] their bow for the lies [they shoot]. And not according to faithfulness do they rule and become strong in the land; for they proceed from evil to evil, and they do not know and understand and acknowledge Me, says the Lord. Let everyone beware of his neighbor and put no trust in any brother. For every brother is an utter and complete supplanter (one who takes by the heel and trips up, a deceiver, a Jacob), and every neighbor goes about as a slanderer.

—Jeremiah 9:2–4

Do you still want to know why we need a new heart? Verses 5 and 6 say:

And they deceive and mock everyone his neighbor and do not speak the truth. They have taught their tongues to speak lies; they weary themselves committing iniquity. Your habitation is in the midst of deceit [oppression upon oppression and deceit upon deceit]; through deceit they refuse to know and understand Me, says the Lord.

What did God say about the heart in Jeremiah 17? He said that above all things, the heart is desperately wicked and deceitful. When you see that wickedness and deceit are prevalent in our churches and in our society, then you know that *the church must seek God for the new heart.*

> Therefore thus says the Lord of hosts: Behold, I will melt them [by the process of affliction to remove the dross] and test them, for how else should I deal with the daughter of My people? Their tongue is a murderous arrow; it speaks deceitfully; one speaks peaceably to his neighbor with his mouth, but in his heart he lays snares and waits in ambush for him.
> —JEREMIAH 9:7–8

I want to repeat this: "Their tongue is a murderous arrow; it speaks deceitfully; one speaks peaceably to his neighbor with his mouth, but in his heart he lays snares and waits in ambush for him." God help us.

This verse indicates that there is a match, a parallel, between Israel in Jeremiah's day and the church in this final hour. For many people, what we say and what we do are two different things. Yet we try to hide who we are and what we do by covering it up with what we say. Eventually that will turn. Why? Because when this wicked heart becomes full and active, having been fed by iniquity, and allows the mind to assume full control, we will see the depths of this old heart operating to its fullest potential.

We will still try to cover it up over and over again saying, "I am not like that." Eventually, though, we will have to face the fact that we have become like the Pharisees in Matthew 12:34, whom Jesus confronted by saying:

> You offspring of vipers! How can you speak good things when you are evil (wicked)? For out of the fullness (the overflow, the super-abundance) of the heart the mouth speaks.

We Cannot Hide From the Truth

You cannot hide who you really are. Eventually, that "old heart" within you will go into full operation. You cannot suppress it. You cannot keep that evil heart from operating. Its nature is to pump. Its nature is to function (operate), and when it begins to operate to its fullest potential, then the words of your mouth are going to speak from the abundance of what is in your heart.

If you want to know what you are full of, and what your heart is full of, listen to your conversation.

Lies, deception and trickery will come out of your mouth. Snares for your brother will escape your lips. Out of your mouth will come greed and lust for the flesh and for things—rather than words reflecting a righteous desire to seek and obey God. If you want to know what you are full of, and what your heart is full of, listen to your conversation.

Everything is naked before Him to whom we must

give an account. (See Hebrews 4:13.) God is calling us today—as leaders—to get *real* and set the pace for others. We must pursue the new heart, or we will not be able to understand and obey what He is telling us to do.

Chapter 4

The Prophetic
Word Deepens

T he Lord continued to forewarn me as He led me to Ezekiel 13. As He spoke to me, I realized that not only did I not want to bring the Word to others, but I also did not want to admit publicly that God had been dealing with me about receiving a new heart. This is the deception.

> Pride goeth before destruction, and an haughty spirit before a fall.
> —PROVERBS 16:18, KJV

I recognized the spirit of pride in my thoughts: *You do not want to say that because you preach the gospel; you do not want to tell people that. When pride comes upon you in this way, the tendency is always to cover up. God has started to reveal to me that covering up is not always the best way to help people.* God has shown me (as mentioned in the previous chapter) that conducting our lives so as to look like "The Untouchables"—looking like we have it all together, like we are perfect—does not leave a straight path for others to follow.

The best route for people to travel is to follow a path that has already been trodden. This is the point of true leadership, the heritage of spiritual fathers and mothers. Since we have already walked the spiritual road that others travel, just like a mother or father in the natural realm, we should be willing to share these experiences with our "children" so that they (and their children) can learn by the same pattern and example.

God explained to me, "I am trying to show you that when you get a new heart, you may be tempted from without, but there is no sin from within. That which is coming 'from without' will not find a match or an identification with anything that is 'within' you. You will be able to stand in times of testing. You will be able to stand against temptation. You will be able to stand against the wiles of Satan."

Then He took me to Ezekiel 13, helping me to understand that as a prophet in this hour, I could no longer keep my mouth shut. I could no longer silence the heartbeat of God.

> And the word of the Lord came to me, saying, Son of man, prophesy against the prophets of Israel who prophesy, and say to those who prophesy out of their own mind and heart, Hear the word of the Lord! Thus says the Lord God: Woe to the foolish prophets who follow their own spirit [and things they have not seen] and have seen nothing! O Israel, your prophets have been like foxes among ruins and in waste places. You have not gone up into the gaps or breaches...
>
> —Ezekiel 13:1–5

In other words, God was saying, "You have not fortified the walls of My people, you have not 'deposited' in them to the degree that their inner man has been strengthened against the onslaught of Satan." Because His prophets have not done this, today we watch as many believers are "taken out" and slaughtered in the battle of the Lord!

Why did Jesus have His disciples with Him at all times? What was the requirement?

What is this battle? The apostle Paul described the battle when he said, "For the desires of the flesh are opposed to the [Holy] Spirit, and the [desires of the] Spirit are opposed to the flesh (godless human nature)" (Gal. 5:17). If walls have not been built up according to Ezekiel 13:5...if no one is standing in the gap...if no one has grabbed the horns of the altar ...if no one has lamented and demonstrated the "pattern" of lament...if no one has shown the saints how to walk, suffer and endure...then there is no example to show people know how to stand during the battle of the Lord.

Have you ever wondered, "Why did Jesus have His disciples walk with Him at all times? What was the requirement?"

It was necessary for the disciples to learn how to follow the steps of Jesus, just as it had been necessary for Jesus to learn how to follow the steps of His Father. They needed to observe Jesus walking in the breaches (paths) of the Father in order to be taught how to operate in signs, wonders and miracles. He had to show them the *pattern* for going through the breaches that He had learned through obedience to His own Father. The disciples learned how to submit by watching Jesus' example. He taught them, by example, how to be persecuted without warring back. He showed them how to be whipped with cat-o'-nine-tails and never say a mumbling word. He showed them how to suffer for righteousness' sake.

- He showed them how to go to the cross and die for the sins of the world.

- He demonstrated how to sacrifice and lay down their lives for a brother.

- He showed them how to "stand in the gap" for someone that needed God.

Jesus lived a pattern. As a result, when Peter was persecuted, he knew how to die. Paul knew how to die. The disciples and early followers of Jesus had all been taught how to die. They understood the pattern and knew how to stand in the battle of the Lord.

Prophets Who Prophesy False Hope

> They have seen falsehood and lying divination, saying, The Lord says; but the Lord has not sent them. Yet they have hoped and made men to hope for the confirmation of their word.
>
> —EZEKIEL 13:6

The prophets who prophesied false hopes to the people caused men to believe that the "peace" about which they were prophesying was possible. They gave the impression that God was "understanding" of the spiritual lethargy present among His people.

Just as in the days of Ezekiel, people everywhere are trusting in the voice of the prophet who comes in God's stead. They are looking for a confirmation of what the prophet has spoken. But in reality, what the prophet has spoken is not what God is saying. Many people have become gripped by false hope, which will bring them into despair and land them in a final state of hopelessness. When hopelessness penetrates their trust in God, they will fall by the wayside.

The Word of the Lord continues in verses 7–11:

> Have you not seen a false vision and have you not spoken a lying divination when you say, The Lord says, although I have not spoken? Therefore thus says the Lord God: Because you have spoken empty, false, and delusive words and have seen lies, therefore behold, I am against you, says the Lord God. And My hand shall be against the prophets who see empty, false, and delusive visions and who give lying prophecies. They shall not be in the secret counsel of My people, nor shall they be recorded in the register of the house of Israel, nor shall they enter into the land of Israel; and you shall know (understand and realize) that I am the Lord God. Because, even because they have seduced My people, saying, Peace, when there is no peace, and because when one builds a [flimsy] wall, behold, [these prophets] daub it over with whitewash, say to them who daub it with whitewash that it shall fall!

Once again, God is warning against taking on the cloak of the outward appearance. Many are deceived into indulging in the seduction of glamour that Christendom brings. Yet God's prophets, His watchmen, do not speak the truth to these people about their need to go deeper in God.

When we stand back and watch people build flimsy walls on things that have no substance, and then turn around and daub them with whitewash, we are saying, "That is good. At least you are not where you used to be...that is wonderful. You are doing fine."

God is saying that if I refuse to preach this new heart message...if I refuse to give you truth to help you understand that we all need a new heart, then I am setting you up for a fall, because that flimsy wall in Christendom shall fall.

> There shall be a downpour of rain; and you, O great hailstones, shall fall, and a violent wind shall tear apart [the whitewashed, flimsy wall].
> —EZEKIEL 13:11

When the enemy comes in and when the storms of life are blowing, many fall by the wayside. They had only the outward appearance of a flimsy wall that had been whitewashed by a false prophet. They have no depth in God because they have not yet received the new heart.

Ezekiel 13:12 continues:

> Behold, when the wall is fallen, will you not be asked, Where is the coating with which you [prophets] daubed it?

When people fall into error and cannot find their way out...when they are launched into an era of darkness, then are you certain that you will not be approached again by these same people, who will say, "You are a man or a woman of God. I thought you said that 'this' or 'that' was all right. I thought you said that nothing was wrong with this. I thought you said that God understood. Why am I in the situation that I am in right now? Why am I being attacked the way that I am being attacked now?"

As men and women of God...as God's spokesmen in this dark world, we must be certain that we have not prophesied false hope to a spiritually lethargic people.

You Cannot Lead People Farther Than You Have Gone

God revealed to me that when He has set you into a position, but you do not have depth in Him, you can only preach from the realm in which you walk. You can only raise a person up to the level on which you stand. The depth of your deliverance is the depth of deliverance you can offer to another. There has to be purification in the priesthood, purification in leadership.

Leaders must begin to seek God for the new heart, so that, by way of example, they can provoke the people to want the new heart.

> Therefore thus says the Lord God: I will even rend it with a stormy wind in My wrath, and there shall be an overwhelming rain in My

anger and great hailstones in wrath to destroy
[that wall].

—EZEKIEL 13:13

God is saying, "You think that you are secure and
that you have it all together. But I am telling you that
if you have no depth in Me, and if you do not receive
this new heart..."

There has to be purification in the priesthood, purification in leadership.

The Word of the Lord is coming to you to say, "I
am going to send a wind, and that wind is going to
blow. I am going to release the hailstones to come in
an awesome, overwhelming rain. I am doing this
because I love you. I am doing this to break down
the wall so that you can see you are not as strong as
you think you are. You do not need structure only—
you need a deposit. You need to be transformed. You
need to be converted.

"When I look and see those that I have chosen
before the foundation of the world to be born again
and transformed, and I see a false prophet trying to
help them construct something that is not going to
be able to stand, then I have no other choice but to
send a wind to blow it down. That wind will keep
blowing it down. It will keep you in the fiery fur-
nace...in the realm of affliction...to show you that
there is another depth, another height, to which I

am calling you." *Thus says the Lord!*

In Ezekiel 13:14, God said:

> So will I break down the wall that you have daubed with whitewash and bring it down to the ground, so that its foundations will be exposed; when it falls, you will perish and be consumed in the midst of it. And you will know (understand and realize) that I am the Lord.

God is reiterating, "You will know, you will understand and realize that it was not Me, that it was not of God, because that which is of God is eternal. That which is of God stands the test of time. That which is of God has already been tried in the fire and has come out as pure gold."

> Thus will I accomplish My wrath upon the wall and upon those who have daubed it with whitewash, and I will say to you, The wall is no more, neither are they who daubed it, the [false] prophets of Israel who prophesied deceitfully about Jerusalem, seeing visions of peace for her when there is no peace, says the Lord God. And you, son of man, set your face against the daughters of your people who prophesy out of [the wishful thinking of] their own minds and hearts; prophesy against them, and say, Thus says the Lord God: Woe to the women who sew pillows to all armholes and fasten magic, protective charms to all wrists, and deceptive veils upon the heads of those of every stature to hunt and capture human lives! Will you snare the lives of My people to keep your own selves alive?
>
> —EZEKIEL 13:15–18

In this last hour we are being confronted with an order of priesthood that chooses to ensnare people's lives by prophesying and preaching lies—by not giving them the Word of the Lord according to the meat of the Word—in order to keep *themselves* alive.

God Led Me Into a Death Walk

When God began to say, "I want you to preach the new heart," then there had to be a death realm for me. There had to be an "exposing" for me. I had to come to the realization "publicly" that I needed a new heart and that there were things going on inside of me that did not please God.

If you come to the place where you say, "I am called of God to prophesy," "I am called of God to be a teacher," or "I am called of God to preach the gospel to the poor and to open blind eyes and set the captives free," then at some point, you will be compelled to give up your own life, even your reputation if necessary, to save the lives of God's people. If you hold on to your own life, walking around as if you have never done anything wrong, as if everything in your life is perfect, you will set a snare and hang a veil that will blind people to the truth. If people are veiled, they cannot see God. If their hearts are snared, they will surely die. Ezekiel 13:19 reads:

> You have profaned Me among My people [in payment] for handfuls of barley and for pieces of bread, slaying persons who should not die and giving [a guaranty of] life to those who

should not live, by your lying to My people, who
give heed to lies.

In other words, "Because you cannot get to the
point..." He said to me, "Because people are bringing you offerings and giving you gifts, and because
they are willing to do this for you..." God did not
have to say any more.

Think about it. We are part of a priesthood that
drives the best cars and wears the finest suits, alliga-
tor shoes and St. John knits—and we are giving
"peace" to people whom God has already cursed and
who should die. And we are telling people who should
live that they are going to die!

If people are veiled, they cannot see God. If their hearts are snared, they will surely die.

We have the gospel backward. We say to those who
are compromising and living close to the edge of the
world, "You are wonderful; you are going to be all
right." Yet they have no desire to "sell out" to God.

But to people who are dying to the flesh and giving
up all to follow God, we tell them—through a false
revelation and evaluation of their circumstance—
"You are going too deep." "You pray too much." "You
are a little too righteous." "You are going a little too
far off the deep end." "Be careful; you'll drive yourself
crazy by praying every day for two or three hours."

We are pronouncing death to people who are selling

out to God, and we are pronouncing life to people who walk in carnality according to the spirit of this world. We are blinded by our own deception. We are blinded by the "old heart." Ezekiel 13:20 continues:

> Therefore thus says the Lord God: Behold, I am against your pillows and charms and veils with which you snare human lives like birds, and I will tear them from your arms and will let the lives you hunt go free, the lives you are snaring like birds.

We are blinded by our own deception. We are blinded by the "old heart."

"You may think you are getting away with it," God is saying, "but it's *only for a season!*"

Hear the Word of the Lord as it comes across this page into the heart of every preacher and teacher: "If you do not begin to teach the full gospel…if you do not begin to warn My people about their ways and provoke them to make sure that they have the heart that is pure…then I am going to snare them from you, and I am going to cause those that have been snared by you to go free. You yourself will be destroyed."

> Your [deceptive] veils also will I tear and deliver My people out of your hand…Then you shall know (understand and realize) that I am the Lord.
>
> —EZEKIEL 13:21

God's people will no longer remain in the hands of those who do not lead them to the new heart. If you have failed to deliver God's people, your ministry will fall. If I have failed, my ministry shall surely fall.

> Because with lies you have made the righteous sad and disheartened, whom I have not made sad or disheartened, and because you have encouraged and strengthened the hands of the wicked, that he should not return from his wicked way and be saved [in that you falsely promised him life], therefore you will no more see false visions or practice divinations, and I will deliver My people out of your hand. Then you will know (understand and realize) that I am the Lord.
>
> —EZEKIEL 13:22–23

The Time for Change Has Come

Trust me when I tell you that we have not seen the falling away. We have not seen the judgment of God as we will see it one day. God is speaking to leadership in this chapter, calling us to fulfill our destiny in ministry by provoking His people to walk in the Spirit so they do not give heed to the things of the flesh. We must redirect this walk of faith to a "heart" thing, not a "flesh" thing…a righteous experience, not a worldly one.

As pastors, teachers or prophets in this hour of preaching the gospel, we should be feeling the temperature of the Spirit realm. We must cry out to the hearts of God's people, according to Hebrews 3:12–13, and say:

[Therefore beware] brethren, take care, lest
there be in any one of you a wicked, unbelieving heart [which refuses to cleave to, trust in,
and rely on Him], leading you to turn away and
desert or stand aloof from the living God. But
instead warn (admonish, urge, and encourage)
one another every day, as long as it is called
Today, that none of you may be hardened [into
settled rebellion] by the deceitfulness of sin [by
the fraudulence, the stratagem, the trickery
which the delusive glamour of his sin may play
on him].

We are living in the final hour, and the glamour of
the world is causing us to be tricked by the enemy.
The "outer cloak" is deceiving us. The Word of the
Lord is constantly ringing in my spirit that we have
the "form of godliness," but we are "denying the
power thereof" (2 Tim. 3:5, KJV). We have everything
that it takes to make up the "image" of God, but the
real power is being able to say *yes* to God and *no* to
the devil.

Even while you are reading these words, as a
prophet of God I bind the hand of the enemy that
would try to come upon you with fear to keep you
from making a righteous stand.

Preach the New Heart Message

Now just as Jannes and Jambres were hostile to
and resisted Moses, so these men also are hostile to and oppose the Truth. They have
depraved and distorted minds, and are reprobate and counterfeit and to be rejected as far as
the faith is concerned. But they will not get very

far, for their rash folly will become obvious to everybody, as was that of those [magicians mentioned]. Now you have closely observed and diligently followed my teaching, conduct, purpose in life, faith, patience, love, steadfastness...

—2 TIMOTHY 3:8–10

Timothy is describing a person who has received the new heart. This is the only kind of person who can preach this message. You cannot preach diligence, conduct, purpose in life, faith, patience, love and steadfastness unless you have first received these characteristics from God. I encourage you to keep reading, and you will discover the truth that I found about this "new heart." This revelation literally shocked me into silence as I sat in awe of God, pondering the depths of His handiwork.

What comes from the heart goes to the heart, as we read in Psalm 42:7: "Deep calleth to the deep" (KJV).

> We have everything that it takes to make up the "image" of God, but the *real power* is being able to say *yes* to God and *no* to the devil.

In the third chapter of 2 Timothy we read: "Now you have closely observed and diligently followed my teaching, conduct, purpose in life, faith, patience, love, steadfastness..." Watch out; it is getting ready to go deeper: "...persecutions, sufferings—such as occurred to me at Antioch, at Iconium, and at Lystra, persecutions I endured, but out of them all the Lord delivered me" (2 Tim. 3:10–11).

That's right. As you stand and provoke people to go after the new heart, you will be persecuted. God, however, has promised in His Word that He will deliver you out of every one.

> Indeed all who delight in piety and are determined to live a devoted and godly life in Christ Jesus will meet with persecution [will be made to suffer because of their religious stand]. But wicked men and imposters will go on from bad to worse, deceiving and leading astray others and being deceived and led astray themselves. But as for you, continue to hold to the things that you have learned and of which you are convinced, knowing from whom you learned [them], and how from your childhood you have had a knowledge of and been acquainted with the sacred Writings, which are able to instruct you and give you the understanding for salvation which comes through faith in Christ Jesus [through the leaning of the entire human personality on God in Christ Jesus in absolute trust and confidence in His power, wisdom, and goodness].
>
> Every scripture is God-breathed (given by His inspiration) and profitable for instruction, for reproof and conviction of sin…
>
> —2 TIMOTHY 3:12–16

The Scriptures were not written to make people jump and shout, or to make them believe things like: "Oh, I am going to get a car." "I am going to get a house." "My life is going to be perfect when I get saved." No! The power that is coming—and this new level of the Word that is about to hit this twenty-first century—is going to be the kind of gospel that will help you to determine who has been in the prayer closet with God, who has received a new heart and who knows the heartbeat of God. The gospel that they will preach will be according to 2 Timothy!

It will be "profitable for instruction, for reproof and conviction of sin..." Watch out! It is not for acquiring houses and cars. It is not for acquiring prosperity, although prosperity is a part of righteous living. It is true that when you "seek ye first the kingdom of God, and his righteousness...all these things shall be added" (Matt. 6:33, KJV). Absolutely! The balance of that Word, and the balance of the power of that message, is the fact that GOD "breathed" it!

Scripture says, "Every scripture is God-breathed (given by His inspiration) and profitable for instruction, for reproof and conviction of sin." Though God inspired the writing of all Scripture, there are seasons when He "breathes" on a certain text. There are times and seasons in our world when God "breathes" on a certain Word in order to get a certain assignment done for a certain season and era. He does this because He knows what is up the road.

If we are preaching a gospel in this hour that is not a God-breathed Word for this season, there will be no conviction of sin even though we slap our hips, turn up the organ and get people to shout back at us. Without that conviction of sin, we are merely covering them up with sheets while they speak in tongues, run around the church or fall to their knees.

When God took me down through this passage, I had no other choice but to hear the Word of the

Lord. I even wrote a little footnote on the side of this scripture that said *yes* to God. When He said, "Read on, daughter," and I did, He declared, "Now I charge you…"

There are times and seasons in our world when God "breathes" on a certain Word in order to get a certain assign-ment done for a certain season and era.

Just as He charged me with that truth, I charge you today, reader. If you have this book in your hand, God is redirecting *your* spirit! Second Timothy 4:1–2 says:

> I charge [you] in the presence of God and of Christ Jesus, Who is to judge the living and the dead, and by (in the light of) His coming and His kingdom; herald and preach the Word! Keep your sense of urgency [stand by, be at hand and ready], whether the opportunity seems to be favorable or unfavorable. [Whether it is convenient or inconvenient, whether it is welcome or unwelcome, you as preacher of the Word are to show people in what way their lives are wrong].

This is my assignment—not to encourage people in doing wrong, but to show God's people where their lives are *wrong*. And to:

> Convince them, rebuking and correcting, warn-
> ing and urging and encouraging them, being
> unflagging and inexhaustible in patience and
> teaching. For the time is coming when [people]
> will not tolerate (endure) sound and wholesome
> instruction, but, having ears itching [for some-
> thing pleasing and gratifying], they will gather to
> themselves one teacher after another to a con-
> siderable number, chosen to satisfy their own
> liking and to foster the errors they hold.
> —2 Timothy 4:2–3

It is our charge to teach people how to take responsibility for their errors. People should not say, "The
reason I am this way is because Pastor So-and-so told
me that it was all right," or "The reason I operate the
way I do is because Pastor So-and-so told me that God
understood."

It is also our charge—first and foremost—to say
and do exactly what God commands. We are not to
preach what we *think* the people need or want to
hear. We are to preach and teach at God's direction,
and let Him take care of the rest. In 2 Peter 2:15–19,
the Lord said:

> Forsaking the straight road they have gone
> astray; they have followed the way of Balaam
> [the son] of Beor, who loved the reward of
> wickedness. But he was rebuked for his own
> transgression when a dumb beast of burden
> spoke with human voice and checked the
> prophet's madness. These are springs without
> water and mists driven along before a tempest,
> for whom is reserved forever the gloom of dark-
> ness. For uttering loud boasts of folly, they
> beguile and lure with lustful desires of the flesh
> those who are barely escaping from them who

are wrongdoers. They promise them liberty, when they themselves are the slaves of depravity and defilement—for by whatever anyone is made inferior or worse or is overcome, to that [person or thing] he is enslaved.

We cannot allow ourselves to be enslaved to deception, especially while we are doing God's work! We must serve God from a new heart, one that only He can give and that we must maintain. He is charging us to turn it around, to set our faces like "flints" toward His divine purpose in this final hour. Second Timothy 4:4–5 concludes our charge:

...and will turn aside from hearing the truth and wander off into myths and man-made fictions. As for you, be calm and cool and steady, accept and suffer unflinchingly every hardship, do the work of an evangelist, fully perform all the duties of your ministry.

Chapter 5

The Heart: **Who Can Know It?**

Yes, we have a problem, and ministers of God bear a great responsibility. This, however, does not abort the individual's responsibility to pursue the new heart. Each one of us will be required to give an account to God for our words and actions (Matt. 12:36; Heb. 4:13). We have all been infected with a diseased, old heart, which is trying to rule us. How can we "know" this deceived heart?

I have already touched on certain aspects of the old heart. In order for you to understand fully God's message in this hour, I must continue to build the case that the old heart does exist. It is important to understand that there are people in the world—and in the church—who have the old heart. We all need the new heart.

Jeremiah 17 is the foundation for what God is saying. He is trying to get—and keep—our attention. It is vital that we understand this truth. The very first thing we discover about the heart in Jeremiah 17:9 is that it is "deceitful above all things."

When the Lord first began revealing this Word to

me, I did not want to hear it. I had already seen the signs of my own shortcomings, but I felt they were just part of my character. In reality, I was taking the easy way out.

The Grace Factor

Many times believers abuse the fact that there is a "grace factor" in our walk with God. We assume a comfortable position where we do not have to change certain behaviors because we know that grace is there. Through our own spiritual laziness, we are using the liberty of Christ as an occasion for the flesh.

> What shall we say [to all this]? Are we to remain in sin in order that God's grace (favor and mercy) may multiply and overflow? Certainly not! How can we who died to sin live in it any longer? Are you ignorant of the fact that all of us who have been baptized into Christ Jesus were baptized into His death? We were buried therefore with Him by the baptism into death, so that just as Christ was raised from the dead by the glorious [power] of the Father, so we too might [habitually] live and behave in the newness of life.
>
> —ROMANS 6:1–4

After God birthed this truth into my spirit, I began recognizing personality traits manifesting from within me that were evidence of the old heart. Each time this happened, I would simply say, "Lord, forgive me." But after a period of time, they would resurface—sometimes on a daily basis! Even though

I repented each time, they would come to the surface again.

I know that God was giving me *opportunities* to allow my mind to be transformed. But, like many other people, rather than spending quality time to find out why these shortcomings kept surfacing and trying to understand why I kept failing in those areas, *for the sake of comfort* I attached those things to myself and said, "This is just a part of my personality." "This is just the way I am." "God understands the way I am." I had made myself comfortable, and I settled into this lethargic frame of mind.

When you fall into this trap, it extends to your inner circle and to your immediate surroundings. Then the deception worsens. Rather than you having to adjust and change some things about your personality and character, your friends and associates begin to accept that behavior as just being "you" because it has become such a part of you. They reposition their personalities and characters to adjust or make room for that part of you, which has not been purified.

As a result, you stay the way you are. Once people become accustomed to your "old heart" behavior, they avoid it. Everybody makes sure they do not do anything to bring that part of your temperament to the surface. If it surfaces, they say, "Well, that is just the way she is."

And you do the same thing about their "old heart" behavior. You end up saying the same thing about them. We forget that the Bible has told us not to know anyone "after the flesh" (2 Cor. 5:16, KJV).

The Lord began to make me understand that He

was not requiring me to *adjust* these shortcomings for *acceptance sake*—He was requiring me to *change*.

Self-Deception

The first thing God had to break was my deception about myself, because "the heart is deceitful above all things" (Jer. 17:9). My own heart was deceiving me. That got me! After being raised in the church and being saved, I constantly "fell away," doing things that were outside of God's will. I came to this realization—your heart can be deceived without your knowing it, because you live for God from the "religious factor."

What do I mean by a *religious factor*? It's when we compare our righteousness to the righteousness of other people, rather than to God's. We measure who we are as compared to another person. You will always find someone who you "feel" is worse off, or "less all right," than you. Evaluating yourself by comparing against others (who are equally as imperfect as you are) is a subtle trick of the enemy.

When you compare yourself with someone else, your heart deceives you into thinking, *I am not all that bad. Look at how bad So-and-so is.* Or you could compare yourself with someone and think, *Well, he and I, or she and I, are a lot alike, so I am not all that bad.*

You begin to identify with the behavior of others, attempting to mimic "the going personality" in Christendom at the time. Everybody does the same thing—that which is *familiar* and *acceptable*. We are all stuck in a bucket like a bunch of crabs, saying, "This is the 'Christian' way, and everybody is like this." Everyone settles in and gets comfortable with that particular lifestyle until the Lord reveals to someone that there is more. There is much more to following Him than stumbling and blundering around with the crowd.

Your heart can be deceived without your knowing it, because you live for God from the "religious factor."

The sad thing is that your mind will do anything to protect itself—even conflicting things. For example, it pushes blame toward some while at the same time identifying with others, all to justify itself. The reason for this is the fact that everything entering the brain is first processed through our emotions. Our emotions, like it or not, decide what is or is not *relevant* before logic sorts things out. This is the danger of the old heart.

Only the new heart can see through this. If you ask God for the new heart, you can begin to pursue the perfection of God and walk out what you believe to the extent that your heart becomes "perfected" in Him.

When this happens, you will stop comparing yourself to others. You will allow God to evaluate you properly. He can inspect your heart and give you the right grade. If He gives your heart an F, then you know it is failing, as mine was. But God will give you a new heart!

Unsaved or Fallen Away?

Revelation 2:4–5 (KJV) warns:

> Nevertheless I have somewhat against thee, because thou hast left thy first love. Remember therefore from whence thou art fallen, and repent, and do the first works; or else I will come unto thee quickly, and will remove thy candlestick out of his place, except thou repent.

How do you know when you need a new heart? How do you know the difference between making a mistake and falling away from your first love?

A Step-by-Step Process

Ephesians 4 gives us a step-by-step process to teach us to recognize when we have fallen away from our first love and need a new heart.

> So this I say and solemnly testify [in the name of] the Lord [as in His presence], that you must no longer live as the heathen (the Gentiles) do in their perverseness [in the folly, vanity, and emptiness of their souls and the futility] of their minds.
>
> —EPHESIANS 4:17

1. A "futile" mind is incapable of producing any result.

Remember that a "futile" mind is incapable of producing any result; it is ineffective, useless and unsuccessful. The thought patterns of this mind do not yield anything that is fruitful or beneficial. This first step is when we look at things our own way and pervert the Word of God.

2. Our moral understanding is darkened.

"Their moral understanding is darkened and their reasoning is beclouded" (v. 18). This is the second step. When you start doing ungodly things and yet try to justify why you are doing it, your moral understanding is darkened, and your reasoning is beclouded.

3. We explain away our actions according to worldly knowledge and carnal information.

"[They are] alienated (estranged, self-banished) from the life of God [with no share in it: this is] because of the ignorance (the want of knowledge and perception...)" (v. 18). We are living in a brain world. This world moves according to knowledge, not according to the new heart. It is propelled by our mind and the lust for knowledge, which brings personal power. Everybody is in a sweat to gain more information and knowledge. Yet they are still ignorant about God and His ways; they are like the people described in 2 Timothy 3:7, who "...are never able to arrive at a recognition and knowledge of the Truth."

As a result, we try to cover our actions by "explaining them away" according to worldly knowledge and carnal information. Gaining this knowledge and information can, once again, deceive the old heart into thinking, *I am filled with great knowledge; therefore, I have an understanding of God.* Not so. You may read the Bible and comprehend it according to the English language, but the only way that you can understand it according to the Spirit is by virtue of the new heart.

4. We persistently do things our own way.

Ephesians 4:18 continues, "(...the willful blindness) that is deep-seated in them, due to their hardness of heart [to the insensitiveness of their moral nature]." This is step 4—persistently doing things our way. We have become *willfully* blinded, not *incapable* of seeing. We have chosen it. That is why this verse says the blindness is "deep-seated." We have been doing something a certain way for years and years, until we finally *believe* that we are walking in God's ways when in fact we are in error. Our hearts have become hardened and insensitive to what is right before God.

> In their spiritual apathy they have become callous and past feeling and reckless and have abandoned themselves [a prey] to unbridled sensuality, eager and greedy to indulge in every form of impurity [that their depraved desires may suggest and demand]. But you did not so learn Christ!
>
> —Ephesians 4:19–20

This is saying that from all of the understanding and knowledge that you have gained, these "sensual" things continue to manifest in your life on a daily basis. I am not talking about when you make a mistake every now and then. You do these things on a daily basis—to the point that you have become "willfully blind." Your heart has been hardened, and you have become insensitive to the fact that you are living a reckless life before God.

5. You indulge in every impurity that comes your way.

You may have learned the vocabulary of Scripture, but you have not learned Christ. You have not spiritually comprehended the purpose and reason why He died. Therefore, as I said in chapter two, you have become prey to the influences of the world and the enemy. Since you have not learned Christ, you indulge in every impurity that comes your way. This is the fifth, and final, step. Verses 21–24 say:

> Assuming that you have really heard Him and been taught by Him, as [all] Truth is in Jesus [embodied and personified in Him], strip yourselves of your former nature [put off and discard your old unrenewed self] which characterized your previous manner of life and becomes corrupt through lusts and desires that spring from delusion; and be constantly renewed in the spirit of your mind [having a fresh mental and spiritual attitude], and put on the new nature (the regenerate self) created in God's image [Godlike] in true righteousness and holiness.

Do you see a negative pattern forming in your life? If so, you need a new heart.

The Deception of the Flesh

~~~

Before I move on to the works of the flesh, I want to make sure that you understand the fullness of what *flesh* means. It refers either to the physical body or the human nature (as opposed to the nature of God) with its "frailties...and passions." The flesh is you—in the natural—inside and out. The "internal" flesh is part of your old heart and your unrenewed mind, which causes the "external" flesh to disobey God.

> But I say, walk and live [habitually] in the [Holy] Spirit [responsive to and controlled and guided by the Spirit]; then you will certainly not gratify the cravings and desires of the flesh (of human nature without God). For the desires of the flesh are opposed to the [Holy] Spirit, and the [desires of the] Spirit are opposed to the flesh (godless human nature); for these are antagonistic to each other [continually withstanding and in conflict with each other], so that you are not free but are prevented from doing what you desire to do. But if you are guided (led) by the [Holy] Spirit, you are not subject to the Law.
>
> —GALATIANS 5:16–18

Verses 19–21 spell out the works of the flesh—*read closely:*

> Now the doings (practices) of the flesh are clear (obvious): they are immorality, impurity, indecency, idolatry, sorcery, enmity, strife, jealousy, anger (ill temper), selfishness, divisions (dissensions), party spirit (factions, sects with peculiar opinions, heresies), envy,

drunkenness, carousing, and the like. I warn you beforehand, just as I did previously, that those who do such things shall not inherit the kingdom of God.

These are just *some* of the characteristics of the heart that are being made manifest. Jeremiah 17:9 said that the heart is desperately wicked; who can know it? This must mean that we can only name some of the traits. Attached to these things, and behind them, are other things that have been "lodged" in the "old heart," things that have not yet come to light.

The Deception of "Control"

Have you ever been in a situation where you said to yourself, "I will never do this" or "I will never do that"? I cannot tell you how many times I said that I would never do something, and then ended up doing just that. This is because the old heart is on a timetable, to the degree that when it is allowed to remain within you, it becomes stronger by being fed the worldly knowledge from the brain. We "house" this old heart until every evil work from the bottom of the pit comes to the surface.

Think about it. How can a man walk into a school and start stabbing small children? Where does it come from? How can a person get a shotgun, walk into a McDonald's and just start firing away and killing people? What do you think gets inside of a terrorist, causing him to ram a plane into the Twin Towers in New York City? These people did not simply plan to do these things. The depths of that evil heart were manifesting.

It starts small, with the things that you "think" you can control—which becomes the next deception of Satan. He allows you to think that you are in control of this "old heart." He allows you to think, *I have it under control. I only drank one drink.* Or, *I only smoked one cigarette.* He knows that if you keep going—keep letting that heart go unchallenged, unchanged and unconverted—everything in that old heart (that he has birthed into the world) will be made manifest in your life.

Who can know this heart? Who would want this heart to remain in them, not knowing the full ability of evil that sits inside of us?

We have become walking time bombs. We have become accidents waiting to happen. We have become "accessible" to anything that Satan desires to do in the earth—a prey for his next assignment. How can you tell him *no* when he is the ruler of that heart? Going back to my friend's comment, it saddens me to think that the enemy's ways seem to be more "attainable" than the gospel—only because we have failed to ask God for a "new heart."

The Spirit of the Lord does not govern the old heart because it does not belong to Him. It is the heart of Satan. So anything that Satan puts forth for us to do, if we have the old heart, we cannot rebuke it. We cannot say, "I refuse to do that," because we are housing his heart.

We must realize this heart is destined for eternal judgment. It has already been prepared, because of what it carries, to go to eternal damnation.

Therefore, it will never lead you to life, because it does not have life in it. It will never lead you to eternal truth, because this heart does not have the ability to house the Word of the Lord.

Transformation takes place when our minds are brought to the understanding that we need God.

I can always tell when an individual is coming to the end of self. Death fights to remain in control as life begins the transformation within—and the struggle comes to the surface. As light emerges, God says:

> You are the light of the world. A city set on a hill cannot be hidden. Nor do men light a lamp and put it under a peck measure, but on a lampstand...Let your light so shine before men that they may see your moral excellence and your praiseworthy, notable, and good deeds and recognize and honor and praise and glorify your Father Who is in heaven.
>
> —MATTHEW 5:14–16

God has put His light within us to shine before the world, not to suppress and hide it from others. He does not want to remove the candlestick "from its place" (Rev. 2:5). He is calling us to repent.

We do not recognize God's mercy in His plan of salvation. What a privilege and an honor it is when He calls us out of sin and gives us the opportunity to become acquainted with Him! This is the biggest miracle that can happen in your life, because—in the midst of having a mind that has been "conceived" in sin and "shaped" in iniquity, trained by the world and the enemy to the point that you have come into the world *prepared* to die an eternal death—God is still able to penetrate it.

God allows us to hear the gospel, and at that very moment, in that split second of time, He penetrates the mind that had been trained by Satan. He puts His Word in our mind, so that it tells us to "...be not conformed to this world: but by ye transformed by the renewing of your mind, that ye may prove what is that good, and acceptable, and perfect, will of God" (Rom. 12:2, KJV).

Transformation takes place when our minds are brought to the understanding that we need God.

The Spiritual Emergency Room

When we do not "renew" our minds, we can "fall away" into the old heart. In my studies, I have learned that the brain never stops working. It never settles down, nor does it ever shut up. Even when you are sleeping, the brain is in motion. The brain (not the heart) constantly races, moves, talks, plans and visualizes. Without stopping for a breath, it takes us to where we have been, where we are and where we are going. It is constantly receiving information at breakneck speed. The majority of the time, the heart cannot, and will not, keep up with the pace of the mind.

I recently had to be taken to the emergency room because I did not understand this principle. You see, many times we are so busy moving and doing things that we do not consider our hearts. I didn't, and I started experiencing the symptoms. I ended up in the emergency room with chest pains. The doctors started talking to me about heart attacks. As they talked, they explained how defibrillators jump-start a heart that has stopped beating.

This incident reminded me of the church. There are so many Christians racing around with spiritual "heart problems" that we need to be resurrected when we get to church! The choir, the preacher and the praise and worship team have been our spiritual defibrillators—they get powered up and anointed with oil, and they send out an electrical charge into the congregation. They are trying to jump-start hearts that have literally stopped beating. The treatment keeps you going for a couple of days, but that heart is still "mortally sick" (Jer. 17:9). It needs to be replaced.

The Bible says that we were "...dead in trespasses and sins" (Eph. 2:1, KJV). We have living, functioning, breathing hearts that keep our physical bodies alive, but spiritually, we are dead. So we depend on church "mechanics" to bring life. But only a new heart will cause us to live forever.

In the natural realm, when someone has a heart attack, there are signs, sounds and different things that the diseased heart allows to happen in the physical body. There is pain that goes down the arm and down the legs because the arteries are having a hard time pumping blood to and from the heart.

We must also look at the causes for a heart attack. Many times we eat the wrong thing, such as foods that are high in fat and cholesterol. We often do not get proper rest. After my trip to the emergency room, I had to change my diet and quit eating meat and other things that would affect my blood flow. I could not carry the outside weight of my schedule, doing everything that needed to be done, and eat as heavily as I was eating. I had to let something go.

The Spiritual "Vital Signs" of Breakdown

God is saying the same thing in this hour.

> O Jerusalem, wash your heart from wickedness, that ye may be saved! How long shall your iniquitous and grossly offensive thoughts lodge within you? For a voice declares from Dan [in the north] and proclaims evil from Mount Ephraim [the range dividing Israel from Judah].
> —JEREMIAH 4:14–15

In other words, God is saying that if you do not wash your heart, the very thing that you once enjoyed with this old heart will ambush you. Before you know it, the thing that you have built up and enjoy will become your enemy. This passage continues:

> Warn the [neighboring] nations [that our adversary is coming]; announce to Jerusalem that besiegers are coming from a far country, and they shout against the cities of Judah. Like keepers of a field they are against her round

about, because she has been rebellious against
Me, says the Lord.

—JEREMIAH 4:16–17

When everything starts folding in and coming
against you, God has not done this. Our own rebellion toward God causes our atmosphere to turn.
These changes are our *vital signs*, letting us know
that it is time to receive a new heart.

Your ways and your doings have brought these
things upon you. This is your calamity and doom;
surely it is bitter, for surely it reaches your very
heart! [It is not only the prophet but also the people who cry out in their thoughts] My anguish,
my anguish! I writhe in pain! Oh, the walls of my
heart! My heart is disquieted and throbs aloud
within me; I cannot be silent! For I have heard
the sound of the trumpet, the alarm of war.

—JEREMIAH 4:18–19

If you do not wash your heart, the very thing that you once enjoyed with this old heart will ambush you.

This is the sound of spiritual vital signs crying out.
Our chest cavities cave in because of our own
doings! Verse 20 states, "News of one violent disaster and calamity comes close after another."

We cannot turn on the news anymore without
hearing about disaster. People are starving; cities are

being flooded; fires cannot be put out; there are terrorist attacks. In other countries people are using
their own bodies to blow up malls and shopping centers. Children are being raped, and the homeless are
going unfed. God help us to discern the "signs" of
worldwide heart failure.

The same types of things happened in the Bible
when people ignored God and refused to learn His
ways. Romans 6:23 says, "For the wages which sin
pays is death."

If we look back at Jeremiah 4:20, we discover that
"the whole land is laid waste; suddenly are my tents
spoiled and destroyed..." Homes are broken up—
mothers and fathers are divorcing, fathers are turning against sons, daughters are turning against
mothers. This verse continues by saying, "Suddenly
are my tents spoiled and destroyed, and my [tent]
curtains ruined in a moment."

When you walk in rebellion, everything can be
going great, and you can have it all together. But I am
a witness of the fact that it can be brought down in
a second.

> [O Lord] how long must I see the flag [marking
> the route for flight] and hear the sound of the
> trumpet [urging the people to flee for refuge]?
> [Their chastisement will continue until it has
> accomplished its purpose] for My people are stu-
> pid, says the Lord [replying to Jeremiah]; they
> do not know and understand Me. They are thick-
> headed children, and they have no understand-
> ing. They are wise to do evil, but to do good they
> have no knowledge [and know not how].
> —JEREMIAH 4:21–22

We have knowledge about doing good, but we do not know how to do it. The know-how to "do good" requires a combination of a new heart and a transformed mind. The heart understands, and the mind knows. When both are in operation, the good in the heart flows to the mind and trains it with "know-how" to live according to God's Word. This renewed mind passes on the manifestation to the physical body.

The Lord is saying from Jeremiah 5:22–23:

> Do you not fear and reverence Me? says the Lord. Do you not tremble before Me? I placed the sand for the boundary of the sea, a perpetual barrier beyond which it cannot pass and by an everlasting ordinance beyond which it cannot go? And though the waves of the sea toss and shake themselves, yet they cannot prevail [against the feeble grains of sand which God has ordained, by nature to be sufficient for His purpose]; though [the billows] roar, yet they cannot pass over that [barrier]. [Is not such a God to be reverently feared and worshiped?] But these people have hearts that draw back from God and wills that rebel against Him; they have revolted and quit His service and have gone away [into idolatry].

According to His sovereign will, God has ordained that small things can overcome the mighty—because everything is in His hand. However, as we learned in chapter one, the problem is that our priorities are out of order. Many of us still have an old heart, so we cannot love God or fear Him unto obedience.

Divine Warnings

~~◦~~

> Say to them, Thus says the Lord, the God of
> Israel: Cursed is the man who does not heed
> the words of this covenant or solemn pledge
> which I commanded your fathers at the time
> that I brought them out of the land of Egypt,
> from the iron furnace, saying, Listen to My
> voice and do according to all that I command
> you. So will you be My people, and I will be
> your God, that I may perform the oath which I
> swore to your fathers, to give them a land flow-
> ing with milk and honey.
>
> —JEREMIAH 11:3–5

God does not want us to be destroyed. He does not
desire for us to be tormented by the ways of this
world. Instead, He gives His people divine warnings
to get their attention and to compel them to change
their ways. Jeremiah records His warning to the people in verses 5–7:

> Then I answered, Amen (so be it), O Lord.
> And the Lord said to me, Proclaim all these
> words in the cities of Judah and in the streets
> of Jerusalem: Hear the words of this covenant
> or solemn pledge and do them. For I earnestly
> protested and warned your fathers at the time
> that I brought them up *out of the land of
> Egypt*...
>
> —EMPHASIS ADDED

Do you see this? God never releases judgment
without first sending a warning. This is why He is
warning us, right now. He is telling us, "It is time to
receive a new heart."

...even to this day, protesting to and warning them persistently, saying, Obey My voice. Yet they did not obey or incline their ear [to Me], but everyone walked in the stubbornness of his own evil heart. Therefore I brought upon them all [the calamities threatened in] the words of this covenant or solemn pledge, which I had commanded, but they did not do.

—JEREMIAH 11:7–8

When that time comes...when God sends a "miracle" from the spirit realm that allows us to escape the old heart and we disobey His voice, He has no alternative. If we rebel against Him, we will reap disaster, just as Jerusalem did. Verse 11 says:

Therefore thus says the Lord: Behold, I am bringing evil and calamity upon them which they will not be able to escape.

God is saying, "I warned you when I sent you the Word of God and revealed to you how to get out of it, but you disobeyed Me."

Divine warnings are the advance symptoms of heart failure. Therefore, when you receive a divine warning, *you know* when it is time for a change of heart. You know when that old heart is starting to break down.

Did you know that in today's medical industry it is virtually impossible to receive a new heart unless the old heart fails you? You cannot get a new heart until the old one breaks down—until it is starting to destroy your life. Then, and only then, will doctors recommend you for a heart transplant. Even in the natural realm, new hearts are in short supply.

Examine your heart right now. Ask yourself, "Is my heart destroying my life?" If so, you are a *candidate* for a heart transplant...but it does not stop there. You have to get up and go to the doctor in order to receive treatment. The doctor does not have a way of knowing that you need a heart transplant. You have to initiate the treatment, or the doctor cannot help you.

God is saying, "I warned you when I sent you the Word of God and revealed to you how to get out of it, but you disobeyed Me."

When I arrived at the emergency room, I had to go through Admitting before they could treat me. I had to go through the process—sign the papers, tell them my name, address and what my problem was. I had to "confess" these things before the doctor could help me. Are you seeing the revelation?

Lamentations 1:20 says:

> Behold, O Lord, how distressed I am! My vital parts (emotions) are in tumult and are deeply disturbed; my heart cannot rest and is violently agitated within me, for I have grievously rebelled. Outside the house the sword bereaves, at home there is [famine, pestilence] death!

In other words, when I go out or when I am at home, I am being attacked. There is no relief.

[My foes] have heard that I [Jerusalem] sigh and groan, that I have no comforter [in You]. All my enemies have heard of my trouble; they are glad [O Lord] that You have done it. You will bring the day [of Judah's punishment] that you have foretold and proclaimed; [it involves also my foes' punishment] and they will become like me. Let all their wickedness come before You; and deal with them as You have dealt with me because of all of my transgressions; for my sighs and groans are many and my heart is faint.

—LAMENTATIONS 1:21–22

The most powerful sign of your need for a new heart is these four golden words: *"My heart is faint."* God's vital signs of breakdown will bring you to this place. *This is God's heart*—that you would understand and know that you need a new heart. He is waiting for you to say, "I cannot survive with this old heart. It has destroyed everything around me. It is destroying everything within me, and the number one thing that I cannot bear is the fact that I find no comfort in You, God. You are not my Comforter, so how can I survive without You?"

When that is the cry of your heart, God is telling you that you need a new heart.

Chapter 6

A Scientific
Point of View

Have you ever used something for a long time before you read the directions? Then when you read them, you discovered how it should *really work* and how much more that thing was capable of (than what you knew). After using it according to the directions, you became amazed at what you had been doing right all the time, and also at what you had missed that kept you from using it to its fullest potential.

When I started studying about the heart and brain, I was literally amazed—at times shocked into silence. More than this, I stood in awe of God, realizing how incredibly He has built us. As we move forward in this chapter you are going to see the Word of God being confirmed over and over again in brand-new ways.

Like me, I pray that you will give God the glory and honor that He deserves. I pray that by learning these incredible truths, your love for Him will grow deeper. We are truly "fearfully and wonderfully made" (Ps. 139:14, KJV). David also said in this verse,

"Marvellous are thy works; and that my soul knoweth right well." Understanding God's works changed his soul! It can change yours.

I pray that, like me, you will read on and say to God, "I lay my life—*everything that I am*—down at Your feet." I pray that you will ask Him for a new heart.

The new heart transformation is very scriptural, as you have been able to see as you read the previous chapters. Everything that God does (in the spirit realm) has an explanation, symbol or example in the natural realm.

> But it is not the spiritual life which came first, but the physical and then the spiritual. The first man [was] from out of earth, made of dust (earthly-minded); the second Man [is] the Lord from out of heaven. Now those who are made of the dust are like him who was first made of the dust (earthly-minded); and as is [the Man] from heaven, so also [are those] who are of heaven (heavenly-minded). And just as we have borne the image [of the man] of dust, so shall we and so let us also bear the image [of the Man] of heaven.
>
> —1 CORINTHIANS 15:46–49

When you look at what scientists have discovered about the heart, you will be amazed at how far behind the eight ball believers *really are*. The secular world has gained a thorough understanding of the heart's anatomy and functions, explaining it to the point that believers can look at the information from scientists and know that it had to be revealed to *them* by God.

God is so determined for us to get this message that when He could not find anybody in the Christian world to seek Him long enough—to get in His presence to receive the revelation—He revealed it to scientists so that we (His children) could understand what He is trying to tell us about this new heart.

The Natural Heart

Allow me to start by giving you a few "heart facts." The heart generally functions for seventy to eighty years without maintenance or replacement. During this time, it beats around one hundred thousand times a day, roughly forty million times a year—almost three billion beats in a lifetime. The heart pumps two gallons of blood per minute, adding up to more than one hundred gallons per hour, through a vascular system that is long enough to wrap around the earth two times—over sixty thousand miles. That powerful organ sits inside of each person.[1]

The heart is like a nuclear power plant. It generates five thousand times more energy than the brain. This is one of the main reasons why the heart has been called the "center" of our being. Even more amazing, it has its own nervous system that is called the "brain of the heart." This "heart brain" has more than forty thousand nerve cells, the same number of cells contained in many of the brain's subcortical centers. Research has proven that the heart brain can and does act independently of the brain in your head![2]

The heart can even beat without being connected to the brain. For example, when someone has a heart transplant, the surgeons have to sever the nerves that run from the brain to the heart. When they put the heart into the new body, they do not yet know how to reconnect the nerves. So the surgeons restore the heartbeat, and it keeps beating—even though there is no "nerve" connection to the brain.[3]

When heart rhythms are in balance, like a mighty waterfall, it releases a balanced flow that resonates throughout our being.

The natural heart is also able to feel, sense, learn and remember. From this, scientists have also observed that the heart sends emotional and intuitive signals to the brain and body that help to govern our lives.

The heart produces a strong substance called "atrial natriuretic factor" (ANF) or atrial peptide, nicknamed "the balance hormone," that "regulates" many of our brain's functions—as well as our organs.[4] Scientists are now finding that the balance hormone also motivates our behavior.[5] The heart's power center directs and aligns many of our bodies' systems and helps them to function in harmony. When heart rhythms are in balance, like a mighty waterfall, it releases a balanced flow that resonates throughout our being.

Heart Vision
~⌒~

> The light of the body is the eye: if therefore
> thine eye be single, thy whole body shall be full
> of light.
>
> —MATTHEW 6:22, KJV

The word *eye* means "vision."[6] The word *single*
means "folded together...to twine or braid."[7] How can
we achieve this balanced, complete vision? How can
we see from a heavenly perspective, according to the
Word of God? We must be born again and receive a
new heart, which causes heavenly vision to flow from
the center of our being to our brains and throughout
the rest of our bodies.

The heart is the center of our understanding—
where concepts and balanced intelligence are introduced to every part of us. It can send waves of rational,
considerate instruction to the brain. If the busy brain
receives this instruction, it brings a balanced perspective, which can strengthen our conscience. However,
the old heart does not have the spiritual power to override the brain's constant activity. This is why even our
human conscience can be deceived.

For example, let us look at John 8 where the
scribes and Pharisees brought a woman to Jesus who
had been caught in the act of adultery. The religious
leaders reminded Him of the Law—she should be
put to death (vv. 3–5). After listening to their argu-
ment, finally Jesus stood up (from where He had
been writing in the dirt) and said to them, "He that
is without sin among you, let him first cast a stone at
her" (v. 7, KJV).

Suddenly their consciences kicked in: "And they which heard it, being convicted by their own conscience, went out one by one, beginning at the eldest, even unto the last: and Jesus was left alone, and the woman standing in the midst" (v. 9, KJV). The Word from Jesus' mouth penetrated their "old hearts" and revealed their hypocrisy—so they left with their old hearts intact. How do I know this?

Their old hearts could understand their own guilt, but they did not have the power to convert and save their souls! They had enough "conscience" to convict someone else of sin, but they still did not have the ability to repent and ask Jesus to give them a new heart. Why? Titus 1:15–16 says:

> To the pure [in heart and conscience] all things are pure, but to the defiled and corrupt and unbelieving nothing is pure; their very minds and consciences are defiled and polluted. They profess to know God [to recognize, perceive, and be acquainted with Him], but deny and disown and renounce Him by what they do; they are detestable and loathsome, unbelieving and disobedient and disloyal and rebellious, and [they are] unfit and worthless for good work (deed or enterprise) of any kind.

The scribes and Pharisees had a "form" of godliness, but they denied His power. They were in the full swing of deception. They had become people pleasers—comparing themselves *by* themselves. They had forgotten that they were God's children and should *serve* others, not *crucify* them. As a result the Israelites could not look at their leaders and see their Savior—because these leaders had not pursued the new heart. Therefore, no matter what they did, these leaders could not please God.

It takes a pure, new heart to create a pure, undefiled conscience. The revelation does not stop there. Jesus turned to the woman in John 8 and gave her the solution: "'I am the light of the world: he that followeth me shall not walk in darkness, but shall have the light of life" (v. 12, KJV). In other words, He was saying, "The men who accused you were walking in the deception of their own, darkened, earthly consciences. But I am able to give you a new heart that will fill your mind, and every part of you, with light—a balanced, complete, heavenly vision and understanding." That is powerful!

The heart understands, and the mind knows. This is why the Book of Proverbs, the book of wisdom, opens with these words:

> The Proverbs (truths obscurely expressed, maxims, and parables) of Solomon son of David, king of Israel: that people may know skillful and godly Wisdom and instruction, discern and comprehend the words of understanding and insight, receive instruction in wise dealing and the discipline of wise thoughtfulness, righteousness, justice, and integrity, that prudence may be given to the simple, and knowledge, discretion, and discernment to the youth.
>
> —PROVERBS 1:1–4

Throughout the Bible, the line of distinction is drawn between "knowing" and "understanding" because there is a distinct difference.

The Natural Mind
~⌒~⌒~

The brain begins to develop after the heart is formed. It grows from the bottom up—the brain stem (medulla oblongata), emotional center (amygdala) and then the logic centers (cerebral cortex and frontal lobes).

The medulla contains the nerve systems that regulate our heart rate, breathing and other body functions. This means that the first part of the brain is created to link it with the heart and to direct or adjust how fast it beats. It monitors and facilitates communication to the heart, lungs, nervous system and parts of the body.

The amygdala develops next. It stores emotional memories and compares these experiences with new information. It determines what is relevant to each individual and forms the brain's basis for our perceptions. As the brain develops, it grows out of this emotional center to develop our logical capabilities. This is why what we perceive and what is *real* can be two different things. It is also why our imagination, strategies and decisions are colored by our emotions. When emotions are balanced, they give life and meaning to facts, objectives and logic. When unbalanced, they distort the truth.

The third section of the brain, the cerebral cortex, develops next. It reasons and reflects, evaluates and considers, strategizes, plans and imagines. It takes the relevant information passed on from the amygdala and makes sense out of it. It can also make nonsense out of it if the imagination goes wild. Whether balanced or unbalanced, this information gets passed on to the next brain center.

The frontal lobes are the fourth, and final, section of the brain. This is where our decision making is done. The lobes also determine which emotional response is appropriate for each situation. It feeds from the emotions and sends the updated instructions back to the emotions.[8]

God created the heart to govern the brain. The heart is outside of the brain and, technically, is not subject to brain processes. However, when we choose to ignore our heart's direction, the brain assumes control. It takes over, operating from a linear and logical perspective, always ready to defend its own interests. The brain has no understanding, so it is territorial—nothing foreign (spiritual) can enter without a fight.

The brain is always active, even while you are sleeping, trying to get your attention through dreams. It stays in a position of alertness to defend or attack when it, or your body, senses a threat—real or perceived—to its existence and development.

The brain tries to pass on information to the heart, but the heart does not have to accept it. And this is where we encounter the mystery of the new heart. Logically, our old heart (by virtue of how God created it) should be able to override the brain. However, Adam and Eve perverted this ability when they followed their brains instead of their hearts (the enemy's great deception) in the Garden of Eden (Gen. 3). Now, in order to balance and control the mind, we must receive the new heart.

As our brains form perceptions and react to the

outside world, neural messages travel down through the medulla that can affect the rhythms of our hearts. The heart, however, has been designed to send messages back to the brain. (Scientists have already observed that the brain both identifies and obeys these messages!) The new heart can filter life-giving information to the brain that not only alters our consciousness, but also our actions.

It has also been medically proven that when we focus on our hearts, the balance of the functions between the heart and brain increases.[9] When this synchronization takes place, every other bodily function operates to its fullest capacity. When we focus attention on our brains, however, our whole body comes under stress and falls out of balance. Maybe that is why stress has been called "the silent killer." It is a matter of the heart—the choice is yours.

Jesus said that unless we become simple, like a child, we cannot enter His kingdom (Mark 10:15). We have to reject our logic and emotions, and with wide-open eyes, turn around and embrace the spiritual truth that flows from our new hearts.

> The law of the Lord is perfect, restoring the [whole] person; the testimony of the Lord is sure, making wise the simple. The precepts of the Lord are right, rejoicing the heart; the commandment of the Lord is pure and bright, enlightening the eyes. The [reverent] fear of the Lord is clean, enduring forever; the ordinances of the Lord are true and righteous altogether.
>
> More to be desired are they than gold, even than much fine gold; they are sweeter also than honey and drippings from the honeycomb. Moreover, by them is Your servant warned

(reminded, illuminated, and instructed); and in keeping them there is great reward. Who can discern his lapses and errors? Clear me from hidden [and unconscious] faults. Keep back Your servant also from presumptuous sins; let them not have dominion over me! Then shall I be blameless, and I shall be innocent and clear of great transgression. Let the words of my mouth and the meditation of my heart be acceptable in Your sight, O Lord, my [firm, impenetrable] Rock and my Redeemer.

—PSALM 19:7–14

Formation of the Heart and Mind

Let us go back to the genesis of the heart and mind in a human fetus. When a child is conceived in the mother's womb, the first thing that develops is a heartbeat. After determining that a woman is pregnant, the heartbeat is the first thing the doctor goes after. He does not examine the mother, first looking for the eyes, nose, brain and nervous system. He listens for a heartbeat, and if there is a heartbeat, the child is alive.

People who live from old heart reasoning—including pro-choice advocates—believe that life does not begin until the brain is functioning. But people who listen to and obey their new heart understand that the heart is where life begins. In fact, the heart begins to store its memory code from being connected to the mother's umbilical cord.

Expectant mothers are told to talk gently and lovingly to their unborn child and to gently stroke the outside of their womb. These words and actions are recorded into that child's memory code before it is ever born. When the child is birthed out into the world, he or she already has a record of everything that it has experienced since its first heartbeat.

As that baby begins to grow, by the time that child is six months old, the record of its experiences has escalated at an unbelievable rate. This is where the problem begins—the heart inside a six-month-old baby has already had six months' accumulation of memories in the world. That baby's brain, with its four different sections, is constantly being fed instant information from society. Already, more information is coming into the brain than the immature heart can handle. Because the brain is receiving more information than the heart can process, the brain "perceives" that it should govern that heart and body.

Remember that our hearts also have a "brain," which integrates and processes intuitive information and signals from the brain and body. However, it is young and already out-of-balance because of the sin nature it inherited from Adam and Eve's fall. Coupled with this, the body and the brain are exposed the most to society. When the brain sends constant information to that young heart, the heart tries to process it (in order to regulate the response), but the brain keeps bombarding it with more and more information—which leaves the young heart miles behind.

This sets the pattern that runs throughout our lifetimes unless we receive the new heart. By the time our hearts can process new information, the brain has already sent messages to the body, and both body and brain have responded to *knowledge*—the way that the world handles things—and not to heart understanding. This puts the old heart in constant jeopardy of spiritual heart failure.

The next stage of a Christian's development is the formative years. Psychologists have proven that, without fail, by the time a child reaches five years of age, his or her heart and mind patterns are basically set for life. This same stage applies to our spiritual lives. It is imperative—especially during the first five years of your walk with God—that you spend time in the Word, worship and prayer in order to transform your mind.

The heart must be converted before you can have a change of mind and a new perspective.

The converted heart longs to walk in the ways of God, which means that it "declares war" on the resident mind. Then the spiritual battle begins:

> Do not be conformed to this world (this age), [fashioned after and adapted to its external, superficial customs], but be transformed (changed) by the [entire] renewal of your mind [by its new ideals and its new attitude], so that you may prove [for yourselves] what is the good and acceptable and perfect will of God, even the thing which is good and acceptable and perfect [in His sight for you].
>
> —ROMANS 12:2

When you are more mature, have learned your heart's rhythm and experienced what happens when you react to information that has been "spit out" by the brain—real or perceived—the results you have suffered teach you not to do that again. However, young Christian hearts have the greatest battle. They are birthed into the church and know the Lord, but the information from the brain still overflows their hearts. (This also happens to saints who refuse to be weaned from the "milk" of the Word. They cannot grow up to eat the "bread," and then the "meat," of the Word.)

With heart and brain unified (aligned), you will experience a natural flow, rhythm and peace within—no matter what is going on in the natural world.

You do not have to wonder anymore why we are so tuned into our thought patterns and why we let our minds govern our lives. As I said before, we are living in a brain world. The information our brains receive tells us that we can change our heart and change our lives if we change our mind. This is not what God intended. The mind does not *change*. It jealously fights to keep everything "the way it has always been." The heart must be converted before you can have a change of mind and a new perspective.

The mind needs to be retrained with the

understanding that is built into the new heart—
which is the heart of God. The mind must be
retrained through the Word of God. Then the emotional and rational memory banks will be refilled
with godly information from the Bible.

Synergy of Heart and Mind

The new heart and the renewed mind are a powerful
combination. When understanding flows from the
heart to the renewed mind, it identifies with what is
already there and causes the body to receive the
blessing. The mind is first "emotional," so the Word
of God must enter the amygdala on a constant basis
and create an emotional connection to the heart of
God within you. Then, and only then, will your decisions be balanced by God's Word. Light and harmony will flood your entire being. With heart and
brain unified (aligned), you will experience a natural
flow, rhythm and peace within—no matter what is
going on in the natural world.

Jesus exemplified this uncommon existence. The
apostle Paul describes this existence and instructs
us to seek the same for ourselves:

> Let this same attitude and purpose and [hum-
> ble] mind be in you which was in Christ Jesus:
> [Let Him be your example in humility:] Who,
> although being essentially one with God and in
> the form of God [possessing the fullness of the
> attributes which make God God], did not think
> this equality with God was a thing to be eagerly
> grasped or retained, but stripped Himself [of all
> privileges and rightful dignity], so as to assume

the guise of a servant (slave), in that He became
like men and was born a human being.

And after He had appeared in human form,
He abased and humbled Himself [still further]
and carried His obedience to the extreme of
death, even the death of the cross! Therefore
[because He stooped so low] God has highly
exalted Him and has freely bestowed on Him
the name that is above every name. That in (at)
the name of Jesus every knee should (must)
bow, in heaven and on earth and under the
earth, and every tongue [frankly and openly]
confess and acknowledge that Jesus Christ is
Lord, to the glory of God the Father.

—PHILIPPIANS 2:5–11

This "Christ-life" existence takes us back to giving
up our right to "be right," because this is what Jesus
did. When He humbled Himself in obedience to God,
His name became something that Satan recognized
as power.

We cannot let the mind control us. We must ask
for a new heart and then begin to obey the divine
messages that God sends from within us. When we
do, we will walk in divine authority because we will
be in sync with the way God intended us to be.
And when we are in sync with what God intended,
the devil has to flee from us when we resist him
(James 4:7).

When you have been born again, you may constantly look for and seek God in prayer for anointing
and authority over the enemy because you do not
understand that you already have the power to
defeat him within you. The only thing that gives you
control over the enemy is the synergy of the new

heart and a renewed mind that is fully submitted to God and His will.

When your mind is submitted to the will of God, which flows from your new heart, then this heart begins to rule and dominate your flesh and influence your surroundings. Since God resides in your new heart, and the character of God is already in it, you are automatically placed in a seat above Satan! You do not have to pray to get there. Your new heart transforms you to your rightful place. As you surrender your mind on a daily basis, it keeps you there.

The only thing that gives you control over the enemy is the synergy of the new heart and a renewed mind that is fully submitted to God and His will.

Jesus came to the earth with the heart of God inside of Him. He still, however, could have aborted His assignment if He made the wrong choices. He could have walked around, allowing His mind to dictate what He did or did not do and what He had the right to be. Since He was the Son of God, He could have demanded to be given a mansion, servants, wealth and everything else—and it all would have happened—but He didn't. He chose, instead, to obey His Father's heart.

Jesus came into the earth with a dying heart. His goal was to die—to fulfill an eternal assignment. His converted heart was built with an assignment already in it. He submitted to His heart and obeyed the will of the Father, which already resided there.

When we are born again and receive the new heart, it comes with an assignment already in it. We need to do what Jesus did instead of letting our minds and bodies dictate what we have "the right" to do and be. We can let *go* and *let God*.

Our heavenly Father is saying, "I want you to submit to obedience, because when you give up your right to 'be right' in the natural realm, your new heart will govern what you do from the spirit realm, and that is when you will have victory. That is when you will receive power to do what Jesus did."

God is telling us like never before—*we need a new heart.*

Chapter 7

Results of a **Heart Transplant**

We have learned how the old heart is conceived and developed, and that it forms the basis of who we are. Now we will take a look at it from another angle. We all have a natural heart, but not many have new hearts that they have received from God. In the natural realm, when a surgeon says that a heart transplant is necessary, it is a matter of life and death.

The new heart brings new warfare because the enemy wants to keep you bound and ineffective.

This is the same in the spiritual realm. God has already said that the heart "is exceedingly perverse and corrupt and severely, mortally sick! Who can know it [perceive, understand, be acquainted with his own heart and mind]?" (Jer. 17:9). We desperately need a spiritual heart transplant!

God has already provided a Donor for all who desire to undergo this vital procedure. The heart that rested inside of Jesus is available for transplant into your life. It is a heart of power. Jesus' heart came with an eternal assignment—and when we receive His heart, we receive our part of that mission. But just as the person who receives a transplanted natural heart must engage in a fight to keep his or her body from rejecting that transplanted heart, so too the enemy fights us tooth-and-nail to try to make us reject our new heart. He knows that the only way he can delay or cause us to abort our divine assignment is to cause us to reject our new heart. The new heart brings new warfare because the enemy wants to keep you bound and ineffective.

The new heart sets us free, dresses us for battle and puts us right back into active duty.

Whether you have realized it or not, there has always been a battle for your soul. Sadly, many of us have functioned like prisoners of war. Stripped of our weapons and uniforms, the enemy has chained us and thrown us into a pit of bondage. There is little to no food (Word) there, and there is definitely no rest. The enemy's cruel forced labor drains every ounce of your strength. The new heart sets us free, dresses us for battle and puts us right back into active duty.

Some spiritual POWs never overcome the trauma of war. Even after they have been rescued and brought back home, their minds torment them with reruns of what used to be. Though they have been set free, they are spiritually paralyzed. Through torment and deception, the enemy has disabled them. They do not even try to walk in their newfound freedom. They need a new heart—just like the generation of Israelites who died in the wilderness because they were afraid to obey God's voice (Num. 32:13).

A Divine Charge

When you receive a new heart, you can expect a battle. Your flesh, and the outside world, will not give up control without a fight. When God spoke to the Israelites, who because of the continual disobedience flowing out of their old hearts and unrenewed minds had been taken captive and scattered out of the Promised Land, He gave them a divine charge:

> Therefore say, Thus says the Lord God: I will gather you from the peoples and assemble you out of the countries where you have been scattered, and I will give back to you the land of Israel. And when they return there, they shall take away from it all traces of its detestable things and all its abominations (sex impurities and heathen religious practices). And I will give them one heart [a new heart] and I will put a new spirit within them; and I will take the stony [unnaturally hardened] heart out of their flesh, and will give them a heart of flesh [sensitive and responsive to the touch of their God].
>
> —EZEKIEL 11:17–19

God promised to gather His people and to give them back their land. But it wouldn't be without a fight! Along with their new heart would come the courage to take possession of their land and clean out all the impurities.

When Jesus talked with His own followers about living the "Christ life" with their new hearts, He said:

> If the world hates you, know that it hated Me before it hated you. If you belonged to the world, the world would treat you with affection and would love you as its own. But because you are not of the world [no longer one with it], but I have chosen (selected) you out of the world, the world hates (detests) you. Remember that I told you, A servant is not greater than his master [is not superior to him].
>
> —JOHN 15:18–20

The good news is that Jesus overcame the world (John 16:33). He died to give us a healthy, new heart, and when that heart is transplanted inside of us, we have part of Jesus—the One who died and rose again—in our innermost being!

Every memory Jesus has of the Father, from before the foundation of the world, is inside of you. His experiences of walking with power and authority on earth and casting Satan down are stored in your new heart. Memories of when He rose from the dead and then ascended to sit on the right hand of the Father flow through your veins. Everything that God is—*since the dawn of eternity*—lives inside of you. If you have a new heart, you have supernatural power! The question is, *If we have truly received this new heart, how can we fail?*

If we trust and obey our new heart, Jesus will help us to get rid of all the "detestable things" and "abominations." Philippians 1:6 says:

> And I am convinced and sure of this very thing, that He Who began a good work in you will continue until the day of Jesus Christ [right up to the time of His return], developing [that good work] and perfecting and bringing it to full completion in you.

In other words, Jesus will work inside of you until you do consistently what is pleasing to God (Phil. 2:13). If you obey the Lord, your new heart will lead you through this life and into eternity. It is actually your *deposit* of eternity, because Christ has already passed through death and ascended to heaven.

> He has made everything beautiful in its time. He also has planted eternity in men's hearts and minds [a divinely implanted sense of a purpose working through the ages which nothing under the sun but God alone can satisfy], yet so that men cannot find out what God has done from the beginning to the end.
> —ECCLESIASTES 3:11

God has an *appointed time* and a *purpose* for you on the earth. The only way you will fulfill that purpose and assignment is to trust and obey Him.

> Therefore also now, says the Lord, turn and keep on coming to Me with all your heart, with fasting, with weeping, and with mourning [until every hindrance is removed and the broken fellowship is restored]. Rend your hearts and not your garments and return to the Lord, your

God, for He is gracious and merciful, slow to
anger, and abounding in loving-kindness; and
He revokes His sentence of evil [when His conditions are met].

—Joel 2:12–13

A Divine Transition
~⌒⌒⌒~

If you set six different pendulum clocks close together
and start them swaying at different times, ultimately
they all come into alignment—swaying in the same
direction and on the same beat. Scientists call this
process entrainment.

The question is, *If we have truly received this new heart, how can we fail?*

In your physical body, your most powerful organ
will pull the others into its force of energy. It is the
same in the spirit realm. Your new heart, being the
heart of God, has infinitely more power than anything else does. Change will come if you allow it. Are
you ready to change?

Though powerful, the old heart has been over-
programmed (by the brain) from birth. Its natural
rhythm has been distorted, so it pulls everything
into an out-of-sync pattern. It does not maintain a
healthy balance. Organs are in place but not functioning the way they should. That is why we need

a new heart. We need the Lord to help us put everything into balance.

> Diverse and deceitful weights are shamefully vile and abhorrent to the Lord, and false scales are not good.
>
> —PROVERBS 20:23

Your new heart has been designed to clear out everything that is unbalanced and deceitful. This transplant moves you from *one place* to *another place*. It changes you, step by step, from one stage into another. God is moving you toward your new assignment. Things may feel strange at first, but if you will submit to God, He will do His "perfect work" in you (2 Tim. 3:16–17; James 1:4).

Since your new heart is no longer connected to your brain, it lives totally from the power of God! It receives its "messages" from the "information" that has been stored deep in His heart. Whatever is programmed in your new heart when God sets it into your chest cavity is the assignment that you will begin to carry out.

"Natural" Heart Transitions

I recently read a story about a girl who received the heart of another young girl who had been murdered. The murder case could not be solved, so the police had closed the case. Months later the little girl began to have dreams and visions about the incident— down to the smallest detail. When she told her mother, they filed a report with the police, describing the man who killed her donor—down to where he lived. She even told them what the little girl had said to her killer. The murderer was arrested.[1] It is amazing, but true. The donor's heart held that vital information and passed it on to its new mind and body.

I heard another story from a syndicated radio program where they were interviewing a doctor who specializes in heart transplant case studies. He shared that he had talked with a man who started having a recurring dream after his heart transplant. Over and over again he saw a young woman who had fallen to her death down a flight of stairs. Troubled, he came to the doctor, and they started tracing the origins of his new heart. They discovered that the donor's daughter had fallen down a flight of stairs and died from a broken neck.[2]

There are many other stories of strange things happening when people received new hearts, including changes in appetite and relationship changes. The important thing to remember is that your new heart will create change that your mind cannot control.

The new heart stops taking the "information overload" from your old brain because it does not need it. It functions from the miracle power of God. He will begin to purge those things from within you that do not line up with His Word.

> Consider it wholly joyful, my brethren, whenever you are enveloped in or encounter trials of any sort or fall into various temptations. Be assured and understand that the trial and proving of your faith bring out endurance and steadfastness and patience. But let endurance and steadfastness and patience have full play and do a thorough work, so that you may be [people]

perfectly and fully developed [with no defects], lacking in nothing.

—JAMES 1:2–4

The Mind Declares War

The new heart has come to assume its rightful place of authority, and the brain is painfully aware of this. Scientists have said that the brain *fears* the heart, and I believe this is especially so once it is severed from its nerve connection.[3] The old mind knows that Someone else is in control. The new assignment in that heart is going to be fulfilled—with or without the brain's help.

When we are no longer obeying the old mind, it is being put to death. A paradigm shift is occurring. While the old mind is being put to death (as the result of reading and obeying God's Word), the new heart is replacing the old actions and patterns in the brain. As you sow to the Spirit, it is taking back the ground that Satan once occupied.

The mind perceives this as a threat to its existence, so it declares war on the new heart…and the battles continue. The apostle Paul said:

> So I find it to be a law (rule of action of my being) that when I want to do what is right and good, evil is ever present with me and I am subject to its insistent demands. For I endorse and delight in the Law of God in my inmost self [with my new nature]. But I discern in my bodily members [in the sensitive appetites and wills of the flesh] a different law (rule of action) at war against the law of my mind (my reason) and

making me a prisoner to the law of sin that dwells in my bodily organs [in the sensitive appetites and wills of the flesh].

—ROMANS 7:21–23

The mind is used to speeding, racing and responding to the worldly way of doing things. In other words, if you walk up to me and slap me, then my brain says, "I have been trained by society to slap you back."

But the new heart says, "Turn the other cheek." It tells you, "If a person wants your coat, give him your cloak also." The new heart tells us to walk a mile for peace (Matt. 5:39–41).

When an enemy comes against you and wounds you, the old mind says, "I do not want to have anything to do with you."

But the Word that flows from the new heart says, "Love your enemies, bless them that curse you, do good to them that hate you, and pray for them which despitefully use you" (Matt. 5:44, KJV). So you enter into immediate warfare, because the Word of God is piercing that old mind and literally "canceling out" worldly thought patterns.

A Two-Pronged Counterattack

When you obey the new heart's rulership, the Word actually begins to renew the mind from without and from within. The brain is sandwiched. You have the Word *inside* of you and are putting the Word *into* you (from outside) by reading the Bible—which travels through your eyes and goes directly to the brain! So the old heart pattern is literally being squeezed out. That is why the battle rages and you feel the conflict inside of you. Your thought patterns have been "dug in" for years and years.

It is important to understand the process of receiving the new heart. It begins one day as you sit in a church service. Someone asks you if you want to be saved, and you go to the altar and receive the new heart. At that moment, everything changes, sending signals to the brain that it is going to die. The first explosion goes off in the mind, which hates being out of control. It loathes being disconnected.

> That is why the battle rages and you feel the conflict inside of you. Your thought patterns have been "dug in" for years and years.

Even as you kneel at the altar deciding to follow Christ, thoughts begin to dart through your mind: *I cannot give this up. I am not ready to do this. I am afraid that So-and-so will not understand.* This is your first battle in the war of your new heart. Your mind continues to perceive and conceive evil, but it does not have an old heart into which to plant the evil anymore. The new heart does not need the brain's input. It will not receive that earthly garbage. It is connected to eternity.

So the mind keeps throwing out its "alarm signals" to the flesh, for the body to obey its instructions and carry out the ungodly actions. The new heart responds by sending a wave of conviction, and the battle goes on. Soon the flesh determines that it no longer enjoys the assignment it has received from the mind because the new heart is convicting it.

Do Not Quench the Spirit

In 1970, Doctors John and Beatrice Lacey observed the following phenomenon. They were able to document that when the brain sent alarm signals to the body, the heart did not automatically obey (as did the other organs). While the other organs began to function in an alarm state, the heart would continue to beat slowly. Not only this, but they also observed that the heart appeared to be sending messages back to the brain, which the brain not only understood, but also obeyed. They even documented that it appeared that these heart messages could influence a person's "motivated behavior."[4]

Your new heart will bring you to a *valley of decision* as you go through the process of purification.

Your new heart is a powerful, yet gentle ruler. If you submit to its promptings in spite of your brain's resistance, the heart will send a message back to the brain that says, "I am not going to do it that way. I am not going to answer that way." As you submit to God, these messages will become so powerful that the body will divorce the brainwaves and begin to line up with your new heart. This is not just a spiritual truth; it is a physical fact.

If the heart sends a clear, intuitive signal with a feeling that says, "Don't do this," the head may vigorously resist, demanding to know "Why? How? When?" so persistently that the heart's signal is cut off.[5] In Christendom, we call this "quenching the Spirit." This can also explain why it can be so difficult at times to pray or enter into true, heartfelt worship. First Thessalonians 5:19 says, "Do not quench (suppress or subdue) the [Holy] Spirit."

God continues to purge the "detestable things" in our flesh as we read and obey His Word. Everything "hidden" begins to be exposed and discarded as the Word digs up each impure thought and motive. Your battle will be to submit to the Spirit's direction, and this can be an awesome fight. If you do not submit to your new heart, ultimately you will be stripped by the enemy and thrown into a cold, dark place. Your new heart will bring you to a *valley of decision* as you go through the process of purification.

For example, if you read the scripture (outside information coming into your mind) that says, "Love thy neighbor as thyself," and your new heart (information from the heart of Christ) is already programmed to love your neighbor, when the evil thought arises to say, "Hate your neighbor," it will be ineffective. The message *coming in* that says, "Love thy neighbor," combines with the new heart desire to love *already inside of you* and attacks that evil thought from both sides, squeezing it out. When you disobey, the opposite happens. Your heart becomes "faint" because you are rejecting it. (See Lamentations 1:20–22.)

God's Measuring Line

It is God who determines how well we are progressing on our transformation into the Christ-life after we receive our new hearts. When He brought His people out of captivity and returned them to the land of promise, He told them He was going to measure the progress they made on rebuilding His temple.

> Therefore say to them [the Jews of this day], Thus says the Lord of hosts: Return to Me, says the Lord of hosts, and I will return to you; it is the utterance of the Lord of hosts...So the angel who talked with me said to me, Cry out, Thus says the Lord of hosts: I am jealous for Jerusalem and for Zion with a great jealousy. And I am very angry with the nations that are at ease; for while I was but a little displeased, they helped forward the affliction and disaster. Therefore thus says the Lord: I have returned to Jerusalem with compassion (loving-kindness and mercy). My house shall be built in it, says the Lord of hosts, and a measuring line shall be stretched out over Jerusalem [with a view to rebuilding its walls].
>
> —ZECHARIAH 1:3, 14–16

When God begins to restore and construct the real temple within us, it will be done according to His measuring line, not our "false" weights and measures. This is why we desperately need the new heart. Verses 17–21 continue:

> Cry yet again, saying, Thus says the Lord of hosts: My cities shall yet again overflow with prosperity, and the Lord shall yet comfort Zion and shall yet choose Jerusalem. Then I lifted up my eyes and saw, and behold, four horns [symbols of strength]. And I said to the angel who talked with me, What are these? And he answered me, These are the horns or powers which have scattered Judah, Israel, and Jerusalem. Then the Lord showed me four smiths or workmen [one for each enemy horn, to beat it down]. Then said I, What are these [horns and smiths] coming to do? And He said, These are the horns or powers that scattered Judah so that no man lifted up his head. But these smiths or workmen have come to terrorize them and cause them to be panic-stricken, to cast out the horns or powers of the nations who lifted up their horn against the land of Judah to scatter it.

When we surrender our hearts to God and say, "No more!", He will do battle on our behalf. He has already prepared a host of angels to fight for us. He has also prepared the Holy Spirit to stretch out the "measuring rod," *so that this time* when we come to Him, we will be built properly. We will be constructed according to the right measurements and fulfill the purpose and assignment that He has already placed in our new heart.

> So shall My Word be that goes forth out of My
> mouth; it shall not return to Me void [without
> producing any effect, useless], but it shall
> accomplish that which I please and purpose, and
> it shall prosper in the thing for which I sent it.
>
> —ISAIAH 55:11

When God sends a Word from the abundance that
is in His heart, it always prospers. This is why we
must not reject the new heart. When "evil treasure"
is inside of you (in your old heart), you cannot
expect to *confess* good things and get what you
want! This is perversion, because you are doing
things exactly opposite of the way that God
intended. (See Jeremiah 17:9.)

> The upright (honorable, intrinsically good)
> man out of the good treasure [stored] in his
> heart produces what is upright (honorable and
> intrinsically good), and the evil man out of the
> evil storehouse brings forth that which is
> depraved (wicked and intrinsically evil); for out
> of the abundance (overflow) of the heart his
> mouth speaks.
>
> —LUKE 6:45

God searches our hearts. He knows when our
words come from the abundance of righteousness
that He has stored within us. And *these* words—not
the empty confessions from the brain—will yield
eternal results, and our Father will be pleased.

He is faithful to tell us when we are doing well, not
through somebody else's words and standards, but
by speaking directly to our new heart, saying, "Well
done, good and faithful servant" (Matt. 25:23, KJV).
God's voice is the only one that *really counts*.

We can compliment each other, compare our-selves against one another and say many things—but we must realize that many who encourage us are still "guppies" in the Spirit. They are not "big fish" to God. They just seem to be because they are stroking our flesh. According to God's measuring line, they are not where they need to be. The danger of comparison surfaces again! In the ocean, a guppy would be so tiny that it would say to a goldfish, "Oh, you are such a big, beautiful, bright fish!" A shark, on the other hand, would see it differently.

God's voice is the only one that *really counts*.

Let us not think of ourselves "more highly" than we ought to think (Rom. 12:3). We are utterly dependent upon God and the new heart that He puts within us. If we fail to trust and obey Him as He begins to purify our earthly temples, we can be taken prisoner again by the enemy. We can submit to God's rebuilding process, or we can go back to the pit. The choice is ours. We need to embrace the new heart.

Chapter 8

The New **Heart**

T he new heart is an amazing mystery, and we must walk in the Spirit to understand its depths. We hold the feelings and purposes of God within us! That is awesome.

> For who has known or understood the mind (the counsels and purposes) of the Lord so as to guide and instruct Him and give Him knowledge? But we have the mind of Christ (the Messiah) and do hold the thoughts (feelings and purposes) of His heart.
>
> —1 Corinthians 2:16

Even more, our new heart leads us into the counsel of God as we submit to its direction. Yes, our new heart has a brain, and that brain is the mind of Christ.

The old heart can function independently of the brain. The new heart also has this ability, but even more so—because it is *supernatural*. The old (natural) "nerve" connection has been severed, so this heart is able to rule your old brain because it was not with your original body at conception. It was never oversaturated with information by your old brain, so it has the power to take authority. This heart has not been naturally conditioned to bow to your mind

135

through years of familiarity. Your new heart has the undeniable ability to walk in the statues of God.

When you say, "I have been born again in Christ Jesus," the first thing that begins to function and rule in that space is the heart.

Your new heart has the undeniable ability to walk in the statutes of God.

> And I will give them one heart [a new heart] and I will put a new spirit within them; and I will take the stony [unnaturally hardened] heart out of their flesh, and will give them a heart of flesh [sensitive and responsive to the touch of their God]. That they may walk in My statutes and keep My ordinances, and do them. And they shall be My people, and I will be their God.
>
> —EZEKIEL 11:19–20

It is incredible to me that God has allowed scientists to prove (to Christians) the difference between a person that says, "I have been touched," and somebody that has truly been converted. When you have been converted *for real*, you receive a new heart, and that heart takes you back to the beginning—to when you were a fetus—because your new heart beats without being connected to the brain, just like in the unborn child.

Nicodemus, a ruler of the Pharisees and one of the wisest men of his day, was stumped by the mystery of the new birth.

Jesus answered him, I assure you, most solemnly I tell you, that unless a person is born again (anew, from above), he cannot ever see (know, be acquainted with, and experience) the kingdom of God. Nicodemus said to Him, How can a man be born when he is old? Can he enter his mother's womb again and be born? Jesus answered, I assure you, most solemnly I tell you, unless a man is born of water and [even] the Spirit, he cannot [ever] enter the kingdom of God. What is born of [from] the flesh is flesh [of the physical is physical]; and what is born of the Spirit is spirit...If I have told you of things that happen right here on the earth and yet none of you believes Me, how can you believe (trust Me, adhere to Me, rely on Me) if I tell you of heavenly things? And yet no one has ever gone up to heaven, but there is One Who has come down from heaven—the Son of Man [Himself], Who is (dwells, has His home) in heaven.

—JOHN 3:3–6, 12–13

Nicodemus had earthly wisdom, not the wisdom of God. If we are to embrace the new heart, we must receive and believe the Word of the Lord.

More on the Anatomy of the Heart

By the twenty-fifth day of a woman's pregnancy, the heart has formed and started its rhythm. Outside of any legal definition, some doctors say that death really occurs when the heart stops beating, because the heart is alive before the brain is formed and can continue beating after the brain is dead.

Through its beating patterns, the heart sends pressure waves that move through our arteries to create our pulse rhythms. Heartbeats also influence brainwave activity and provide oxygen, nutrients and electrical energy to every organ and gland in our bodies.

Researchers have documented that when a pulse of blood gets up to the brain, it changes the brain's electrical activity. It alters the flow of that brain's process! Your new heart is also able to send "waves" of life, quickening your brain and the rest of your being to the ways of God.

> But if the Spirit of him that raised up Jesus from the dead dwell in you, he that raised up Christ from the dead shall also quicken your mortal bodies by his Spirit that dwelleth in you. Therefore, brethren, we are debtors, not to the flesh, to live after the flesh. For if ye live after the flesh, ye shall die: but if ye through the Spirit do mortify the deeds of the body, ye shall live.
> —ROMANS 8:11–13, KJV

Of the trillions of cells in the human body, heart cells are the only ones that can pulsate. With every pulsation, "intelligent communication" takes place. According to cardio-energetics (a newer field of science), our heart *mediates* our thoughts, feelings, fears and dreams. It also keeps our bodies in chemical balance. (See "the balance hormone" in chapter six.) Research has also revealed that the heart has a powerful impact outside of the body as well. For example, when nurses played a recorded heartbeat in a hospital nursery, the crying was reduced by almost 55 percent. The beats become their rhythm—an emotional "life support" system.[1]

Unlike the brain, or any other organ in the body, we can feel, hear and sense our hearts. Our heart not only affects every cell in our bodies, its electromagnetic field also has been measured to radiate outside of the body, even up to ten feet away.[2] Any way you look at it, the heart is magnetic.

The Atmosphere of the New Heart

God tells us that He has a pattern for us to follow that will keep our new hearts alive. It is an atmosphere where our new hearts will thrive. It restores everything to a state of balance and harmony with God. It is the atmosphere of worship.

> Therefore also now, says the Lord, turn and keep on coming to Me with all your heart, with fasting, with weeping, and with mourning [until every hindrance is removed and the broken fellowship is restored]. Rend your hearts and not your garments and return to the Lord, your God, for He is gracious and merciful, slow to anger, and abounding in loving-kindness; and He revokes His sentence of evil [when His conditions are met].
>
> —JOEL 2:12–13

There is another amazing fact about the beating heart that ties into this. If you place several heart cells together (but not touching) in a dish, with no nerve cell connecting them, they will fall into the same beating pattern, one that is different from the beat of each individual cell.

This is the same balancing principle that I mentioned in chapter seven, only greater. The "clock" balance represented everything in your body aligning with your heart—since the heart has the most energy. This "heart cell" balance ties the heart to its Creator.

God desires that we dedicate ourselves fully to Him, trusting in and obeying His instructions. As we do this, our new hearts are strengthened, and an atmosphere of righteousness, worship and purification is created that reminds your heart of its heavenly home.

> Therefore say to them [the Jews of this day], Thus says the Lord of hosts: Return to Me, says the Lord of hosts, and I will return to you; it is the utterance of the Lord of hosts...I appeal to you therefore, brethren, and beg of you in view of [all] the mercies of God, to make a decisive dedication of your bodies [presenting all your members and faculties] as a living sacrifice, holy (devoted, consecrated) and well pleasing to God, which is your reasonable (rational, intelligent) service and spiritual worship.
> —ZECHARIAH 1:3; ROMANS 12:1

Your new heart comes from a purified place, so in order for it to be strong enough to stay in a willing position, you have to keep it in this type of atmosphere.

When a baby is delivered out of its mother's womb, the nurses wrap the baby up and hand it to the mother, who holds her baby close to her heart. This makes the newborn feel warm and protected, just like when that baby lived in the womb.

If you take a fish out of the ocean, it can survive as

long as you put it back in water within a short period of time. You cannot take a fish out of the ocean, its place of origin where it survives and thrives, bring it home and lay it on your living room table. It will never live like that. If you take it from water where it is accustomed to living, you have to put it back into water in order for it to stay alive.

Your new heart comes from the Spirit realm, so you have to keep it in the atmosphere of the Spirit in order for it to exist.

A baby fights to stay in the womb, and a fish will fight when you take it out of the water. It is the same with the new heart. It "hungers and thirsts" after righteousness—it will suffocate if you take it out of God's presence. If you have a new heart, you should get to the point that you cannot get enough of God, church or God's people—because this heart lives and thrives in the atmosphere of worship.

Your new heart desires the things of God above the things of this world. You will find yourself saying, "I have to wash dishes, but I feel like glorifying God!" No longer will you have the thought ringing in your heart, *Oh no, I* have *to pray*, or *I* have *to go to church*, or *I* have *to worship*. Instead, as you prepare to go about your daily duties, getting ready for work, you will think, *I have to go to work, but I want to stay here in His presence!*

Your new heart will no longer sit in your pew at church and have to be forced to worship! No longer will you watch the clock as you hurriedly take three minutes to pray as your day begins. No longer will you have to deal with feelings of dislike or hatred toward your fellow man. Your new heart will compel you to love others.

This heart is bursting with the characteristics of Christ and longs for opportunities to express Christ through your actions. Because it "hungers and thirsts" for God, you must nourish it and feed it through your "Christ-life" living. Your new heart comes from the Spirit realm, so you have to keep it in the atmosphere of the Spirit in order for it to exist.

The new heart comes from glory—from God Himself, from heaven—where the heavenly host worships and praises Him continually. His glory, purification, righteousness and awesome presence surrounded your heart like a warm blanket before He gave it to you. This heart cannot rest in the midst of junk. You have to put it in the same atmosphere that it was birthed out of.

> My son, attend to my words; consent and submit to my sayings. Let them not depart from your sight; keep them in the center of your heart. For they are life to those who find them, healing and health to all their flesh. Keep and guard your heart with all vigilance and above all that you guard, for out of it flow the springs of life.
>
> —PROVERBS 4:20–23

Responding to the Rhythms
of the New Heart

There is another amazing thing about your heart-beat: It responds to music. Just as the heart influences the *autonomic* (subconscious, automatic) functions of your body (like breathing, for example), the new heart will gently begin to influence your behavior. You will desire to do something that will please God, sometimes even before you have learned the scripture that tells you that is what you should do! (See 1 Thessalonians 4:1.)

I have seen people who were converted who did not know the first thing about God before their conversion. They had not been raised in the church, yet they had an experience with God. After their conversion they started saying things like, "He told me to turn that movie off." "He told me to take those clothes off and not to wear that because it was too seductive." "He told me to take the earring out of my lip."

Sometimes I would ask, "You found that in the Scriptures?"

They would reply, "No, I have not read about it, but that is what God told me to do." They began to respond automatically to the new information flowing out of their new hearts. In Galatians 5:16 we read:

> But I say, walk and live [habitually] in the [Holy] Spirit [responsive to and controlled and guided by the Spirit]; then you will certainly not gratify the cravings and desires of the flesh (of human nature without God).

This verse refers to the fact that you have been *disconnected* from your brain because you are no longer responding to its demands. You are obeying the gentle promptings of Almighty God! Because of that, you no longer follow the carnal, fleshly prompting of the flesh. Verses 17–21 describe those fleshly desires:

> For the desires of the flesh are opposed to the [Holy] Spirit, and the [desires of the] Spirit are opposed to the flesh (godless human nature); for these are antagonistic to each other [continually withstanding and in conflict with each other], so that you are not free, but are prevented from doing what you desire to do. But if you are guided (led) by the [Holy] Spirit, you are not subject to the Law. Now the doings (practices) of the flesh are clear (obvious): they are immorality, impurity, indecency, idolatry, sorcery, enmity, strife, jealousy, anger (illtemper), selfishness, divisions (dissensions), party spirit (factions, sects with peculiar opinions, heresies), envy, drunkenness, carousing, and the like. I warn you beforehand...that those who do such things shall not inherit the kingdom of God.

Do not be like a fish out of water. God does not want you to die! Submit to the ways of God, and your new heart will thrive, bringing life to every other part of your being. Verses 22–24 continue by describing the life your new heart brings to you:

> But the fruit of the [Holy] Spirit [the work which His presence within accomplishes] is love, joy (gladness), peace, patience (an even temper, forbearance), kindness, goodness

(benevolence), faithfulness, gentleness (meekness, humility), self-control (self-restraint, continence). Against such things there is no law [that can bring a charge]. And those who belong to Christ Jesus (the Messiah) have crucified the flesh (the godless human nature) with its passions and appetites and desires.

If we live by the Holy Spirit, how do we crucify the flesh with our new heart?

If we live by the [Holy] Spirit, let us also walk by the Spirit. [If by the Holy Spirit we have our life in God, let us go forward walking in line, our conduct controlled by the Spirit.] Let us not become vainglorious and self-conceited, competitive and challenging and provoking and irritating to one another, envying and being jealous of one another.

—GALATIANS 5:25–26

All of these things have been described by *scientists* (not by the church) as being the workings of the mind! Because this is a competitive world, and our old brains have been trained (according to medical doctors) to *compete*, Christians have become "... self-conceited, competitive...challenging...jealous of one another."

Our minds are determined to stay on top, be number one over our hearts and bodies. So our minds have learned to keep gathering more and more information. The old mind tries to run the old heart into the ground as your brain attempts to keep up with the latest information, technology and everything else, just to stay competitive.

When this happens inside of you, when you

become aware of the fact that you are jealous of people and competitive, it is time to make a change. Something is wrong if you are having these kinds of thoughts: *Do I preach better than this person? Who sings the best? Whose church is larger?* Such thoughts are the workings of your mind. They do not flow from the heart of God.

Across this nation, the church must become aware of her need to crucify the flesh with our new hearts. The church has not yet tapped into the heart of God. In too many instances, our brains are leading us.

It has been scientifically proven that when people undergo lobotomies, a procedure where part of the brain is removed, they can still survive. *Yet you cannot remove a person's heart and expect that person to live.* The same is true of our new hearts. Your life is hidden in God, which is the essence of your new heart. You cannot remove the new heart and expect to live spiritually.

Another interesting fact about the brain is that it has no feeling. If we apply this spiritually, we can discover why people can curse you out and not feel it. They can do evil things and think evil thoughts, and not be spiritually aware or pained by their actions. The reason is because they have cut off the intelligent language of their new heart. The Scriptures tell us repeatedly to "hearken" unto the word of the Lord. (See Leviticus 26; Deuteronomy 15:5; 1 Kings 11:38; Proverbs 8:32; Isaiah 46:12.) In the Hebrew, this word *hearken* means "to hear intelligently."[3]

The brain, on the other hand, has so much information coming into it, that it overloads and paralyzes the old heart. The old heart could not compete against it. This is one of the main reasons why your new heart has to be disconnected from the mind. Your new heart has come loaded with divine information that has not yet been revealed to man! So it always tells that old brain, "I know stuff that you do not know. I know things that your intellect could never comprehend! The only way you will ever be able to understand is if God reveals it to you!"

Only the Blood Can Save Us

There is another, even more amazing thing about the new heart, old mind disconnection. Since the arteries, which transport the blood, are no longer connected by nerve endings to the old heart, they establish the connection to our new hearts. Praise God! Only by the blood can the heart rule the mind. The blood is how the new heart stays purified, because it is continuously cycled through the heart on its way to the rest of the body. The blood of Jesus can literally "wash away your sin," making you "white as snow" (pure) in His sight!

There is life in the blood! So when Jesus said, "You are cleansed and pruned already, because of the word which I have given you," He was revealing a spiritual process (John 15:3). The Word enters the mind and cleanses it; then the blood flows through and gives it life. The Word of God is alive because Jesus shed His blood and transformed typed pages into a living reality! His blood brings the Word alive. It makes the gospel work.

Even more than this, just as a heart transplant

patient must receive life-giving blood transfusions as a part of the transplant process, so when you receive a new heart, you have also received *new blood*—Christ's blood!

This new blood identifies you with the Father and sets the atmosphere for the new heart. It cleanses you as it fills every part of your being with the character of Christ. That character (which defines who you are) is passed to you through your heavenly Father's DNA. Jesus was the identical image of God because He diligently followed His new heart. He said, "Anyone who has seen Me has seen the Father" (John 14:9).

For this reason we must be "born again" and receive the new heart. The spiritual DNA in our new blood is eternally new. It makes us "sons" and "daughters" of God, causing us to look more like Him as we obey our new heart. DNA always reveals who the real father is!

The Heart Cry of God

Understand [this], my beloved brethren. Let every man be quick to hear [a ready listener], slow to speak, slow to take offense and to get angry. For man's anger does not promote the righteousness God [wishes and requires]. So get rid of all uncleanness and the rampant outgrowth of wickedness, and in a humble (gentle, modest) spirit receive and welcome the Word which implanted and rooted [in your hearts] contains the power to save your souls.

—JAMES 1:19–21

Your new heart is the heart of God. It comes with His will, His ways, His purpose, assignment and obedience already in it! This heart, and *only* this heart, contains the *power* to change the way you live.

So ask yourself these questions: "Am I really saved? Though I cried on the altar, did I really get converted? Though I am in church, faithful to attend services...I sit on the second pew every Sunday...has my heart been changed? Did I really receive a heart transplant from God?"

Do I really have the new heart?

Chapter 9

The Renewed **Mind**

If you have received the new heart, chances are you remember when it happened. Suddenly your responses to the world began to change—sometimes to your own surprise. The spiritual transformation begins to manifest itself in your physical body. To do so, it must be processed through your brain.

When God gives you a new heart, it is the deposit, or assurance, from God that He is also going to make your mind new. The old (natural) brain is formed, step by step, into four different sections. Although you get a whole new heart at once, the mind must be transformed in stages and in levels. Going back to conception, the heart forms and beats before the brain is created. Then it grows from the bottom up, starting with the medulla, amygdala, cerebral cortex and finally the frontal lobes. According to medicine, the heart transplant is immediate, but the mind transformation is progressive.

The Four Stages of Mind Transformation

~~~

For Christians, our daily battleground is the progressive state of renewing our minds.

> Therefore, my dear ones, as you have always obeyed [my suggestions], so now, not only [with the enthusiasm you would show] in my presence but much more because I am absent, work out (cultivate, carry out to the goal, and fully complete) your own salvation with reverence and awe and trembling (self-distrust, with serious caution, tenderness of conscience, watchfulness against temptation, timidly shrinking from whatever might offend God and discredit the name of Christ). [Not in your own strength] for it is God Who is all the while effectually at work in you [energizing and creating in you the power and desire], both to will and to work for His good pleasure and satisfaction and delight.
>
> —PHILIPPIANS 2:12–13

As you submit to God through your new heart, He balances your entire being. Your body starts to pulse with the new rhythms from your new heart, blood pressure waves hit your brain, and the old mind begins to respond to the new flow of your heart. And although the immediate effect may be subtle, you discover that you no longer think the same way anymore. Subtly, but consistently, the way you think and the way you do things change.

Let us briefly review the development of the mind as we learned in chapter six. The mind begins to develop after the heart is already in place, and it grows from the bottom up. The *medulla oblongata* establishes the link between the automatic functions of the heart, mind and body. Then the *amygdala* develops, which stores emotional memories and forms the basis of your perceptions. Out of the amygdala, the *logic* centers form, beginning with the cerebral cortex, where complex thought patterns like planning, strategizing, reflection, inspiration and imagination emerge. Lastly, the *frontal lobes* develop, allowing you to make decisions based on emotional and logical input. This section feeds back into the amygdala, telling it how to react or respond from the emotional memories.[1]

According to medicine, the heart transplant is immediate, but the mind transformation is progressive.

Each stage of your mind's development must be renewed. The Word must "pierce" each part of the mind, transforming thought and emotion on the subconscious and conscious levels.

The Four Levels of Consciousness

Just as there are four sections of the brain, there are four levels of consciousness called *brainwaves*, or electrical currents that cycle through it. We know them as *Beta, Alpha, Theta* and *Delta*. They are measured by the power of the impulse, or frequency, as well as speed, which determines the category. Beta cycles through your brain eighteen to thirty times per second; Alpha is next at eight to twelve cycles, followed by Theta at four to seven cycles, and finally to Delta waves at less than six cycles per second. The faster the cycles, the higher your level of consciousness will be.[2]

Most people function on the Beta level while they are awake. This level is fast, but not the most efficient. The logic and problem solving of the frontal lobes and cerebral cortex are easiest in Beta; however, your thoughts often "collide" on this level. Researchers say that you cannot stop or slow Beta waves down long enough to focus on just one thought, causing you to miss important details. This is how the old mind deceives you. Logic and decision making, which require crystal-clear thinking, cannot be clear and focused when your heart and mind are out of balance.

Americans live in an instant society, so Beta thinking is very welcome here. We want things to happen fast, so we take things into our own hands. God is not pleased. Beta thoughts wear and tear on your heart (and your entire body) if you remain on this level too long. Yet the "ruling" brain loves Beta; it will keep you from slowing down and listening to your heart whenever it can. Like stress, Beta thinking can be a silent killer. Before you realize it, your thought patterns are in overdrive, and breakdown is imminent.

Alpha bridges your conscious and subconscious minds. It has been called the most productive cycle, and it was the first that people learned to identify

Cerebral Cortex
Thinking center that strategizes, plans, reflects, inspires and imagines

Beta
18–30 cycles/sec.

A state of normal to panic thoughts, racing and colliding in the brain

Frontal Lobes
Decision-making center that determines appropriate emotional responses

Alpha
8–12 cycles/sec.

Bridges the conscious and subconscious mind; a state of relaxed, detached awareness and receptiveness that includes daydreaming, fantasizing and visualizing

Amygdala
Emotional memory center that compares emotionally familiar experiences with new information

Theta
4–7 cycles/sec.

Signals onset of emotional stimulation or flashes of insight; a state of light sleep

Medulla
Contains nerve centers that regulate breathing, heart rate and other bodily functions

Delta
<6 cycles/sec.

The largest waves with the lowest signal; a state of deep sleep

Adapted from Childre and Martin, *The HeartMath Solution*, 31, Figure 2.2, "Neurological Communication from the Heart to the Brain."

and control. Alpha is an alert, daydreaming state, a relaxed, detached awareness that reflects a receptive mind. Alpha seems to function primarily between the cerebral cortex and the amygdala. If Alpha is lost, the link to your subconscious mind is broken. You will not be able to remember details about your dreams or visions from God. Alpha is the link between "knowing" and "doing."

> Stand in awe, and sin not: commune with your own heart upon your bed, and be still.
> —PSALM 4:4, KJV

The Alpha state is where you have chosen to "be still" and know that God is in control (Ps. 46:10). It is the *meditative* state, where you are aware of your surroundings, but more tuned into your inner consciousness. Problem solving becomes easier, and your intuitions run deeper. You catch the thoughts that are missed in Beta.

Many have been hurt, bruised and offended because their minds— *not* their hearts—were leading them.

Theta is the next level, occurring while you are in a light sleep. Theta waves are slower than Alpha waves, but more intense, usually indicating emotional stimulation. They are linked with childlike thoughts and insecurities (children up to the age of puberty have high readings of Theta waves).[3] Theta waves seem to operate hand in hand with amygdala thinking, and they can also tap into deeper thought patterns. Flash insights come from the Theta realm. For example, have you ever thought, *Something is not right here...I do not know what it is, but something is wrong.*

Sometimes Theta brainwaves relate to those *gut feelings* we all have from time to time. Have you ever thought, *Do not go that way*, but you went anyway? Then something happened that could have been avoided. Most likely, your new heart was connecting with Theta brainwaves. So many times when something goes wrong, we think back on the incident and say, "I had a gut feeling!" In reality, our heart was forewarning us of danger—already having perceived what was going to happen—but we were not in the right state of consciousness to receive the full revelation. We cannot speed around in Beta thinking and expect to have new heart insight. Many have been hurt, bruised and offended because their minds—*not* their hearts—were leading them.

Delta thinking is where "deep calleth unto deep" —the subconscious mind—where "all thy waves and thy billows are gone over me" (Ps. 42:7, KJV). This is the abyss, the deepest depth of your mind; you cannot measure, understand or control it. This is where God can change your temperament and behavior without you even knowing it! There is a saying: "A leopard can't change its spots." It can, and it will, if the Word of God is allowed to pierce on the Delta level.

Delta is where your mind can receive the "meat" of the Word as it pierces to the depths of your innermost being—where Delta and Theta waves unite. Like a child, you embrace the truth and trust God with a deep, calm awareness. David said, "Even at night my heart instructs me" (Ps. 16:7, NIV). On the Delta thought level, "all things are possible with God" (Mark 10:27). This deep, subconscious transformation flows up—through your emotions and logic—to illuminate your entire being. When the new heart is in complete control, electric impulses are *supernatural*—because the natural link has been cut. This mind is controlled by the power of God!

The Emotional Mind

As you have read, *conscious thought* begins and ends in your emotions. Emotions give meaning to facts generated by your logic—that is why our logical centers grow out of our emotions. The word *emotion* literally means "energy in motion." It is a strong feeling—like love, anger, joy or sorrow—that moves us. Basically, emotional energy is neutral. It is our logical thoughts and physical reactions that make our emotions either positive or negative.

People tend to think that emotions come from the heart. The truth is that both our mind and heart drive them.

Head emotions are self-centered and defensive. They are moved by "what you can do for me." They want instant gratification. They are like conditional love, which says, "I'll love you, if you love me and meet my needs." Brain emotions will *drive* you to do things that are unwise or dangerous.

Heart emotions run deeper and are selfless. They express themselves without expecting anything in return. Heart emotions reflect emotional maturity; they are balanced and offer solutions to problems rather than participating in them. They are like *agape* love, which is the love God shows to us. God, who understands our weaknesses, sees the problems we bring upon ourselves and helps us find solutions, yet He does not become entangled in our problems. He loves us in spite of ourselves, and He expects nothing from us in return.

Circumcision of the Heart

Because God understands us so thoroughly, He has chosen to rule in our lives through our new heart. When He established a covenant relationship with Israel (through Moses), He did it through circumcision—a cutting of the flesh, which drew blood. When God began to teach us the spiritual implications behind this physical act of circumcision, He taught us about the circumcision of the heart.

God could not establish a covenant relationship with us through the brain. The brain says, "I will do something for you only if you will do something for me." The love and obedience that flow from our brains are conditional—dependent upon "what's in it for me!"

But the new heart says, "I will love you...obey you...care for you even if you will not respond to me. I will, in spite of what I see from you. I will, regardless of the way you treat me...I am still able to love you." The church has not yet been perfected in love, because the minute we are offended by people, we stop loving them. The minute we see something in our church, or in our pastor, that we do not like, we leave the church. Our brains are leading us.

The brain gathers all of the facts, information and emotions. Then it rationalizes or reasons them out. When it gets through calculating, it says, "I like you, for now." The new heart (which comes from our Father) looks at everything, but because it is eternal, it sees beyond who a person is now to what he is going to become—and loves him until he gets there. This can only be done when you are equipped with knowledge that is beyond this earth. Believers should not see things as "natural" people do. We should see things as God sees them, because we are looking through the eyes of our new heart.

Without the governing influence of the new heart, we can fall prey to negative emotions like fear, anger, blame or insecurity. When this heart comes into a person's body, that person begins to see with a new perspective, even if he or she does not understand why. When we have a new heart, we learn to respond instead of react. For example, if someone offends you, the *natural* reaction would be anger because the emotion would be charged by the natural thought pattern. But a mind that has been renewed according to the Word can look at an offense and call it a blessing. The renewed mind is powerful.

Sometimes when a person is in the physical healing process, a doctor will say, "She's fighting..." The person may have been wounded by a gunshot and may have all the probable signs indicating death. Yet in spite of the injury, the doctor says, "…but she's fighting." That person's mind is saying, "I know that I am shot. I know that I am bleeding to death, but I am fighting to live." Very often it is the mind's response to an incident that determines the outcome.

The same is true spiritually. When the heart and brain are out of alignment (resulting in an unrenewed mind), the thought patterns that are released into the world by way of the flesh will always be negative. This deceptive thinking can mean the difference between life and death.

Your new heart reveals the truth. Its substance is Truth, so it reveals the truth. That is why we can look at something that Satan has camouflaged to look like God and call it a lie. We are also able to look at something that has the "form of godliness" and know that it denies the "power thereof." Why? There is no truth in it. Why? Eternal love does not live there. Jesus said, "And you will know the Truth, and the Truth will set you free" (John 8:32).

Why Didn't I Think?

Scientists have observed that *feeling* is faster than *thought*, so our emotional reactions show up in brain activity before we have time to think. As soon as we perceive something, our emotions are active. We think, or process the perception, afterward. This is the reason we say things before we realize why we have said them. Emotions, even though they are influenced by our thoughts, *act* much faster. Doctors have concluded that we cannot manage our emotions through our rational mind. We react, and then we think.

Remember the four sections of the mind—the medulla (breathing, heart rate and other body functions), the amygdala (storehouse of emotional memory), the cerebral cortex (plans, strategies, reflection, inspiration and imagination) and the frontal lobes (decision making). The heart pumps blood through the medulla to the amygdala and changes its electrical activity. This confirms that our emotions move faster than our logic centers, or the slow brainwave patterns associated with our subconscious mind. Our brains cannot manage our emotions—and transform our lives—without the heart's regulating influence.

Unless we receive the new heart, we will always react through our amygdala via the old, evil heart. So I may blow your brains out and then later think with my logic, *I should not have done that.* You could slap somebody because your old heart runs offensive information straight to your emotion center. If you have an old heart (which is of Satan), and you cuss somebody out, the amygdala may get you slapped! Later (*always* later) the logical centers would say, "I should have thought first. I should have gone for a walk. I should not have slapped her. Then I would not have lost my job."

When you have received a heart transplant from God, your first response from the amygdala should be what God would do. Upon seeing your response, a person operating from the cerebral cortex, frontal lobes area of his or her mind would ask, "Why didn't you slap her? Why didn't you cuss her out?"

Standing there (with the heart of God) you would say, "I could not open my mouth. The Holy Spirit would not let me say a word."

A cerebral, frontal person would ask, "Why did you give her a ride [when it is raining] when you know she cannot stand you?"

You would respond, "The Holy Spirit told me to stop my car and let her get in."

When you get home, your mind would say, "I do not even know why I did that, because I know that she does not like me."

Scientific study has proven that the emotions get messages directly from the heart. This means the first response you see will reveal the nature of a person's heart.

I know this is true from my own experiences. God has put me in predicaments where I *knew* I should have gone off about something, yet He would not let me open my mouth. I *knew* that I had been wronged, but God still led me to bless the people who wronged me. Now I understand, from my fresh understanding of science, how God makes this happen. It is not easy for the flesh, but the more you submit to your new heart, the easier it will become.

Unraveling the Mystery of the Mind

Since the new heart is no longer connected to the brain by the nerves, it can control every part of the mind with its power—its pulsating authority. This is how a new heart can take up residence in a person's body and *cause* the mind to do *strange* things. The

old mind has begun to be controlled by the power of
the new heart and is *no longer* controlled by the limited power of the nerve endings. Nerve endings can
only release measured amounts of power at a time to
that brain. When the new heart controls the brain
with its pulsating power, it can send spiritual power as
strong as is needed in order to change that mind.

> For with the heart a person believes (adheres
> to, trusts in, and relies on Christ) and so is jus-
> tified (declared righteous, acceptable to God),
> and with the mouth he confesses (declares
> openly and speaks out freely his faith) and con-
> firms [his] salvation.
>
> —ROMANS 10:10

Your new heart is already equipped with the ability to believe God. It comes "built with faith." The
mind must learn to demonstrate, on every level,
what the heart believes. A powerful confidence flows
out of the new heart, a confidence Jesus demonstrated when He came into the world.

Jesus said confidently, "I am the door...I am the
way...I am the resurrection." He did not say, "I
think I am the door...I *think* I am the way...I *think*
I am the resurrection." And if Jesus Christ, indeed,
is the Word "made flesh" that has dwelled among
us—and now the Word lives inside of us—we can
now make the same confessions. Confidently we can
declare, "I am healed; I am delivered; I am set free!"
If I believe "unto salvation," then this is how I am
able to say that I am saved. God knows when He is
alive and well inside of us.

The Bible says, "Out of the abundance of the heart
the mouth speaketh" (Matt. 12:34, KJV). Whatever

your heart is full of…whatever overflows from it…is what your mouth is going to speak. When you say, "I am saved," it is because your heart is full, overflowing with abundance and salvation.

The Mind/Body Connection

The second chapter of 1 Corinthians gives an awesome understanding of the mind/body connection. Let's take a close look at what the Word is teaching us in this chapter.

The apostle Paul was a highly educated man in traditional religion. Yet as he begins this chapter, he clearly states that he was determined that his new heart would not be reconnected to his philosophy or to anything that he had studied in the past. He opted for a permanent disconnection!

> As for myself, brethren, when I came to you, I did not come proclaiming to you the testimony and evidence or mystery and secret of God [concerning what He has done through Christ for the salvation of men] in lofty words of eloquence or human philosophy and wisdom. For I resolve to know nothing (to be acquainted with nothing, to make a display of the knowledge of nothing, and to be conscious of nothing) among you except Jesus Christ (the Messiah) and Him crucified.
>
> —1 CORINTHIANS 2:1–2

In verses 3–7 he teaches us about *heart wisdom*—something very different from the knowledge from the mind. It was a wisdom available only to those who have received a new heart. Paul describes this experience by saying:

> And I was in (passed into a state of) weakness and fear (dread) and great trembling [after I had come] among you. And my language and my message were not set forth in persuasive (enticing and plausible) words of wisdom, but they were in demonstration of the [Holy] Spirit and power [a proof by the Spirit and power of God, operating on me and stirring in the minds of my hearers the most holy emotions and thus persuading them], so that your faith might not rest in the wisdom of men (human philosophy), but in the power of God. Yet when we are among the full-grown (spiritually mature Christians who are ripe in understanding), we do impart a [higher] wisdom (the knowledge of the divine plan previously hidden); but it is indeed not a wisdom of this present age or of this world nor of the leaders and rulers of this age, who are being brought to nothing and are doomed to pass away. But rather what we are setting forth is a wisdom of God once hidden [from the human understanding] and now revealed to us by God—[that wisdom] which God devised and decreed before the ages for our glorification [to lift us into the glory of His presence].

Paul stated, "None of the rulers of this age or world perceived and recognized and understood this, for if they had, they would never have crucified the Lord of glory" (v. 8). Why did he say this? Because by crucifying Christ, the Lord of glory, they gave Jesus the power to live inside of us. This enabled people to receive divine wisdom and revelation from the "new heart"—things that had not yet been revealed to man. This new heart wisdom would eventually out-run them and supersede the mind knowledge upon which they based their whole lives. It would expose them and bring glory to Christ—the very glory they tried to destroy.

Through Paul, God is teaching us that we cannot grab hold of God—or of the knowledge and wisdom that is God's alone—with our natural minds. To understand God we must receive the new heart. In Joel 2:13 God tells us the only way to receive this new heart. We must "rend [our] hearts and not [our] garments and return to the Lord."

In verses 9–11 of 1 Corinthians 2, Paul points out the utter futility of trying to grab hold of God in any other way:

> But, on the contrary, as the Scripture says, What eye has not seen and ear has not heard and has not entered into the heart of man, [all that] God has prepared (made and keeps ready) for those who love Him [who hold Him in affectionate reverence, promptly obeying Him and gratefully recognizing the benefits He has bestowed]. Yet to us God has unveiled and revealed them by and through His Spirit, for the [Holy] Spirit searches diligently, exploring and examining everything, even sounding the profound and bottomless things of God [the divine counsels and things hidden and beyond man's scrutiny]. For what person perceives (knows and understands) what passes through a man's thoughts except the man's own spirit within him? Just so no one discerns (comes to know and comprehend) the thoughts of God except the Spirit of God.

Paul continues by explaining the role of the Holy Spirit in receiving our new heart:

> Now we have not received the spirit [that belongs to] the world, but the [Holy] Spirit Who is from God, [given to us] that we might realize and comprehend and appreciate the gifts [of divine favor and blessing so freely and lavishly] bestowed on us by God. And we are setting these truths forth in words not taught by human wisdom but taught by the [Holy] Spirit, combining and interpreting spiritual truths with spiritual language [to those who possess the Holy Spirit].
>
> —1 CORINTHIANS 2:12–13

This heart wisdom that comes from our new heart is available only to those who possess the Holy Spirit. The Holy Spirit does not baptize our mind! We receive the baptism of the Holy Spirit in our hearts, and when this happens, God teaches and trains us how to combine the spiritual "deposit" with the new, spiritual language.

> But the natural, nonspiritual man does not accept or welcome or admit into his heart the gifts and teachings and revelations of the Spirit of God, for they are folly (meaningless nonsense) to him; and he is incapable of knowing them (of progressively recognizing, understanding, and becoming better acquainted with them) because they are spiritually discerned and estimated and appreciated. But the spiritual man tries all things [he examines, investigates, inquires into, questions, and discerns all things], yet is himself to be put on trial and judged by no one [he can read the meaning of everything, but no one can properly discern

or appraise or get an insight into him]. For who has known or understood the mind (the counsels and purposes) of the Lord so as to guide and instruct Him and give Him knowledge? But we have the mind of Christ (the Messiah) and do hold the thoughts (feelings and purposes) of His heart.

—1 CORINTHIANS 2:14–16, EMPHASIS ADDED

The mind of Christ is the mind of the Word! God has given us the Bible literally to "possess" His mind—the mind of Christ—the Word made flesh. Once we possess His mind, we "do hold the thoughts (feelings [emotions!] and purposes) of His heart" (v. 16).

Evidence That We Have a New Heart

Paul helps us to recognize the evidence that we have received a new heart and possess the heart wisdom about which he is speaking in 1 Corinthians 2. A newborn infant cannot understand the intelligent language of his adult parents, but must learn to speak as he grows. So too a spiritual "infant" in Christ must learn a "spiritual language." Paul continues:

However, brethren, I could not talk to you as to spiritual [men], but as to nonspiritual [men of the flesh, in whom the carnal nature predominates], as to mere infants [in the new life] in Christ [unable to talk yet!]

—1 CORINTHIANS 3:1

Paul was not speaking about using sentences or words in a natural language. He was indicating that these new believers were unable to talk "spiritual language." He continued by saying:

> I fed you with milk, not solid food, for you were not yet strong enough [to be ready for it]; but even yet you are not strong enough [to be ready for it], for you are still [unspiritual, having the nature] of the flesh [under the control of ordinary impulses]. For as long as [there are] envying and jealousy and wrangling and factions among you, are you not unspiritual and of the flesh, behaving yourselves after a human standard and like mere (unchanged) men?
>
> —1 CORINTHIANS 3:2–3

Paul was saying that these new believers were still controlled by "ordinary impulses," the nerve endings leading to and coming from the old heart. They adopted "human standards" because they did not have the new heart. A few verses later, Paul warned these spiritual "infants" to be prepared to be tested.

> But if anyone builds upon the Foundation, whether it be with gold, silver, precious stones, wood, hay, straw, the work of each [one] will become [plainly, openly] known (shown for what it is); for the day [of Christ] will disclose and declare it, because it will be revealed with fire, and the fire will test and critically appraise the character and worth of the work each person has done.
>
> —1 CORINTHIANS 3:12–13

We need to heed these words from Paul. It's foolish to go around "thinking" you have a new heart when indeed you have not yet received it. As the old adage says, "Don't talk the talk until you can walk the walk!" A day of testing is coming, and when you get in the fire, when it is time to be tested to see what you are made of—the fire is going to reveal your work. The fire will reveal whether your heart is made of gold, silver and precious stones (the new heart) or if it is composed of hay, wood, stubble or straw (the old heart). The fire of walking in what you believe and the fire of being tested come to "appraise" your character, to see of what you are made.

We will be tested in the fire of our daily living. The enemy will throw his fiery darts at us. But the fire does not come to harm us—it comes to appraise us. It is in the crucible of God's fire of testing that the evidence of our new heart begins to shine forth. It is as though God is saying, "Just checking. Just checking to see if My heart is still in there. Just checking to see if My blood is still running through your veins."

The fire of walking in what you believe and the fire of being tested come to "appraise" your character, to see of what you are made.

The test of fire allows the new heart to shine forth. For those who pass the test and reveal the new heart, there will be a reward.

If the work which any person has built on this Foundation [any product of His efforts whatever]

survives [this test], he will get his reward.
                              —1 Corinthians 3:14

But for those who do not reveal a new heart life,
Paul gave a serious warning:

> But if any person's work is burned up [under the
> test], he will suffer the loss [of it all, losing his
> reward], though he himself will be saved, but
> only as [one who has passed] through fire. Do
> you not discern and understand that you [the
> whole church at Corinth] are God's temple (His
> sanctuary), and that God's Spirit has His per-
> manent dwelling in you [to be at home in you,
> collectively as a church and also individually]?
>   —1 Corinthians 3:15–16

We will be tested. This is God's "checks-and-
balance" way of seeing what rules in our lives. Is it
your mind or your heart? I believe the test determines which part of you is in control. Do the thought
patterns of your mind, which say "Fight back," "Be
jealous" or "Be envious," determine your response? If
so, you have reacted from your flesh and have sown to
the fleshly realm, which is your mind, soul and body.

Or does your new heart overrule the old thought
patterns? If your new heart controls your response,
you have come out of the fire walking in the Spirit.
You are truly minding the things of the Spirit.

Meditation and Renewal

If you simply *read* the Word, it will travel through the
first, second and third regions of your mind. In order

for it to penetrate the fourth center, the frontal lobes, you have to *meditate* on the Word—consistently keep it there until it permeates the fourth realm of decision. Then, as you study the Word, it will travel down your nerve endings and cause your body functions to relax and line up with the will of God.

As you keep putting the Word inside of you, it will pierce on the subconscious level and begin to heal your emotional memories. Then you will be able to stop comparing against negative, *emotionally familiar* experiences. As the Word pierces the depths of your mind, it will compare and replace these old memories according to the Word of God. You will gain a new perspective—one that will amaze you. Instead of being tormented by your old mind, you will be able to say, "No, I want the Word."

You have to keep meditating on the Word day and night (Ps. 1:2). Digest the Word over and over again until it gets through the cerebral cortex where you think, strategize, plan, reflect and become inspired as God takes your vision for the future to an incredible, new level. Then your imagination takes over from there, and you start seeing yourself succeed and prosper—until you have become an overcomer! As you consistently meditate on the Word, it will go to the frontal lobes, where the power of your decision will declare, "As for me and my house, we are going to live for God!"

David knew the power of meditating on God's Word. He said:

> Your word have I laid up in my heart, that I might not sin against You.
>
> —PSALM 119:11

In Romans 12:2, Paul added, "Do not be conformed to this world...but be transformed...by the
[entire] renewal of your mind [by its new ideals and
its new attitude], so that you may prove [for your-
selves] what is the good and acceptable and perfect
will of God." The "[entire] renewal of your mind"
will lead you through a transformation in all four
regions of your brain.

I believe that when you receive the new heart, its
power breaks the shackles of things that possessed
you as a sinner (things that you hated and
denounced). Yet there are still things that you love
and do not want to release. Then it becomes the
power of your decision to surrender those things to
the Lord, which is done during your mind's *renewing* process. This is the first level—confronting the
old habits (those things you love) just as God confronted me in Chicago.

Take cigarette smoking, for example. Though your
heart has been converted, your mind still wants a
cigarette. It wants that old habit. Therefore, it has to
go through the four stages of deliverance by way of
the Word.

Deliverance Step by Step

Let's investigate each step. The medulla, which contains the nerve centers that regulate breathing, heart
rate and other body functions, begins to get taken
care of at conversion. It starts to regulate and balance. The second stage involves the amygdala
(storehouse of emotional memory), comparing the

new information with what your emotions have already experienced. This is where the new heart information says, "I do not want to smoke. I want God. I live for God..." There has to be a showdown between the new heart and the old mind, which is where your internal battle begins.

When you begin to read the Word of God, the pressure waves from your new heart become so powerful that your heart rejects what is stored in your mind (in the amygdala). The warfare that comes back to the mind is so powerful that it causes you to get in the Word to see what the Bible says about it. When that Word comes in contact with your emotional memories, it begins to cancel that "smoking memory" and replace it with the new, sanctified thought pattern from your new heart.

When you receive the new heart, its power breaks the shackles of things that possessed you as a sinner.

Now your new heart is refusing to give up, because it cannot be overthrown. It is, after all, the heart of God. So it presses through to the third realm, the cerebral cortex, where it thinks, strategizes, reasons, plans and inspires, and it causes the brain to imagine what it is like not to smoke. It causes that brain to plan, strategize and be inspired to live for God. How does it do this?

It uses the Word to inspire the mind! It dissects

the Word in order to strategize how you are going to keep your mind stayed on God. This reaches the frontal lobes, which are involved in decision making. You decide, "I am not going to do this anymore," and say "My response to this cigarette is *no!* " The lobes then send waves back to the amygdala to reflect the appropriate emotional response.

Your new heart exerts pressure on the old brain to receive and digest the Word. It goes completely through all four stages. By the time the Word reaches the decision-making center, it has rejected the memory and inspired the mind. After the decision is followed through, the body begins to line up in sync with the new heart rhythms that have passed through the frontal lobes back to the amygdala. This completed process is transmitted back to your physical being through the medulla as it pierces on the subconscious level.

> # When you begin to read the Word of God, the pressure waves from your new heart become so powerful that your heart rejects what is stored in your mind.

Let's relate this to church. Your body goes to services because your new heart is overpowering the mind. It has divorced the mind and linked up with the heart to say, "I am going to church." The problem is that although many people have allowed their new hearts to exert the control necessary to get their bodies to church, their minds still sit in the pews unresponsively. The purpose for going to church should be to get the Word of God into the four sections of the mind, allowing the mind to reach the point of decision!

Which stage of mind renewal describes where you are today? Is your mind being renewed?

Are you working out your own salvation with fear and trembling before God?

Have you embraced your new heart?

Chapter 10

Rejection of the
New Heart

A new heart comes with many godly attributes, including a strong conviction of what it believes. God already "believes, accepts and receives" Himself. He has every confidence that His Word is true. He knows it will accomplish His divine purpose. (See Isaiah 55:11.) We fall into error when we think of ourselves "more highly" than we should and then fail to trust and obey God. Isaiah 55:7–9 says:

> Let the wicked forsake his way and the unrighteous man his thoughts; and let him return to the Lord, and He will have love, pity, and mercy for him, and to our God, for He will multiply to him His abundant pardon. For My thoughts are not your thoughts, neither are your ways My ways, says the Lord. For as the heavens are higher than the earth, so are My ways higher than your ways and My thoughts than your thoughts.

Many in the church do not have the mind of Christ, so they live in a perpetual state of sin, saying,

179

"I do not feel convicted about this. I do not feel bad about that." Their consciences have become darkened, and they habitually do things that displease God. They do not love God or fear Him unto obedience. If this describes you, then I am sorry. You do not have the new heart.

When you have the new heart—*God's heart*—and you do anything that is contrary to God's Word, it will automatically send a wave of conviction. And because you love and fear God and believe in His name, you will repent.

> He who believes in Him [who clings to, trusts in, relies on Him] is not judged [he who trusts in Him never comes up for judgment; for him there is no rejection, no condemnation—he incurs no damnation]; but he who does not believe (cleave to, rely on, trust in Him) is judged already [he has already been convicted and has already received his sentence] because he has not believed in and trusted in the name of the only begotten Son of God. [He is condemned for refusing to let his trust rest in Christ's name.] The [basis of the] judgment (indictment, the test by which men are judged, the ground for the sentence) lies in this: the Light has come into the world, and people have loved the darkness rather than and more than the Light, for their works (deeds) were evil. For every wrongdoer hates (loathes, detests) the Light, and will not come out into the Light but shrinks from it, lest his works (his deeds, his activities, his conduct) be exposed and reproved.
>
> —JOHN 3:18–20

There is a penalty for sin, one way or the other. If you habitually do things that are ungodly and sense no conviction, but just say, "God understands," the old heart has deceived you. You are walking out a death sentence. *Remember*:

> The heart is deceitful above all things, and it is exceedingly perverse and corrupt and severely, mortally sick! Who can know it [perceive, understand, be acquainted with his own heart and mind]? I the Lord search the mind, I try the heart, even to give to every man according to his ways, according to the fruit of his doings.
>
> —JEREMIAH 17:9–10

If you can continue in a pattern of sin, you have not received the new heart. The new heart changes you completely, even if you cannot explain it. You cannot "coin" the new birth experience any more than a person can explain exactly what happens when he has undergone a heart transplant. Jesus said:

> The wind blows (breathes) where it wills; and though you hear its sound, yet you neither know where it comes from nor where it is going. So it is with everyone who is born of the Spirit.
>
> —JOHN 3:8

The little girl in chapter seven could not explain why she kept seeing a murder after she received a heart transplant. The older man could not explain why he kept dreaming about a young woman who fell down a flight of stairs.

The new heart is a miracle. I cannot explain how I stopped doing certain things or exactly how I got the victory in some areas. I cannot explain why I am a "new creation," but the Holy Spirit has led me every step of the way. God put a new heart inside of me, and I have never been the same.

Your heart will always tell you who your father is and from where your motivations come.

God's new heart comes with divine passion for the things of the Spirit. The new heart craves what God craves, loves what He loves and hates what He hates. So how is it that we can say we have received the heart of God, yet we do not love what God loves, we do not hate what He hates or we do not crave after righteousness as He does?

If you do not love God or fear Him unto obedience, you do not have the new heart.

When we receive God's heart, it should birth a passion within us for holiness, worship and everything that pleases Him. It should automatically reject anything that does not sound, look, taste or feel like God. If it does not do this, something is wrong.

The Word says that we have been made "the righteousness of God in him" (2 Cor. 5:21, KJV). Unless we train our minds (and, as a result, our flesh) to line up with who we have already become, we will fall into deception.

In the Garden of Gethsemane, Jesus said this: "My Father, if it is possible, let this cup pass away from Me" (Matt. 26:39). At that moment, Jesus' mind was fighting the warfare for what His physical body would soon have to endure, so that He would be able to fulfill the assignment of His new heart.

If Jesus had disobeyed the Father and rejected His new heart, God's eternal plan would not have been fulfilled—and His new heart would have died (just as a natural heart's signal is cut off by constant refusals from the brain). This is how a person falls into a backslidden state. The new heart says, "Do not do this." But the mind refuses over and over again, saying, "I am going to do what I want."

The Danger of Habitual Sin

When you reject the Word and do not put it into your heart and mind, the old nature assumes control—and you shut down the power and the activity of your new heart. God will not stay in this temple. You will have forced the Holy Spirit to leave, and not because you have done "one little thing" wrong. He will have left because you have refused to store the Word of God in your mind, enabling it to progress through all four stages of deliverance. You have refused to meditate on the Word. Therefore, your "emotional memories" and the stubbornness of your old mind can draw your heart to do something that offends God.

Anyone can make a mistake. Falling into temptation and sin does not mean that you are not saved. But when ungodly behavior becomes habitual to the point that you no longer sense the heart's conviction, the new heart has been repelled. Because you have ignored the new heart's correction—deliberately annihilating its message, which says that you no longer desire God—you have rejected your new heart. To consistently refuse the new heart's direction, you are sending a signal back saying, "I do not want you here." And the Spirit of the Lord will never stay where He is not wanted.

Overtaken in Sin, or a Reprobate Mind?

If you allow your flesh (mind) to lead you into sin, and then you repent, God is just and able to forgive you. Why? You have been overtaken in a fault. Overtaken by what? You have been overtaken by memories of the brain. Man looks on the outside, but God sees your heart (1 Sam. 16:7). He knows that sin action did not come from your heart. It cropped up from your emotional memories. This is why it is critical for you to renew your mind.

In all his victories through the help he received from the Lord, King Uzziah had become a mighty ruler. Scripture says, "As long as he sought (inquired of, yearned for) the Lord, God made him prosper" (2 Chron. 26:5). As king, Uzziah "did right in the Lord's sight," until he began to think "too highly" of himself, thus usurping God's established authority in the priesthood.

Uzziah had become wealthy, strong and famous. Obviously, he had started to believe that nothing was impossible to him—even if it perverted God's ways. This is where his heart deceived him. As king, he should have recognized the Torah as God's final authority. As a "son," he should have humbled himself under God's mighty hand—but his heart had become filled with pride. Uzziah forced his way into the temple to offer incense despite the priests' strong objections, and God struck him with leprosy. (See 2 Chronicles 26:16–19.) Uzziah was deceived by powerful emotional memories, which led to his greatest—and final—defeat.

When God turns someone over to a "reprobate" mind, more often than not it is someone who has declared that he has a new heart. Although that person receives convicting messages from God, he ignores them…*continuously*. His actions become a mockery against God. God has no other choice but to turn that person over to a reprobate mind.

> And even as they did not like to retain God in their knowledge, God gave them over to a reprobate mind, to do those things which are not convenient.
>
> —ROMANS 1:28, KJV

Saul was crowned the first king of Israel. Very tall and handsome, he had probably become accustomed to being the center of attention—and he was, until he sinned against God. A young shepherd boy became his most influential protégé. David served Saul with all of his heart and received great favor from the Lord. Yet because Saul was a "man of the people," he grew more and more jealous of David—to the point that he relentlessly hunted him down like a wild animal.

God had already stripped Saul of his kingly authority, but instead of repenting, Saul used every ounce of his power to save face before the people over and over again. His actions and condition kept getting worse. He lied, murdered and manipulated—all while putting on the "form" of kingship and royalty! God turned him over to his wicked thoughts, and the man who had begun his reign by prophesying with the prophets ended up seeking psychics and dying at the hands of his enemies. (See 1 Samuel 9–31.)

Uzziah was deceived by powerful emotional memories, which led to his greatest—and final—defeat.

This is the danger that faces the church today. Many people are still saying, "I am saved," as they willfully and continually do things that displease God. That offends Him, to the point that He turns them over to a deceived and debased mind. This kind of mind is "deceitful...perverse...corrupt...and severely, mortally sick."

It would be better for these people to say, "I was saved, but I am in a backslidden state right now. I need prayer. My memories remind me what it felt like to be in an adulterous situation, and I just cannot say *no* to my brainwaves. The memory is too strong. I cannot overthrow it." There is grace and mercy for these individuals. But when you have a new heart (that constantly sends waves of conviction), and you constantly reject the conviction while declaring how righteous and holy you are, the Spirit of the Lord will leave...just as He left Saul.

> For if anyone only listens to the Word without obeying it and being a doer of it, he is like a man who looks carefully at his [own] natural face in a mirror; for he thoughtfully observes himself, and then goes off and promptly forgets what he was like.
>
> —JAMES 1:23–24

They are committing spiritual suicide by willingly "putting to death" the "breath of life" that God has sovereignly placed in their hearts. They know the truth, but over and over again they reject it. Then they walk away and pretend that everything is OK. This leaves God with no alternative.

The New **Evil** Heart

As we learned in chapter six, when we have the new heart and are studying the Word consistently, we have the ability to "squeeze out" ungodly thought patterns. If we refuse to accept the directions of God's Word and act upon that evil thought, God has no alternative but to leave. He cannot dwell in the same place as sin.

This puts you in imminent danger. When you backslide, your latter state becomes worse than your original state before receiving the new heart. Therefore, you will begin to experience the depths of the evil realm, which is worse than you have ever dreamed. Hear me. If you have followed the command of Joel 2:12–13 to rip out your old heart, and God has given you a new heart according to Ezekiel 11:19–20, and yet you reject that new heart, you will not merely revert back to the old heart that you had before.

You will receive another heart from Satan, one that is prepared to receive seven times the amount of evil that you once held in your old heart. This "evil" heart will also not connect to your nerve endings, so you could end up becoming a murderer! As the evil battle begins, your old mind may say, "I have never killed anybody before." But the evil heart you have received from Satan has also come programmed with an assignment for evil—and you will end up doing evil and wicked things that you never dreamed you would do.

When you tear up and rip out your old heart, the Bible says that God casts it into the depths of the sea (Mic. 7:19). He removes it from you as far as the east is from the west, so you cannot go back and get that old heart (Ps. 103:12). When you backslide, leave God and say, "I do not want to hear the Word of God. I do not want to transform my mind so that it can line up with my new heart," then you do not get your old heart back! It has been cast into outer darkness. It is gone!

When you reject God, Satan brings you an evil heart, and you do not know what is in that heart, either. It is even more deceitful, because it "looks like" it is in perfect order—until it begins its evil transformation.

> When the strong man, fully armed, [from his courtyard] guards his own dwelling, his belongings are undisturbed [his property is at peace and is secure]. But when one stronger than he attacks him and conquers him, he robs him of his whole armor on which he had relied and divides up and distributes all his

goods as plunder (spoil). He who is not with Me [siding and believing with Me] is against Me, and he who does not gather with Me [engage in My interest], scatters. When the unclean spirit has gone out of a person, it roams through waterless places in search [of a place] of rest (release, refreshment, ease); and finding none it says, I will go back to my house from which I came. And when it arrives, it finds [the place] swept and put in order and furnished and decorated. And it goes and brings other spirits [seven of them], more evil than itself, and they enter in, settle down, and dwell there; and the last state of that person is worse than the first.

—LUKE 11:21–26

Like the first heart transplant, your evil heart will not be connected to your mind. It will not obey you, either.

When you "rend your heart" and give it to God, do you think that He puts it in a bank account and saves it? Do you think that He puts it in cold storage, saying "I will save it just in case you do not want Me later?" No! He destroys it, just like anything else that looks like death. The destiny of that old heart is death and destruction, and since He came to give us everlasting, abundant life, He destroys anything that resembles death. God does not save "death."

"Hearken" to (hear intelligently) the Word of the Lord in this matter. God is sending this Word because we do not realize just how powerful backsliding is! The very reason we get rid of the old heart (the one "housed" in our life until we become saved) is because it is too dangerous to hold on to (because, "Who can know it?"). If you cannot know that heart,

how will you ever know the one that Satan brings—
one seven times worse than the first one?

This ought to make you hold on to God even if you
have to fight tooth and nail. This knowledge should
make you determined to put your old mind to death.
It should make you feed your mind with the Word of
God *every day*, because you do not ever want to
backslide.

Spiritually, the only difference is this: Satan already has donors lined up. *He is ready*.

When a surgeon takes out an old, damaged heart
he does not try to restore it. He discards it. (God is
trying to tell us something. He is trying to show us
through medical science, again, what His process
is!) If your body rejects your new heart, the doctors
would never go back and get your old one. They
couldn't—it is gone! So they would put your name
back on the list to receive a second new heart, and
you would have wait for another donor. Spiritually,
the only difference is this: Satan already has donors
lined up. *He is ready*.

A Deadly Disease

After you have received a new heart (and new
blood), if you "quench the Spirit," rejecting God,
you might as well have injected poison into your

veins. It could be likened to contracting AIDS, which starts to kill your immune system. It travels to the weakest part of your body and starts attacking that area. When that poison starts hitting your blood (because you have rejected the Word of God), you will begin to experience a full AIDS manifestation. And it will kill you.

AIDS usually starts by infecting the lungs, where the "breath of life" keeps oxygen flowing through a person's body. When he can no longer breathe, his lungs fill up with fluid, pneumonia sets in and his condition becomes critical. At this stage (in the spirit realm), he starts to "drop weight" and slowly begins to lose power—his punch, kick and overall strength. The enemy is destroying his "breath of life."

A Fatal Attack

At one time, my pastor was eating things that were unhealthy for his body. The arteries leading to his heart became clogged because of things he had eaten (that his mind had told him he should have). This was not his heart's desire. His *mind* said, "I want bacon." Did his heart completely fail him? No. He had a stroke, so there was nothing wrong with his heart. Yet there was something wrong with the artery that led to his heart.

When people fall into temptation, it does not mean their hearts are messed up. They have had a spiritual stroke. The artery can be unclogged through spiritual surgery according to the Word of God. The valve can be restored so that the blood can continue to flow to the heart. Only the blood can wash and make you clean and keep that new heart purified. This same blood flows to the heart and goes back up to the brain with oxygen so that the brain is able to think clearly again.

When a doctor tells his patient what to do in order to stay healthy, and she refuses to obey his orders, eating everything that she can get her hands on, it will ultimately affect her heart. If she has a stroke, she can become paralyzed and possibly lose the ability to think clearly, move or talk. Her body and face could become twisted and distorted. On the spiritual side, this means she would no longer resemble Christ.

This same blood flows to the heart and goes back up to the brain with oxygen so the brain is able to think clearly again.

Some people are paralyzed for life due to a physical stroke. In the spirit realm, this is why some people sit in church unable to lift up their hands! They cannot dance, sing or worship because they have suffered a stroke. The heart is still intact, but the stroke indicates that unhealthy things have been put into their bodies. Thus the new heart rejects that polluted blood. If their arteries remain clogged and they do not change, a spiritual heart attack could kill them.

The Time for Change Has Come

~~⌒~~

God is saying, loud and clear, that if we intend to live throughout eternity—if we intend to live for Him in this world—we need to change. If we don't, we will have massive heart failure and die a spiritual death. This is definitely a *matter of the heart*. Proverbs 4:23 says, "Keep and guard your heart with all vigilance and above all that you guard, for out of it flow the springs of life."

We must be vigilant, constantly examining our own hearts. Otherwise, we will continue to be the "great pretenders." One day the Lord may say to us, "Begone from Me...I never knew you" (Matt. 25:41; 7:23).

The Word of the Lord speaks to us from Revelation 2:5:

> Remember then from what heights you have fallen. Repent (change the inner man to meet God's will) and do the works you did previously [when first you knew the Lord].

As I close this chapter, heed this warning to care for your new heart diligently. Follow this advice from 2 Corinthians 13:5–11:

> Examine and test and evaluate your own selves to see whether you are holding to your faith and showing the proper fruits of it. Test and prove yourselves [not Christ]. Do you not yourselves realize and know [thoroughly by an ever-increasing experience] that Jesus Christ is in you—unless you are [counterfeits] disapproved on trial and rejected? But I hope you

will recognize and know that we are not disapproved on trial and rejected. But I pray to God that you may do nothing wrong, not in order that we [our teaching] may appear to be approved, but that you may continue doing right...

For we can do nothing against the Truth [not serve any party or personal interest], but only for the Truth [which is the Gospel]...And this we also pray for: your all-round strengthening and perfecting of soul. So I write these things while I am absent from you, that when I come to you, I may not have to deal sharply in my use of the authority which the Lord has given me [to be employed, however] for building [you] up and not for tearing [you] down.

Finally, brethren, farewell (rejoice)! Be strengthened (perfected, completed, made what you ought to be); be encouraged and consoled and comforted; be of the same [agreeable] mind one with another; live in peace, and [then] the God of love [Who is the Source of affection, goodwill, love, and benevolence toward men] and the Author and Promoter of peace will be with you.

God will be with us if we trust and obey our new heart. Above anything else, we must know that *we have it*.

Chapter 11

Prayer **Keys**

We know the problem, we have read the prophetic word, and we have examined the depths of the heart and mind. Now it's time to put what we know into practice. It's time to take the *keys* of God's Word and, from the deep chambers of our hearts, unshackle our minds—and ultimately the world—from the enemy's bondage. Remember what Jesus said in Matthew 16:19:

> I will give you the keys of the kingdom of heaven; and whatever you bind (declare to be improper and unlawful) on earth must be what is already bound in heaven; and whatever you loose (declare lawful) on earth must be what is already loosed in heaven.

We are to "bind" what God has already bound in His Word and to "loose" what He has already loosed. We are not supposed to bind and loose what we desire or anything that has not first been revealed to us by God. If we have received the new heart, both heart and mind should be totally submitted to God's Word and ways. This is how we begin to experience and walk in the "counsel" of God.

> Blessed (happy, fortunate, prosperous, and envi-
> able) is the man who walks and lives not in the
> counsel of the ungodly [following their advice,
> their plans and purposes], nor stands [submis-
> sive and inactive] in the path where sinners
> walk, nor sits down [to relax and rest] where the
> scornful [and the mockers] gather. But his
> delight and desire are in the law of the Lord, and
> on His law (the precepts, the instructions, the
> teachings of God) he habitually meditates (pon-
> ders and studies) by day and by night. And he
> shall be like a tree firmly planted [and tended]
> by the streams of water, ready to bring forth its
> fruit in its season; its leaf also shall not fade or
> wither; and everything he does shall prosper
> [and come to maturity].
>
> —PSALM 1:1–3

God is saying that we are to break old, fleshly
habits and build a new habit of meditating on His
Word…day and night. Let me bring this down to
earth. It takes about twenty-one days to establish a
new habit in your mind. So why don't you challenge
yourself—for the next twenty-one days—to study
and ponder the Word of God day and night? You will
get results…and your battle will be won. When
Daniel sought God for a message, the angel appeared
and told him:

> Fear not, Daniel, for from the first day that you
> set your mind and heart to understand and to
> humble yourself before your God, your words
> were heard, and I have come as a consequence
> of [and in response to] your words. But the
> prince of the kingdom of Persia withstood me
> for twenty-one days. Then Michael, one of the
> chief [of the celestial] princes, came to help me,

> for I remained there with the kings of Persia.
> Now I have come to make you understand what
> is to befall your people in the latter days, for the
> vision is for [many] days yet to come.
> —DANIEL 10:12–14

This could not be a coincidence! If you want to change, you have to "sow to the Spirit," consistently and persistently, to complete the transformation according to God's Word. That is when understanding comes. This is what God is after. This is what God wants to "unlock" through your new heart in order to renew your mind.

In Hebrews 4:12 we discover that an understanding of God's Word is released through our heart, which pierces the brainwaves and flows through our emotions to transform our thoughts, plans and imagination. We read:

> For the Word that God speaks is alive and full of
> power [making it active, operative, energizing,
> and effective]; it is sharper than any two-edged
> sword, penetrating to the dividing line of the
> breath of life (soul) and [the immortal] spirit,
> and of joints and marrow [of the deepest parts
> of our nature], exposing and sifting and analyz-
> ing and judging the very thoughts and purposes
> of the heart.

Based on this verse, you *decide* to obey the Word, and your brainwaves flow back through your emotions to your body and into the depths of your subconscious mind. The transformation is complete: soul, spirit, joints and marrow.

As you seek God in prayer, the Holy Spirit will begin to lead you into the counsel of God's Word.

When you hear the voice of God in prayer, He will either speak to you through His Word (using His Word) or by speaking in harmony with what He has already revealed. The more you seek God, the deeper His counsel will become, and the more "secrets" He will reveal. You will gain more and more understanding. James 1:5–8 says:

> If any of you is deficient in wisdom, let him ask of the giving God [Who gives] to everyone liberally and ungrudgingly, without reproaching or faultfinding, and it will be given him. Only it must be in faith that he asks with no wavering (no hesitating, no doubting). For the one who wavers (hesitates, doubts) is like the billowing surge out at sea that is blown hither and thither and tossed by the wind. For truly, let not such a person imagine that he will receive anything [he asks for] from the Lord, [for being as he is] a man of two minds (hesitating, dubious, irresolute), [he is] unstable and unreliable and uncertain about everything [he thinks, feels, decides].

Being *double-minded* is a state of conflict between the "brain of the heart" and the brain in your head. It is spiritual schizophrenia! It is proof that your new heart is still fighting for the victory. So how do you identify the wisdom that comes from God?

> But the wisdom from above is first of all pure (undefiled); then it is peace-loving, courteous (considerate, gentle). [It is willing to] yield to reason, full of compassion and good fruits; it is wholehearted and straightforward, impartial and unfeigned (free from doubts, wavering, and insincerity).
>
> —JAMES 3:17

When you respond to your new heart, obeying its "intelligent communication" so that the Word penetrates your mind and brings your body into subjection to God's Word, you have won the victory.

> Who is the man who reverently fears and worships the Lord? Him shall He teach in the way that he should choose. He himself shall dwell at ease, and his offspring shall inherit the land. The secret [of the sweet, satisfying companionship] of the Lord have they who fear (revere and worship) Him, and He will show them His covenant and reveal to them its [deep, inner] meaning.
>
> —PSALM 25:12–14

Once you have gained the victory of the new heart, you can consistently receive and respond to the undefiled wisdom of our Father. He can trust you with His secrets.

If you are living in sin, the only thing that God will likely tell you is to repent. Once you have repented from habitual sin, you can then receive the "deep, inner" meaning of His heavenly counsel.

Sometimes you will receive wisdom in prayer that conflicts with everything you see and feel, but it covers you like a warm blanket. This is the wisdom of God. As you go deeper in God, He will begin to lead you in everything you do. He will give you intercessory "assignments" and tell you what to pray according to His Word. Other times, He will lead you to lie silently at the altar or to dance and sing before Him. The most important thing is to do what He leads you to do and to remember what He has already said.

Write the vision and engrave it so plainly upon tablets that everyone who passes may [be able to] read [it easily and quickly] as he hastens by. For the vision is yet for an appointed time and it hastens to the end [fulfillment]; it will not deceive or disappoint. Though it tarry, wait [earnestly] for it, because it will surely come; it will not be behindhand on its appointed day.

—HABAKKUK 2:2–3

Once you have repented from habitual sin, you can then receive the "deep, inner" meaning of His heavenly counsel.

If you do not have one already, it is time to start keeping a prayer journal. Make sure that you write the day, date and time (and sometimes even the place) when God speaks to you. Write the scriptures that He reveals to you. Sometimes He will give you a verse that describes a problem. When this happens, ask Him to reveal how you can intercede for His solution. He will show you. It is always His will for the power of sin to be broken so that His people can be delivered from bondage.

Seek, inquire for, and require the Lord while He may be found [claiming Him by necessity and by right]; call upon Him while He is near. Let the wicked forsake his way and the unrighteous man his thoughts; and let him return to the Lord, and He will have love, pity, and mercy for

> him, and to our God, for He will multiply to him
> His abundant pardon...For you shall go out
> [from the spiritual exile caused by sin and evil
> into the homeland] with joy and be led forth
> [by your Leader, the Lord Himself, and His
> word] with peace; the mountains and the hills
> shall break forth before you into singing, and all
> the trees of the field shall clap their hands.
> Instead of the thorn shall come up the cypress
> tree, and instead of the brier shall come up the
> myrtle tree; and it shall be to the Lord for a
> name of renown, for an everlasting sign [of jubi-
> lant exaltation] and memorial [to His praise],
> which shall not be cut off.
> —ISAIAH 55:6–7, 12–13

God wants to "heal our land" (2 Chron. 7:14). He longs to deliver us from the problem that has emerged from our old, deceitful hearts (Jer. 17:9). Yes, we have been deceived to the point that we have fallen into a pattern of sin that threatens to paralyze the church if we do not turn to God and sincerely repent.

We must receive the new heart and begin to seek God while He can still be found. We must forsake our own thoughts and put on the humble mind of Christ. (See Philippians 2:5–8.) Then, and only then, will God release true "prosperity." And it will not only heal us; it will heal our land.

Principles of Prayer and Intercession

Before you can begin to pray effectively, you need to understand exactly what prayer is, so let us begin with *praise* and *petition*. Yes, I started with praise,

and, yes, it works together with petition! You enter
God's presence through your praises, because thank-
ing God proves your faith in Him to perform His
Word. After all, if you do not believe that God
answers prayer, you might as well not even ask—
because He does not answer "double-minded"
requests. Philippians 4:6–7 says:

> Do not fret or have any anxiety about anything,
> but in every circumstance and in everything,
> by prayer and petition (definite requests), with
> thanksgiving, continue to make your wants
> known to God. And God's peace [shall be yours,
> that tranquil state of a soul assured of its salva-
> tion through Christ, and so fearing nothing
> from God and being content with its earthly lot
> of whatever sort that is, that peace] which tran-
> scends all understanding shall garrison and
> mount guard over your hearts and minds in
> Christ Jesus.

There is also an intensified prayer of *consecration*
where you press into God with a need to know or to
do God's will. (See Matthew 26:39.) Another type of
prayer is the prayer of *faith*, or an urgent request for
God to intervene in a situation that usually requires
an immediate answer. (See James 5:15.) The prayer
of *agreement* is joining your faith with two or three
others before God. (See Matthew 18:19–20.) Finally,
intercession is when you pray and believe for someone else. (See Isaiah 59:16.)

According to Matthew 7:7–8, there are also levels
(or increasing intensities) of prayer:

> Keep on *asking* and it will be given you; keep
> on *seeking* and you will find; keep on *knocking*

[reverently] and [the door] will be opened to
you. For everyone who keeps on asking
receives; and he who keeps on seeking finds;
and to him who keeps on knocking, [the door]
will be opened.

—EMPHASIS ADDED

The kingdom of God is like "something precious
buried in a field" (Matt. 13:44). Sometimes we have to
dig deeper, wait longer and press in harder to get the
full revelation.

Simply put, to *ask* is to petition God for your
needs or to intercede for the needs of others. To seek
means to ask God for deeper wisdom and, at the
same time, to search the Word for deeper insight.
Seeking can also mean that you study other
resources or look more deeply into the things
around you. It can also mean that you receive godly
counsel in order to get a full understanding of what
God is saying.

Knocking is pressing in further through persistent
prayer, fasting and obedience to God's revealed and
written Word. When you fast, you willingly give up
food and anything else that stands in God's way in
order to hear God, obey Him and accomplish His
purpose.

[Rather] is not this the fast that I have chosen:
to loose the bonds of wickedness, to undo the
bands of the yoke, to let the oppressed go free,
and that you break every [enslaving] yoke? Is it
not to divide your bread with the hungry and
bring the homeless poor into your house—
when you see the naked, that you cover him,
and that you hide not yourself from [the needs
of] your own flesh and blood?

Then shall your light break forth like the morning, and your healing (your restoration and the power of a new life) shall spring forth speedily; your righteousness (your rightness, your justice, and your right relationship with God) shall go before you [conducting you to peace and prosperity], and the glory of the Lord shall be your rear guard. Then you shall call, and the Lord will answer; you shall cry, and He will say, Here I am. If you take away from your midst yokes of oppression [wherever you find them], the finger pointed in scorn [toward the oppressed or the godly], and every form of false, harsh, unjust and wicked speaking, and if you pour out that with which you sustain your own life for the hungry and satisfy the need of the afflicted, then shall your light rise in darkness, and your obscurity and gloom become like the noonday.

—ISAIAH 58:6–10

Fasting from food is extremely powerful because your new heart is bypassing your mind (which is bent on survival) and going directly to your body, which tells the brain, "Man shall not live and be upheld and sustained by bread alone, but by every word that comes forth from the mouth of God" (Matt. 4:4). To coin a phrase, fasting is "putting your body where your heart is" to squeeze out any form of mind control.

This is also why it is good to meditate even more deeply on the Word during a fast. It escalates the two-pronged counterattack (discussed in chapter seven) to an all-out, three-pronged assault against the enemy. In other words, denying yourself food can help you to see that other "earthly" things are not that important—which opens the door to obedience in every area of your life. Ecclesiastes 4:12 says, "A threefold cord is not quickly broken."

To coin a phrase, fasting is "putting your body where your heart is" to squeeze out any form of mind control.

When you overcome in a fast, the devil has to flee; there is a clear path—*within you and outside of you*—for God's will and purpose to be done. Let me say this a different way: When you overcome by denying yourself food, time, money, convenience and whatever you value most, the devil will not be able to tempt you because you have already rejected everything that he can throw in your direction. And he cannot stay in the light; he has to run from it, because his evil deeds are immediately seen and exposed for what they truly are.

Getting to the Heart of Prayer

Obviously, prayer is not what it needs to be in the body of Christ because we are operating from wicked, deceived hearts (Jer. 17:9). Prayer will be restored as we obey our new hearts and renew our old, stubborn minds. Today, in this season and final hour of the church, prayer will be the final test of any genuine believer or work for God:

Dwell in Me, and I will dwell in you. [Live in Me,
and I will live in you.] Just as no branch can
bear fruit of itself without abiding in (being
vitally united to) the vine, neither can you bear
fruit unless you abide in Me. I am the Vine; you
are the branches. Whoever lives in Me and I in
him bears much (abundant) fruit. However,
apart from Me [cut off from vital union with Me]
you can do nothing. If a person does not dwell
in Me, he is thrown out like a [broken-off]
branch, and withers; such branches are gathered up and thrown into the fire, and they are
burned. If you live in Me [abide vitally united to
Me] and My words remain in you and continue
to live in your hearts, ask whatever you will,
and it shall be done for you.

—JOHN 15:4–7

Prayer is our vital connection to God through the
vehicle of our new hearts. If we do not pray, we will
not have the life of Christ within us. We will be unpro-
ductive and, even worse, could be told on that Day, "I
never knew you."

You must decide whether to hear and embrace
this word of prophecy—and inherit eternal life—or
to continue walking in your own thoughts and ways,
and reap destruction. The choice is yours.

I pray and trust that you will choose to obey God
and reap eternal life.

To get you started, the following are a few steps to
develop your daily devotions, as well as a few
Scripture keys on the heart and mind.

The Practice of Prayer

~ᑲ~

I adapted this daily "prayer practice" from a powerful, in-depth teaching called "The Power of Positive
Prayer Points" in Matthew Ashimolowo's special edition Bible.[1]

1. Start each day loving God and people.
    This means your relationship with God
    is good, and that as far as you are able,
    your relationships with family mem-
    bers, friends, coworkers and others are
    in line with the Word.

2. Start each day communing with God
    through Bible study and prayer.

3. Thank God, praise Him for answering
    your prayers and worship Him for who
    He is.

4. Repent, asking God to forgive you and
    to cleanse your heart from every sin,
    known and unknown.

5. Thank God for your spiritual armor, as
    listed in Ephesians 6:10–18.

6. Surrender yourself to the Holy Spirit
    so He can pray through you, according
    to Romans 8:26–27.

7. Be ready to obey the Holy Spirit's lead-
    ing, to petition (for your needs) or
    intercede (for others); declare God's

Word; lie still, or do whatever God
leads you to do.

8. Ask God to build a hedge of protection
    around your life, family and all others
    who are praying with you against the
    enemy's devices.

9. Ask God to rebuke Satan and all his
    servants.

10. Take authority over the enemy's work
    and his attempts to attack your new
    heart (spirit), your mind (emotions,
    logic, and decision making) and body.

11. Repeat these steps until you know that
    you have broken through in the Spirit
    realm and that God is leading you in
    prayer and intercession.

A Few Prayer Keys for the Heart

Here are a few scriptures to get you started as you
seek God in prayer daily, learning to embrace your
new heart. Put yourself in these scriptures as you
meditate on the Word. For example, "I shall love the
Lord my God with all my mind and heart..."

> Create in me a clean heart, O God, and renew
> a right, persevering, and steadfast spirit within
> me...Let the words of my mouth and the med-
> itation of my heart be acceptable in Your sight,

O Lord, my [firm, impenetrable] Rock and my
Redeemer.

—Psalm 51:10; 19:14

A new heart will I give you and a new spirit will
I put within you, and I will take away the stony
heart out of your flesh and give you a heart of
flesh.

—Ezekiel 36:26

Search me [thoroughly], O God, and know my
heart! Try me and know my thoughts! And see
if there is any wicked or hurtful way in me, and
lead me in the way everlasting.

—Psalm 139:23–24

Teach me Your way, O Lord, that I may walk
and live in Your truth; direct and unite my
heart [solely, reverently] to fear and honor Your
name.

—Psalm 86:11

I delight to do Your will, O my God; yes, Your
law is within my heart.

—Psalm 40:8

As for what was sown on good soil, this is he
who hears the Word and grasps and compre-
hends it; he indeed bears fruit and yields in one
case a hundred times as much as was sown, in
another sixty times as much, and in another
thirty.

—Matthew 13:23

And you shall love the Lord your God with all
your [mind and] heart and with your entire
being and with all your might.

—Deuteronomy 6:5

A Few Prayer Keys for the Mind

As I was studying, I found that the word *heart* is used at least seven times more in the Bible than the word *mind*. Many of these uses of the word *heart* refer to both heart and mind, but I believe this is because the heart comes first—in the natural and spiritual realms. Begin to meditate on these scriptures:

> For who has known or understood the mind (counsels and purposes) of the Lord so as to guide and instruct Him and give Him knowledge? But we have the mind of Christ (the Messiah) and do hold the thoughts (feelings and purposes) of His heart.
>
> —1 CORINTHIANS 2:16

> Do not be conformed to this world (this age), [fashioned after and adapted to its external, superficial customs], but be transformed (changed) by the [entire] renewal of your mind [by its new ideals and its new attitude], so that you may prove [for yourselves] what is the good and acceptable and perfect will of God, even the thing which is good and acceptable and perfect [in His sight for you].
>
> —ROMANS 12:2

> And be constantly renewed in the spirit of your mind [having a fresh mental and spiritual attitude], and put on the new nature (the regenerate self) created in God's image, [Godlike] in true righteousness and holiness.
>
> —EPHESIANS 4:23–24

You will guard him and keep him in perfect and constant peace whose mind [both its inclination and its character] is stayed on You, because he commits himself to You, leans on You, and hopes confidently in You.

—Isaiah 26:3

I will imprint My laws upon their minds, even upon their innermost thoughts and understanding, and engrave them upon their hearts; and I will be their God, and they shall be My people.

—Hebrews 8:10

For God did not give us a spirit of timidity (of cowardice, of craven and cringing and fawning fear), but [He has given us a spirit] of power and of love and of calm and well-balanced mind and discipline and self-control.

—2 Timothy 1:7

So brace up your minds; be sober (circumspect, morally alert); set your hope wholly and unchangeably on the grace (divine favor) that is coming to you when Jesus Christ (the Messiah) is revealed.

—1 Peter 1:13

Again, these verses will get you started. As you continue to seek, study and meditate upon God's Word, He will finish the work that He has started in you.

God Can Still Deliver Us

Yes, the new heart message is a mandate for me to preach, because so many believers have been deceived (as I was) about their own hearts. So many *think* they are saved, but they still do not know Christ. Many leaders and preachers have not yet been born again, or they are not telling the whole truth and causing others to stumble. Yes, knowing Christ has become "unattainable," but God can still deliver us.

God turned me around, so I know that He will do the same for you. Like me, you need to ask God to give you a new heart.

> Therefore also now, says the Lord, turn and keep on coming to Me with all your heart, with fasting, with weeping, and with mourning [until every hindrance is removed and the broken fellowship is restored]. Rend your hearts and not your garments and return to the Lord, your God, for He is gracious and merciful, slow to anger, and abounding in loving-kindness; and He revokes His sentence of evil [when His conditions are met].
>
> —JOEL 2:12–13

It is time to return to the Lord, because nothing is more important than *the matters of the heart*.

Notes

Introduction
How It **All Began**

1. "Give Me a Clean Heart," public domain.

Chapter 1
We Need a **New Heart**

1. James Strong, *The New Strong's Exhaustive Concordance of the Bible,* (Nashville, TN: Thomas Nelson, 1984), s.v. 5315, "soul."
2. Ibid., s.v. 5368, *"phileo."*

Chapter 6
A Scientific **Point of View**

1. Doc Lew Childre and Howard Martin, *The HeartMath Solution* (San Francisco, CA: HarperSanFrancisco, 2000), 9.
2. Ibid., 33.
3. Ibid., 9.
4. Ibid., 32.
5. Ibid., 10.
6. Strong, *The New Strong's Exhaustive Concordance of the Bible*, s.v. 3788, "eye."
7. Ibid., s. v. 573, 4120, "single."
8. Childre and Martin, *The HeartMath Solution*, 31.
9. Ibid., 34.

Chapter 7

Results of a **Heart Transplant**

1. Paul Pearsall, "The Heart That Found Its Body's Killer," *The Heart's Code* (New York: Broadway Books, 1998), 7.
2. *The Art Bell Show* (syndicated), as aired on New Talk Radio, 570 KLIF, Dallas, Texas, March 21, 2002.
3. Pearsall, *The Heart's Code*, 24–25.
4. Childre and Martin, "The Brain in the Heart," *The HeartMath Solution,* 10.
5. Ibid., "Let's Make a Deal," 41.

Chapter 8

The New **Heart**

1. Pearsall, *The Heart's Code*, 66.
2. Childre and Martin, *The HeartMath Solution*, 34.
3. Strong, *The New Strong's Exhaustive Concordance of the Bible*, s.v. 8085, "hearken."

Chapter 9

The Renewed **Mind**

1. Adapted from Childre and Martin, *The HeartMath Solution,* 31.
2. Elaine Farris Hughes, *Writing from the Inner Self* (New York: Harper Perennial, 1992), 4.
3 Childre and Martin, *The HeartMath Solution*. Also, source retrieved from Internet: The High-Performance Mind and encyclopedia.com.

Chapter 11
Prayer **Keys**

1. The Daily Prayer Practice was adapted from a special
    edition King James Bible by Matthew Ashimolowo, in
    a section titled, "The Power of Positive Prayer
    Points," page 17. For more information regarding this
    resource, contact Matthew Ashimolowo Media
    Ministries, London, England, or go to his website at
    www.kicc.org.uk.

Book II

My
*S*piritual
Inheritance

Juanita Bynum

Charisma
HOUSE
A STRANG COMPANY

DEDICATION

*A*lthough I have many fathers in the Spirit, I would like to dedicate this book to my first spiritual father, my dad, Evangelist Thomas Bynum, as well as my mother, Katherine Bynum—for raising me in holiness.

> —To Pastor Terrell and Veter Nichols for birthing spiritual character in me.
>
> —To Dr. John H. Boyd Sr. for imparting into me the love for souls.
>
> —To Pastor James Swinson for protecting and guarding my ministry during warfare.
>
> —To Pastor Rod Parsley for being the wind in my back and a shield to my face.
>
> —And to Pastor John Hagee for putting the salve on the wound, for ministry just plain hurts.
>
> —To Bishop Thomas and Dr. Leona Weeks for your covering and loving counsel…

ACKNOWLEDGMENTS

*F*irst of all, I would like to thank God, my heavenly Father, who gave me the strength to give birth to this spiritual assignment.

And to one of His angels on earth, Paula Bryant. Without her dedication, her consecration, and, most of all, her intercession over me and this project, I could not have gotten this done. Paula, you are not just an editor; you are an intercessor-editor. In my book, the words "Thank you" are not enough—so I'll just say, "May God forever bless you."

CONTENTS

FOREWORD

By John Hagee

Welcome to Juanita Bynum's latest release titled *My Spiritual Inheritance.* In this exciting and unpredictable book you will discover how to find the power of God. You will discover the destiny God has uniquely planned for you from the foundations of the earth.

In this life-changing book, Juanita Bynum, with personal illustrations and examples from prophets, priests, and kings, points the way to your divine destiny. *My Spiritual Inheritance* will find its place as one of the most relevant books you read this year.

—JOHN HAGEE
SENIOR PASTOR, CORNERSTONE CHURCH
SAN ANTONIO, TEXAS

INTRODUCTION

I first received this word from the Lord during a time when I was walking through a hard trial—not a trying of my faith, but a trying of my character. At the time, I wanted to leave my church home because I felt as though I wasn't being fed spiritually—I felt as if I had outgrown what my pastor was preaching. Above this, everything that I was seeing behind the scenes was offensive to me. My inner warfare was so intense that I cried out to the Lord. Was it really my time to go, or was God trying to take me to another level of revelation?

As time passed and God continued to do a work in my heart, I knew that I would share this experience with others. Initially, I thought I would only end up preaching the message. I had no idea that God was in the process of birthing a book.

I have a strong conviction about preaching messages that I haven't walked out in my own life. So I knew that by the time the Lord finished processing this word in me, it would be a powerful message that would definitely change lives—including my own. As I began to study and read, and ultimately to preach this message, it was like opening up Pandora's box—a multidimensional jack-in-the-box. The more I preached it and the more I experienced it, the more this word of the Lord began to unravel.

More and more, my thoughts went back to situations and circumstances I had experienced myself in the body of Christ. Interestingly, I began to realize the direct relationship these situations and circumstances had to my own relationship with my pastor. Even though I had been extremely active in church for years, I had never before been able to understand how very relevant my relationship with my pastor was to my relationship with my heavenly Father. I had never seen the association . . . so I began to go back and take a closer look.

Suddenly I was confronted with the realization that although I was able to give testimony to the fact of having been in church for years—indeed, I was *raised* in the church—I had never before really thought about whether or not I was receiving everything my heavenly Father intended for me to have as my spiritual inheritance. This lack of knowledge about His portion for me had robbed my life and hindered me from reaching my full potential in Him.

I see the onset of a mighty revival across this nation. People everywhere are being embraced and ushered into the body of Christ. As brand-new baby members of Christ's body, these people look for local churches where they can be nourished and fed with the Word of God. As I watch these baby Christians begin to grow, I cannot sit back and let them miss out on an authentic experience in God. You see, you can have the experience of salvation and receive a new heart, but still miss the experience of walking into your spiritual destiny—your spiritual inheritance—the portion that is supposed to be implanted into your new heart.

After receiving a new heart, that heart must continually be fed by your heavenly Father. Receiving your spiritual inheritance is an ongoing process. You can miss out on all He has for you if you try to diminish this experience by isolating it to a one-time experience. Just as you need daily nourishment to keep your physical body alive, you need to receive your daily spiritual portion from your heavenly Father to reach your full potential in Christ.

For this reason, my purpose for writing this book is even stronger now than before. It is vital that you know when you have met your spiritual parents, and after meeting them, to recognize they are preparing you to receive your spiritual inheritance from God. This will help you to guard against losing that inheritance.

As the Lord led me through the process of examining my own heart, I went all the way back to how I felt as a young teenager when my first pastor, Luke Austin Sr., passed away. Although his son took over the ministry, still, I felt lost, disconnected. From that point on, I began to wander spiritually. Soon to be eighteen, I asked my mom for permission to move to Milwaukee, Wisconsin. I was searching for more but did not know it. Since my pastor had been an older man, he had been like a spiritual grandfather to me—and I didn't understand the weight of his influence upon my life. My parents understood, but I hadn't come to terms with it. I truly did not understand what the loss of his influence meant in my spirit man. In fact, I did not even recognize that it had created an empty place within. So I started searching for something, not knowing what I was searching for. Along the way, I came across several pastors, but it wasn't until 1982, when I moved to Port Huron, Michigan, that the divine destiny of the Lord connected me to my spiritual parents, who certainly were a blessing to my life.

In all honesty, that was the first time I realized that God had placed in my life a man who functioned as a spiritual father to me. I knew it the moment I walked into the office of Pastor William and Sister Veter Nichols because he immediately became concerned about me as a person. He observed my life and saw some issues that needed attention. Though I came across as an awesome young evangelist, and the people at the church were impressed by the move of God in my life, Pastor Nichols dove right into my personal life and dealt with my personal issues.

I believe it was at this point when God became concerned that I would not miss out on my spiritual inheritance. He wanted me to receive the full portion of what He wanted to give me—and He wants you to receive the full portion of your spiritual inheritance, too.

His portion will change you. It will birth you into destiny. When you are receiving your spiritual portion from God, it will feed your spirit. As your spirit grows, you will come to maturity in Christ. And as Christians everywhere mature in Christ, maturity comes to the body of Christ. So we must be sure we are really getting the Father's portion.

If you are a pastor or leader, this book will help you to recognize the great responsibility we have as leaders to rise to a new level in our own relationship with God so that we are able to impart God's portion to the people who are coming to us for spiritual leadership. When you stand in front of others, you must ask: Are people receiving their portion, or are they just getting another message? If they are receiving their portion from God through you, then it must be a message given as a result of your brokenness before the Lord, or it will only go to the ears and not to the heart. It will not change their lives!

I believe a lot of people are asking, even right now, *"Where is my spiritual inheritance?"*

It is God's desire to change the world one person at a time. When a person walks into a ministry—your ministry—and sits under your spiritual leadership, God's sole motive for that person is to birth him or her into destiny through your leadership.

> A LEADER IS ACCOUNTABLE, NOT JUST FOR SPEAKING THE WORD OF THE LORD TO A CONGREGATION, BUT ALSO FOR IMPARTING THAT WORD INTO THE HEARTS OF THE PEOPLE.

On the other hand, if you are the one seeking spiritual leadership and nourishment in the body of Christ, your introduction to a local ministry should be based upon a divine connection, communication, and relationship that you have with the leadership of that local ministry. Your connection to that church should not be based upon the choir or the praise and worship team, the basketball club or the usher's board, and certainly not because you like the fact that they throw big birthday parties for their members. In short, you should not join a church for its activities.

Too many people have done this. They haven't linked to the divine portion of their spiritual fathers and the deposit of their spiritual mothers. God's Word gives us this advice:

> My son, hear the instruction of your father; reject not
> nor forsake the teaching of your mother. For they are
> a [victor's] chaplet (garland) of grace upon your head
> and chains and pendants [of gold worn by kings] for
> your neck.
>
> —PROVERBS 1:8–9

Introduction

People—like sheep—must be led. Why? People can easily become entangled with their peers in situations that magnify issues they have not dealt with. They come to church, but their hearts are not in the right posture. Leaders have been called to feed, which means you must eat.

Jesus addressed our need for spiritual leadership when He talked to His disciples (future leaders) in the twenty-first chapter of John. In the following verses we can identify the posture we must have as believers desiring to obtain our Father's portion.

> Jesus said to them, Come [and] have breakfast. But none of the disciples ventured or dared to ask Him, Who are You? because they [well] knew that it was the Lord. Jesus came and took the bread and gave it to them, and so also [with] the fish. This was now the third time that Jesus revealed Himself (appeared, was manifest) to the disciples after He had risen from the dead.
>
> When they had eaten, Jesus said to Simon Peter, Simon, son of John, do you love Me more than these [others do—with reasoning, intentional, spiritual devotion, as one loves the Father]? He said to Him, Yes, Lord, You know that I love You [that I have deep, instinctive, personal affection for You, as for a close friend]. He said to him, Feed My lambs. Again He said to him the second time, Simon, son of John, do you love Me [with reasoning, intentional, spiritual devotion, as one loves the Father]? He said to Him, Yes, Lord, You know that I love You [that I have a deep, instinctive, personal affection for You, as for a close friend]. He said to him, Shepherd (tend) My sheep.
>
> He said to him the third time, Simon, son of John, do you love Me [with a deep, instinctive, personal affection for Me, as for a close friend]? Peter was grieved (was saddened and hurt) that He should ask him the third time, Do you love Me? And he said to Him, Lord,

You know everything; You know that I love You [that I
have a deep, instinctive, personal affection for You, as
for a close friend]. Jesus said to him, Feed My sheep.
—JOHN 21:12–17

The Father's portion is a meal that satisfies, and it must be digested
in order to work in our lives. So when we walk through the doors of
the church, it's time for a feeding. We should come prepared to worship the Father and receive a meal from His table. A dietician will tell
you the best time to eat isn't when you're starving—because you will
eat anything. That's our problem. Too many
in the body of Christ are starving because we
only eat a healthy meal once or twice a week.
In other words, we don't maintain intimacy
with God on a daily basis, so we can't even
digest properly what we receive from Him.
We are malnourished.

THE BIBLE'S
PATTERN IS
CLEAR—SPIRITUAL
LEADERS ARE TO
LEAD, AND WE ARE
TO SUBMIT UNDER
THEIR SPIRITUAL
LEADERSHIP
FOR SPIRITUAL
DIRECTION.

Recently I have been changing my diet
and lifestyle. The first time I went to the
dietician's office, they inquired about what
I had been eating. I told them that I had
been eating one big meal each day, though
I snacked on potato chips and other quick
foods throughout the day. Then when I
wanted to lose weight and started removing snacks and sodas from
my diet, I still couldn't lose the excess pounds—and I was still eating
just one meal a day.

After I shared this, they told me why I hadn't been able to lose the
weight. My body knew that it would only get one full meal a day, so it
kicked into survival mode. In other words, it held on to that one meal
and turned it into fat reserves. Therefore, that one daily meal wasn't
fuel for my body. It wasn't giving me the energy I needed to do what
I had to do.

They told me to start eating at least six mini-meals a day, and
along with that to increase my water intake. That way, my body would

know that it didn't have to turn each meal into fat storage. It would understand that another meal would be coming in two hours, so in turn, it would turn each meal into energy. As I was faithful to this new diet and lifestyle, my metabolism started kicking in. And when this happened, everything began to change, even the appearance of my skin. Even better, the excess weight started dropping off.

This same dynamic happens in the spirit realm. If your spirit man knows that it is only going to get one meal, you won't be able to lose the "excess flesh" that you have been carrying around. One meal a week is not enough to make your spiritual metabolism kick in and burn off everything that is not pleasing to God. You must increase your intake of balanced meals in order to digest the Word of God properly. Through this consistent intimacy with the Father, your character will begin to change. You will become a mature Christian.

Like those small meals, a healthy walk with the Lord cannot be developed on a one-day-a-week meal…it must be nurtured every hour of every day. This is why the Bible tells us that we must always pray and not faint (Luke 18:1–8). Because not only will the Lord answer the cries of His people, but also we will stay in communication with Him throughout the day.

How does this tie into our relationship with leadership? Since our heavenly Father requires constant communion, we must come as often as we can to eat from the table of the "messenger" that God has sent to stand in His stead on earth. It is all part of the process.

I must say it again. Spiritual leaders stand in the stead of the Father. This is why I'm certain that if you do not have a relationship with your spiritual leaders, God will not stop until He establishes that relationship. The Father is concerned about every individual sitting in the pews, but His primary goal is relationships—with Him and with those who stand in His stead in leadership. He is a God that moves through divine order.

That is also why He didn't simply send an angel or another created being to fulfill His plan of redemption. He sent His very own Son. In doing so, God was helping humanity to understand that deliverance must come through the relationship of family. Deliverance comes through the bloodline. Deliverance comes through God being our heavenly Father—and we being children of the Royal Family.

Leadership is supposed to be set up in our hearts as well as in our churches. This is His order. And when the body of Christ receives this revelation, our spiritual metabolism will kick in and cause us to shed the excess flesh that has hindered our growth and development as a family in Christ.

While reading this Introduction, your thoughts may be racing back to the conditions in your own church. I can feel that you might be saying, "But you don't know what I've been through. You don't know about the Jezebel that is taking over our church. You don't know how many times I have been humiliated and embarrassed by people in leadership positions. You don't know how many times I have gone to church and didn't get anything out of it. Do you know how many of the wrong people I see in leadership positions, and everybody else acts as if they don't see what I see?"

But I answer by saying, "Do I know what you're feeling?" Of course, I do. I am about to write some of your thoughts because I have walked in all of those positions. What I didn't know is that God had a remedy to every condition that I was experiencing. I had to come to grips with this important fact: if God didn't tell me to leave my church, then I couldn't go anywhere. Hear the Lord, reader. If *God* is not telling you to leave your church, then you might as well buckle your seatbelt, because He is preparing you for your next level. Believe me when I tell you, He is about to birth something great in you, and you cannot give birth while running.

You may think that it is time to switch ministries, but it may just be time for you to switch your "spiritual seat" and begin to see through the revelatory eyes of the Spirit. That's what I did…and it changed my life.

CHAPTER 1

The Voice of the Father

When I moved to Port Huron, Michigan, it was the beginning of an intense, nine-year process of spiritual growth. At the time, I was young in the Lord and immature in the Spirit. I needed the mentorship of my new spiritual parents. Actually, I went through all of those years calling them *Mom* and *Dad*, because that's what we normally did in church. Even still, I didn't truly embrace the power of this experience or the portion the Father was trying to give me.

God was trying to impart a new level of revelation in my spirit. He was introducing me to His order, but I couldn't see it because of things that were going on in my life. I was battling a lot of emotional issues and had my own ideas about what I wanted to do. As a result, the Nichols had to correct me constantly. At the time, I didn't understand the power and anointing that were being imparted to me with every correction. The mystery of spiritual parenting had not yet been revealed to me.

I left Port Huron before it was time, and as a result, I ran into some very bad situations. As a matter of fact, after just two months outside of the will of the Lord and the divine covering of my spiritual parents, I began to see signs that everything I had been processed through for nine years (and delivered from!) was beginning to resurface in my life. Ultimately, I had to call Pastor Nichols and repent. I asked for his forgiveness because, in spiritual rebellion, I had walked out from under his leadership and away from my divine calling. He received my apology, as any father would, and in turn prayed with me that God would lead me to the church of my next level.

Please know that unfortunate situations can come up in your life, not only as a result of leaving your church at the wrong time, but also as a result of leaving the wrong way. In fact, while it may be time for you to leave, the way that you leave your spiritual parents is just as important as the timing. Clearly, I didn't have it right at that stage of my walk with the Lord. When I think about how this situation played out, I realize how awesome our God is.

When you really belong to the Lord, when you are a child of the King, it becomes the Father's responsibility to make sure you get your spiritual inheritance. It's His responsibility to make sure you don't miss it. So even though I messed up in one sense, I didn't miss His portion. He is the God of the second chance—and that's exactly what He did. He gave me another chance.

When I arrived in New York City, I was impoverished in my spirit and in my bank account. I had holes in my shoes, and I was going through depression. My self-esteem had been shot out of the window as the result of my involvement in some relationships that were not the will of the Lord for my life. Above this, I was experiencing that "lost feeling" in the church. I had been in church all of my life, yet I still felt as though I didn't really know God. I certainly didn't understand His purpose for saving me. Up to this point in my life, it had seemed that no matter what I did, I could not find His purpose.

I had already done the preaching thing; I had been preaching since I was sixteen years old. My popularity was starting to grow. Yet on a personal level as a young woman of God, I still felt unfulfilled. I still felt lonely in my spirit, longing for something and not knowing what that something was.

During these times in New York City I would leave my radio tuned to a gospel station. Music would play for a couple of hours, and then there would be preaching. On one of these occasions I heard Dr. John H. Boyd Sr. speak for the first time. I almost can't describe the experience: I was lying across my bed, and when he began speaking, the power of God literally came through that radio. There was something about his voice that made me feel as if I were back at home during my early days in Chicago with Pastor Austin.

I remembered Pastor Austin's church. I had been born into his ministry and grew up under his leadership. Everybody knew him as "Papa." When he died, I sat in back of the church at his funeral, feeling completely lost and not knowing why. Years later, when I heard Dr. Boyd on the radio, something quickened in me. My spirit identified with the sound of his voice even though technically he didn't sound like Pastor Austin. It was something more than just his voice. In the Spirit realm it was a sound I recognized, the sound of impartation with the same sense of comfort I had felt during those early years with Papa Austin. I felt as if I were in my grandma's kitchen with the smell of apple pie baking in the oven. The sound of Dr. Boyd's voice on the radio that day definitely gave me that "at home" feeling.

When I was relocated to New York City as a flight attendant for Pan American Airlines, the only place I could find to live was a rented room right in the middle of the projects. But even from the room in the projects—miles away from where I began—my bedroom was filled with a sense of "home." When I wasn't working, I listened to Dr. Boyd's radio programs. God is so faithful. I was in a new city, traveling all the time, yet God was introducing and connecting me in the Spirit realm to my spiritual inheritance through the man who would become my new spiritual father. This man, Dr. Boyd, was going to reflect the voice of my Father in heaven.

I didn't yet understand the purpose of spiritual fathers and mothers. I didn't know they actually impart our spiritual inheritance from God as they show us His ways and teach us how to respond to Him. I didn't have a revelation of this spiritual truth. But God was faithful and made sure I didn't miss His portion.

As a job requirement, I had to travel all the time. Many times I would be out of town for work, and from wherever I was at the moment, I would hear Dr. Boyd's voice on the radio. This happened to me on more than ten occasions when I walked into a hotel room, turned on the radio, and scanned for a gospel station. As soon as I located a gospel station, I'd hear "The Voice of Bethel" broadcast with Dr. John Boyd.

Those moments when Dr. Boyd's voice came through my radio into my spirit were powerful confirmations to me of God's will for my life. It seemed that everywhere I went the Spirit of the Lord was making sure I didn't miss my Father's feeding. For six months, God continued this process of connecting me with my new spiritual father on earth.

There Is a Portion for You

There are many people who believe they became the people they are because of experiences they had with an earthly father figure. Some of these are good, positive experiences. In other cases, it has been negative, abusive experiences with a father figure that have shaped a person's life. People have had all kinds of experiences with fathers. Some people have no father. Others never knew their fathers. But it doesn't matter what kind of relationship we have had, or haven't had, with our natural fathers. Our heavenly Father is THE ultimate Father, and He desires that we know Him. It is the responsibility of our heavenly Father to make sure we experience divine fatherhood. This is His gift to us.

> **YOUR HEAVENLY FATHER WANTS YOU TO RECEIVE YOUR SPIRITUAL INHERITANCE.**

If you have had a good relationship with your father, your Father in heaven wants to impart His portion to you. But every person can receive this gift, even those who have been abused by a natural father, those who never knew their fathers, and those who may have lost their fathers. No matter what you may have missed in life, what you may have, or what you desire for your future—the ultimate desire of the Lord is for you to experience true spiritual fatherhood. Those radio broadcasts from Dr. Boyd were just the beginning. In order to initiate

His divine plan for my life, God turned a frustrating situation into an appointment with destiny. You may have heard me tell this story before; it's one I will never forget. One Sunday morning I woke up around 4:00 a.m., knowing I needed to get ready for work. I had read my flight schedule the night before, which said, "6:45 report." I got dressed and headed for the airport, planning to arrive, as usual, about an hour before crew check in.

I arrived at the airport at 5:45 a.m., and by 6:45 I was walking into the Pan American briefing room. The purser (lead flight attendant) came in and started reading the names of all the crew to make sure everybody was present. When she had read all of the names, she looked at me and said, "Who are you?"

"I'm Juanita Bynum."

"You're not on my list," she said.

I explained to her that my schedule told me to report in at 6:45 a.m.

"Are you sure?" she asked.

"Yes," I replied. "I have it right here..." I pulled the paper out of my purse, and it said 6:45 a.m. So we called the supervisor of scheduling and were told, "That was a misprint. You don't report until *6:45 p.m.*" So after getting all the way to the airport, I had to turn around and head back home. That particular morning, it was below zero. The wind chill factor was so cold that it felt like the water in my eyelids was freezing. Needless to say, I was frustrated.

When I was one block from home, I noticed a lady standing at a bus stop with three little kids. They were all bundled up. The Spirit of the Lord said, to me, "Turn around, and ask that lady if she needs a ride."

So I turned around, in obedience to God (we're going to get to the power of obedience later), and pulled up to the curb. "Ma'am," I said to her, "are you on your way home?"

"No, I'm on my way to church," she told me. "I just missed our church bus, so I'm going to catch the regular bus to church."

"It's really cold out here for your kids," I said, "Are you sure you don't want a ride?" Finally she agreed, saying, "I'll take a ride, if you don't mind."

Believing God to help me find my way, I told her, "I don't know my way around New York. If you tell me how to get to your church, then I'll find my way back." I had less than a quarter tank of gas. I can still remember thinking to myself, *I'm giving this lady a ride, and I don't even know if I'm going to have enough gas to make it back to work tonight.* I kept driving. We had almost reached the church when she said, "There's a gas station on the corner. Pull into that station, because the least I can do for you, sister, is fill your tank." I shouted a praise to God for that tank of gas, because, in those days, money was definitely scarce for me.

Then we pulled up in front of the church. I wasn't really paying attention to the sign in front. I asked, "This is where you go to church?"

"Yeah," she said.

"What is the name of your church?" I asked.

"New Greater Bethel."

The blood rushed to my face. "New Greater Bethel!" I exclaimed. "Dr. John H. Boyd Sr.?"

"Yes! That's my pastor."

How ironic was that? It wasn't chance—it was my heavenly Father. He had already given me an association to Dr. Boyd through the times I *just happened* to listen to the radio outreach. Now, divinely, my work schedule had been confused that day so that I could pick up a lady who was on her way to the same church I had been listening to for six months!

I parked my car, walked into the church, and sat in the sixth row from the front on the left side. Pastor Boyd was already preaching his message. Not even ten minutes passed before he looked out into the audience directly at me and said, "Little lady, right there in that uniform. I don't know who you are or where you come from. But God told me that you're an eagle with broken wings, and there's a ministry down inside of you. Your worst days are behind you, and your best days are yet to come."

Without Pastor Boyd even touching me, the power of God knocked me out. I hit the floor. When I got up, I put out a fleece to the Lord and said, "One more thing, God. They're getting ready to call for the offering. When I walk to the offering table, if the man of God says anything else to me, I'm going to know that I'm in the right place."

The offering music started, playing, "We're blessed, we're blessed, we're blessed…" Everybody started to march around the offering table. The ushers started from the back of the church, so it took a while for them to get to my row. When they got to me, I was ready. With my $5.00 offering in my hand, I started making my way to the offering table. As I walked down the aisle, the pastor came down from the pulpit to the bottom steps (behind the offering baskets). Just as I was putting my offering in the basket, he reached out, grabbed my hand, and said, "Welcome to Bethel."

"OK, this is it," I said to the Lord. "This is where You've placed me."

Come Out of the Wilderness

For much of my life, from the time I left Port Huron until the time God led me to that Sunday morning service at Dr. John Boyd's church, I felt as though I had been wandering in a spiritual desert. No doubt you have experienced your own spiritual wilderness. I believe a wilderness experience is a journey to find our spiritual destiny. In the midst of my wilderness, God reached out and gave me a spiritual home. The children of Israel wandered in the wilderness until they found the divine place. Egypt wasn't it. Egypt had been their place of bondage.

> REMEMBER THIS: ANY PLACE WHERE YOU ARE NOT RECEIVING THE MANIFOLD BLESSINGS OF GOD IS YOUR SPIRITUAL EGYPT.

The Israelites belonged to their heavenly Father. Because they were His chosen children, God was obligated to get them out of Egypt. He had a divine place for them—*Canaan*—but they had to go through the wilderness.

You know the story. The vast majority of that first generation never made it to the Promised Land because they were disobedient. A few, however, were brought into their destiny. Joshua and Caleb became leaders for the next generation. They reached the Promised Land.

If you have received Jesus and are still going through that *wilderness experience*, be confident that you belong to God. If He is your heavenly Father, God will make sure you receive His portion. As long as you obey Him, you are destined to find your spiritual parents.

CHAPTER 2

The Power of Obedience

*K*nowing I had found a new spiritual home at New Greater Bethel Ministries, I started rearranging my flight schedule to be in services on Friday night and Sunday morning. After being at Bethel for about a month, I was prompted by the Spirit of the Lord to help the church on my off days. I felt very strongly that I was supposed to volunteer. So I called Dr. Boyd and said, "I'd like to start volunteering and working in the church."

This desire to serve is a true sign that you are really *at home*. When you are in the house of your spiritual father, you are not content with being simply a bench member. Think about it. Natural children have a responsibility to maintain the upkeep of their father's house. In my family, we were trained from childhood to wash dishes, vacuum the carpet, clean out the refrigerator, clean out the garbage can, and clean the entire house. We were also trained from childhood that the oldest child is a babysitter for the others. In short, we were taught to look after each other.

There are so many strong comparisons from the natural life of a family to the spiritual. If you are a lazy child, it means you have no respect for your parents. You don't appreciate what they have provided for you. The spiritual fathers (and mothers) that God places in your life to help you move into your spiritual inheritance are a precious gift. When God demonstrates His love for you by revealing His desire to deepen your relationship with Him through the counsel and teaching of a spiritual father or mother, then you automatically want to show appreciation to God by becoming a servant in the house of that spiritual father or mother.

Your Portion Is Your Measure

I believe the first desire of a child of God is to be a servant in His kingdom. Mark 10:42–45 says:

> But Jesus called them *[all of the disciples]* to [Him] and said to them, You know that those who are recognized as governing and are supposed to rule the Gentiles (the nations) lord it over them [ruling with absolute power, holding them in subjection], and their great men exercise authority and dominion over them. But this is not to be so among you; instead, whoever desires to be great among you must be your servant, and whoever wishes to be most important and first in rank among you must be slave of all. For even the Son of Man came not to have service rendered to Him, but to serve, and to give His life as a ransom for (instead of) many.

This is the reason why an individual cannot just "join" a church. We must be born by way of a relationship with Christ (through receiving salvation), because again, the first manifestation of new life in Christ is the desire to serve. Servanthood proves the fact that you have truly become a child of God. For example, the gift of tongues is a manifestation that you have been baptized in the Holy Spirit. Servanthood and faithfulness are manifestations that say, "I have been given the measure of faith in God. I am a child of the kingdom." Jesus was speaking about this spiritual principle when He responded to His disciples' questions about their positions in glory.

When I joined New Greater Bethel, the manifestation of this spirit in me was a sign that I was home. I knew that I had met the "spiritual father" my heavenly Father had prepared for me because I had an immediate desire to serve in a place I had never been before. My first reaction wasn't, *I don't know these people; I don't know this building. I don't know this church or anything about it.* Immediately my response to God was, "What can I do? Can I sweep, mop, or staple papers? Can I do something to help?"

From the time I started attending Bethel, I was being driven by the measure of faith. I had received a supernatural trust in God, and as a result, I believed He had bestowed upon me a new spiritual father. Immediately, I wanted to do whatever I could to build His kingdom through my church. I wanted God's kingdom to become great because of what I had been given.

The Servant—Your Spiritual Assignment

Listen to me. One of the first signs that you are in the right spiritual home isn't that you feel like withdrawing or being indifferent. It's when your spirit becomes humbled to the point that you ask, "What can I do?" Jesus said, "The Father knows Me and I also know the Father—and I am giving My [very own] life and laying it down on behalf of the sheep" (John 10:15). In John 4:34, He said, "My food (nourishment) is to do the will (pleasure) of Him Who sent Me and to accomplish and completely finish His work." Jesus did everything according to the Father's will. His heartbeat was to make sure He fulfilled His Father's assignment.

When I walked into Bethel, I knew that Dr. Boyd had a worldwide radio ministry. This was part of his assignment. So my responsibility as a child of his ministry—just as Jesus is responsible to the Father—became to make sure that the vision, desires, and assignment of my spiritual father (as spoken to him by God) were fulfilled.

Two weeks after becoming a member, I went to Pastor Boyd and asked, "How can I get involved in the ministry, and what can I do?" He asked me if I had to work the next day, and, when I confirmed that I didn't, he told me to report to him at 9:00 the next morning. When I arrived at the office the next day, I started stuffing envelopes that contained announcements for an upcoming church revival and performing other small tasks.

Eventually, my assistant pastor recognized that I had an ability to write. So Pastor Boyd began asking me to write letters whenever he needed to send a letter to a company or to invite an evangelist to minister at our church. At the time, my finances weren't where I desired them to be to be able to sow into the ministry, so I sowed all of my off days to working in the office. I reported to work from 9:00 a.m. to 5:00 p.m., just as if it were a regular paying job.

I felt very comfortable doing this. I never thought about getting paid. There were days when the person who cleaned the bathrooms was ill, so I would go from stapling papers and writing letters to cleaning toilets. But I knew that God had a purpose in it. I never felt a grudging spirit about doing any type of work needed to help the ministry. I was happy to do whatever I could. Sometimes I would be working with others at the office and didn't go home until 9:00 or 10:00 at night. I just felt that I needed to do whatever it took to see Pastor Boyd's vision go forth, because he truly had a heart for souls.

God gives our leaders a vision, a purpose, and a plan—and then He births children into the kingdom who are capable of helping them to fulfill it. For example, if your spiritual father's assignment is to paint the largest mural in New York City, then the heavenly Father will send him children who can help him to fulfill the vision.

This reveals another way you can know when you are in the right place. Whatever the vision of your father is, you have been equipped with a calling, gifts, and talents that correspond to his vision. What does this mean? The anointing you have is not for you. It is to make sure the vision your heavenly Father has given to your spiritual father and mother will be fulfilled.

Many Christians don't have a revelation of this. We think our job is simply to sing in the choir or to be an usher. We don't understand that we are an intricate part of the puzzle that moves a vision forward and causes it to flourish. So in the end, when the man of God lies down, closes his eyes, and meets his heavenly Father, his corporate assignment for that season, era, and time in history has been completed.

Looking back, as my ministry was taking off and I began to be known around the world, the Lord dropped my home church into my spirit very strongly. He started saying to me that I needed to remain sensitive and responsive to serving in the house of my father. And now that I am a married woman and a pastor's wife (my husband has no objection), I still make sure that my spiritual father's house is doing well and is in good order.

As a matter of fact, four years ago when I started holding 5:00 a.m. prayer meetings at New Greater Bethel, I did it because I knew that winning souls through prayer was the heartbeat of my spiritual father, Dr. Boyd. I started the prayer meetings with around four people, and God has now allowed them to grow in attendance to at least two thousand every Tuesday morning.

I am thankful that to this day, even being married and serving as the first lady of my husband's church, my husband still permits me to hold 5:00 a.m. prayer meetings at New Greater Bethel every week. It has brought such blessings and stability to that house. From my experience, you can never get to the point where you outgrow your concern or passion for that which belongs to your spiritual father.

There Is Power in Obedience

As God's children, we must be confronted with the fact that there is power in obedience. Obedience is vital to your walk with God. Whatever you believe God is calling you to accomplish as an individual, it's not for you, and it's not about you. It's about a spiritual vision that is being passed from generation to generation. It's about serving as part of one body, doing specifically what God has created and equipped you to do.

Jesus came in the form of a Son in order to redeem man back to God. This was the only way that the Father's vision could be fulfilled. As a Son, Christ remained in complete obedience to the Father's vision. Hear me. Jesus did not come with His own vision. He did not come with His own plan. When He was sitting in glory with the heavenly

Father, they looked out over the world and saw sin and degradation. Then the Father said, "I desire that My creations will be joined to Me and desire to serve Me, but because of sin, they're separated from Me. I have to save the world that I've created. But whom can I send?"

Jesus said, "I'll go." And when He came, it wasn't to start His own ministry. He didn't come to earth trying to start His own praise team, create His own ministry, and build His own dynasty. He came to build the kingdom of God; He came to fulfill His Father's vision. Everything Jesus said and did constantly referred people back to the Father. He constantly gave the glory back to the One who sent Him—even when Judas was about to betray Him:

> Then after [he had taken] the bit of food, Satan entered into and took possession of [Judas]. Jesus said to him, What you are going to do, do more swiftly than you seem to intend and make a quick work of it.... When he had left, Jesus said, Now is the Son of Man glorified! [Now He has achieved His glory, His honor, His exaltation!] And God has been glorified through and in Him.
>
> —JOHN 13:27, 31

When Jesus said "glorified," He meant the workings of the Father would be seen, admired, and praised by the world. Jesus didn't want the praise for Himself. He constantly performed miracles and said, "Don't tell anybody," because He didn't want to be the center of attention. He was on earth to complete an assignment from His Father. Jesus didn't want His Father's glory.

True sons and daughters in the kingdom are focused on the will and vision of their spiritual fathers. That is why Jesus told His disciples in John 4:34, "My food (nourishment) is to do the will (pleasure) of Him Who sent Me and to accomplish and completely finish His work." The disciples were hungry after a full day of work, and when they came back to Jesus with food, they asked, "Master, did You eat?"

What He was saying to them in a revelatory sense is that doing the will of the Father strengthened Him more than physical meat. His human frame was able to survive from the power source of doing the will of the Father. It was as if Jesus were telling them, "As long as I am in pursuit of doing the Father's will, I'll get the same results as if I had eaten the food you are offering to Me—because when I pursue after the will of My Father, I am strengthened by My Father."

When Jesus finished fulfilling the Father's plan, He moved out of the way and sent the baptism of the Holy Spirit to keep the divine plan of obedience. He entered the world wrapped in the blanket of time and a fleshly body (which had a time limit on it), and then He died. This is why Paul was able to say, "I have been crucified with Christ [in Him I have shared His crucifixion]; it is no longer I who live, but Christ (the Messiah) lives in me; and the life I now live in the body I live by faith in (by adherence to and reliance on and complete trust in) the Son of God, Who loved me and gave Himself up for me" (Gal. 2:20).

> WHEN WE BELIEVE IN THE LORD AND IN THE WORKINGS OF THE FATHER—WHO SENT THE SON—WE CAN FULFILL HIS VISION AND WILL BECAUSE CHRIST LIVES IN US.

Paul could affirm that he lived by faith in Christ's sacrifice, and we can affirm it, because of Jesus. Christ was so determined to finish the Father's will that He gave up the fleshly frame, which hindered the full expression of His obedience. You see, before He died, Jesus could only be in one town at a time, performing one miracle at a time. Because His Father's vision was so huge, Jesus was willing to let go of the natural realm (the fleshly realm) that confined Him. He released Himself unto death so that He would be able to live inside of every living being that would believe on Him—regardless of the time or place. He did all of this just so that His Father's plan would be completed.

Christ's ultimate goal is to finish the work of His Father. This is the reason that He continues working in us today—because He is yet on a mission for His Father. So you see, salvation isn't only for our benefit (though we benefit by being saved from hell and gaining a heavenly position). While we live in these fleshly frames, we have the ultimate goal of finishing the will of the Father—because Jesus is working in us. (See Philippians 2:13.) His number one goal will never change. He will never stop until the Father's plan is complete.

> After that comes the end (the completion), when He delivers over the kingdom to God the Father after rendering inoperative and abolishing every [other] rule and every authority and power....However, when everything is subjected to Him, then the Son Himself will also subject Himself to [the Father] Who put all things under Him, so that God may be all in all [be everything to everyone, supreme, the indwelling and controlling factor of life].
>
> —1 CORINTHIANS 15:24, 28

What does this mean to us today? When our spiritual leaders get up and preach the Word of God, they are really saying, "You have to finish the work." When they correct us, they are saying, "You have to move your flesh out of the way as Christ did. Now that Christ lives in you, He can't be hindered again by a fleshly frame. He died once. He's not going to die again. Now, you have to die to your flesh so the will of the Father can be done."

The power of submission and obedience to our spiritual parents is much deeper than just saying "He's my pastor" or "She's my pastor." We are part of a vision that is much greater than anything we know. When we disobey and don't submit to the Father's will, then we hinder His plan and crucify Christ afresh according to Hebrews 6:4–8. This binds Him to the state of being crucified, which means we haven't released Him to His supernatural ministry—fulfilling the will of the Father in our lives.

By completing His Father's will, Jesus was saying, "I'll go to the cross...whatever it takes. I'll let them whip Me, spit on Me, and pierce My side. I'll let them put a crown of thorns on My head—and I won't open My mouth." For Jesus, performing the Father's will for His eternal kingdom was greater than experiencing pain or discomfort from anything that was done to Him in the fleshly realm. He became so focused and determined that what was done to Him could not be compared to the glory that was about to be released through Him.

Don't Get Disgruntled

The body of Christ hasn't reached the purpose of doing the Father's will because we stay too offended to build His kingdom. Our attention stays focused on what's being done to us in the fleshly realm. To be honest with you, the only way we can prove authentically that we are the body of Christ is to have scars. If we are His body, then we have to have nail prints. We have to be whipped, spat upon, and talked about to be authentic sons and daughters.

You will have to go through some things, walk through difficult situations, and deal with hard issues—things the enemy tries to use to wipe you out—and still survive, because you belong to the body of Christ. You survive because you belong to the Father and obey the Son, doing what He called, anointed, and appointed you to do.

We may get hit in the natural, but 2 Corinthians 4:16 says this:

> Therefore we do not become discouraged (utterly spiritless, exhausted, and wearied out through fear). Though our outer man is [progressively] decaying and wasting away, yet our inner self is being [progressively] renewed day after day.

The most important part of us is being renewed—the spiritual part that fulfills the plan of the Father—so that we can build the kingdom.

This is also why no two churches are alike. Each church is like a fingerprint. If you tried, you couldn't find two that are identical. Remember this when God adds you to a ministry (your spiritual father's church) and you get mad because, "We don't have a soup kitchen." Maybe God hasn't called this ministry to have a soup kitchen! He may have called the ministry across town to do that.

Every vision that God has given to His leaders is part of the puzzle. Think about it. If you were able to stand up in glory and look down upon the earth realm, seeing every church that is being established and called of God, you would see the bigger plan. No two churches are supposed to be alike. They are not supposed to have the same ministry! Some churches have drug ministries, some have soup kitchen ministries, others have hospital ministries, and so on.

Don't get disgruntled at the vision of your spiritual father. We are all here to do one thing, and that is to build the kingdom of God and do our part.

Jesus wasn't called to establish His own vision. That's why the Bible tells us we must be faithful in another man's work before God will give us our own. Jesus came to fulfill the work of His Father; He was faithful unto death, and because of this, no work can be done without using His name. Jesus made Himself of no reputation. God saw His faithfulness and said, "From this point on, no man comes to the Father but by Jesus." And nothing can be done except we use His name.

> PASTORS ARE FOLLOWING ONE DIVINE PLAN— THE PLAN OF THE HEAVENLY FATHER, OF WHAT IS HIS WILL.

Do you see the revelation? While we're out seeking to build our own thing and trying to get recognition for ourselves, we don't understand the way a ministry is built. The way we obtain the respect of having a ministry is by being faithful to that which belongs to our spiritual father. Faithfulness can only be birthed in a person when he or she is willing to obey the voice of the Father, no matter what the price. There is power in obedience. Luke 16:12 says:

> And if you have not proved faithful in that which belongs to another [whether God or man], who will give you that which is your own [that is, the true riches]?

Obedience Is Taught

The Bible says that Jesus was a miracle worker. He opened blind eyes and cast out devils—but there was one thing He had to be taught.

Hebrews 5:8–9 says, "Although He was a Son, He learned [active, special] obedience through what He suffered and, [His completed experience] making Him perfectly [equipped], He became the Author and Source of eternal salvation to all those who give heed and obey Him." Obedience to the Father's will brought power to His name. Let me say that again—obedience to the *Father's will* brought power to His name.

Too many of us are trying to build a name. Many in the body of Christ are doing things and establishing things that God never told them to do—because they are trying to build a name. Listen to me. You will get recognition when you establish and respect the workings of your father.

Verses 1 and 14 of the first chapter of John say, "In the beginning was the Word, and the Word was with God, and the Word was God. . . . And the Word was made flesh, and dwelt among us" (KJV). Jesus is the Word of God, but the heavenly Father established the name of Jesus in the earth by obedience.

You may join a church and say, "Yes, I go to church every Sunday." "I'm an evangelist." "I've been licensed under a ministry." Now, you bear the ministry's name. But hear me, your name will never be empowered unless you operate under the authority of your spiritual parents, unless you "suffer" in obedience to gain power!

> For though we walk (live) in the flesh, we are not carrying on our warfare according to the flesh and using mere human weapons. For the weapons of our warfare are not physical [weapons of flesh and blood], but they are mighty before God for the overthrow and destruction of strongholds, [inasmuch as we] refute arguments and theories and reasonings and every proud and lofty thing that sets itself up against the [true] knowledge of God; and we lead every thought and purpose away captive into the obedience of Christ (the Messiah, the Anointed One), being in readiness to punish every [insubordinate for his] disobedience,

when your own submission and obedience [as a church] are fully secured and complete.

—2 CORINTHIANS 10:3–6

That's why demons became subject to Jesus! He could command their obedience because His obedience was complete. This is also why many are ministering but have no power. They failed the test of obedience. Unless you have walked in your own obedience and fulfilled it—meaning you have obeyed everything God has told you to do—then you lose power and authority.

The Bible tells us that when John baptized Jesus, He rose up out of the water and a dove descended from heaven. Then a voice spoke out from heaven and said, "This is my beloved Son, in whom I am well pleased" (Matt. 3:17, KJV). When the Father said this, Jesus hadn't yet been spat upon or gone to the cross and died. Was God pleased just by the fact that Jesus obeyed Him in baptism? No! God was pleased by His Son's willingness to submit to His Father's plan and say, "Here I am, send Me."

When Jesus said that, God knew that His Son had submitted to doing His will. It is not your actions that get God's attention—because you can do the right things in the wrong spirit. Not only did Jesus do the Father's will, but He also kept His spirit right…even in persecution.

Let me explain. At the beginning of Creation, God said, "Let there be light: and there was light" (Gen. 1:3, KJV). When He said, "Let the waters bring forth abundantly the moving creature that hath life, and fowl that may fly above the earth" it happened *immediately* (v. 20, KJV). Just so, when Jesus, the living Word of God, said, "I will go," He *immediately* became slain before the foundation of the world. God was already pleased with Him before He came to earth. By the time Jesus hit the earth realm, He had already gone through the process of fulfilling His spiritual assignment. That's why nothing could throw Him off course; He had already fulfilled His Father's will before He left heaven. His answer was already, "Yes." And *yes* gave Him power with God *and* power over the enemy.

Jesus' submission pleased the Father. Even before He started His ministry on earth, He was already submitted to it. In kind, the church has to learn how to submit and do the will of our heavenly Father. That's why Jesus is constantly speaking out, "Let Me show you the way to power. You get power through the things you suffer." But the church tries to escape from pain and discomfort.

Now, we are waiting for the greatest revival ever to hit this country. And it will never happen in its fullness until the body of Christ comes into a state of spiritual readiness. When our own submission and obedience as a church are fully secured and complete, the awesome power of God will be released. We have no power because we have no obedience. We are not willing for our flesh to suffer in order to fulfill the Father's will.

Coming Into Spiritual Order

When you obey, you are complying with someone else's wishes or orders. You are acknowledging someone else's authority. God perfectly designed the plan of salvation through Jesus when He said, "No man cometh unto the Father, but by me" (John 14:6, KJV). We can't ignore earthly authority and think we're going to reach the Father. How can we? God designed His plan so that we would walk in spiritual order.

Look at the tabernacle of God in the Old Testament. He designed the outer court, the holy place, and the most holy place. (See Exodus 25–27.) God's way always involves a process of coming through something in order to get to Him. He built the temple structure so we would have to come through the East Gate, which represents the completed works of Jesus Christ, in order to come into the outer court (where we stop at the brazen laver and brazen altar). Then we enter the holy place, which houses the golden candlestick, the table of shewbread, and the golden altar, before reaching the ark of the covenant behind the veil in the holy of holies.

It was also the design of God that priests would maintain the tabernacle on behalf of the nation of Israel. Expanding this spiritual principle further, Jesus went into the heavenly tabernacle on our behalf, and the veil to the most holy place was ripped from top to bottom.

Now the Holy Spirit makes intercession for us. Yes, there is still a plan of order.

> He Who descended is the [very] same as He Who has also ascended high above all the heavens, that He [His presence] might fill all things (the whole universe, from the lowest to the highest). And His gifts were [varied: He Himself appointed and gave men to us] some to be apostles (special messengers), some prophets (inspired preachers and expounders), some evangelists (preachers of the Gospel, traveling missionaries), some pastors (shepherds of His flock) and teachers. His intention was the perfecting and the full equipping of the saints (His consecrated people), [that they should do] the work of ministering toward building up Christ's body (the church).
>
> —EPHESIANS 4:10–12

This means that before you can even understand God, you have to go through spiritual order. For example, God didn't send the children of Israel rampaging out of Egypt. He gave them a leader to get them out. And when that leader disobeyed Him, He gave them another leader to take them into the Promised Land. Leading is God's way.

It was as if He was saying to the Israelites, "You're in Egypt. You're in bondage, eating leeks and onions—*but obey*. Come into compliance with Moses. Agree with the plan that I gave to him, respect and acknowledge his authority, and you'll come out." They got out of Egypt and into the wilderness, and then they usurped that authority with Aaron and the "golden calf." (See Exodus 32.) In short, when Israel tried to put an "image" as their leader instead of the man of God, God cursed them.

When you exchange the manservant of God for an image, when you exchange the revelation and the Word of God that come from your pastor and diminish him to an image—a tie, a suit, an office, and a title—then you will keep wandering, never reaching your divine destiny. You will go to church every Sunday and still be wandering in a spiritual wilderness.

Looking at God's plan and how everything unfolded in the Bible reveals another problem. Every time the Israelites got into rebellion, they said, "Moses, tell us what God is saying." But other times they said, "We want to talk to God ourselves." Then when the heavens and the earth started trembling, they would turn around and say, "No, we don't want to talk to God; we'd rather hear you."

Today many are saying, "I'm hearing from God." You are not hearing from God if you are in rebellion! The children of Israel couldn't stand to be in the presence of God. Moses had to go up on the mountain. And God had to set him in the cleft of a rock and cover him, showing only His hinder parts (Exod. 33:17–23). *We are not ready to see God!* That's why He gives us only what we can handle—*our leaders.* God is saying, "If you can't handle *that* person, then you can't handle Me. If you can't find Me by being led, you can't find Me by yourself, because My way," says the Lord, "is leadership." It is a very dangerous thing to kick against the person God has set before you as your leader.

When Moses' sister, Miriam, came against Moses, God struck her with leprosy. Many people today think, *Well, I'm a preacher, or I'm an evangelist, so I can do what I want to do. I'll be all right.* When Moses' brother and sister came against him in the wilderness, God struck her with leprosy. And as for Aaron, as long as he was in the priestly garment—in his office—God maintained him. But when God said, "Enough is enough," Aaron took off his priestly garments, and he died. (See Numbers 20:22–29.) The fact that he held a spiritual office didn't mean that he was getting away. God had a set time for Aaron to be dealt with.

Miriam and Aaron thought they were speaking for the people. "And they said, Hath the LORD indeed spoken only by Moses? Hath he not spoken also by us? And the LORD heard it" (Num. 12:2, KJV). We do the same thing when we say to our pastors, "You are not doing things right. We should be over here. Why do we have this?"

When you look at it, it didn't matter how much the children of

Israel cried out to God; nothing happened for them until Moses went before the Father. When Moses said, "They're hungry," that's when the quail fell (Num. 11:21–22, 31). When Moses said, "They're thirsty," the people got water (Exod. 17:3–7; Num. 20:2–11). When Moses held up his arms, the Red Sea opened up (Exod. 14:21–22).

Many Christians are at the end of their roads and can't go any further because a "Red Sea" is in front of them and the enemy is behind them. And they have no leader to hold up his hands on their behalf.

Embrace Authority

God's way is the leader way. Throughout the history of the Bible, from beginning to end, God always used a leader to bring victory to His people. You have to understand, there is a power of impartation that comes from leadership. So when you truly understand that obedience is to be in compliance with someone else's wishes or orders—to acknowledge their authority—then you must associate that thought pattern with leadership.

> IF YOU ARE GOING TO ACCOMPLISH ANYTHING FOR GOD, YOU HAVE TO BE IN DIVINE ORDER.

When you acknowledge somebody else's authority, it means this person has the power and the right to give orders and make decisions. When you respect the authority that has been placed over your life, you don't have to wander in the valley of decision. You don't have to be without direction—because God has given someone the right to give orders and make decisions that cover you. He can order the enemy out of your life, and he can unlock your destiny.

And because he stands higher in the spirit realm, his vision is broader. He can look down the road and see that you already have the victory. That's why, when you come into the house of the Lord and the man of God brings a word, saying that you have the victory, you have the right to praise God regardless of what you see.

Samuel's mother, Hannah, went to the temple because she had wanted a baby for years and couldn't have one. She got down on her face and prayed to God. But the Bible didn't say, "Then she got pregnant." Eli (the high priest) came to her and said, "What are you talking about down there?" She told him, "I want to be pregnant." That's when something happened. Eli told her, "May God grant your wish." The next day, she left the temple, and, not long after that, her husband "knew" her, and she became pregnant (1 Sam. 1:4–20). Nothing happened until her leader spoke it over her life!

Hannah gave birth to Samuel, a prophetic servant of the Lord who changed the course of the nation of Israel. Hear me. If you are going to accomplish anything for God, you have to be in divine order.

A person has authority in the spirit realm because he or she is living in submission to the Father. Therefore, a leader who is doing the will of the Father has this *God-given grace*. And for this reason you should willingly comply with his or her direction.

In essence, every leader walks under the same principle as every son and daughter. Nobody escapes the process of obedience and submission. God is the ultimate authority. He is every leader's authority, and our leaders are our authorities. There are also authority structures in our homes. In everything and in every area of our lives, our spirits and everything in the flesh must submit under the authority and power of God.

The power of obedience is always in operation, in everyone, at the same time. Therefore, a leader does not require you to do something that he or she will not do—because in order for leaders to carry God's power and authority, they must be submitted under authority. A leader cannot enforce authority unless that leader is under authority and his or her obedience is complete. (See 2 Corinthians 10:6.) We are empowered by submission. When we submit to authority in obedience to God, then we have the power to command the enemy. We have power over anything that comes to attack or destroy our destiny.

The Principle of Satan

Let's look at the principle of Satan. When he was still called *Lucifer*, he was in the heavenlies serving God. Every being knew he was a worshiper; his whole being was built to worship God. But the Book of Isaiah says he wanted to become "equal" with God. He said in his heart, "I will ascend to heaven; I will exalt my throne above the stars of God; I will sit upon the mount of assembly in the uttermost north. I will ascend above the heights of the clouds; I will make myself like the Most High" (Isa. 14:13–14).

The minute Lucifer began the whole *I* thing, he became an individual without God. Hear me. The power of the Godhead is in the Trinity: Father, Son, and Holy Spirit. The conversation of Christ is always *We*, *Us*, and *Our*. So whenever you hear a person say "*I*," he or she is canceling out the principle of God and is disconnected from the Source of power. Anything that is operating in the *I* realm is in the flesh realm. And anything that is in the flesh realm will never prosper in the Spirit.

The day we were born, we began to die. We are growing up to die, because the flesh is taking us to the end of its biological and genealogical journey—the end of our life span. By our accepting Christ, who was fully obedient to the Father, God is able to transform us and stop the death pattern. He has the power to say, "Flesh, keep dying, because now that I live here, the spirit that lives in this body will live forever."

The minute you cancel out God and start saying, "I...I...I...," you diminish yourself back to the flesh realm. And the only thing the flesh can do is die. That means your ministry will die; everything that you operate in will die as long as you're saying "I." Remember, Paul said, "I have been crucified with Christ...it is no longer I who live, but Christ (the Messiah) lives in me" (Gal. 2:20).

Listen closely. Lucifer's principle became, "I will lift myself above the heavens...I will be exalted...I will be as God...I will know as much as God knows...." He became a being that, although he didn't mind worshiping God and praising God, *would not and did not want to submit to God*. When we disobey God any time He requires that we do a certain thing, and He commands and orders us in a certain way, then we are operating under the principle of Satan—worshiping in disobedience. At that point, the only alternative is for God to cast us down.

The principle of Satan is running rampant in the church today. We worship God in praise and worship, we preach, we prophesy, and we pray—but we won't obey. Disobedience is rebellion, and the Bible says that "rebellion is as the sin of witchcraft" (1 Sam. 15:23). Oh, yes, disobedience has power, too—counterfeit power. One day, Jesus will look at people who declare that they have prophesied and cast out devils and say, "Depart from me, ye that work iniquity" (Matt. 7:21–23, KJV).

What Christ was communicating in that passage was, "My relationship with you is greater than anything you can perform in My name. You do all of these things, yet you are still not in relationship with Me because you are disobedient. You don't hear what I say and do it." (See Matthew 7:24–27.)

As a result, that which should be glorifying the Father is sin in His sight, because when you do these things without being submitted to the authority of Christ, He disregards everything you do. None of it is counted. How much are we doing in the kingdom that we are not getting credit for? First Samuel 15:22 says, "Behold, to obey is better than sacrifice, and to hearken than the fat of rams."

The enemy is not afraid of a person who preaches. He is not afraid of our messages! He is not scared of the person who is shouting and speaking in tongues in church. He is not even threatened by someone who can quote the Bible verbatim, from cover to cover. But he is terrified of the person who has submitted his life under the obedience of Christ. Satan is petrified of obedience, because an obedient person knows how to follow the order, and the orders, of the Lord. God's order says, "Let God arise, let his enemies be scattered"…and let the kingdoms of this world come down (Ps. 68:1, KJV)! The enemy is afraid of the person who would dare to follow these orders.

Are You Really Saved?

That's why you must truly understand: Jesus learned obedience by the things He suffered in order to become the author of eternal salvation (Heb. 5:8–9). Satan fights the body of Christ in the area of obedience, according to 1 Peter 1:1–2:

> Peter, an apostle (a special messenger) of Jesus Christ, [writing] to the elect exiles of the dispersion scattered (sowed) abroad in Pontus, Galatia, Cappadocia, Asia,

and Bithynia, who were chosen and foreknown by
God the Father and consecrated (sanctified, made
holy) by the Spirit to be obedient to Jesus Christ (the
Messiah) and to be sprinkled with [His] blood:...

Let me break it down. We were consecrated, sanctified, and made
holy by the Spirit for the purpose of being obedient to Jesus Christ and
sprinkled with His blood. Then there's a colon. (When a colon is used,
it means that whatever is stated after the colon is dependent upon that
which was stated before the colon.)

We were chosen and foreknown by God the Father, and then consecrated, sanctified, and made holy by the Spirit. Then we are to be
obedient to Jesus Christ and be sprinkled with His blood. Note that
all those actions are "pre-colon" spiritual principles. Only when those
actions have been taken can we move past the colon to the next part of
this spiritual principle. Then verse 2 continues by saying:

...May grace (spiritual blessing) and peace be given
you in increasing abundance [that spiritual peace to
be realized in and through Christ, freedom from fears,
agitating passions, and moral conflicts].

Catch the significance of this spiritual principle. This says that
most of the things we are battling against in the body of Christ, and
trying to keep ourselves free from, come along with—are fringe benefits of—being obedient to Christ! In our obedience to Christ, blessings
are increased, our peace is increased in abundance, and this obedience
brings to us freedom from fears, agitating passions, and moral conflicts.
When we realize all of these things come through Christ and by being
obedient to Him, we can be free indeed.

Verses 3–5 continue:

Praised (honored, blessed) be the God and Father of
our Lord Jesus Christ (the Messiah)! By His boundless
mercy we have been born again to an ever-living hope
through the resurrection of Jesus Christ from the

dead. *[Born anew] into an inheritance which is beyond the reach of change and decay [imperishable], unsullied and unfading, reserved in heaven for you,* who are being guarded (garrisoned) by God's power through [your] faith [till you fully inherit that final] salvation that is ready to be revealed [for you] in the last time.

—EMPHASIS ADDED

This is powerful! Not only do you receive all of these things—the increase of peace, abundance of blessing, and freedom from fears, agitating passions, and moral conflicts—but also the garrison of God, His archangels, are guarding it so that you can maintain it all the way into everlasting life. So if you don't have money, when you walk in obedience, it will increase you in abundance. The favor of the Lord rests upon you when you understand that you have been saved, sanctified, and consecrated to obey. There is power in obedience!

Then the question remains: are you really born again? Hear me. *Born again* comes with both the desire and power to obey.

After being born again, we are part of the body of Christ. When Jesus was on the earth, His physical body lived in submission to the Father, even to death on the cross. So think about it. On a spiritual level, are you really part of His body? When you were born again, you were equipped to obey the Father—even to the death of the flesh—because of what Christ has already done.

Just as Jesus came and was obedient to the Father, all the way to the cross…so His body—you and I—must go through the same experience in order for God's power and vision to be revealed and carried out. And this can be done because it already has been done. The pattern is there; we only have to follow it. So are we really the body of Christ, when God is saying, "Go left," and we go right? When God is saying, "Be quiet," and we talk? When God is saying, "Fast," and we eat? When God is saying, "Pray," and we watch television? When God is saying, "Be still," and we move? When God says, "I know the way you should go, and when I've tried you, you'll come out as pure gold," but instead, we do things our own way?

The questions remain: Are you really the body of Christ? Are you really submitted? Jesus yielded His body to the will of the Father. You don't need anybody to seduce you with a false prophecy! You just need to obey. The power to obey comes with the Christ in you.

You don't need to pray for peace, because peace comes with obedience. You don't need to pray for abundance. Abundance comes with obedience. You don't have to pray for favor. Favor comes with obedience. And you don't have to fight the devil to keep from sinning, because deliverance from the fear of *agitating passions* and *moral misconduct* comes with obeying. Oh, yes, there is power in obedience.

CHAPTER 3

Receiving the Father's Portion

*T*here is a pattern for receiving the Father's portion that we can learn from the story of Samuel anointing Saul as the first king of Israel. (See 1 Samuel 9.) As we examine this story, you will discover that the first step in making sure you don't miss this portion is to pay close attention to the pattern, not just the excitement of the story.

When you go all the way back to the beginning of your life in Christ, back to where you first were born in Him, most likely you will find that you followed the same pattern as Saul—you started out as a nobody. First Samuel 9:2 says that Saul was the son of Kish. Other than being very handsome, he hadn't done anything great. He was just the son of a Benjamite.

As the story of Saul's encounter with Samuel begins, Saul was going to look for donkeys in obedience to his natural father. "Kish said to Saul, Take a servant with you and go, look for the donkeys" (v. 3). In his pursuit to obey his father, he and the servant stayed and looked for so long that he finally said to the servant, "Maybe we ought to go back so my father won't worry about us." (See verses 3–5.) His servant said:

> Behold now, there is in this city a man of God, a man held in honor; all that he says surely comes true. Now let us go there. Perhaps he can show us where we should go.
>
> —1 Samuel 9:6

This demonstrates how important it is to be careful about the people you are acquainted with. Any time your natural parents or your parents in the Spirit, say, "Do it this way," and you have friends and associates telling you to do it the opposite way, you are in trouble. Saul's father sent a servant with Saul to help him finish his father's business. You have to hear this, because it's a revelation. Saul's father sent two men: one was a son, and the other was a servant. The son was in obedience, and the servant understood authority.

Since the servant understood authority, he provoked the son to stay in obedience. When Saul was ready to give up, the servant said, "Let's keep looking for the donkeys." If Saul had given up his search and returned to his father, he would not have found Samuel. He may not have encountered the spiritual father who could lead him into his spiritual inheritance.

Even before they met Samuel, Saul realized something vital. He said to the servant, "But if we go, what shall we bring the man? The bread in our sacks is gone, and there is no gift for the man of God. What have we?" (v. 7). During Bible times, if you went to inquire of the man of God, you took with you gifts out of respect that he had lain before God and served Him.

The servant replied, "I have here a quarter of a shekel of silver. I will give that to the man of God to tell us our way" (v. 8). And they started up the hill to the city. When they ran into the water girls, they asked, "Is the seer here?" The maidens said:

> He is; behold, he is just beyond you. Hurry, for he came today to the city because the people have a sacrifice today on the high place. As you enter the city, you will find him before he goes up to the high place to eat. The people will not eat until he comes to ask the blessing on the sacrifice. Afterward, those who are invited eat. So go on up, for about now you will find him.
>
> —1 SAMUEL 9:12–13

Is the person that you are in pursuit of to help you in your assignment a seer? Think about that.

How can you know when you are approaching a spiritual parent? When you get there, he or she will already be doing God's assignment. Samuel was already in the right posture because he was in the city to offer up a sacrifice for God's people. Here's what happened:

> So they went up to the city, and as they were entering, behold, Samuel came toward them, going up to the high place. Now a day before Saul came, the Lord had revealed to Samuel in his ear, Tomorrow about this time I will send you a man from the land of Benjamin, and you shall anoint him to be leader over My people Israel; and he shall save them out of the hand of the Philistines. For I have looked upon the distress of My people, because their cry has come to Me.
>
> —1 SAMUEL 9:14–16

Understand that spiritual relationships are divine. The man of God or the woman of God should already know, before you get there, who you are in the Spirit. When Philip was bringing Nathanael to meet Jesus, Jesus saw him coming and said, "Behold an Israelite indeed, in whom is no guile" (John 1:47, KJV). In other words, Jesus was saying, "He doesn't have a double spirit. He is a man with a single focus, and there is no guile and no iniquity in him. I already know his spirit. I know who that is." You must understand: people who are anointed to see can see *for real*.

On the day before Saul came to Samuel, the word of the Lord had already come to Samuel's ear, saying, "Tomorrow, a man is going to come looking for you...and you will anoint him as a leader, because My people have cried unto Me." (See 1 Samuel 9:16.) Let's understand something: Saul came to Samuel looking for donkeys, not to be anointed as king of Israel. He came trying to fulfill his obedience to his father, not to get a position in the kingdom. As he obeyed in the small things, the Spirit of the Lord aligned him for greater things.

Entering Into Purpose

When you come into the knowledge of your spiritual parents, they are going to give you destiny. You will come to them with one purpose, and because of their nature as spiritual parents, they will begin to introduce you to destiny. Why? Because *they know* you don't know it. You are too busy doing the "work of the church," but your spiritual parents are called to show you the will of God for your life.

Saul came looking for donkeys, but God had already shown Samuel, "Saul is going to deliver Israel from her enemies. His call is greater than donkeys." Hear me. Your call is greater than what you think. Whether you play the piano, sing on the worship team, or are starting up a kitchen, your calling is significant. Saul was looking for donkeys, and God was preparing him for destiny.

The man of God had to anoint him for purpose. He couldn't do it himself! He couldn't even find donkeys by himself because he didn't have enough discernment in his spirit to even know where they were. If he had that level of discernment, he would have known to look on the right side of the mountain. Only a person who is under the obedience of God, under a mighty anointing, can see in the Spirit far enough to lay hands on you and anoint you for a worldwide, universal call.

Why does God do things this way? He does it because He hears the cry of His people. It is not because you are ready in all aspects of your life. God anoints you because you have yielded to His will, which says whatever isn't right, you are willing to be led in order that you may finish the work. You must always remember, and I must say it again: He hears the cry of His people, and because of that cry, He calls into destiny the answer to His people's cry. He does this by picking out people who don't know how to fulfill His purposes. He sends them to anointed leaders who will anoint those people into something greater than either of them can control—destiny. He will do this with you if you allow Him to. He will send you to your spiritual father or mother who will anoint you for your spiritual destiny. But both you and your spiritual leader must seek the Lord constantly to avoid messing up this mantle.

This principle reveals obedience by way of relationship in its highest form of operation. Saul was in obedience to his father, looking for donkeys. Samuel had come into obedience to his heavenly Father, who told him, "Tomorrow, look for this man, because you have to anoint him."

Always remember that when your spiritual leader is introduced to you, that leader will not be surprised by who you are. Samuel was not surprised by Saul. We read:

> When Samuel saw Saul, the Lord told him, There is the man of whom I told you. He shall have authority over My people. Then Saul came near to Samuel in the gate and said, Tell me where is the seer's house?
> —1 SAMUEL 9:17–18

Did you catch that? Saul was staring the seer in the face and didn't have enough discernment to recognize him!

If Samuel had disobeyed God and gone up to eat without waiting for Saul to come to him, there would have been no King Saul. His kingship came into existence because God had spoken to Samuel and told him Saul was coming the next day.

One of the first true signs that an individual has been called to lead in the Spirit is when you see signs of his ability to follow instructions in the natural. You see, the Lord has to show you whether you can vacuum the church right and let you see if you can be committed to the praise team before He gives you a worldwide singing ministry. Though He gives you great "talents," He still expects you to be faithful in that which is little. (See Luke 19:12–17.)

This is why Christians go from church to church looking for their spiritual parents and cannot find them. They don't have the spiritual discernment to recognize who they really are. This is also the reason many don't value spiritual leadership. We don't value our leaders because our spiritual eyesight isn't mature enough to discern what they mean to our lives. We have eyesight but no insight. That's why we see our pastor as just a man in a suit. That's why we see our first lady as just a wife wearing a pretty outfit, with a cute hairstyle and makeup. Then we wonder why we are still wandering in a spiritual wilderness.

Saul was looking straight at the seer, asking him, "Where is the seer?" Samuel answered, "I am the seer. Go up before me to the high place, for you shall eat with me today, and tomorrow I will let you go and will tell you all that is on your mind" (1 Sam. 9:18–19). These verses reveal two important spiritual principles about your spiritual father. How do you know who is to be your pastor? How do you know your future spiritual father? That which he feeds you will be a satisfying portion in order to determine your spiritual depth and to what length the Holy Spirit has prepared you for.

It does not matter what kind of image you try to show to your spiritual father. It does not matter how hard you try to convince him of your spiritual depth or power. He has discernment about you already. He will confirm what's in your spirit—because he will be able to identify the real you.

Discovering True Riches

When Saul confronted Samuel, Samuel also addressed the matter of the lost donkeys. He said to Saul, "As for your donkeys that were lost three days ago, do not be thinking about them, for they are found" (v. 20). Let me translate this into your situation: "As for you, who just came out of the wilderness of disobedience, the Lord will have them to speak into your life concerning your past, your present, and your future."

When I met Pastor and Sister Nichols in Port Huron, they told me things about myself that I had not said to anyone. They couldn't have known these things, because nobody in Port Huron, Michigan knew me. Bottom line. The same thing happened when I met Pastor Boyd at New Greater Bethel Ministries. He started to speak things about me that he could not have known in the natural. He didn't know me.

Samuel continued speaking to Saul by saying, "And for whom are all the desirable things of Israel? Are they not for you and for all your father's house?" (v. 20). After confirming to Saul that his father's donkeys had been found, Samuel raised Saul's vision to the bigger picture of his spiritual inheritance. Samuel moved Saul's thinking from donkeys to his father's house and then to his destiny. Even in his prophetic word to him, he followed prophetic protocol and provoked Saul to continue to have a concern for his father's house, despite the fact that he was going to be made king. He did not allow him to forget where he came from.

What about all of the stuff that's going on in your family—your mother, father, sisters, brothers, finances, emotions…marriage? God sent Jesus to give you authority in all areas. When your spiritual father finds you, he will anoint you to receive victory over everything that threatens to hurt your family or to destroy your lineage. This is the real purpose for which you need a spiritual father. You don't meet him so that you can get a better job or a better house. You don't encounter a spiritual leader so that you can drive a Mercedes. That's not why God led you this far. God has introduced you to a spiritual father so that through him the Lord can draw you into destiny.

> A SPIRITUAL FATHER RAISES YOUR VISION.

Your spiritual father will say, "The Lord has spoken to me about you even before we met. I didn't meet you to cater to your comfort. I can look right into your spirit and see who you are. Our relationship is bigger than that. We have met so the generations coming after you can walk in the abundance of blessing and peace. We have met so that you can increase in the power of the anointing, to change your name into one that will be respected as having authority over the power of the enemy. This is what I'm called to give you." This is where your life will take a turn.

Saul responded to Samuel, "Am I not a Benjamite, of the smallest of the tribes of Israel? And is not my family the least of all the families of the clans of Benjamin? Why then do you speak this way to me?" (v. 21). The man of God was speaking to him that way because he had been given the authority by God to decree something new over Saul's life. He was anointed to give Saul's family something they never had.

"Then Samuel took Saul and his servant and brought them into the guest room [at the high place] and had them sit in the chief place among the persons" (v. 22). Samuel said, "Come this way...come up before me...come and sit here." This required Saul's obedience.

> And the cook lifted high the shoulder and what was on it [indicating that it was the priest's honored portion] and set it before Saul. [Samuel] said, See what was reserved for you.
>
> —1 SAMUEL 9:24

Samuel took Saul to the "chief place" and sat him down among people Saul had never met before. This was Samuel's private chambers, a guesthouse reserved for the man of God, prepared for the honor of the priest and the prophet. (The other people feasted outside.) You see, this is a very vital piece of information for our growth. Many sons and daughters don't mind being told, "Come this way...come up here with me." They are always ready to go here and there and sit in places of high stature with their leadership. They are always so very ready to walk with leadership because it adds status to them by association.

But, oh, please let me inform you that without a proper diet, pride and arrogance will be the result of just walking and sitting. Eating is a whole horse of a different color—and this is where we err by not combining all three of these ingredients: walking, sitting, and eating.

You may have enough knowledge by association in your head and enough confidence in the stature of your leaders to sustain you for a moment. But trust me when I tell you this: at this early stage of your ministry, you do not have enough power in the belly of your spirit to hold you for eternity. And right now, the impartations that are coming from those whom God has called to be spiritual leaders are an eternal word for an eternal work. So don't get caught up in the moment. This isn't an event—it's a lifestyle.

Let's look at this. Once there, Samuel said to the cook, "Bring the portion which I gave you, of which I said to you, Set it aside" (v. 23). Let's backtrack a bit and look at the steps:

- *Come this way*; leave your way of doing things.
- *Come up*; let's go to another place in God.
- *Sit, eat*; now sit down so I can feed you.

To show you how vitally important this principle is, as we study in the next few chapters concerning Jezebel, you will see how this applied to Elijah, one of the most prominent prophets in the Old Testament. After he brought down the prophets of Baal on Mount Carmel, he went away and fell asleep. The angel of the Lord had to come and wake him up and command that he eat, not once but twice. Before he was to go and impart the mantle of the anointing upon Jehu, Hazael, and Elisha, he had to eat—because the next level of his assignment was going to be forty days long, and he did not have enough manna to finish the job. (See 1 Kings 19:1–17.)

No one yet in this hour has done anything that is worthy to be compared to the works of Elijah. And if he had to eat, so do we. Why am I saying this? Why do you feel such passion in my writing about this portion? Because so many of us feel that where we operate for God automatically determines where we are in our spirit and in our level of inner strength.

This takes me back to when I was in Port Huron, Michigan, under the spiritual oversight of Pastor and Sister Nichols. (The reason that I keep referring to specific places and times is that I have had several fathers in the spirit and many experiences under the tutelage of each one. So it helps me to identify, and you to understand, where I was spiritually by repeating their names.)

At the time, I was engaged to be married and going through the process of getting ready for the wedding, getting myself prepared, and so on. In the meantime, Pastor Nichols kept reminding me about my spiritual commitments. "You missed Thursday night service," he'd say, or "You weren't at noonday prayer," or "You were late for Saturday night service." I felt that because I was directing the choir and God was really using me, they weren't considering who I was in the Spirit and what I needed to do during that time.

I remember one night while I was directing the choir at an outside event that the Spirit of the Lord really came in and used me. I took the microphone and began to exhort the people in the praise service, and it was a mighty move of God. Then when the service was over, Sister Nichols looked at me and said, "I know everybody is complimenting you and telling you how powerful the service was, but you know that God is not finished with you yet."

I almost felt that she might have been jealous, or that maybe she didn't want to see people giving me honor for what God had done in my life. So I said to myself, *OK, in her eyesight, I'm not ever going to be ready for God to use me.* Maybe I was caught up in the fact that after I had taken the microphone, the service seemed to go to another level in praise, so I thought some type of recognition was due to me.

Hear me. This is what the enemy wants. He will set your mind up to make you believe that your leadership will allow God to move through you so powerfully in services, then suddenly, they will sit you down and act like they don't even see you. You will begin to feel it is so unfair for them to intentionally ignore you. If you are looking through satanic vision, it will appear that they are trying to keep their feet on your neck to suppress the call of God that's on your life—but that's not the truth, and I found that out very quickly.

When my engagement was broken, it was extremely painful. And there I was, the director of the choir and other church activities, expediting the services, leading praise and worship—but the night I found out that my engagement was off, I found myself sitting down by the river with the biggest bottle of whiskey I could find. I sat there drinking, drinking, and drinking until I started up my car and headed back to Sister Nichols' house. (At the time they lived in a very large house that was almost completely isolated outside of the city.)

I pulled my car up all the way across the lawn to their front steps—then I passed out on the horn. I didn't know that they were entertaining a visiting pastor and his wife at their house for dinner. They all came outside. Pastor and Sister Nichols physically picked me up out of my car and carried me to an upstairs bedroom where Sister Nichols' mother (our church mother) slept. When I came to, I was still drunk, crying and throwing up everything I had taken in. They were very sympathetic. They comforted me, saying things like,

"I know it hurts…" That night, Mother Hill rubbed me all night, and Sister Nichols wept with me and comforted me.

The next morning, I heard somebody banging on the door. It sounded like ten thousand pounds of lightning. Sister Nichols came in the room and said, "Last night, we sympathized with where you are. But this morning, get yourself up, and get your clothes on. You'd better be downstairs in the next twenty minutes ready to go to church." I didn't see that same loving, kind person from the night before. When I walked in the church, Pastor Nichols was on the platform. He looked at me and said, "Sister Juanita, come down and sit on the front row."

I didn't direct the choir that day, and everybody was looking and whispering. When the time came for Pastor Nichols to finish his message and start praying for the people at the altar, he called me. (It's funny when I think of this now, but it wasn't funny then.) I had the worst hangover that anybody could ever have. My head felt like it had been pounded into the ground.

When I reached the altar, our two church mothers, Mother Hill and Mother Lott (who was the head of our intercessory prayer board), took over. One was in front of me, hitting me in my stomach and telling me to surrender to God, and the other one was shouting in my ear and hitting me in my back, telling me, "God wants to deliver you. God wants to take you back." I was being knocked in my stomach forward and then hit in my back, sending me in the other direction, to the point that I passed out.

They thought I had gone out under the power. But Mother Hill kept hitting me in my stomach until I started throwing up alcohol. They believed I was being delivered—but they were beating me to the point that I was physically sick! I didn't know whether God was setting me free or if the world was coming to an end. The room was spinning, I had vomit all over me, and the church mothers were hollering, "God is doing it!" Every time they shouted, my head vibrated.

Now, I can't tell you during which part of this experience that my deliverance came, but I vowed to myself from that day on that I never, ever wanted to experience that again! To have two sanctified, Holy

Ghost–filled (from the old school) church mothers beating and hollering the devil out of you is an experience you would never forget—because they have energy many today don't know anything about! They
don't give up. We call on Jesus and our mouths get dry, but "old school"
church mothers never stop. And our church mothers were doing all of
these things wearing high-heeled shoes, completely dressed in white.

I learned from that experience that though I had power in my
gifts, when a fiery trial came, I hadn't eaten enough of the Word to
sustain me through the hard times. This lesson was invaluable: my
spiritual diet was far more important than what I was able to exhibit
through my talents. You see, talent can put you on the platform... but
only your diet can keep you where God places you.

The Lord is also revealing through this story that we can't afford to
get caught up in one isolated experience. We can't afford to get caught
up in our own greatness. Because right after you receive an anointing, right after you gain recognition, and right after you exercise the
mantle of the Lord, you are going to be faced with issues in your personal walk that have nothing to do with grabbing a microphone. Far
more important than your "gifts" is the fact that your spirit man has
to be able to sustain you. For Proverbs 18:14 says:

> The spirit of a man will sustain his infirmity; but a
> wounded spirit who can bear?
>
> —KJV

Infirmities and offenses are sure to come, but if your spirit has
been fed the right diet, it will sustain you. If you have not "dieted" on
the Word, you won't be able to bear through times of trouble. You
won't be able to stand.

Though we walk and sit with our leaders, and all of that is impressive, your leaders can't follow you everywhere you go. They can't be
with you in every situation, which means there are going to be times
when their status and position aren't going to mean a hill of beans
when it comes down to you being sustained through a fiery trial. Hear
me. This is going to be the result of *your diet*, which means it becomes

your responsibility to eat and digest the portion that they have prepared, just as it was for Saul.

Remember, Saul did not even have the ability to recognize who the seer was when he was standing before him. So the only way Saul could receive the privilege and honor of becoming a king in Israel was to be taken up to a higher place by Samuel. His spiritual father ushered him into destiny. This reveals how important it is for our leaders to first know and recognize who their sons and daughters are in the Spirit, as my leadership did that day. They must have the discernment of knowing those to whom they have been called to impart the inheritance of God. If they didn't know, then we would all be lost—because we don't have what it takes to know and see the fullness of what God requires.

> IT IS THE DIVINE REVELATION GIVEN TO OUR LEADERS THAT ENABLES US TO REACH OUR DIVINE DESTINIES— BECAUSE WE CANNOT SEE DESTINY.

The story of Samuel and Saul is a prime example of the difference between the sheep and the shepherd. Sheep are dumb. They're blind. They can't see afar off. That's why they need a shepherd. And the shepherd has to be on a divine assignment, because there's nothing more frustrating than trying to lead a herd of sheep that don't even recognize who the shepherd is.

This was one of Moses' difficulties. He was trying to lead the children of Israel, as best as he knew how, from the spiritual assignment he had received from the Father—but the people couldn't recognize the Father in him. So on many occasions, God had to speak up on Moses' behalf, and the nation ended up being confronted by God without the covering of a mediator . . . without Moses.

It's Time to Change

Another illustration can be drawn from the twenty-first verse. In essence, Saul was saying to Samuel, "Why are you speaking such powerful and deep things to me? You're saying I'm going to be a deliverer over Israel when I'm just a Benjamite. I'm just Kish's son. Nobody in my family has that kind of calling on their lives." This shows us that when we are brought into purpose and our leaders reveal to us who we are, then we have to be *taught* who we really are. We have to be trained according to the vision of those God has placed over us. If not, we would be limited by our own capacity.

So Samuel prophesies to Saul and tells him, "The Lord has spoken this thing in my spirit. He's revealed this to me; He's told me who you are. Now, immediately you have to change not only where you eat, but also how you eat. You can no longer eat from the lower place; I have to bring you up to where I am. Now, you must eat what I eat." If the food of the prophet is what launches you to a place, then it will only be by that level of eating that you will remain. Where the Spirit of the Lord calls, the Spirit and only the Spirit will sustain. You cannot be called from the realm of the Spirit and then eat from the realm of the flesh. You will not last. You will come down quicker than you went up.

When God has revealed to our leaders who we are in the Spirit, then our feedings will lead us to where we are going. In other words, this new spiritual food shouldn't be reduced to being something "common." As their spiritual children, we must be able to go to new levels in God, to the level of our spiritual parents. We must adapt our appetite and learn to digest the same meat. This is one way we must change our posture.

This story also reveals a lesson for the body of Christ. There were thirty other people at the table, and others feasting outside (1 Sam. 9:22). This reveals that there may be other people in your church or in the body of Christ to whom God has divinely connected you—but it is your leader who sees God's divine purpose in your life. There's a prepared portion for you. Yes, a special portion has been set aside just for you. It doesn't matter who else may or may not get blessed in the services. You are almost guaranteed a word from the Lord, because you are called out and appointed. There's a divine assignment on your life, so a portion has been set aside for you.

Apparently, when the Lord had revealed to Samuel that Saul was coming, it became Samuel's responsibility to prepare a portion. Samuel had told the cook, "God has revealed to me that I have a special guest coming. Set this portion apart. It will be reserved for him." Listen to me. This means the things God has prepared for the priests will be given to those He has called to anoint. So you have to be in divine obedience in order to not miss your divine connection—because before you get there, the atmosphere is already being prepared. The meal has been reserved. It was handpicked before you came.

That's why when you come to a church, and God divinely connects you with a ministry, you feel as if you have been there for years. It seems that you have known the pastor for a long time, because the Lord has already revealed in the spirit realm that you are coming. The atmosphere has been prepared. That's why you can sit down when you first walk into a church and say, "Wow, that was just what I needed." The Holy Spirit knew you were coming.

Samuel said to Saul, "See what was reserved for you. Eat, for until the hour appointed it was kept for you, ever since I invited the people. So Saul ate that day with Samuel" (v. 24). In other words, you can't reach your spiritual assignment before it is time. The Father appointed the time when you should show up, just as He did for me. It was appointed for me to show up at New Greater Bethel Ministries. *Unto the hour appointed*, it was kept for me, to see if I was going to be obedient and end up at the right destination.

When you have met your spiritual parents, and they begin to impart that divine assignment into your life, it will also require a change in some of your relationships. After Samuel and Saul had finished eating:

> When they had come down from the high place into
> the city, Samuel conversed with Saul on the top of
> the house. They arose early and about dawn Samuel
> called Saul [who was sleeping] on the top of the house,
> saying, Get up, that I may send you on your way. Saul
> arose, and both he and Samuel went out on the street.
> And as they were going down to the outskirts of the

> city, Samuel said to Saul, Bid the servant pass on be-
> fore us—and he passed on—but you stand still, first,
> that I may cause you to hear the word of God.
> —1 SAMUEL 9:25–27

No doubt you will need to let some people "pass on before you" also so that you can "stand still…to hear the word of God." People that started out with you won't be the ones you end up with. Samuel told Saul, "Send the servant on, because this isn't for his ears. This isn't his grade; this isn't his divine appointment. He just happened to be with you, but you stand still, because before I send you, I have to tell you what God is saying over your life."

This is where many of us miss the mark. We meet the right divine connection, we are in the right church, and we have the right pastor—but we don't wait on the word of God. We are not still enough so that the full word of the Lord concerning our life can be imparted unto us. So we "go" before our time instead of waiting on the timing of the Lord. We begin to operate by association. This is false authority.

What do I mean by this? We begin to operate in the fact that "I've been brought to the high place, and Pastor has drawn me close to him. I can go in his office and talk to him, carry his briefcase, and help in the church. When he goes out to preach, I'm his armorbearer. I'm able to sit among preachers and teachers of the high echelon…I'm in the company of great men and women of God."

In short, we think we've arrived. The fact is, we have moved out before our time. We left before we were *still enough* to hear the word of the Lord and receive His true assignment for our lives.

Then we get into real danger by beginning to use authority that we don't really have, authority that comes by name association, not by waiting…not by eating. This is why Colossians 1:12 says, "Giving thanks to the Father, Who has qualified and made us fit to share the portion which is the inheritance of the saints (God's holy people) in the Light." The Father qualifies and makes us fit to share the portion, which is our inheritance as the saints of God. The *full portion* of the Lord is your spiritual inheritance…you just have to wait for God's timing.

In waiting for God's timing, we have to be careful (as spiritual leaders) to impart a proper protocol to those who have been called to walk in greatness. I started a mentorship class about four years ago, and in this class I still have several students whom the Lord has allowed me to call closer to me. I can recall on different occasions when we went out of town that we would emerge from the airport to find a limousine and a truck or van parked out front. I remember hearing several of them ask whether a second limousine would be picking them up.

Then we would arrive at the hotel and walk into the suite that the host ministry had prepared for me. I would go into the bathroom, and when I came out, they would have opened my greeting basket and started eating my fruit, cookies, and whatever else the hosts had given me. The fact remains that those who walk with leadership must be taught that what leaders have been birthed into, and what the Lord has allowed them to embrace at their level in ministry, is *their level*. So I had to teach these students that though they walked with me, it didn't mean they merited the same reward.

You have to remember that when you are called to walk closer to your leadership and are being mentored by them, you are supposed to be catching the diet—not the status. Your interest and focus must remain on what you are to receive out of their spirits, not what your flesh desires to receive from their hands. When you get off focus and start gazing and grabbing at the status of the person whom God has called you to serve, that's when you will start walking into places and demanding that people give you front row seats or open doors for you (because you're with the prophet, the pastor, or the evangelist).

These things are danger signs, because they signify that you are not catching the spirit of your leaders. You are not catching the real purpose for which you have been called. Your focus is how you can become great when you are really walking with your leaders to learn servanthood and brokenness. When you walk with leaders, you are learning how to catch the vision.

This is why, on many occasions, I have had to strongly rebuke and correct those who walk with me. We would walk into places where the hosts had prepared food for us after I had finished ministering, and just like at the hotel suite, half of my people were sitting down already eating when I arrived. And I had to tell them, "This wasn't prepared for you. This was prepared for me. And if I invite you to sit down and have something to eat, that's proper protocol. But you don't sit down and eat before me; that's improper." The leader, the prophet, must invite the servant to come to the table. And the Bible tells us it is better to be called to the king's table than to be turned away in shame.

The process of this principle is learning to understand how things are to be handed down to you—not handed up to you. If you sit down at a table before your pastor or leader sits down, then you are no longer sitting in their presence; they are sitting in your presence. You shouldn't eat before they do, because they'll be eating what was prepared for you when you are supposed to be eating what was prepared for them.

We don't recognize little things like this as being strong principles of spiritual protocol. You also shouldn't get in a car before your leaders do, because they'll be sitting in the presence of where you're sitting, and not vice versa. There are principles you have to maintain in the natural as examples of how you are trying to receive in the Spirit. A leader can watch the way you act in the natural and rightfully be able to determine what it is you are really gleaning from him or her in the Spirit.

The Bible even gives us example of this when Jesus spoke of the scribes in Luke 20:45–47:

> And with all the people listening, He said to His disciples, Beware of the scribes, who like to walk about in long robes and love to be saluted [with honor] in places where people congregate and love the front and best seats in the synagogues and places of distinction at feasts, who make away with and devour widows' houses, and [to cover it up] with pretense make long prayers. They will receive the greater condemnation (the heavier sentence, the severer punishment).

The scribes served the Pharisees, yet they desired what they could receive from their hands. They wanted to be where their leaders were and to get the same recognition—they merely wanted a physical portion. This is also why, when the mother of Zebedee's children came and asked Jesus if her sons could sit at His right hand and left hand in His kingdom, Jesus responded by saying:

> You do not realize what you are asking. Are you able to drink the cup that I am about to drink and to be baptized with the baptism with which I am baptized?... You know that the rulers of the Gentiles lord it over them, and their great men hold them in subjection [tyrannizing over them]. Not so shall it be among you; but whoever wishes to be great among you must be your servant, and whoever desires to be first among you must be your slave—just as the Son of Man came not to be waited on but to serve, and to give His life as a ransom for many [the price paid to set them free].
>
> —Matthew 20:22, 25–28

Let me rephrase. Jesus was saying to them, "You want the benefits of My level, but are you able to walk on My level of sacrifice?" He made it clear that those who are called to greatness must follow proper spiritual protocol.

True Riches Are in Your Father's House

We see an illustration of this spiritual principle in the story of the prodigal son in Luke 15:11–32. He lived in his father's house and, like his brother, had an inheritance. He knew who he was, that he was above the servants—but he made a mistake. He began to ask for the financial portion of his inheritance without understanding who he was in the Spirit. We do this all the time today. We want to drive the same kinds of cars our pastors are driving. We want to wear the same kinds of clothes. We want to preach using their body gestures. We want to sound like them and move in the Spirit as they do.

We want the physical portion, not knowing that if we get that portion and run, we have forfeited the inheritance. We must be careful that we are not forcing our spiritual fathers to give us a physical inheritance, while at the same time we are missing who we are in the Spirit. We take on the physical "image" of sons and daughters of the gospel, but our true inheritance is the divine, birthed-out word that comes through suffering and trial. Just think about Job. He had sons and daughters, but he constantly had to offer up sacrifices because his children went to each other's houses, having parties and forgetting about God. (See Job 1:1–5.)

They were able to do this because Job was wealthy. They were partaking of the physical inheritance of their father. But they didn't yet know or respect the spiritual nature of who he was. So being a righteous man, Job constantly offered up sacrifices to God on their behalf. Job's children were partaking of his physical substance, not understanding the weight of what God was doing in their lives.

In order for Job to have sons and daughters that were of a different nature, God had to take him through a time of suffering. And when Job went through that suffering, he lost all of his children. He went through a process of purification until he said, "Behold, I am of small account and vile! What shall I answer You? I lay my hand upon my mouth" (Job 40:4). After this, Job received seven more sons and three more daughters (Job 42:13). And the Bible said that his new children were more excellent than his former children, because they were birthed out of his purification and suffering.

So when we look at the story of Job, and that of the prodigal son, we see that at times it takes losing a financial portion to gain your spiritual inheritance. The prodigal son actually took his inheritance and wasted it by going into the world and trying it out on his own. Then he realized his error. He came back home and said, "I missed God. I missed it altogether."

Then he said something even more profound: "I'd rather be a servant in my father's house. If I could just go back and become a servant." (See Luke 15:19.) He had to swallow the fact that he had wasted his financial portion. As a result, he was able to understand the significance of being in his father's house. This was a valuable lesson. He had come to the place where he valued being in his father's house more than what he had in his hand. He understood, *I received my father's substance—his walk, his talk, his name, his money—but I did not get his wisdom.*

In this generation, we have to train up sons and daughters in the kingdom to value being in their father's house more than what they can do on their own.

There were three very important actions that Samuel took to prepare Saul to receive his spiritual inheritance.

1. When God revealed to Samuel that Saul was coming, the first thing Samuel did was to bring Saul to the high place.
2. His second act was to help Saul understand that a portion had been set aside for him.
3. His third act was to see if Saul understood the power of what was about to happen in his life to the point that he would be willing to separate himself from one who admired him, the one who was instrumental in helping him find Samuel.

Saul's servant obviously must have had great respect for him, which reveals something else. The people whom God is preparing to take to another level always have admirers around them. But listen to me. You will never get to your next level until you are willing to give up those who think you are wonderful in order to stand in the presence of somebody who can discern the areas that you are awful in.

Samuel said, "Bid the servant pass on before us [*because this word isn't for him*]...but you stand still, first, that I may cause you to hear the word of God" (1 Sam. 9:27).

> Then Samuel took the vial of oil and poured it on Saul's head and kissed him and said, Has not the Lord

anointed you to be prince over His heritage Israel?

—1 SAMUEL 10:1

In other words, Samuel's actions were revealing his prophetic role. They demonstrated the call of a prophet on his life. He made Saul stand still, he poured oil on him, and he kissed him. Immediately, he began to prophesy from the prophetic mantle on his life. At that point, everything Samuel had labored for and walked under was poured into a nobody: a person with no past history, dealings, or even a concept of being a prophet. Did you see that? The oil of the prophet was poured upon the head of the one who was under the spout.

> **WHAT WAS THE PROBLEM WITH THIS WHOLE STORY? SAUL WAS ANOINTED BY GOD, BUT HE HAD NO RELATIONSHIP WITH GOD.**

As Samuel began to prophesy, he said, "This will be your new role. You are about to become the prince, the anointed one, over Israel. And by the way, the donkeys that you're looking for . . . don't even worry about it, because your daddy won't be needing them anymore."

Yes, it was time to change. Saul was walking into a new day of destiny.

CHAPTER 4

The Anointing: Divine Order

*S*aul's story confirms that when you truly meet your divine connection, that person will have the anointing to help resolve your past while ushering you into the future. Samuel initiated the flow of spiritual inheritance into Saul's life.

> When you have left me today, you will meet two men
> by Rachel's tomb in the territory of Benjamin at Zelzah,
> and they will say to you, The donkeys you sought are
> found. And your father has quit caring about them
> and is anxious for you, asking, What shall I do about
> my son? Then you will go on from there and you will
> come to the oak of Tabor, and three men going up to
> God at Bethel will meet you there, one carrying three
> kids, another carrying three loaves of bread, and an-
> other carrying a skin bottle of wine. They will greet
> you and give you two loaves of bread, which you shall
> accept from their hand.
>
> After that you will come to the hill of God, where
> the garrison of the Philistines is; and when you come
> to the city, you will meet a company of prophets com-
> ing down from the high place with harp, tambourine,
> flute, and lyre before them, prophesying. Then the
> Spirit of the Lord will come upon you mightily, and

you will show yourself to be a prophet with them; and
you will be turned into another man.

—1 SAMUEL 10:2–6

The three things that happened to Saul in this passage of Scripture are all direct signs for you.

1. Saul's past assignment was brought to closure.
2. People were already being prepared and sent to sow into his life.
3. He received divine direction on how to reach and operate on this next level.

In six verses, from the time Samuel said, "Stand still and let me tell you what the will of God is for your life," Saul was transformed from a man chasing donkeys into a man proclaiming the future. His physical needs were met; a divine assignment was spoken over his life; he was anointed for that assignment; and with one prophecy, one kiss, and one vial of oil, he was turned into a different man. The same prophetic gift that was upon Samuel instantly came upon Saul.

Let me explain the historical significance of this impartation. Samuel was a miracle child granted to Hannah when she went to the temple to pray. So his conception and birth were rooted in the prophetic. Then, when he was a small boy, Hannah dedicated Samuel to the temple and left him there, to fulfill her vow to God. This was during a time when the word of the Lord was shut up in Israel, and God wasn't talking to anybody. When God spoke and called Samuel's name, Eli said, "If you hear your name being called again, that's God— answer Him!" (See 1 Samuel 1:1–3:10.)

When Samuel was dedicated in the tabernacle unto God, it caused God to speak out over Israel once again. Samuel's ear was trained to hear the Lord. He was raised in the tabernacle—weighed and birthed out in that prophetic anointing. Samuel's conception, birth, and lifestyle were entirely prophetic. Then years later, he met a man who had nothing prophetic in his background. And because Samuel had paid the price, because God had birthed him out, Saul came by way of the prophetic. His whole lifestyle demonstrated the making of a mighty prophet. Saul received an anointing by being in the right place at the right time.

Saul never had to be birthed out into the prophetic. He had never lived in the tabernacle to learn the voice of God on his own. He simply had to stand still and let the man of God reveal the word of the Lord over his life. And in six verses he received an anointing, provision, and divine placement in the right company. One man of God changed everything about his life.

Too many of us are in the right place under the right leader, but we haven't allowed *that leader* to find us the *right company*. It is as though Samuel was saying, "In order to walk in this assignment, you're going to have to change your company. You have to get among the kind of people that have the same kind of anointing. And you're going to know who they are, because first of all, they're going to be coming down from a high place."

In other words, these new associations won't be coming from a low place. They won't be coming from somewhere filled with grumbling and complaining. They will be coming down from the high place with harps, tambourines, flutes, and lyres—and they will come prophesying. Your spiritual parent will always work to get you in the right celebratory atmosphere to keep the prophecy over you alive. He will get you in a place where the Spirit of the Lord is moving all the time, with people who will have like spirits and the same anointing.

Many years ago (even prophetically), before I was formed in my mother's womb, Jeremiah 1:10 had already become a significant part of my life.

> See, I have this day appointed you to the oversight of the
> nations and of the kingdoms to root out and pull down,
> to destroy and to overthrow, to build and to plant.

This scripture was actually making a declaration concerning who I was to become. And as the years went by and I was passed through the hands of many spiritual fathers and mothers, I can remember as if it was yesterday when I received my final impartation and my final "shot to the nations," as we referred to it then, according to 2 Kings 13:17. One of my spiritual mothers (who was known by many very prominent people across the nation), Mother Estella Boyd, laid hands on me in February 1996 while I was attending a revival at New Greater Bethel.

Mother Boyd and Bishop Jesse T. Stacks, who have both now gone on to be with the Lord, had called a "solemn assembly," or what was also known as a fellowship meeting. Once a month, these fellowships would go from church to church, and all of the sons and daughters that sat under Mother Boyd's and Bishop Stacks's ministries would attend, flying to the different cities where these fellowship meetings were being held.

We all were reaching for the same thing—our destiny. We were all in high pursuit of the will of God for our lives. So when we got into those meetings, even though masses of people were not there (the majority of the time, attendance ranged from between 150 to a maximum of 400 people) and there were no cameras and lights, the power of God that fell in those meetings was something that I cannot begin to explain. There were great men and women of faith like Bishop Collins and Pastor Curlin from Sacramento, California, both who have gone to be with the Lord. A woman named Bea was one of the most powerful readers that I have ever heard.

When I look back over those services, it was almost as if we were sitting inside of a big stewing pot, and because everybody had a purpose and everybody was reaching for his or her purpose, it didn't take long for the power of God to fall. It didn't take long in every fellowship for us to experience a divine visitation from the Lord. There were things that we felt and experienced in those meetings that, if I live to be a hundred years old, my soul will never forget.

In 1996, during the month of February, the fellowship meeting came to New Greater Bethel in New York. I still remember that night: The service was just about over, and Mother Boyd had prayed for hundreds of people in the building that night. I walked up to Mother Boyd just to give her a hug good-bye…and the power of God struck her.

Her hands went up, and they were shaking like electricity was flowing through them. When her hand came down on my belly, I hit the floor. And when I hit the floor, I felt a racing feeling in the center of my belly that moved up and shot through my body (like I was being electrocuted).

At that very instant, it was as if my spirit shot out of my body, and I began to fly above the service. My body was still on the floor because I could look down to the floor and see the whole service. It literally felt like my spirit was in the ceiling. And then as my spirit began to move, it shot straight through the ceiling, and I began to fly. I saw myself wearing a long, white gown as I was flying…and I went to countries all over the world. I flew to Japan, I flew to Africa…I was flying to every corner of every nation, even the United States. I saw myself flying high over auditoriums with thousands and thousands of people in them. By the time it ended, it looked as if I had flown in a complete circle. I can still see it right now.

When I came back and my spirit man hit my body, I went into a realm of tongues that I had never spoken before, and I can't begin to explain to you what that power felt like. As I came to, I could hear Mother Boyd shouting, "She's gone to the nations. This shot sent her to the world." At that time, I had been preaching in small congregations but had not yet mounted a major platform. Mother Boyd said, "Before the year is over, God is going to mount her feet on a major platform because the Holy Ghost just sent her to the nations." The church and those who remained in that service began to praise and worship God. I had never experienced the power of God like that in my life, and I have not experienced it since that time.

That night, they had to pick me up physically and carry me out of the service. And for twenty-four hours straight, they had to sit by my bed and watch me—because I spoke in tongues and traveled all night, seeing visions—seeing myself laying hands on people, sick bodies being healed, and the dead being raised.

Two months later, Bishop T. D. Jakes sent me a letter asking me to teach a class for single women at the Woman, Thou Art Loosed conference. I went to the conference prepared to teach a class that was to run for two days. But after the first class, while we were eating at a restaurant, I started to take a bite of food, and the same tongues that I had received in February returned to my mouth. I looked across the table at my mother and said, "Momma, remember the night that Mother Boyd laid hands on me? Those tongues have returned." And she said, "Don't eat, because God isn't through using you."

We left everybody else at the table, and I returned to the hotel room and lay down. Two hours later, the phone rang. It was the administrator for Bishop Jakes' ministry, saying, "God told Bishop that you have the word for the night." That night, I mounted the platform in front of thirty-six thousand people—and I had never been on a major platform. From that moment, my ministry went to the world.

What I am trying to impart to you is the fact that you are not just a reader. You have this book in your hand because it is a divine connection to where you are about to go. And remember, though the Lord had already started using me, I had to submit myself to attending these fellowships—paying my own way to get there, paying my own hotel cost, and sitting anywhere they sat me. It was Mother Boyd's and Bishop Stacks's responsibilities to keep my life in the level of atmosphere that would keep the prophecy alive until God was ready to birth it forth to the nations. I had traveled around the country not knowing that I would receive that arrow of deliverance that sent me to the world in my own home church.

Yet in pursuing after my destiny, I had to forget about my title, because at that point, I was holding my own women's conferences and drawing three thousand to five thousand people in each meeting. So I had to humble myself and be willing to go to a smaller setting with a few hundred people. I had to be broken enough to forget about my makeup, hairstyle, title, and whatever I was trying to be...because my heart desired my next level. I wanted destiny; I didn't merely want a portion.

If I had continued to do my conferences, preaching everywhere I saw fit, I would have only experienced a portion—and I knew that God had destiny for me. I wanted my full inheritance!

As I said before, Mother Boyd, Bishop Stacks, Pastor Collins, and Pastor Curlin have all gone on to be with the Lord, but I received my inheritance from each one of their lives. I have received something in my spirit that I walk with in ministry even now, which testifies to the fact that I have received an impartation. As Scripture says, I have made each of their ministries authentic by the power of God that has been exemplified in my life.

The point is, if God can't trust your character enough to "take" a shot (from your leaders) as an arrow of deliverance, He certainly can't trust you to "give" a shot to someone else. When you are in a battle, and you are in the ring, you have to be able to take a blow in order to give a blow. And what you take, what you're willing to let leadership impart into you, will only testify of the level that you will be able to impart. You must understand that the most important factor is for you to remain in the right atmosphere, in the company of those who can usher you to your next level. When people say to me, "You really have a mantle for prayer" or "The anointing of prayer is really on you," I look back on what God has done.

I remember one season when Mother Boyd was sick, and my schedule was really tight, so I couldn't make it to her fellowship services. But when I held my conference in Pensacola, Florida, the Spirit of the Lord impressed me to invite her to be a speaker. I remember somebody saying, "You're going to ask Mother Boyd to speak? The nation really doesn't know who Mother Boyd is." I replied, "I don't care. I know what God told me."

Mother Boyd came into that second service of the conference, and when I got up to speak, I turned around and said, "Mother Boyd, do you have something to say?" She got up and told her assistant to hand her an orange robe. Then she walked up to me and said, "God told me when I came here to get you dressed." She put that robe on me and said, "For over thirty years this was the robe that I prayed in during intercessory prayer." Her hand went up, her fingers began to quiver, and when her hand came down on my belly she said, "You're going to pray…because God has just anointed you for prayer."

That happened in August, and by January of the following year, the Lord directed me to call my first intercessory prayer service at New Greater Bethel. Five people showed up to pray at 5:00 a.m. Now, five years later, we have had up to two thousand people in early morning prayer—all because I received a mantle for prayer. I thank God for giving me the wisdom to keep myself submitted in the right atmosphere under the right leadership in order to receive my next level of impartation.

Remember this, reader. It is atmosphere that will lead you to the next level of impartation.

Can God Trust You?

Now, it's important that you see this. God is saying that before you can be birthed out from your leaders, several things need to take place. They have to see if you can separate yourself from anything that is less than you are. They have to find out whether or not you are able to follow instructions. After Samuel anointed and kissed Saul, there were several instructions from Samuel that Saul could not afford to miss. Listen carefully to this statement that I am about to make. These instructions were not all spiritual, but they all had spiritual significance.

> **KEEP YOURSELF IN THE COMPANY OF THE RIGHT PEOPLE AND THE RIGHT ATMOSPHERE IF YOU EXPECT TO GO TO YOUR NEXT LEVEL IN GOD.**

From the second to the fifth verse, Samuel gave him detailed instructions. He was saying, "I'm going to tell you where you need to go, where you need to stop, and what you need to take from which people. I'm telling you clearly what you need to do—and don't mishandle any of it."

Let's look closely at this. First of all, you have to be taught and instructed. Your leaders have to see you follow direction. This starts immediately after you are called and anointed. Remember the second verse: "When you have left me today, you will meet two men by Rachel's tomb in the territory of Benjamin at Zelzah, and they will say to you, The donkeys you sought are found. And your father has quit caring about them and is anxious for you, asking, What should I do about my son?" (1 Sam. 10:2).

In other words, Saul had to go to Rachel's tomb. He couldn't go where he wanted to go. He couldn't go to the left side of the mountain. He could not tell Samuel, "Graveyards are not my calling," or like us, "I don't sweep, clean pews, or do hospitals." No! You don't say anything. You do what you're told. Saul had to go exactly where Samuel told him to go. He had been anointed, kissed, and given the word of the Lord. It was a new day.

This is a place where many people mess up. This is the point where we will miss God every time! Once we get a prophecy, and once our leaders look at us and say, "You're anointed of God. You're going to preach. I see you traveling all over the world," then *bam!* Immediately, the next phase begins, when our spiritual fathers say, "Let me pull all that in now and teach you how to follow instructions."

Samuel was saying to Saul, "Don't start being the prince of Israel yet. Go to Rachel's tomb to meet your divine connections. Go and let God bring closure to the old mantle—the old you."

> Then you will go on from there and you will come to the oak of Tabor, and three men going up to God at Bethel will meet you there, one carrying three kids, another carrying three loaves of bread, and another carrying a skin bottle of wine. They will greet you and give you two loaves of bread, which you shall accept from their hand.
>
> —1 Samuel 10:3–4

Listen closely, because I want you to see this. Samuel said, "You're going to meet three men. Together, they will be carrying three kids, three loaves, and a skin of wine. Can I trust you not to take more than what you need? Can I trust you with offerings? Can I trust you not to take advantage of this situation? Will you say to them, 'Samuel prophesied to me…he's my spiritual father. He just anointed me,' knowing that I'm a prophet in the land?"

Samuel was mighty in the Lord and greatly feared. So he tested Saul. "Can I trust you not to use your association with me to get more than what I told you to take?" This reminds me of Elisha's servant, Gehazi, when Elisha wouldn't take an offering from Naaman after God healed him of leprosy. Gehazi went behind the prophet's back and told Naaman, "Just give it to me." God dealt with Gehazi (through Elisha) for this. He and his entire family were cursed with leprosy. (See 2 Kings 5:15–27.)

Can your spiritual father trust you when he is not around? Can he trust you not to be manipulative? Can he trust you to take only what he told you to take—that even though there are a host of things you could probably take, you choose to uphold his word and follow instructions? Can he trust you to keep your divine assignment and association with him to yourself until the time appointed?

Keep It to Yourself

This leads into the next spiritual principle we must learn from the story of Saul's introduction to spiritual destiny. Christians need to learn how not to become braggadocios toward people in their circle of influence who have not been called to the same level of destiny. Notice Saul's response in the following verses:

> Saul's uncle said to him and to his servant, Where did you go? And Saul said, To look for the donkeys, and when we found them nowhere, we went to Samuel. Saul's uncle said, Tell me, what did Samuel say to you? And Saul said to his uncle, He told us plainly that the donkeys were found. *But of the matter of the kingdom of which Samuel spoke he told him nothing.*
> —1 SAMUEL 10:14–16, EMPHASIS ADDED

Did you hear that? In the matter of his spiritual destiny, he told his uncle nothing.

A Word Out of Season

Saul illustrates a level of spiritual understanding that young Joseph failed to grasp. Joseph got himself in trouble because the Lord had revealed his destiny in a dream, but he spoke it at the wrong time, in the wrong place, and in the wrong way. He walked over to his brothers and said, "I had a dream that I was going to be over all of you and that you are all going to be my servants." (See Genesis 37.) These statements introduced him to his pit experience.

Genesis 37:3 says:

> Now Israel loved Joseph more than all his children because he was the son of his old age, and he made him a [distinctive] long tunic with sleeves.

Joseph was his father's chosen one. Jacob had already made Joseph a robe of "many colors," so it was already apparent to his brothers that he was special. In reading the story, though the brothers were bothered by their father's special attention to Joseph, they had more or less accepted that Joseph was precious to his father. It wasn't until Joseph started declaring his dreams that a real problem emerged:

> Now Joseph had a dream and he told it to his brothers, and they hated him still more. And he said to them, Listen now and hear, I pray you, this dream that I have dreamed: We [brothers] were binding sheaves in the field, and behold, my sheaf arose and stood upright, and behold, your sheaves stood round about my sheaf and bowed down! His brothers said to him, Shall you indeed reign over us? Or are you going to have us as your subjects and dominate us? And they hated him all the more for his dreams and for what he said. But Joseph dreamed yet another dream and told it to his brothers [also]. He said, See here, I have dreamed again, and behold, [this time not only] eleven stars [but also] the sun and the moon bowed down and did reverence to me!
>
> —Genesis 37:5–9

Joseph became a braggadocio. He was almost rubbing it in his brothers' faces that God had a call upon his life! So he had to go by way of the pit so that God could purify his mantle. Joseph had to be put in a position where he was falsely accused, where he was running for his life. He had to sit in prison, prophesying and helping others. When the one who had promised not to forget him was released from prison, he forgot all about Joseph. He had to wait until God brought him out at an appointed time, through serving another man. (See Genesis 37–50.)

Joseph had to develop character and learn obedience through suffering so that the mantle God had placed upon him could become a blessing to his family—not a knife in their sides. When you lack wisdom, and when you speak those things that were spoken to you in private, it can cause your journey to divine destiny to be painful. This happens when your motive is not spiritual growth—instead it is self-recognition.

That's why many Christians are going through what we call "spiritual warfare" in their churches. They have announced themselves and proclaimed their own importance instead of acting according to the teaching of Proverbs 27:1–2, which says, "Do not boast of [yourself and] tomorrow, for you know not what a day may bring forth. Let another man praise you, and not your own mouth; a stranger, and not your own lips."

After Samuel had met with Saul and initiated the flow of his spiritual mantle into Saul's life, Samuel came out before the people of Israel and announced: (Reader, did you get that? Saul did not make his own announcement. He did not go out before the people and announce himself to be the king of Israel. He was announced by the one who was anointed before he came.)

> You have this day rejected your God, Who Himself saves you from all your calamities and distresses; and you have said to Him, No! Set a king over us. So now present yourselves before the Lord by your tribes and by your thousands.... And Samuel said to all the people, Do you see him whom the Lord has chosen, that none like him is among all the people? And all the people shouted and said, Long live the king! Then Samuel told the people

the manner of the kingdom [defining the position of the king in relation to God and to the people], and wrote it in a book and laid it up before the Lord. And Samuel sent all the people away, each one to his home.

—1 SAMUEL 10:19, 24–25

Regardless of the circumstances, it's your leader's responsibility to make an announcement about you. You should never announce yourself. Not even Jesus, the Son of God, the Word made flesh, announced Himself. John the Baptist announced Him. (See John 1.) Proverbs 13:3 says, "He who guards his mouth keeps his life, but he who opens wide his lips comes to ruin." Saul did not tell his uncle everything about his meeting with Samuel, a direct illustration of Proverbs 10:19, which says, "In the multitude of words there wanteth not sin: but he that refraineth his lips is wise" (KJV).

I believe the whole process of Samuel giving Saul instructions and telling him how to handle himself reveals another important lesson. In the midst of receiving a great anointing, Saul had to be taught *balance*. He had to receive wisdom in the area of his new anointing. Proverbs 11:1–3 says:

> A false balance and unrighteous dealings are extremely offensive and shamefully sinful to the Lord, but a just weight is His delight. When swelling and pride come, then emptiness and shame come also, but with the humble (those who are lowly, who have been pruned or chiseled by trial, and renounce self) are skillful and godly Wisdom and soundness. The integrity of the upright shall guide them, but the willful contrariness and crookedness of the treacherous shall destroy them.

The Test of Character

As we develop this principle further, we will see that Saul was being tested in the area of balance through character. Samuel told him to take two loaves and keep going. Saul needed to demonstrate that his character was being strengthened through obedience. God was building integrity in Saul, and Saul was receiving upright guidance to keep him walking uprightly. The "daughters of Zion" and the "sons of thunder" must be taught character. (See Isaiah 3:16–17; 4:4; Mark 3:17.) When the anointing is placed upon us…when the word of the Lord is spoken over our lives…*when we have received our divine assignment,* character must be worked in us through obedience. And we can't "learn obedience" until we have been instructed in the way of the Lord. His knowledge comes "precept upon precept; line upon line…here a little, and there a little" (Isa. 28:10, KJV).

We must not be allowed to get away with anything once we have received the mantle and anointing for a divine assignment. The Bible says, "A little leaven leaveneth the whole lump" (Gal. 5:9, KJV). Before you know it, a little lying will lead to a lot of lying; a little cheating will lead to a lot of cheating; and a little stealing will lead to a whole lot of stealing. The flesh has to be cut. Let me reiterate: we learn obedience through the things we suffer.

> AT EVERY DIVINE TURN IN OUR LIVES, WE MUST BE CORRECTED IN OUR CHARACTER.

These spiritual values revealed through Saul's encounter with Samuel demonstrate the true value of the impartation. This is our real inheritance, the authentic portion of the Father according to Proverbs 13:22: "A good man leaves an inheritance [of moral stability and goodness] to his children's children, and the wealth of the sinner [finds its way eventually] into the hands of the righteous, for whom it was laid up."

The portion God wants us to receive isn't material wealth. He is trying to walk us through the process of inheriting morality, stability, integrity, and right standing with God and man from our spiritual parents. That's when the wealth of the sinner finds its way to us as spiritual children of our spiritual fathers. In that position we obtain favor from the Lord.

After we have received our father's mantle of the anointing, we must become spiritual children—daughters of Zion and sons of thunder—and be willing to submit to instruction. Remember Proverbs 15:22: "Where there is no counsel, purposes are frustrated, but with many counselors they are accomplished." Many people have great anointings and giftings, but they don't reach their divine destiny because their purposes are frustrated. So they wander around in the body of Christ because they have refused counsel and instruction. They don't know how to walk in obedience because they will not hear the counsel of their spiritual fathers and mothers.

There are many in the body of Christ who have had great anointings placed upon them, but they are beating the air with no aim. That's why Paul said:

> Do you not know that in a race all the runners compete, but [only] one receives the prize? So run [your race] that you may lay hold [of the prize] and make it yours. Now every athlete who goes into training conducts himself temperately and restricts himself in all things. They do it to win a wreath that will soon wither, but we [do it to receive a crown of eternal blessedness] that cannot wither. Therefore I do not run uncertainly (without definite aim). I do not box like one beating the air and striking without an adversary. But [like a boxer] I buffet my body [handle it roughly, discipline it by hardships] and subdue it, for fear that after proclaiming to others the Gospel and things pertaining to it, I myself should become unfit [not stand the test, be unapproved and rejected as a counterfeit].
> —1 Corinthians 9:24–27

We are running around without counsel, proclaiming ourselves, and calling it spiritual warfare. But Proverbs 20:18 tells us, "Purposes and plans are established by counsel; and [only] with good advice make or carry on war." We cannot war after our own purposes. We cannot war for our spiritual assignments without counsel, because it is through counsel that the purposes and plans of the Father are established.

The anointing alone doesn't establish our purposes. Our destiny cannot be established from just having a "high time" in church. It cannot be established from goose bumps and tears. These things are only the beginning. Your divine purpose can only be established by counsel and discipline, or else you will be fighting without aim. I heard it takes twice the energy to throw a punch and miss than it does to connect with the target. So hear me. When you walk without the counsel and instruction of a spiritual father, the devil is going to wear you completely out.

CHAPTER 5

Stepping Over Authority

*R*eader, I know you are saying by now, "This is very heavy." If you feel at this moment anything like the way I felt while I was writing this book, you should feel as if a brick is sitting in your chest and a skyscraper is resting on your back. I realize that this subject is somewhat weighty. But I would like to encourage you with this fact: because this book is in your hands, it tells me that God has placed a heavy call on your life and you need to get used to carrying weight. Now, let's continue...

In this chapter, I want to make something crystal clear: one of the major problems in the kingdom of God is not the failure to anoint people into *positions*, but instead, in teaching or training them how to stay in their grace. People need to know how to stay in position.

This can also serve as a warning. Why? Knowing the story of Saul, we must be careful that upon being changed into another man, we don't assume false authority and change ourselves into the *wrong man*. In other words, when someone anoints you, you don't become *that* person. You become a partaker of his or her grace. We can see this principle in operation as we look at ministries across the country. There are ministries that carry the same characteristics of their spiritual parents because DNA is inevitable—just as my parents conceived me, and according to medical science, we have the same DNA.

How do I know this? Because the shape of my head, my eyes, and my nose resemble my dad. My mouth, my personality, and the rest of my physical body resemble my mom. When people see me, they can see my parents in me, just as Jesus said, "Anyone who has seen Me has seen the Father" (John 14:9). So, of course, you will resemble the ministry that births you out and raises you in the Spirit—but not to become them. Eventually, you will develop into the full maturity of the call that God has for you, and there will always be signs to remind you of where you came from. And if by chance other ministry gifts are aware of who your parents are, they will also see your parents in you and respect the fact that you have come from a powerful lineage.

When Timothy was concerned about his age, Paul told him, "When I call to remembrance the unfeigned faith that is in thee, which dwelt first in thy grandmother Lois, and thy mother Eunice; and I am persuaded that in thee also. Wherefore I put thee in remembrance that thou stir up the gift of God, which is in thee by the putting on of my hands" (2 Tim. 1:5–6, KJV). Timothy didn't have an anointing on his own; it was given to him through the spiritual DNA of his mother and grandmother, and by the laying on of Paul's hands it was activated.

I said this earlier, but it bears repeating here. Understand that when God uses a man or woman of God to place an anointing upon you, the next step of receiving that anointing is to come under submission. The anointing in you must be channeled and guided. It must be placed under great counsel, because you are wearing something that you are unfamiliar with. And though it may feel good that the mighty hand of God is resting upon you, one fact remains—you haven't been trained to operate effectively in that particular anointing or gift.

Take a surgeon, for example. A doctor can go to school for many years learning how to become a surgeon. He can learn which sutures to use and which way the blood flows through the body. He can learn about veins, where arteries can be located, and exactly where the heart is situated. All of these elements, and many more, make up the human body. So when it's time for a surgeon to operate, he must have been thoroughly trained—even in how to suture correctly—because he is using a mighty instrument. His intellect has been power-packed with a lot of information, yet if his hands aren't skilled with the expertise of much "hands-on" training, he could cut right through the skin and hit an artery, killing a person on the operating table.

How does this relate to the body of Christ? Too many times, people are "murdered" by those who carry a heavy anointing but who have never been spiritually trained to become a skillful surgeon. This takes us right back to Jesus, who gave us the correct pattern. The Bible says He was anointed by God to heal the sick, raise the dead, open blinded eyes, set those who were in captivity free, and to heal all that were bruised. (See Isaiah 42:6–7; Luke 4:18.)

However, remember that in Hebrews 5:8 we read: "He learned [active, special] obedience through what He suffered." As we learned in chapter two of this book, the power in which Jesus walked was so awesome that it required Him to obediently stay under the constant tutelage of His Father. It was required of Him to keep asking when and how to use that power, what to say, what not to say, when to speak, and when not to speak. Even when Jesus was brought before Pilate, He did not open His mouth and try to defend Himself; instead, the Father was compelling Him to be silent. He consistently reminded us that He came to do as His Father commanded, not as He Himself willed.

When the devil approached Jesus after He had fasted for forty days, he said, "Let me lead You up on the mountaintop...." (See Matthew 4:1–11.) From that mountaintop the devil taunted Jesus to cast Himself down, tempting Him to call ten thousand angels to help Him. He could have dashed Himself down and then called upon the ministering angels to come and destroy the foul things that were coming up against Him, but He held His peace. Why? Jesus understood His anointing.

Though He had a powerful anointing, He knew it was under subjection to the Father. And He couldn't step out from under that anointing at any time, or He would disconnect Himself from the Father and start following His own will. He preferred to stay focused on the purpose for which He was sent rather than to allow the enemy to provoke Him to some sort of spiritual Olympics. He understood that the purpose for this level of the anointing was to set the captive free, not to prove His power.

While Jesus was in the earth realm, He said that everything He did was done to glorify His Father—not to glorify Himself (though the Father was using Him powerfully to get the work done). He always pointed the attention and the respect back to His heavenly Father. He always acknowledged the fact that the anointing in which He operated belonged to the Father. He did this because He was submitted.

When Saul Stepped Over Authority

When you look at the example of Saul through the mirror of the way Jesus glorified His Father, you need to understand that Saul came under Samuel's anointing. Yet something that's all too common today happened to Saul after he was anointed. It has happened countless times during the course of the kingdom, and it is still happening now. Saul stepped out of his anointing by stepping over Samuel's authority.

> **PLEASE GET THIS! BECAUSE OF HIS SUBMISSION TO GOD, JESUS HAD ACCESS TO EVERYTHING THAT BELONGED TO THE FATHER.**

At the beginning of the thirteenth chapter of 1 Samuel, Saul began his reign as king of Israel. Saul was grown—at forty years old, he wasn't a little boy.

At this point of his reign, the children of Israel were about to go to battle, and they found themselves in a tight situation. They were outnumbered by their enemies, and they were shaking and trembling as they followed Saul. The eighth verse says that Samuel had required that Saul wait for him for seven days in Gilgal until the appointed time. But when the seven days had passed, Samuel had not yet arrived, and the people were scattering. Saul was in fear and felt that he must do something, *right then—with or without Samuel.*

When the ministry work you believe God has called you to do is *about you,* it will force you to step out of the will of God. When you step out of the will of God, you step over into self, because pride is in operation. Pride says, "The people are leaving me. They no longer want to follow me or to be subject to me. *I have to do something.*" This thinking is not the will of God, and believe me, pride automatically comes before destruction...a haughty spirit comes right before a fall.

The first thing pride does is to give you a false delusion, making you feel as if you are more important than you really are. Pride convinces you that your spirit is in a certain place, and, as a result, you can walk in that place doing things God has not authorized you to do. This is what happened to Saul. He reacted to the people's actions and took that step out of authority: "So Saul said, Bring me the burnt offering and the peace offerings. And he offered the burnt offering [which he was forbidden to do]" (1 Sam. 13:9).

Saul wasn't a priest! And because he wasn't a priest, he couldn't function in the office of a prophet (though he had received a prophetic anointing from Samuel). In short, Saul was not ordained by God to step into that position. Let's go back to Scripture:

> And just as he finished offering the burnt offering, behold, Samuel came! Saul went out to meet and greet him. Samuel said, What have you done? Saul said, Because I saw that the people were scattering from me, and that you did not come within the days appointed, and that the Philistines were assembled at Michmash, I thought, The Philistines will come down now upon me to Gilgal, and I have not made supplication to the Lord. So I forced myself to offer a burnt offering. And Samuel said to Saul, You have done foolishly! You have not kept the commandment of the Lord your God which He commanded you; for the Lord would have established your kingdom over Israel forever.
>
> —1 SAMUEL 13:10–13

Now think about it. God would have established Saul's kingdom over Israel forever had he obeyed leadership. Had Saul obeyed the spiritual authority God placed over his life, his kingdom would have been established forever. That's powerful.

The ministry and anointing that God imparts into you is eternal. His calling and gifts are irrevocable (Rom. 11:29). When you receive an impartation from your spiritual father, it is meant to last from generation to generation—because it comes from a spiritual lineage. It is your portion…your spiritual inheritance. For example, I am who I am in Christ right now because an anointing was imparted into me, not because I went on a fast and prayed and sought the Lord.

First of all, I was called of God even before I was discovered in my mother's womb. Jeremiah 1:5 says, "Before I formed you in the womb I knew and approved of you [as My chosen instrument], and before you were born I separated and set you apart, consecrating you; [and] I appointed you as a prophet to the nations." Yet in completing that calling on my life, God had to send along another prophet—one who had carried the mantle in the earth before I came, to impart that anointing unto me. This "eternal" anointing makes me understand my purpose, because when hands were laid on me, *that* anointing was passed down.

The deposit and transmission of this power is eternal because it originates from God, our heavenly Father—which means my life will end, but the mantle will never die. Hear me. *The anointing never dies!* The impartation never dies! That's why I must walk according to the will of God and according to His precepts, so that when the time comes (and God begins to bring the people into my life that He has ordained to walk with me), then I'll be able, through the laying on of hands, to impart that mantle upon them. In turn, they will lay hands on others at the appointed time and impart the same anointing upon them.

If the next generation is to be able to receive a divine impartation, the people who currently carry that impartation must walk in divine obedience. They must walk strictly according to the will of God in every aspect of His will.

This spiritual principle was the focus of chapter two of this book.

But it runs like a golden cord throughout this entire book. We must constantly be reminded of it. To be in *obedience* means to be in compliance with someone else's wishes or orders—to acknowledge his or her authority. To be in compliance, we must yield to the will of others. So when we walk in obedience to God and yield to the will of others (i.e., our spiritual leadership), then we are truly submitting to His authority.

Let's look at John 16:13–15:

> But when He, the Spirit of Truth (the Truth-giving Spirit) comes, He will guide you into all the Truth (the whole, full Truth). For He will not speak His own message [on His own authority]; but He will tell whatever He hears [from the Father; He will give the message that has been given to Him], and He will announce and declare to you the things that are to come [that will happen in the future]. He will honor and glorify Me, because He will take of (receive, draw upon) what is Mine and will reveal (declare, disclose, transmit) it to you. Everything that the Father has is Mine. That is what I meant when I said that He [the Spirit] will take the things that are Mine and will reveal (declare, disclose, transmit) it to you.

Learning Submission

The Spirit of Truth transmits everything to us in perfect divine order…so you must be willing to receive from those who carry His authority on earth. You must be in compliance with what God says and prophesies to you through your spiritual fathers, so that when they lay hands on you, you will receive the imparted anointing to operate in the calling and purpose of God.

Our spirits must be willing to receive the truth, because if we deny and reject the truth that comes on the wings of correction, rebuke, and instruction, then we will be shut off from the threefold power of God. And when we are shut off from being successful under authority, we become mere Bible teachers, not those whom God has called to *impart truth* into other people's lives. This comes only by the Spirit as we receive and walk in truth. Many people can teach a lesson, but only those who walk in submission to the Father can transmit power.

That's why so many are teaching Bible studies but people aren't receiving a transmission from the Spirit of Truth—because you can't impart what you don't have. You can't impart the Spirit of Truth when you are not willing to receive or walk according to this same spirit. It is only by the Spirit of Truth that we receive the authority and power of God. Now, follow me here. The same power and authority God gave to Jesus is now transmitted through the Holy Spirit to us...so again, the only way we can use it is to stay in obedience. We can't afford to "tap in and out" of obedience. We can't afford to do things the way we want to do them!

The Father gave power to Jesus, and He submitted. Therefore, it enabled Him to send the Holy Spirit to earth, who now makes intercession for us. Look at the pattern. The Father gives the Son power. The Son submits that power back to the Father, enabling the Son at the appointed time to send the Holy Spirit. In turn, the Holy Spirit submits to interceding for us. So, do you see, reader? Power is given; power is submitted. Power is given, and power is submitted. So therefore, the manifestation of the real power of God is that wherever it is displayed, it comes through service.

Do you see, reader? Jesus came with all power, and what did He do? He served. Then the Holy Spirit came with power, and He served. So when you really display the power of God, we should see a willingness to serve in everything that you do. Whatever assignment has been passed on to our spiritual fathers or mothers (that has been spoken into our lives) requires a process of staying under that anointing in order to walk in it. We must walk in obedience, whether we agree or not.

Bear with me, as I explain further. People have made submission a matter of submitting to *a person*; they have not understood that submission is a matter of submitting to *the authority of God*. We have made submission about the leader—the type of person he or she is, and whether or not we like what we see in his or her life. We need to understand that submission is not about the person. Submission is not about whether we like something or not. Submission is about the incorruptible portion we are trying to obtain from our heavenly Father.

Submission is about what I am trained *into*. In other words, it is about what God is training me to do. For me, I know He is training and positioning my spirit so that I can be an oil carrier and, even more, the carrier of a mantle that goes beyond the church, extending His power into the world. I want to be able to transmit this weight of authority, this anointing that I have been given, into somebody else's life. Therefore, I must be willing to pass every test of obedience.

Jesus did not like the fact that He had to go to the cross. He did not enjoy being whipped. I am certain He did not like the fact that while He was on the cross, His Father had to turn away—no longer being able to feel His presence and His covering. He knew that He was in the will of the Father, but still it did not *feel* good.

The process wasn't about whether or not Jesus liked what was happening to Him. He didn't say, "Well, I'm not going to finish this work because You left Me. I'm not going to die. I'm going to call ten thousand angels because I don't feel You with me anymore. It's unfair that You've turned Your back on Me. You knew what I had to do, and I only did what I did because You sent me and told Me to do it. Now suddenly, You've rejected Me."

No! No! No! Jesus understood that if He continued the process of obedience and submission—and respected, recognized, and acknowledged the authority of the One that was over Him—He was well on the way to gain power. Hear me. Being able to walk in the power and authority of God is our ultimate goal. We miss it when we become entangled in the flesh. Think of it in the natural. People in the sports world, like football and basketball players, are trained under a well-organized coaching staff. That's the reason they can be successful. That's why you see them becoming accomplished in their skills and abilities.

No matter how talented an athlete is, regardless of how awesome he or she is, there is an underlying reason for his success. Michael Jordan got to where he is today because, on every level, he had a coach. Denzel Washington became the great actor he is because he had an acting coach. People you see who are successful in any arena have usually been coached.

Christians are the only ones who don't seem to want a coach. We want to succeed in God, we want to become accomplished in the kingdom, but we don't want a coach. We don't want anybody telling us what to do. Please don't miss this. The way to ultimate power is through the direction of divine counsel. Sound spiritual counsel is our safety net.

This takes me back to Saul. When he stepped over the anointing of Samuel, he assumed a position that had not been given to him. When he was operating in the Spirit of the Lord among the prophets, he was operating in an imparted anointing. But he violated a spiritual principle when he crossed the line and made the sacrifice on his own. When you begin to operate in something that hasn't been imparted into you, you are crossing the line, and you can lose the anointing.

I am not saying that Saul wouldn't eventually have been called, ordained, and anointed of God to become even more than a king with a prophetic anointing. He was an anointed king, because the spirit of the prophetic (not the office of a prophet) also came with the kingly anointing. But when he violated and stepped over the authority of Samuel, he lost the anointing yet remained the king—but his kingdom didn't last forever. God removed the eternal blessing.

Saul's kingdom would have been established in Israel forever. Instead, he was left to live out the season of his life that God had appointed without the prophetic anointing. Saul lost the anointing to become popular with the people. He stepped on top of the person whom God called to anoint him. Nothing could flow down into him anymore because he was no longer down—no longer under the spout. Samuel was Saul's "flow," and as long as Saul stayed under Samuel, the prophetic anointing flowed down into him. When he stepped on top of it, it was gone. He was diminished to merely being a king of men, full of torment and grief.

Not only this, when Saul stepped over his spiritual head, he stepped under the "false anointing" of Satan, the prince of the power of the air. Then immediately, he began to reap the fruits of a corrupt lineage.

Today, we have preachers, teachers, evangelists, and people sitting in the pews with anointings on their lives that are being diminished daily. Some have an anointing to become preachers, or maybe pastors. Others have the anointing to become bishops or evangelists. Still others have an anointing to become prophets—but when they stepped out of the will of God, they broke the divine pattern. Regardless of what the anointing is that they received, because they stepped out of the divine counsel and authority over them, they can no longer carry the authority of their anointing. They did not stay under their spiritual authority. That is why the Bible says we must submit one to another, because submission keeps the anointing oil flowing down into your life.

Regardless of how high you go in ministry, no matter how high your calling and title may be, God requires you to be submitted and accountable. Even the president of the United States cannot function in this capacity alone. He has to be accountable. He has to submit himself to others who are more knowledgeable than he is in specific areas. If he is going to rule the most powerful nation in the world, he must do this. Oh, yes! The law of authority can be seen in every area of life.

God did not waste any time in dealing with Saul's disobedience. Right after Saul offered the sacrifice, Samuel showed up and said:

> What have you done?... You have done foolishly! You have not kept the commandment of the Lord your God which He commanded you; for the Lord would have established your kingdom over Israel forever; but now your kingdom shall not continue; the Lord has sought out [David] a man after His own heart, and the Lord has commanded him to be prince and ruler over

His people, because you have not kept what the Lord
commanded you. And Samuel went up from Gilgal to
Gibeah of Benjamin. And Saul numbered the people
that were left with him, only about 600.

—1 SAMUEL 13:11, 13–15

Saul started out with thousands and ended up with six hundred.
This is what happens when you begin to walk in disobedience and step
over the authority God has given you. Instead of gaining, you lose. At
first, you look like a great wonder, but it all begins to diminish—because
only the authentic oil of the anointing causes multiplication. The oil
of the anointing causes you to prosper. What the Lord allows to be
spoken and poured into your life by your spiritual father is what causes
your tent to be expanded. Yes, the Bible does tell us to broaden our
horizons, enlarge our territories, and expand our tents—but it has to
flow down God's way.

When the one who is appointed to pour into your life isn't there,
your capacity to hold the anointing begins to diminish. It's no different than what happens when a person goes for days and days without
eating. Once you fast for many days (let's say forty) without eating
regular food, it is almost impossible to come off of this extended fast
and eat a steak the same day. Your digestive system needs to adjust
in order to house that kind of food again. Those who have tried have
made themselves sick, because they weren't prepared to function on
that level. Their stomachs couldn't expand to digest meat instead of
fluids.

If you can't house and digest the anointing of your spiritual father, then you won't have strength to put out anything of substance.
Your body will be weak, and your ministry will be weak. When the
anointing on your life is weak, the gifts in which you operate will be
anemic. That's why some people get up to minister, singing, playing
instruments, and preaching, and they sound like *sounding brass* and
a *tinkling cymbal*. They have lost the authority of God. They wouldn't
submit themselves to walk the path of obedience.

Saul's Counterfeit Anointing Multiplies

When Samuel discovered Saul's disobedience, he spoke a word to Saul to tell him that he had lost his kingdom forever and that the Lord had chosen someone else who would obey Him. Yet Saul moved on and started regathering his army, trying to pull it all back together. Now look at the pattern that began to unfold. When Saul didn't wait for Samuel to arrive and perform the sacrifice, he rejected divine instruction. And it wasn't long before Saul's chain of command was infected by this same spirit:

> Saul and Jonathan his son and the people with them remained in Gibeah of Benjamin, but the Philistines encamped at Michmash. And raiders came out of the Philistine camp in three companies; one company turned toward Ophrah, to the other land of Shual, another turned toward Beth-horon, and another toward the border overlooking the Valley of Zeboim toward the wilderness. Now there was no metal worker to be found throughout all the land of Israel, for the Philistines said, Lest the Hebrews make swords or spears. But each of the Israelites had to go down to the Philistines to get his plowshare, mattock, axe, or sickle sharpened. And the price for plowshares and mattocks was a pim, and a third of a shekel for axes and for setting goads [with resulting blunt edges on the sickles, mattocks, forks, axes, and goads.] So on the day of battle neither sword nor spear was found in the hand of any of the men who were with Saul and Jonathan; but Saul and Jonathan his son had them. And the garrison of the Philistines went out to the pass of Michmash. One day Jonathan son of Saul said to his armour-bearer, Come, let us go over to the Philistine garrison on the other side. But he did not tell his father.
>
> —1 SAMUEL 13:16–23; 14:1

Though Jonathan fought a great battle against that group of men, Saul was really supposed to gain that victory. Saul was supposed to lead his army to get the job done, but because he had come out from under Samuel's authority and began to "step over" into areas where he didn't belong, that same spirit expanded itself right down to Jonathan. Then Jonathan did the same thing: he went over to the Philistine garrison and didn't tell his father. Jonathan fought a battle without getting his father's direction.

> **THERE IS A SPIRIT OF OBEDIENCE, BUT DISOBEDIENCE IS ALSO A SPIRIT.**

Another incident arose a few verses later after all the men of Israel pursued the Philistines until they fled from battle. (See 1 Samuel 14:6–23.) You see, once you break the rank of submission, everything that is under you will begin to operate in the same spirit. And the Bible says it didn't stop with the first incident. The twenty-fourth verse says:

> But the men of Israel were distressed that day; for Saul
> had caused them to take an oath, saying, Cursed be
> the man who eats any food before evening.

Saul had put his men on a fast, but then in the twenty-seventh verse, something happened:

> But Jonathan had not heard when his father charged
> the people with the oath. So he dipped the end of the
> rod in his hand into a honeycomb and put it to his
> mouth, and his [weary] eyes brightened.

Why didn't he hear what his father said? He was his father's son, his father's assistant. All the men of Israel had heard Saul's decree, but Jonathan didn't because he was nowhere to be found—he was already off fighting a battle that his father was in charge of, and so he knew nothing about the oath. Jonathan had already assumed his father's authority in just the same way his father had taken Samuel's authority. So the process didn't stop with Saul.

> Then one of the men told him, Your father strictly charged the men with an oath, saying, Cursed be the man who eats any food today. And the people were exhausted and faint.
>
> —1 SAMUEL 14:28

The process of disobedience had moved from Saul to his son Jonathan. But the process had not yet stopped. It would continue further.

Jonathan Denounces His Father

Right away, Jonathan started speaking against his father, against his leadership. He began to judge the instruction of his father, not being able to discern spiritually what was really happening inside of him. He was under his father's spirit of disobedience from the prince of the power of the air. He was being influenced by the spirit that challenges and disrespects authority. Notice what he told the men who had come to him:

> Then Jonathan said, My father has troubled the land.... How much better if the men had eaten freely today of the spoil of their enemies which they found! For now the slaughter of the Philistines has not been great.
>
> —1 SAMUEL 14:29–30

This spirit kept getting worse. "They smote the Philistines that day from Michmash to Aijalon. And the people were very faint. [When night came and the oath expired] the men flew upon the spoil. They took sheep, oxen, and calves, slew them on the ground, and ate them [raw] with the blood. Then Saul was told, Behold, the men are sinning against the Lord by eating with the blood" (vv. 31–33).

Jonathan was probably going around saying, "I tasted of the honey, you know. Then I went out and fought the battle just as you did." *Hear me now.* When disobedience started to operate, this cord flowed through everything—starting when the supernatural anointing from

Samuel, Saul's spiritual authority, was interrupted. Then disobedience ran down onto Saul (from the false authority, Satan), and that same spirit of arrogance and rebellion began to operate in Jonathan. Not long after, that same vile spirit started operating in others when they defiled themselves by sinning against God and eating not just blood, but even worse, fresh blood from raw meat. Each time sin multiplied.

Tragically, Saul found himself trying to correct something his own sin had given birth to. So he turned around and built his first altar unto the Lord (v. 35). In other words, Saul continued to operate under Samuel's transmitted mantle and anointing without developing an ultimate experience and relationship with God. He had become totally dependent on the fact that he was under Samuel's leadership, yet obviously he felt he didn't have to pray or develop a personal relationship with God. He had received an impartation, but he was moving by association. I must repeat that. He was moving by association and not relationship.

> Then Saul said, Let us go down after the Philistines by night and seize and plunder them until daylight, and let us not leave a man of them. They said, Do whatever seems good to you. Then the priest said, Let us draw near here to God. And Saul asked counsel of God, Shall I go down after the Philistines? Will You deliver them into the hand of Israel? But He did not answer him that day.
>
> —1 SAMUEL 14:36–37

This indicates that Saul still desired to win the battle over the Philistines, but the opportunity had already been taken away from him. Earlier, he had stepped out from under Samuel's authority, and not long after that, Jonathan stepped out from under his authority by sneaking off and defeating a garrison of men. Therefore, the glory of the battle didn't go to Saul, who was supposed to be the leader. Think what would have happened if Jesus had stepped out from under His Father's authority on the cross. The glory would not have gone to God; it would have gone to Jesus—and Jesus wasn't the source of His own power. Had He died on that cross without the power source being in the Father, there would have been no resurrection. Jesus had to remain under the power that His Father had transmitted to Him.

It is illegal for you to operate in an anointing that doesn't belong to you. Notice what happened next: "Then Saul said, Draw near, all the chiefs of the people, and let us see how this sin [causing God's silence] arose today. For as the Lord lives, Who delivers Israel, though it be in Jonathan my son, he shall surely die. But not a man among all the people answered him" (vv. 38–39). Then Saul began a process of casting lots. When all was said and done, the Bible says, "And Saul and Jonathan were taken [by lot], but the other men went free" (v. 41). Then the story continues to unfold:

> Saul said, Cast lots between me and Jonathan my son.
> And Jonathan was taken. Saul said to Jonathan, Tell
> me what you have done. And Jonathan said, I tasted
> a little honey with the end of the rod that was in my
> hand. And behold, I must die.
>
> —1 SAMUEL 14:42–43

Jonathan already knew that his father had given his word about what would happen to anyone who disobeyed his order to fast. He also knew that his disobedience had caused this chain of events, and that although he had been the only one with energy to overthrow the enemy, he would have to pay the price for his sin.

Jonathan had fallen into disobedience because he didn't stay in position. He didn't stay under authority. He wasn't where the rest of the men were to hear the instructions of leadership. Therefore, he had done what seemed right in his own eyes. Now it seemed as though he must die for his sin.

Saul knew he must carry out his sentence of death—even though it was his own son standing before him. "May God do so, and more also," he said to Jonathan, "for you shall surely die" (v. 44). "But the people said to Saul, Shall Jonathan, who has wrought this great deliverance to Israel, die?" (v. 45).

"Why slaughter him? Why get rid of such a great leader? Jonathan won the battle for us. Oh, Jonathan is so awesome." The verse continues by saying, "So the people rescued Jonathan, and he did not die." Saul didn't obey his own public decree that the person who did this thing would be cursed and that God would surely put him to death.

This is a powerful revelation. Jonathan did a great work and performed a great wonder, so his disobedience was tolerated. We must watch for this pattern in the body of Christ today, because this same cord is flowing down in our generation.

Just because somebody is an awesome preacher or ran a powerful revival and is so anointed of God—maybe the person over your youth group grew it from one hundred to ten thousand, and it's never been that big before—doesn't mean that he or she is walking in the true character of the Holy Spirit. For just as with Saul, a residue from the one who has imparted spiritual destiny into a life may still remain on that person, as it remained on Saul—yet it will only remain for a season.

I have personally seen this happen to people over and over and over again. I have seen young men and women of God walk out from under their spiritual covering, starting their own ministry by seducing the membership of their father's house to follow them—and their ministries seem successful for a season. And when they have finished walking far enough from under that covering, I began to see the demise of that ministry. If you don't believe what I'm saying, I will prove to you through Scripture that there is a mantle of the anointing that radiates from a leader by way of depth, height, and width.

When Saul was chasing David in 1 Samuel 19, and he sent three sets of men to kill him, David ran back to the covering of Samuel. The Bible said that before they even reached David—while they saw him afar off—the anointing that was upon Samuel came upon them from afar off, and instead of killing David, they prophesied to him. So Saul said, "Forget this...I'm going to kill him." And when Saul was yet miles away, he came under the spirit of Samuel's anointing and began to prophesy to David. When he reached Samuel and

David, Saul stripped off his clothes in front of Samuel and lay like that all night.

You can walk a certain distance from under the mantle of your spiritual father, but just as you know when you have reached the boundaries of a city, state, or country, you will know when you have reached the line of limitation in the Spirit because the blessings of the Lord will lift off of you like a blanket being lifted off of you in the dead of winter. You are still within the radius, but if you don't believe what I am saying to be a true prophecy, just keep walking in rebellion.

When you look at this story, we as the children of God had better recognize that the method that works for us will work against us if we come against the will of God. If the anointing of Samuel could be felt before an individual reached him, then why can't you believe the same anointing can be felt when an individual is walking away from him? And again, once you go past the limits of God that are upon your leader, you will be sure to fall under a curse.

Just because you put someone over the Bible study on Wednesday nights (and it's never been as big as it is now), or you put another person over the choir (and the choir is singing more awesomely than ever), it doesn't mean that individual is submitted under authority. You can't assume this person is walking according to the Word. In this last hour, character and integrity must become your first priority.

How will you know? That individual will begin to talk against the instructions of the house. That individual will tear down the vision of the man of God. That individual will begin to draw attention to himself (or herself) and away from the vision and assignment God has given to that particular ministry. That person will disrupt the orderly flow of the anointing.

Even after his sin was exposed, Jonathan became a great warrior. He fought battle after battle, but he wasn't able to hold his own. How do I know this? First Samuel 14:52 says, "There was severe war against the Philistines all the days of Saul, and whenever Saul saw any mighty or [outstandingly] courageous man, he attached him to himself."

Saul's Third Encounter With Authority

God still didn't forget His word to Saul. He sent the same man who had poured oil over him earlier—Samuel—back to him again. Samuel told Saul, "The Lord originally sent me to anoint you king over His people Israel. Now listen and heed the words of the Lord. You have already stepped over the anointing and cut short your reign as king. Now, once again, God is trying you. So hear these instructions carefully." (See 1 Samuel 15:1.)

> Thus says the Lord of hosts, I have considered and will punish what Amalek did to Israel, how he set himself against him in the way when [Israel] came out of Egypt. Now go and smite Amalek and utterly destroy all they have.
>
> —1 SAMUEL 15:2–3

Saul began to do what the Lord had commanded. He assembled the men and went forth to Amalek. There was going to be a great battle. But when it was all said and done, once again Saul failed to do all that God instructed him to do. He spared Agag, the king of Amalek (v. 8). I can just hear God say, "Here we go again."

Saul's earlier disobedience in burning incense against the will of God had caused his son Jonathan to come out from under his father's authority. It had caused Saul to listen to the people and then refuse to rebuke Jonathan because Jonathan had done a mighty wonder. Even after this, God gave Saul a third opportunity: "Now go and smite Amalek and utterly destroy all they have; do not spare them, but kill both man and woman, infant and suckling, ox and sheep, camel and donkey" (v. 3). Let me make this clear. All means all. God said, "Kill everybody." He didn't instruct Saul to take anyone alive! But once again, Saul stepped out from under spiritual authority and stepped into false authority:

> Saul and the people spared Agag and the best of the sheep, oxen, fatlings, lambs, and all that was good, and would not utterly destroy them; but all that was

undesirable or worthless they destroyed utterly. Then the word of the Lord came to Samuel, saying, I regret making Saul king, for he has turned back from following Me and has not performed my commands. And Samuel was grieved and angry [with Saul], and he cried to the Lord all night.

—1 SAMUEL 15:9–11

Don't think that when you walk in disobedience, leadership doesn't feel it, because they do. Even today, any real spiritual father or mother would weep and cry when the anointing is lifted off of someone, because it's as if that person had died naturally. There is nothing worse than having the anointing lifted off of your life because of disobedience—especially when you have received a rich impartation of an untainted anointing.

It's a tragedy. Samuel had transmitted his anointing to Saul after having waited in the tabernacle for years (during a time when the word of the Lord was shut up to Israel). Samuel was the first to hear God speak again, and Saul disobeyed Him three times in a row.

Samuel walked out the word he had been given. He kept himself clean before the Father, and God kept him separated and consecrated. Saul received a pure impartation and allowed his flesh to taint it. Saul took Agag; the people didn't do it. Yet, when Samuel confronted him, Saul passed the blame:

> And Samuel said, What then means this bleating of the sheep in my ears, and the lowing of the oxen which I hear? Saul said, They have brought them from the Amalekites; for the people spared the best of the sheep and oxen to sacrifice to the Lord your God, but the rest we have utterly destroyed.
>
> —1 SAMUEL 15:14–15

The people did what they did because Saul had broken the orderly flow of the anointing. They spared the best of the sheep and oxen because Saul had spared King Agag. Always look at the pattern. Whenever there is disobedience in the leadership, it breeds disobedience in the people. Look at verse 16:

> Then Samuel said to Saul, Stop! I will tell you what the Lord said to me tonight. Saul said to him, Say on.

Now remember, whoever has been given authority to impart also has authority to rebuke.

First, I'd like to point out that pride goes before destruction, and a haughty spirit before a fall...and it always manifests in cockiness and arrogance.

> Samuel said, When you were small in your own sight [*when you didn't have anything and nobody knew who you were...when you were out looking for donkeys*], were you not made the head of the tribes of Israel, and the Lord anointed you king over Israel? And the Lord sent you on a mission and said, Go, utterly destroy the sinners, the Amalekites; and fight against them until they are consumed. Why then did you not obey the voice of the Lord, but swooped down upon the plunder and did evil in the Lord's sight? Saul said to Samuel, Yes, I have obeyed the voice of the Lord and have gone the way which the Lord sent me, and have brought Agag king of Amalek and have utterly destroyed the Amalekites. But the people took from the spoil sheep and oxen, the chief of the things to be utterly destroyed, to sacrifice to the Lord your God in Gilgal.
>
> —1 SAMUEL 15:17–21

True spiritual parents will put you in check. They will provoke you to take your mind back to where God brought you from, to who and what you were before the Father caused this great transmitting of His power to be imparted into your life, in order to show you how far you have gotten off course. Do not think that this is out of order, because Zechariah 13:1–6 says:

In that day there shall be a fountain opened for the house of David and for the inhabitants of Jerusalem [to cleanse them from] sin and uncleanness. And in that day, says the Lord of hosts, I will cut off the names of the idols from the land, and they shall no more be remembered; and also I will remove from the land the [false] prophets and the unclean spirit. And if anyone again appears [falsely] as a prophet, then his father and his mother who bore him shall say to him, You shall not live, for you speak lies in the name of the Lord; and his father and his mother who bore him shall thrust him through when he prophesies. And in that day the [false] prophets shall each be ashamed of his vision when he prophesies, nor will he wear a hairy or rough garment to deceive, but he will [deny his identity and] say, I am no prophet. I am a tiller of the ground, for I have been made a bond servant from my youth. And one shall say to him, What are these wounds on your breast or between your hands? Then he will answer, Those with which I was wounded [when disciplined] in the house of my [loving] friends.

Now, I have to let you read what *The Message* Bible says:

"On the Big Day, a fountain will be opened for the family of David and all the leaders of Jerusalem for washing away their sins, for scrubbing their stained and soiled lives clean. On the Big Day"—this is GOD-of-the-Angel-Armies speaking—"I will wipe out the store-bought gods, erase their names from memory. People will forget they ever heard of them. And I'll get rid of the prophets who polluted the air with their diseased words. If anyone dares persist in spreading diseased, polluting words, his very own parents will step in and say, 'That's it! You're finished! Your lies about GOD put everyone in danger,' and then they'll stab him to death in the very act of prophesying lies about GOD—his own parents, mind you! On the Big Day, the lying prophets will be publicly exposed and humiliated. Then they'll wish they'd never swindled people with their 'visions.' No more masquerading in prophet clothes. But they'll deny they've even heard of such things: 'Me, a prophet? Not me. I'm a farmer—grew up on the farm.' And if someone says, 'And so where did you get that black eye?' they'll say, 'I ran into a door at a friend's house.'"

There is a powerful revelation in Saul's response. Saul didn't say, "Yea, I have obeyed the Lord." He said, "Yea, I have obeyed the voice of the Lord." Saul did not have a relationship with God on a personal, spiritual level. His anointing had been imparted to him through the man of God, Samuel. Saul knew nothing about the prophetic; he knew nothing about prophesying or what to do when the mighty Spirit of God came upon him. But he presumed to operate on that level, even though he knew it wasn't true. That's why he finished his sentence by saying, "... *to sacrifice to the Lord your God*" (1 Sam. 15:21). Did you hear what Saul just said? He didn't say "our God," because he received an anointing to be king from a man who knew God. Saul himself did not have a relationship with God. That's why he was able to say "your God."

Earlier in verse 20, Saul said, "I have obeyed the voice of the Lord and have gone the way which the Lord *sent me*" (emphasis added). He did not say, "I have gone the way God *instructed you* to tell me." This is the root of the problem. When you walk in pride and step out from under leadership, you begin to walk in a spirit of delusion. You think God is saying things to you that He isn't saying. That's why a novice can't be a leader. (See 1 Timothy 3, especially verse 6.)

When you "step over" into an anointing and the mantle isn't yours, it becomes perversion. Once the spirit of perversion has entered in—meaning something that was ordained of God has begun to flow in an incorrect manner—it presents a reflection of the truth of God, but it actually yields the opposite result: it reverses His commands. Perversion is always laced with the truth. It's laced with *some* of the things God has said, but His words get turned around and twisted. Then, what God has spoken is brought outside of His order.

The order of the Lord can be perverted today. So it is critical to understand that His order for your life may not be His order for someone else. For example, somebody you know may be getting along fine spiritually, someone who is living in some remote part of Alaska and doesn't have a pastor. Nobody is up there except two or three little missionary sisters who live in an igloo—so the Lord allows them to become submitted one to another.

But if you live in a populated area and were once a crack addict or a prostitute (or maybe you were caught in a sexual sin), God has appointed somebody to birth you out and put you through a deliverance to free you from these things. That person has been anointed to transmit a "measure" of God into your life. If you break the pattern of what God has sent into your life to govern, guide, and counsel you, and you become your own counsel and "the voice of the Lord" in your own life, you can easily pervert what

> **LEADERSHIP IS GOD'S WAY. IT'S OUR SAFETY NET.**

God is saying because you haven't gone far enough in purification to rightfully discern and divide the Word. In order to hear clearly the Father's voice and receive His portion for you, you must first reach a level of maturity in Christ.

When you interrupt God's orderly flow of the anointing through your leader, what you are really saying is, "I don't need this person." Let me tell you something. I am forty-five years old, but I will always need my mother. As long as God sees fit to place her over my life, there will be some areas where I will always need her. There will also be areas in my life where I will always need my pastor. Why? Spiritual counsel is the order of the Lord.

There is another way that the anointing upon a life can be perverted.

When Saul responded to Samuel's correction, he didn't say, "The instruction that you [Samuel] gave me..." He said, "I...have gone the way which the Lord sent me, and have brought Agag king of Amalek and have utterly destroyed the Amalekites. But the people took from the spoil sheep and oxen, the chief of the things to be utterly destroyed, to sacrifice to the Lord your God in Gilgal" (1 Sam. 15:20–21).

The enemy wants to make us believe that the Lord is more interested in what we sacrifice to Him—how we direct the choir, how good our message might be, everything involved with how we go about "doing good"—than He is in our obedience. We pervert the will of the Lord when we change it into a false glory, because the Lord isn't glorified when we walk in disobedience. I don't care how beautiful it sounds when songs of worship come out of our mouths. It doesn't matter how intellectual the preached word is when it escapes our lips. God doesn't get the glory until we are walking in obedience to what *He says*.

Many people are constantly offering God sacrifices and constantly telling Him things like, "Well, I'm in Sunday school every week. I haven't missed a Sunday in ten years." "I'm the best choir director that anybody has ever seen...I have ten Grammys, nine Dove Awards, and five Stellar Awards. My record is at the top of the charts." But when it comes down to submitting to authority, submitting to the voice of God, and walking in obedience—respecting and acknowledging another man's authority, being yielded to the will of the one that has been called over us—we can't do that. And when we don't, the Bible has the same answer for us that Samuel had for Saul:

> Samuel said, Has the Lord as great a delight in burnt offerings and sacrifices as in obeying the voice of the Lord? Behold, to obey is better than sacrifice, and to hearken than the fat of rams.
>
> —1 SAMUEL 15:22

In other words, it is better to listen and respond to the voice of the Lord than it is to put attention on what you give back to Him. To hearken means to listen attentively.[1] Be attentive to God. Pay attention to every detail He reveals instead of what you sacrifice (i.e., the fat of rams). In other words, being attentive unto God is more consecrated than a physical sacrifice—so it's better to hearken and pay attention to Him than to try pleasing Him with empty works. Remember the example of Martha, who was "overly occupied" with "much serving" when Jesus sat in her home. It was Mary who chose "the good portion" (Luke 10:38–42).

Martha chose to work. She did not recognize when it was time to put down her works and sit at the Master's feet. What happens when a person works more than they eat? He or she begins to complain. Jesus answered Martha's complaint by saying, "You chose to work, but Mary chose the portion that shall never be taken away."

Somebody else can come after you have long gone from a ministry and do what you did, but what you eat in the Spirit is your eternal portion.

CHAPTER 6

The Generational Curse

*D*isobedience runs from generation to generation, bringing curses upon each one. For Scripture says:

> I am the Lord your God, Who has brought you out of the land of Egypt, out of the house of bondage. You shall have no other gods before or besides Me. You shall not make yourself any graven image [to worship it] or any likeness of anything that is in the heavens above, or that is in the earth beneath, or that is in the water under the earth; you shall not bow down yourself to them or serve them; for I the Lord your God am a jealous God, visiting the iniquity of the fathers upon the children to the third and fourth generation of those who hate Me.
>
> —EXODUS 20:2–5

To understand the spiritual principles at work, let's look at the life of Uzziah by taking a closer look at the example of his father, Amaziah.

> Amaziah was twenty-five years old when he began to reign, and he reigned twenty-nine years in Jerusalem. His mother was Jehoaddan of Jerusalem. He did right in the Lord's sight, but not with a perfect or blameless heart.
>
> —2 CHRONICLES 25:1–2

This Scripture portion goes on to tell how Amaziah slew those who had killed his father but spared their children according to the Law of Moses (vv. 3–4). Then he assembled the men of Judah and Benjamin to lead them out for war against Edom. Amaziah made sure he kept the Law of Moses (which he saw as being from God), and then he followed the initial counsel of the prophet before going to war with Edom (vv. 7–10). Let's see what happened next:

> After Amaziah came back from the slaughter of the Edomites, he brought their gods and set them up to be his gods and bowed before them and burned incense to them. So the anger of the Lord was kindled against Amaziah, and He sent to him a prophet, who said, Why have you sought after the gods of the people, which could not deliver their own people out of your hand? As he was talking, the king said to him, Have we made you the king's counselor? Stop it! Why should you be put to death? The prophet stopped but said, I know that God has determined to destroy you, because you have done this and ignored my counsel.
>
> —2 Chronicles 25:14–16

Amaziah heeded one prophetic warning, but then he rejected the Lord's rebuke that came through a prophet in his own house.

We see this same principle in many who are called today. There are leaders who have honored the prophets of old but who fail to honor the prophets God is sending from among them to speak into their lives today. When pride is in operation, it will cause them to disobey the word of the Lord, either because of the mightiness of their ministries or the strength of their talents. There are always, I mean *always*, repercussions, which do not stop with the spiritual parents. These repercussions will flow down from generation to generation as the Scripture has declared.

In anger, Amaziah said, "Don't I own you? You can't speak to me like that, because you'll have to give me a reason why I shouldn't kill you. We put you in the position you're in right now." Nevertheless, the prophet was under the hand of God. Amaziah didn't honor the prophet because he deemed his position to be higher than the Word of God.

You must never depend upon the strength of your ministry gift of position and ignore the word of the Lord. You will lose every time, because Scripture says, "When the enemy shall come in like a flood, the Spirit of the Lord will lift up a standard against him and put him to flight [for He will come like a rushing stream which the breath of the Lord drives]" (Isa. 59:19). When your position becomes your central focus instead of obeying the Lord, you have come under the spirit of dictatorship and control.

God will bring down false authority. Why? Because these individuals are no longer letting the Spirit of God direct them. So they start commanding people to obey the dictates of their flesh, manipulating and coercing them to agree with and do things that aren't the will of the Father.

When this happens, God's people can no longer respond properly to ministry. Then it becomes no more than a club and a cult. Why? The spirit of control has silenced the mouth of God.

So as a leader, when you see these issues running like a cord throughout your ministry, this becomes God's way of revealing to you that there are some unsurrendered areas in your life. You need to check what you are birthing and imparting into your people, because they are giving back what they have received from you.

Remember the prophet's challenge to Amaziah: "I know that God has determined to destroy you, because you have done this and ignored my counsel" (2 Chron. 25:16). In other words, he was saying, "You brought me in so that you could submit unto the anointing of God upon me." Please pay close attention to this. Pastors and leaders are accountable, just like lay members, their children, and the sons and daughters of God. Real authority is always accountable to authority.

When Amaziah conquered the Edomites, the Word of God said he became so lifted up by what he had conquered that he brought their gods back and worshiped them. Amaziah began to boast about his victory, because he was no longer operating in the Spirit of the Lord—he was moving in his own might and power.

Listen closely. When we begin to worship what we have established—how big our ministries have grown, how awesomely the church has been established, and so on—then we have made an idol of what we have conquered. That's what Amaziah (and others) did. And when he did this, the anger of the Lord was kindled against Amaziah, and He sent unto him a prophet.

As you continue reading this story, you will see that Amaziah was eventually overthrown and taken hostage (vv. 15–25). The last verses in the chapter say, "Now after Amaziah turned away from the Lord, they made a conspiracy against him in Jerusalem, and he fled to Lachish. But they sent to Lachish and slew him there. And they brought him upon horses and buried him with his fathers in the city of [David in] Judah" (vv. 27–28). Amaziah was mighty, and his kingdom was strengthened until he became exalted in his own eyes. When he felt that he no longer needed to seek after God or to receive the counsel of the Lord, Amaziah's sins ultimately led to his death.

I know this is a lot for you, reader. But there is a reason why I must lay such a thick foundation in obedience and generational curses. So please bear with me and trust the fact that this is a prophetic word to you—not just another book.

The Fruit of Uzziah

Uzziah was Amaziah's son. The first verse in the twenty-sixth chapter of 2 Chronicles says, "All the people of Judah took Uzziah, who was sixteen years old, and made him king in place of his father Amaziah." Remember that young Uzziah had watched his father, so he saw what happened in the kingdom.

> Uzziah was sixteen years old when he began his fifty-two-year reign in Jerusalem. His mother was Jecoliah of Jerusalem. He did right in the Lord's sight, to the extent of all that his father Amaziah had done. He set

himself to seek God in the days of Zechariah, who
instructed him in the things of God; and as long as he
sought (inquired of, yearned for) the Lord, God made
him prosper.

—2 CHRONICLES 26:3–5

Uzziah submitted himself under the tutelage of Zechariah, *and as
long as he sought the Lord,* God prospered him. Unlike his father, he
received his portion from the man of God. As a result, Uzziah became
strong in the Lord.

He went out against the Philistines and broke down the
walls of Gath, of Jabneh, and of Ashdod, and built cities near Ashdod and elsewhere among the Philistines.
And God helped him against the Philistines, and
the Arabs who dwelt in Gur-baal and the Meunim.
The Ammonites paid tribute to Uzziah, and his
fame spread abroad even to the border of Egypt, for
he became very strong. Also Uzziah built towers in
Jerusalem at the Corner Gate, the Valley Gate, and at
the angle of the wall, and fortified them. Also he built
towers in the wilderness and hewed out many cisterns,
for he had much livestock, both in the lowlands and
in the tableland. And he had farmers and vinedressers
in the hills and in the fertile fields [of Carmel], for he
loved farming.

—2 CHRONICLES 26:6–10

The list of Uzziah's accomplishments continues through the fif-
teenth verse. Uzziah accomplished things that had never been done
before. He was following in his spiritual father's stead, seeking the Lord
and being made able to do great and mighty works.

However, the cord of disobedience from his father had been
planted deep in Uzziah's soul—and he eventually repeated what he
had seen in his natural father. The sixteenth verse says:

> But when [King Uzziah] was strong, he became proud
> to his destruction; and he trespassed against the Lord
> his God, for he went into the temple of the Lord to
> burn incense on the altar of incense.

Do you see the pattern? At the beginning of his reign, King Uzziah was under spiritual authority. He was submitted to the established way for God's house to operate and the oil of the anointing to be released. But then the time came when he stepped over it, attempting to operate in a spiritual office that was not his. When you become so great in your own eyes that you think you can operate in a spiritual office God has not anointed and appointed you for, you are putting yourself in a dangerous position. Uzziah was not a priest; he was a king. So he stepped out of his place and perverted God's divine order.

God has an intended purpose for each of His children. It is clear from the story about Uzziah that God intended for Uzziah simply to be the king and nothing more. The Lord had not anointed him to be a priest. But, like the story of Saul we studied earlier in this book, once again, strength breeds pride, which led to disobedience. We must be careful when the Lord begins to strengthen us in ministry—when we start seeing the fruits of our labor. We must be careful when the Lord starts allowing our names to be spread abroad and we gain recognition, because strength can creep in unnoticed and create a foothold for the spirit of arrogance.

Uzziah trespassed against the Lord when he went into the temple to burn incense on the altar of incense. So Azariah the priest went in after him along with eighty priests of the Lord—men of courage and discipline.

> They opposed King Uzziah and said to him, It is not for
> you, Uzziah, to burn incense to the Lord, but for the
> priests, the sons of Aaron, who are set apart to burn
> incense. Withdraw from the sanctuary; you have tres-
> passed, and that will not be to your credit and honor
> before the Lord God. Then Uzziah was enraged.
> —2 CHRONICLES 26:18–19

When sons and daughters operate under the spirit of pride, they become strong in their own eyes. And anytime they are corrected they become enraged:

> He had a censer in his hand to burn incense. And while he was enraged with the priests, leprosy broke out on his forehead before the priests in the house of the Lord, beside the incense altar. And as Azariah the chief priest and all the priests looked upon him, behold, he was leprous on his forehead! So they forced him out of there; and he also made haste to get out, because the Lord had smitten him. And King Uzziah was a leper to the day of his death, and, being a leper, he dwelt in a separate house, for he was excluded from the Lord's house. And Jotham his son took charge of the king's household, ruling the people of the land.
>
> —2 CHRONICLES 26:19–21

Uzziah stepped over the spiritual authority God had appointed for him and became a diseased king under a false anointing. The same thing is happening in the church today. Many people are still stepping out of their appointed spiritual positions and moving into false authority. Some are preachers, but they are diseased. Others are evangelists, and they have become diseased, also—they have stepped out of the will of the Lord by way of their own strength.

Paul put it this way in 2 Corinthians 12:5–10:

> ...of myself [personally] I will not boast, except as regards my infirmities (my weaknesses). Should I desire to boast, I shall not be a witless braggart, for I shall be speaking the truth. But I abstain [from it], so that no one may form a higher estimate of me than [is justified by] what he sees in me or hears from me. And to keep me from being puffed up and too much elated by the exceeding greatness (preeminence) of these revelations, there was given me a thorn (a splin-

ter) in the flesh, a messenger of Satan, to rack and buffet and harass me, to keep me from being excessively exalted. Three times I called upon the Lord and besought [Him] about this and begged that it might depart from me; but He said to me, My grace (My favor and loving-kindness and mercy) is enough for you [sufficient against any danger and enables you to bear the trouble manfully]; for My strength and power are made perfect (fulfilled and completed) and show themselves most effective in [your] weakness.

Therefore, I will all the more gladly glory in my weaknesses and infirmities, that the strength and power of Christ (the Messiah) may rest (yes, may pitch a tent over and dwell) upon me! So for the sake of Christ, I am well pleased and take pleasure in infirmities, insults, hardships, persecutions, perplexities and distresses; for when I am weak [in human strength], then am I [truly] strong (able, powerful in divine strength).

Paul understood that when you walk in human strength, you are usurping the authority of God. With Uzziah, however, not only did leprosy strike him, but also he was excluded from the house of the Lord. He didn't lose his kingdom, but he lost influence.

For example, you may be reading this book, thinking, *I don't feel a witness that I'm still supposed to be in this church. People don't really accept my ministry. I feel like it's time for me to go.* Noooo! It is *not* time to change churches. It is possible you may have become leprous by stepping out from under proper authority and into your own counsel, which has caused you to lose the spirit of humility. And where there is no humility, there is no brokenness. And without brokenness, there is no room for correction or counsel. Proverbs 16:18 says, "Pride goes before destruction, and a haughty spirit before a fall."

Reflecting on Uzziah, then, we can truly understand that in the midst of being corrected you can still be blinded because you can't see past your own strengths and accomplishments. Uzziah raged against God and the people of God, and he was a leper until the day he died. Sadly, even in death, he had no influence. Because he had become diseased, he had to be buried in the field of the kings outside the royal tombs (2 Chron. 26:23).

In the next chapter, we will take a look at the power of rebuke, because the principles of God will stand. Whatever pattern we live by, we must understand we are not living for ourselves, but we are living to transfer a mantle to the next generation. So my question is, "What mantle are you transferring?"

A review of the story of King Uzziah helps us to see this principle clearly. Amaziah, as king in Jerusalem, stepped into false authority through pride. His son Uzziah assumed the throne and behaved himself the same way his father did. In 2 Chronicles 27 we meet Uzziah's son Jotham, who was twenty-five when he started his reign (like his grandfather Amaziah). He reigned for sixteen years (his father's, Uzziah, age when he began his reign). Jotham was a man of God.

> He built the Upper Gate of the Lord's house and did much building on the wall of Ophel. Moreover, he built cities in the hill country of Judah, and in the forests he built forts and towers.... Jotham grew mighty, for he ordered his ways in the sight of the Lord his God.
> —2 CHRONICLES 27:3–4, 6

Jotham was the third generation. Jotham had most likely heard about what happened to his grandfather, and he also watched his father, Uzziah. He started ruling when his father was leprous, so he guarded what he did and walked in a level of obedience unto God.

But the generational pattern still had an effect on his reign, because Jotham didn't get everything right. He did not restore the hearts of the people back to God. Second Chronicles 28:1–2 says:

> Ahaz was twenty years old when he began his sixteen-year reign in Jerusalem. He did not do right in the sight of the Lord, like David his father [forefather].

> But he walked in the ways of the kings of Israel and
> even made molten images for the Baals.
> —2 Chronicles 28:1–2

The cord ran down to Ahaz because he was still in the lineage of Amaziah. And like his great-grandfather (and grandfather), Ahaz "walked in the ways of the kings of Israel," not in the ways of God. He even made molten images for idol worship.

> And he burned incense in the Valley of Ben-hinnom
> [son of Hinnom] and burned his sons as an offering,
> after the abominable customs of the [heathen] nations
> whom the Lord drove out before the Israelites.
> —2 Chronicles 28:3

To continue the pattern, Ahaz had come to the point where not only was he disobeying God, but also he was twice as corrupt as his forefathers—burning incense to false gods and even burning up his own lineage. He was killing the very sons to whom he was supposed to hand his mantle. Look at the pattern. Amaziah disrespected the prophet and disobeyed God. Uzziah disrespected the temple and the priesthood. Jotham ordered his ways in the Lord's sight, but still the people were corrupt (2 Chron. 27:2).

Now in the fourth generation, the false anointing of disobedience comes into full bloom upon Ahaz. He started sacrificing his own sons because he was a king under a false anointing.

Leadership, hear me. Pastors, evangelists, or teachers without an anointing will begin to destroy what's underneath them with false pressure, putting demands on their followers that they themselves could never adhere to. Many times this process is referred to as, "I'm breaking you." Many

> THIS THING ABOUT BAAL MAY MEAN NOTHING TO YOU RIGHT NOW. BUT IT WILL HAVE SUCH A PROFOUND IMPACT ON YOUR LIFE, LIKE YOU WOULD NOT BELIEVE, WHEN THIS MESSAGE IS FINISHED. SO KEEP THAT NAME *Baal* IN MIND.

of us as leaders must be careful how we handle sheep—for God's way is the way of the skilled surgeon. You cut out the disease, but you save the life. God is the only Breaker. He is the Potter. Because what He breaks, He knows how to put it back together again. Hosea 6:1–2 says, "Come and let us return to the Lord, for He has torn so that He may heal us; He has stricken so that He may bind us up. After two days He will revive us (quicken us, give us life); on the third day He will raise us up that we may live before Him."

False authorities destroy the people under their rule instead of birthing them out. Think about it. That's what the antichrist is trying to do now until the end of time—destroy God's children. He wants every person on the face of the earth to spend an eternity (with him) in the lake of fire.

Let's take a closer look at Ahaz:

> He sacrificed also and burnt incense in the high places, on the hills, and under every green tree. Therefore the Lord his God gave Ahaz into the power of the king of Syria, who defeated him and carried away a great multitude of the Jews as captives, taking them to Damascus. And he was also delivered into the hands of the king of Israel, who smote Judah with a great slaughter.
>
> —2 CHRONICLES 28:4–5

When you look at his demise, history repeated itself. Amaziah had fought against the Edomites and won—but then he brought their gods back to Israel with him and bowed before them (2 Chron. 25:11–14). Now, two generations later, the Edomites defeat King Ahaz:

> At the time King Ahaz sent to the king of Assyria to help him. For again the Edomites had come and smitten Judah and carried away captives. The Philistines had invaded the cities of the low country of the South (the Negeb) of Judah, and had taken Beth-shemesh, Aijalon, Gederoth, and Soco, and also Timnah and

Gimzo, with their villages, and they settled there. For the Lord brought Judah low because of Ahaz king of Israel, for Ahaz had dealt with reckless cruelty against Judah and had been faithless [had transgressed sorely] against the Lord.

—2 CHRONICLES 28:16–19

Please be reminded. Scripture says it is better that you would be tossed into the middle of the sea than to harm one of God's little ones. (See Matthew 18:6.)

Do you see the cord of disobedience and false authority? It keeps getting worse from generation to generation. When you walk in a spirit of disobedience and are not submitted unto God, that spirit breeds itself down onto your sons. It passes from one generation to the next, and the generation that follows becomes even more wicked. By the fourth generation of Amaziah, the entire nation of Israel had gone into captivity.

This is why God cries out for every believer to walk in purification, even if you don't function in a spiritual office. For example, you might be thinking, *I'm not a pastor, so this doesn't apply to me.* I beg to differ. Every member in every church has a following—I don't care if you are a church staff member and practically live at church or if you are busy with work and family and can only attend church once or twice a week. If you are active in the church, somebody admires the anointing on your life. Somebody in that ministry is drawn to the flow of the anointing upon you.

You have relationships in the church, whether or not you are ordained into the ministry. Your lifestyle and the way you handle yourself cause others either to see God and embrace the divine flow of the anointing or to be destroyed by the cord of disobedience. Think about it. People get hurt in the church every day—and they either keep their eyes on God and do what's right unto Him, or they draw back and leave the church because of failed relationships.

God is crying out for sanctification and purification, not just for our sakes, but so that the orderly flow of the anointing would not be hindered. If God's anointing is flowing out of our lives, generations further down the cord of Christendom will not be hindered. People beyond us will be saved and become completely submitted to God. If we can keep the orderly flow of the anointing from generation to generation, what a mighty church we will be!

Ahaz ruled with *reckless cruelty* against Judah and was faithless unto the Lord. So when he sent out to Assyria for help, the Bible says, "So Tilgath-pilneser king of Assyria came to him and distressed him without strengthening him" (2 Chron. 28:20). Why? If you are walking in disobedience, you do not receive help from others—nobody can help you because the Word states you shall reap what you have sown. (See Galatians 6:7.) That is why you need to stay in purity before the Lord.

Do you find yourself praying, "O God, if I just had somebody to help me"? If so, you need to check your submission to spiritual authority. Find out if there is a cord of disobedience, an area where you haven't been walking in submission to God. Heed the instruction in Isaiah 1:18–20:

> Come now, and let us reason together, says the Lord.
> Though your sins are like scarlet, they shall be as white
> as snow; though they are red like crimson, they shall
> be like wool. If you are willing and obedient, you shall
> eat the good of the land; but if you refuse and rebel,
> you will be devoured by the sword. For the mouth of
> the Lord has spoken it.

We are constantly challenged to walk consistently in faith toward God. If we do, we are promised in Psalm 84:11 that the Lord will walk with us: "For the Lord God is a Sun and Shield; the Lord bestows [present] grace and favor and [future] glory (honor, splendor, and heavenly bliss)! No good thing will He withhold from those who walk uprightly." Proverbs 3:5–8 tells us how to be consistent in our walk:

> Lean on, trust in, and be confident in the Lord with
> all your heart and mind and do not rely on your own

insight or understanding. In all your ways know, recognize, and acknowledge Him, and He will direct and make straight and plain your paths. Be not wise in your own eyes; reverently fear and worship the Lord and turn [entirely] away from evil. It shall be health to your nerves and sinews, and marrow and moistening to your bones.

In this hour, we cannot afford to be self-willed. We cannot afford to insist upon our own way, because if we do, everything the Lord has lined up in our lives will be aborted. Hear me. Your life and your anointing do not belong to you alone. You are accountable to the authority of God through the spiritual fathers who have gone before you. And remember, no matter what may have happened in the past, if you are willing and obedient unto God, you will eat the fat of the land. You don't have to stay under a curse!

Elisha's Double Portion

Elisha gives us a positive example of the anointing and mantle of a spiritual father being passed down to his spiritual son. Elijah walked with God. He went through a process of God leading him through different situations, and he reached the point where it was time to pass his mantle on to Elisha.

> And when they had gone over [*the Jordan River on dry land*], Elijah said to Elisha, Ask what I shall do for you before I am taken from you. And Elisha said, I pray you, let a double portion of your spirit be upon me. He said, You have asked a hard thing. However, if you see me when I am taken from you, it shall be so for you—but if not, it shall not be so.
>
> —2 KINGS 2:9–10

Elisha saw Elijah taken away, and the Bible demonstrates that Elisha did indeed double the works that Elijah had done. But Elisha first had to submit himself to training. He submitted himself unto

Elijah, walking with him daily for over twenty years before he received Elijah's mantle. This was not the first time that Elijah had placed a prophetic mantle on Elisha. When they first met, Elijah tossed his mantle on Elisha as he walked through a field where Elisha was plowing—and Elijah did not open his mouth. So Elisha had to be in tune with God and be ready to do something different. (See 1 Kings 19:19–21.)

God has called you to do greater works—and they are usually revealed as you are going about your day-to-day routine. God will come in the midst of whatever you are doing, because at the appointed time, He will send you a spiritual father to impart a new anointing upon your life.

Be careful that the enemy doesn't blind you with pride in what you think you are accomplishing. You need to recognize the new mantle that is standing in front of you—*God is waiting to toss it*. And when He tosses it, your spirit must be willing to drop what you are doing and follow after that mantle, no matter how great your "field" may be.

When your spiritual parents come, you must be willing to drop your old thoughts and ways, and say, "OK, God…there's a reason You have placed this person in my life. There's a reason You have allowed me, out of all the other people in the kingdom, to have an association with someone who is walking in power, someone who is walking closely with You." Then obey God, and submit yourself to the order of the anointing.

When that anointing comes, turn from what you are doing and submit yourself—so that you don't miss the mantle and the charge that you are supposed to receive. By looking at the consistent, faithful way that Elisha followed after the mantle of Elijah, staying under his tutelage, you can understand the purposes of God in raising him up.

Elijah was a man of integrity and a fearless reformer. On three different occasions, he was fed divine supplies from God. He trusted in the Lord and was mighty in prayer. As you read the story of Elisha, you can see how he walked under that same mantle and received a double portion.

Did you catch the revelation? In order to receive double, it has to flow down to you from someone else's measure. Then as God develops you, you begin to walk steadily in the integrity and discipline of His Word. And when you are walking in submission to the point that you are "buffeting your body" and consistently bringing your flesh under the divine will of God, another anointing is placed upon you…because of your level of obedience.

> THIS IS HOW GREATNESS IS BIRTHED: THE PORTION ALREADY WITHIN YOU BALANCES WITH THE PORTION YOU INHERIT FROM YOUR SPIRITUAL FATHER.

That is when you know that you are walking under the divine call and mantle God has placed over your life. The two have become one. Now, the anointing upon your life (and the things you should be able to accomplish in ministry) should be doubled. You should have the capacity to do double what your spiritual mentor has done, double that of the person with whom you have walked in submission to. That is why Jesus said:

> Do you not believe that I am in the Father, and that the Father is in Me? What I am telling you I do not say on My own authority and of My own accord; but the Father Who lives continually in Me does the (His) works (His own miracles, deeds of power)....I assure you, most solemnly I tell you, if anyone steadfastly believes in Me, he will himself be able to do the things that I do; and he will do even greater things than these, because I go to the Father. And I will do [I Myself will grant] whatever you ask in My Name [as presenting all that I AM], so that the Father may be glorified and extolled in (through) the Son.
>
> —JOHN 14:10, 12–13

This is what Elisha experienced through Elijah. A mantle was tossed to him, he walked through his time of tutelage and submission, and he came out speaking with twice the authority. He learned to lean on and trust in God in his entire character. Elisha lived and walked in the Spirit. He was a man of spiritual vision. And when he died, he still got the victory—because the impartation he had received from Elijah was so powerful it was in his very bones. Yes, a godly anointing multiplies.

> Elisha died, and they buried him. Bands of the Moabites invaded the land in the spring of the next year. As a man was being buried [on an open bier], such a band was seen coming; and the man was cast into Elisha's grave. And when the man being let down touched the bones of Elisha, he revived and stood on his feet.
>
> —2 KINGS 13:20–21

That's what I call power to the bone!

Breaking the Curse…for Good

Because Elisha was obedient to the Lord and diligently matured under the spiritual anointing of Elijah, he was able to move on into the destiny to which God had called him. As we discovered earlier in this chapter, however, it did not happen this way with Amaziah. Amaziah had received a false anointing from his father, Joash, who had followed after Ahaziah and Jehoram in their family line. (See 2 Chronicles 21–24.) That cord of disobedience kept flowing from generation to generation until Ahaz died.

Finally, after this fourth generation, Hezekiah was set into power with grace (represented by the number five). By the power and might of the Lord, Hezekiah fully recognized and understood that his forefathers had gravely disobeyed God—because he could clearly see the penalties they had paid.

Hezekiah was twenty-five years old, so he had reached a level of maturity. Not only did he set himself to seek the Lord, but he also started his reign by restoring the temple. He started by putting the things of God back into divine order.

> In the first year of his reign, in the first month, he opened the doors of the house of the Lord [which his father had closed] and repaired them. He brought together the priests and Levites in the square on the east and said to them, Levites, hear me! Now sanctify (purify and make free from sin) yourselves and the house of the Lord, the God of your fathers, and carry out the filth from the Holy Place. For our fathers have trespassed and have done what was evil in the sight of the Lord our God, and they have forsaken Him and have turned away their faces from the dwelling place of the Lord and have turned their backs. Also they have closed the doors of the porch and put out the lamps, and they have not burned incense or offered burnt offerings in the place holy to the God of Israel. Therefore the wrath of the Lord was upon Judah and Jerusalem, and He has delivered them to be a terror and a cause of trembling, to be an astonishment, and a hissing, as you see with your own eyes. For, behold, our fathers have fallen by the sword, and our sons, our daughters, and our wives are in captivity for this. Now it is in my heart to make a covenant with the Lord, the God of Israel, that His fierce anger may turn away from us. My sons, do not now be negligent, for the Lord has chosen you to stand in His presence, to serve Him, to be His ministers, and to burn incense to Him. Then the Levites arose.... They gathered their brethren and sanctified themselves and went in, as the king had commanded by the words of the Lord, to cleanse the house of the Lord.
>
> —2 CHRONICLES 29:3–12, 15

Let me summarize. In the first month of the first year of his reign, Hezekiah opened the doors of the temple (which are symbolic of the heart) and repaired them. Then he made a declaration and charge to the leadership, exposing the work of the enemy and confessing the sins of the fathers that led to their captivity. Finally, he moved into a new day and started the orderly flow of the anointing by declaring a new covenant with God.

Hezekiah reinforced the necessity for the priesthood to be attentive servants unto God, reminding them of their covenant responsibilities. *"Then the Levites arose..."* (v. 12). They sanctified themselves before they dared touch the work of God. That prepared them to go into the inner part of the temple and carry out the unclean things. By the eighth day (the number of new beginnings), the priests came to the porch of the Lord—and on the sixteenth day (the second interval of eight, representing divine agreement), they were finished. (See verses 16–17.)

When the priests reported back to Hezekiah, he immediately took seven bulls, rams, lambs, and he-goats—seven of each—and reinstituted the temple sacrifices to atone for the sins of the nation. After this, the song of the Lord came forth in worship until the burnt offering was complete—and then King Hezekiah and all who were with him bowed and worshiped God (vv. 21–29).

As you read the rest of 2 Chronicles 29, you will see that Hezekiah set the service of the Lord's house into order before he built his own house. And God, the eternal Father in heaven, was restored to His rightful place of glory and authority. So Hezekiah, the fifth from Amaziah, received grace to birth a new day for God's people—but notice, he did everything in "perfect" order. Everyone went back to his or her original positions in God, and the nation prospered.

Proverbs 29:2 says, "When the [uncompromisingly] righteous are in authority, the people rejoice; but when the wicked man rules, the people groan and sigh." It didn't happen until the fifth generation—but through Hezekiah, the cord of disobedience was broken, and the people were restored to order and prosperity.

It doesn't matter whether you are a spiritual father or mother, or a spiritual son or daughter; before you are tempted to jump out of position, follow the advice given by the apostle Paul to Timothy:

> I admonish and urge that petitions, prayers, intercessions, and thanksgivings be offered on behalf of all men, for kings and all who are in positions of authority or high responsibility, that [outwardly] we may pass a quiet and undisturbed life [and inwardly] a peaceable one in all godliness and reverence and seriousness in every way. For such [praying] is good and right, and [it is] pleasing and acceptable to God our Savior.
>
> —1 TIMOTHY 2:1–3

The spirit of disobedience can be broken! The satanic cord can be severed. And you can find and stay in your place in God, no matter what you have been through in the past—because Jesus has gone before you. Turn your face to seek the Lord, and walk after the Spirit, praying acceptably unto God the Father. He will help you set your spiritual house in order and get aligned to receive a heavenly impartation.

CHAPTER 7

The Power of Rebuke

*W*hen the Lord begins to channel our lives and prepare us for our next level, if our spirits haven't been matured to receive rebuke and correction, then we could miss levels in God.

Why must a spiritual leader rebuke? Rebuke keeps the spirit on course, and it ensures that you don't forfeit anything that God has for you. Correction from your spiritual parents will keep you under spiritual authority and will keep you from trusting in your own strength, thereby missing all that God has destined for you. Remember, destiny is at stake. I don't know about you, but I am not just after "a few things" God has for me. I am after all of them. Therefore, I must embrace the power of rebuke. So let's look closely at what the Lord is trying to reveal to us:

> The Lord is far from the wicked, but He hears the prayer of the [consistently] righteous (the upright, in right standing with Him). The light in the eyes [of him whose heart is joyful] rejoices the hearts of others, and good news nourishes the bones. The ear that listens to the reproof [that leads to or gives] life will remain among the wise. He who refuses and ignores instruction and correction despises himself, but he who heeds reproof gets understanding. The reverent and worshipful fear

of the Lord brings instruction in Wisdom, and humility comes before honor.

—PROVERBS 15:29–33

Job 5:17 says, "Happy and fortunate is the man whom God reproves," but Proverbs 9:8 says, "Reprove not a scorner, lest he hate you; reprove a wise man, and he will love you." If you are able to receive correction in your spirit, then you are at the place of wisdom. God helps, saves, and has mercy on fools. But He trains and corrects the wise.

A Loving Father Corrects His Children

Let me make this clear. When God puts you in the position to be rebuked, whether it's for something you have said, done, felt, or believed, He is announcing to you that He loves you. Many times we doubt God's love for us. We expect Him to minister love to us the same way another person would—because we don't have a true concept of His divine nature. God doesn't just express His love to us through presents, houses, cars, or goose bumps. He confirms His love when He corrects and rebukes us. Revelation 3:19 says:

> Those whom I [dearly and tenderly] love, I tell their faults and convict and convince and reprove and chasten [I discipline and instruct them]. So be enthusiastic and in earnest and burning with zeal and repent [changing your mind and attitude].

The Lord was speaking to the church of Laodicea—lukewarm believers who had prospered and felt as if they had "arrived." (See Revelation 3:14–18.) But God told them otherwise, compelling them to embrace correction.

Being enthusiastic and full of zeal when the spirit of rebuke comes your way means you are excited to get it right. You begin to say to yourself, *OK, where did I miss it? I understand now that I'm being corrected because God has a destiny for me.*

If God is in the process of correcting your life, He has a portion for you, and He is getting your spirit ready. Why? If you are going to be used by Him in this last hour, it has to be done according to the method by which God instructed Zerubbabel—"...not by might, nor by power, but by my Spirit...says the Lord of hosts" (Zech. 4:6). By following this method you will remain open to correction, and you will impart life unto others. If you don't impart life, you will impart the spirit of error. Proverbs 10:17 says:

> He who heeds instruction and correction is [not only himself] in the way of life [but also] is a way of life for others.

Imparting the spirit of error happens too easily—and more often than not without the leader even realizing it. This is what happened with King Saul and Jonathan. If you are in the position of a leader, you are communicating to others (even without words). Your life is saying, "The way I'm going is the way you should follow." Most people don't read the Bible; they read your life. So anything that you do incorrectly (because you have rejected the correction of the Lord), you are actually telling them, "This is the way you should act." If you are imparting the spirit of error to them, rebellion will multiply in the lives of your spiritual children.

The Divine Order of Rebuke

In the New Testament, the apostle Paul spoke these words to Titus:

> Paul, a bondservant of God and an apostle (a special messenger) of Jesus Christ (the Messiah) to stimulate and promote the faith of God's chosen ones and to lead them on to accurate discernment and recognition of and acquaintance with the Truth which belongs to and harmonizes with and tends to godliness.
>
> —TITUS 1:1

Let me restate this in common language. Paul was saying, "I'm a servant who has been ordained by God. Understand that I have been called by God to bring correction to you. I want you to understand that my job isn't to be concerned with your gifts, callings, or talents. I'm concerned with 'cutting out' a pattern for character in you."

Even during Paul's time, some were expressing their gifts but having a hard time being servants. Paul was telling Titus, "You might have been an evangelist or prophet at your old church. But if you're going to minister in our church, we're going to watch your servant-hood. If you qualify as a servant, then I know you can be trusted as a prophet." So many believers get too anxious, asserting: "Oh, the Lord gave me a word; He gave me a word." If He gave you that word, it will keep. In the meantime, your spiritual leaders need to carve character in you to bring you to the level where you can handle the word you have received. You must be made to understand that a true leader cannot allow your gifts to take you where your character can't keep you.

Who Can Rebuke?

How can you know when someone has the power to rebuke you? Why do you have to listen to what he or she has to say? What qualifies a leader? Let's start with the office of a bishop. Titus 1:6–8 says:

> [These elders should be] men who are of unquestion-able integrity and are irreproachable, the husband of [but] one wife, whose children are [well trained and are] believers, not open to the accusation of being loose in morals and conduct or unruly and disorderly. For the bishop (an overseer) as God's steward must be blameless, not self-willed or arrogant or presumptu-ous; he must not be quick-tempered or given to drink or pugnacious (brawling, violent); he must not be grasping and greedy for filthy lucre (financial gain); but he must be hospitable (loving and a friend to believers, especially to strangers and foreigners); [he must be] a lover of goodness [of good people and good things], sober-minded (sensible, discreet) upright and fair-minded, a devout man and religiously correct, temperate and keeping himself in hand.

We must understand that the feet of leadership must stand sure in their position in God, not just their authority in God. One of the first inner responses coming from one who is being rebuked is to challenge any weakness or any lack of obedience that he or she has seen in the one who is trying to rebuke. Titus 2:7–8 and Titus 1:9–16 say:

> And show your own self in all respects to be a pattern and a model of good deeds and works, teaching what is unadulterated *[not mixed or watered down; not a compromising gospel that seeks only to fill up a church]*, showing gravity [having the strictest regard for truth and purity of motive], with dignity and seriousness. And let your instruction be sound and fit and wise and wholesome, vigorous and irrefutable and above censure, so that the opponent may be put to shame, finding nothing discrediting or evil to say about us.
>
> —TITUS 2:7–8

> He must hold fast to the sure and trustworthy Word of God as he was taught it, so that he may be able both to give stimulating instruction and encouragement in sound (wholesome) doctrine and to refute and convict those who contradict and oppose it [showing the wayward their error]. For there are many disorderly and unruly men who are idle (vain, empty) and misleading talkers and self-deceivers and deceivers of others. [This is true] especially of those of the circumcision party [who have come over from Judaism]. Their mouths must be stopped, for they are mentally distressing and subverting whole families by teaching what they ought not to teach, for the purpose of getting base advantage and disreputable gain. One of their [very] number, a prophet of their own, said, Cretans are always liars, hurtful beasts, idle and lazy gluttons. And this account of them is [really] true. Because it is

[true], rebuke them sharply [deal sternly, even severely with them], so that they may be sound in the faith and free from error, [and may show their soundness by] ceasing to give attention to Jewish myths and fables or to rules [laid down] by [mere] men who reject and turn their backs on the Truth. To the pure [in heart and conscience] all things are pure, but to the defiled and corrupt and unbelieving nothing is pure; their very minds and consciences are defiled and polluted. They profess to know God [to recognize, perceive, and be acquainted with Him], but deny and disown and renounce Him by what they do; they are detestable and loathsome, unbelieving and disobedient and disloyal and rebellious, and [they are] unfit and worthless for good work (deed or enterprise) of any kind.

—TITUS 1:9–16

Many times, when leaders are rude and insensitive in how they rebuke, it is because their own sword is not sharp. In other words, there are things in their own lives that have not been cut. And when your sword is dull, you have to apply more strength and force, for example, yelling, screaming, using profanity, and calling your children names. This is spiritual abuse. For Ecclesiastes 10:10 says:

If the ax is dull and the man does not whet [sharpen] the edge, he must put forth more strength; but wisdom helps him to succeed.

We will also find a description of what God is trying to reveal to us about the temperament of leadership in 2 Timothy 2:24–26:

And the servant of the Lord must not be quarrelsome (fighting and contending). Instead, he must be kindly to everyone and mild-tempered [preserving the bond of peace]; he must be a skilled and suitable teacher, patient and forbearing and willing to suffer wrong.

He must correct his opponents with courtesy and gentleness, in the hope that God may grant that they will repent and come to know the Truth [that they will perceive and recognize and become accurately acquainted with and acknowledge it], and that they may come to their senses [and] escape out of the snare of the devil, having been held captive by him, [henceforth] to do His [God's] will.

Even Samuel found it necessary to declare himself blameless before the people in 1 Samuel 12:1–5:

And Samuel said to all Israel, I have listened to you in all that you have said to me and have made a king over you. And now, behold, the king walks before you. And I am old and gray, and behold, my sons are with you. And I have walked before you from my childhood to this day. Here I am; testify against me before the Lord and Saul His anointed. Whose ox or donkey have I taken? Or whom have I defrauded or oppressed? Or from whose hand have I received any bribe to blind my eyes? Tell me and I will restore it to you. And they said, You have not defrauded us or oppressed us or taken anything from any man's hand. And Samuel said to them, The Lord is witness against you, and His anointed is witness this day, that you have not found anything in my hand. And they answered, He is witness.

In other words, Samuel was saying to them, "I am a prophet, and I have been brought by the Lord to correct you, but who among you can spot my life? What have you seen of me that is crooked and unrighteous?"

We know that as long as we live in a human body, we are apt to make mistakes; no one at this point is perfect. But those who rebuke must be those whose lives cannot be spotted and whom the congregation knows and believes to be persons who are giving all diligence to walk in righteousness. For the Scripture says in 2 Corinthians 10:6:

> ...being in readiness to punish every [insubordinate for his] disobedience, when your own submission and obedience [as a church] are fully secured and complete.

Now, let's continue to look at the spiritual qualifications for those who must rebuke:

> I warn and counsel the elders among you (the pastors and spiritual guides of the church) as a fellow elder and as an eyewitness [called to testify] of the sufferings of Christ, as well as a sharer in the glory (the honor and splendor) that is to be revealed (disclosed, unfolded): Tend (nurture, guard, guide, and fold) the flock of God that is [your responsibility], not by coercion or constraint, but willingly; not dishonorably motivated by the advantages and profits [belonging to the office], but eagerly and cheerfully; not domineering [as arrogant, dictatorial, and overbearing persons] over those in your charge, but being examples (patterns and models of Christian living) to the flock (the congregation). And [then] when the Chief Shepherd is revealed, you will win the conqueror's crown of glory.
>
> —1 PETER 5:1–4

After a leader has been qualified by means of these particular spiritual standards, this is what empowers him to be able to have strong legs in the place of authority. He is not moved or shaken by what he sees, but his testimony becomes like the apostle Paul's testimony in Philippians 4:12–13 when he said:

> I know how to be abased and live humbly in straitened circumstances, and I know also how to enjoy plenty and live in abundance. I have learned in any and all

circumstances the secret of facing every situation, whether well-fed or going hungry, having a sufficiency and enough to spare or going without and being in want. I have strength for all things in Christ Who empowers me [I am ready for anything and equal to anything through Him Who infuses inner strength into me; I am self-sufficient in Christ's sufficiency].

This, therefore, assists him in being able to accept and execute the charge in 2 Timothy 4:1–4, which says:

I charge [you] in the presence of God and of Christ Jesus, Who is to judge the living and the dead, and by (in the light of) His coming and His kingdom: Herald and preach the Word! Keep your sense of urgency [stand by, be at hand and ready], whether the opportunity seems to be favorable or unfavorable. [Whether it is convenient or inconvenient, whether it is welcome or unwelcome, you as preacher of the Word are to show people in what way their lives are wrong.] And convince them, rebuking and correcting, warning and urging and encouraging them, being unflagging and inexhaustible in patience and teaching. For the time is coming when [people] will not tolerate (endure) sound and wholesome instruction, but, having ears itching [for something pleasing and gratifying], they will gather to themselves one teacher after another to a considerable number, chosen to satisfy their own liking and to foster the errors they hold, and will turn aside from hearing the truth and wander off into myths and man-made fictions.

The Necessity of Open Rebuke

Now that we have established the scriptural purpose of rebuke, let's see what the dictionary says:

To express sharp, stern disapproval of; reprove; reprimand. A sharp reproof; reprimand.[1]

We must understand that the majority of the people who are called
to be spiritual parents more than likely will be parents to more than
one child, especially when it comes down to pastors. For that reason, it
becomes almost impossible to make sure that every person's life is corrected in private. The majority of the time when there is a rebuke to be
given openly, it is oftentimes given to one who has been given enough
opportunity for spiritual maturity. He is one that, by now, understands
the love of his father and does not take the rebuke as an opportunity to
draw away; but if he is wise, he uses it as an opportunity to draw near.

I believe that the Holy Spirit wants us to be aware of the fact that it
is in these times when people are rebuked they use this as an opportunity to say, "I think it's time for me to leave the church," when frankly
speaking, that is not the correct time for you to leave the ministry.
That is the time for you to go in prayer and pray that God would reveal
to you, even more, His will for your life. Because remember, when
you leave a ministry, you are being passed on to your next level. So
how can you successfully receive from your next level when you are
offended by your past? There will come a time, whether now or later,
that you will have to face that person again.

Let me say this. Rebuke is painful, but it is intended to shave the
flesh and mature the spirit. So though my flesh may be hurting, my
spirit man is being matured. If you keep this thought pattern in mind,
you can go on to spiritual perfection.

When your spiritual parent is rebuking you, what he or she is really saying is, "This thing is causing you and I to be separated. And
because there are younger children watching, if I don't use this opportunity as a parent to openly rebuke you, there is a very strong possibil-
ity that a baby Christian would do exactly what you just did and not
survive the experience." So in rebuking openly, one may be pained,
but the flock shall be saved. For Proverbs 27:5 says, "Open rebuke is
better than love that is hidden."

The majority of the time when a person is openly rebuked, his or her actions, which have provoked the rebuke, have openly affected the congregation. Therefore, this rebuke cannot be given in private, because it has affected the body of Christ openly. For Titus 1:10–13 says:

> For there are many disorderly and unruly men who are idle (vain, empty) and misleading talkers and self-deceivers and deceivers of others. [This is true] especially of those of the circumcision party [who have come over from Judaism]. Their mouths must be stopped, for they are mentally distressing and subverting whole families by teaching what they ought not to teach, for the purpose of getting base advantage and disreputable gain. One of their [very] number, a prophet of their own, said, Cretans are always liars, hurtful beasts, idle and lazy gluttons. And this account of them is [really] true. Because it is [true], rebuke them sharply [deal sternly, even severely with them], so that they may be sound in the faith and free from error.

This is why, when speaking of correcting elders, 1 Timothy 5:20 says, "Them that sin rebuke before all, that others also may fear" (KJV).

If an individual does something that affects his or her life personally, and if it's the only life that is being affected by their actions, then that is a private rebuke. But if his or her actions have affected the body of Christ or the local church at large, then this is a probable situation for open rebuke.

Incorrect Rebuke

On the note of open rebuke, many times I have experienced incorrect rebuke. But I thank God that I was mature enough to eat the meat and throw away the bones. However, there are many whom I have witnessed receive the same type of incorrect rebuke and end up back in the world. What do I mean by incorrect rebuke?

First of all, the pulpit is not to be used as a place of "throw off." If the leadership believes that it is the right timing to rebuke an individual openly, then he must be prepared to be a skilled surgeon. In other words, there should not be innuendoes, throw offs, and hints about subject matter. The individual should be told first:

1. About your love for him or her
2. About your respect for their ministry, whatever that ministry is
3. About what you see as the success of his or her future

However, then that person must be told in a "however state" what he or she has done incorrectly. Therefore, cutting out the cancer, but saving the life. By doing it in this fashion, not only do you save that person, but you also save those who look up to and respect him. This is the pattern by which I personally have seen the best results in my life. I have had people come to me after I had been openly rebuked, months later, who were baby saints that said to me, "I almost did exactly what you did, but I remembered how Pastor corrected you—and it saved my life."

When you throw off innuendoes, you ignite the spirit of gossip in your church. People will leave the services after you preach saying things like, "Who is he talking about? That sounds like this one… No, it sounds like that one…" This ignites factions in the church! This is the same behavior for which Paul rebuked the believers in the church at Corinth:

> I fed you with milk, not solid food, for you were not yet strong enough [to be ready for it]; but even yet you are not strong enough [to be ready for it], for you are still [unspiritual, having the nature] of the flesh [under the control of ordinary impulses]. For as long as [there are] envying and jealousy and wrangling and factions among you, are you not unspiritual and of the flesh, behaving yourselves after a human standard and like mere unchanged men?
>
> —1 Corinthians 3:2–3

As a spiritual mother or father, you should have corrected an individual and sent the flock into maturity, rather than tossing an innuendo and sending the flock into immaturity. On another note, leadership must never use innuendoes as an opportunity to divulge any weaknesses of the children who have once confided in them. For example, let's just say one of your sons or daughters has expressed to you that they are having financial problems, and his or her actions have brought it to the point of an open rebuke. It must not be said by the leader on the tail end of the rebuke to that individual openly, "Now, son, that's why you don't have any money." This is a divulging of a personal and confidential conversation being tagged onto an open rebuke.

> NO SPIRITUAL PARENT WOULD INTENTIONALLY TRY TO ABUSE ONE'S SPIRITUAL CHILDREN—BUT REBUKE IS NECESSARY.

This is why Galatians 6:1 says:

> Brethren, if any person is overtaken in misconduct or sin of any sort, you who are spiritual [who are responsive to and controlled by the Spirit] should set him right and restore and reinstate him, without any sense of superiority and with all gentleness, keeping an attentive eye on yourself, lest you should be tempted also.

This scripture reminds me of how many times my mother has said to me before giving me a whipping, "This is going to hurt me as much as it's going to hurt you." I could not understand that until I got old enough to have spiritual children of my own . . . and I have actually gone into another room or gotten into my car and just broke down crying when I have had to rebuke sharply one of my sons or daughters. It is a look that they have in their eyes that breaks my heart—and even though I feel for the one rebuked, I know I have just saved his or her life.

Any leader, after rebuking his or her children, who does not feel compassion for where their children have missed it is not a father or a mother, but a dictator! For what loving spiritual father or mother desires to purposefully hurt and abuse his or her children?

Although I was spanked many times by my parents, they did not abuse me. Their correction matured me…and it is the same in the Spirit. However, this same principle is not necessarily to be applied when you are bringing down the spirit of Jezebel. (See chapter eleven.)

Now, let's see how open rebuke was handled in Numbers 25:1–8:

> Israel settled down and remained in Shittim, and the people began to play the harlot with the daughters of Moab, who invited the [Israelites] to the sacrifices of their gods, and [they] ate and bowed down to Moab's gods. So Israel joined himself to [the god] Baal of Peor. And the anger of the Lord was kindled against Israel. And the Lord said to Moses, Take all the leaders or chiefs of the people, and hang them before the Lord in the sun [after killing them], that the fierce anger of the Lord may turn away from Israel. And Moses said to the judges of Israel, Each one of you slay his men who joined themselves to Baal of Peor. And behold, one of the Israelites came and brought to his brethren a Midianite woman in the sight of Moses and of all the congregation of Israel while they were weeping at the door of the Tent of Meeting [over the divine judgment and the punishment]. And when Phinehas son of Eleazar, the son of Aaron the priest, saw it, he rose up from the midst of the congregation and took a spear in his hand and went after the man of Israel into the inner room and thrust both of them through, the man of Israel and the woman through her body. Then the [smiting] plague was stayed from the Israelites.

Phinehas is an excellent example for the entire church because he was zealous for the honor of the Lord—and did you see his reward? Think about it. Maybe this is why the body of Christ today is in so much warfare. We have broken the covenant of peace with God because we don't allow the leaders with the spirit of Phinehas to thrust people through with the word of the Lord!

Many will say when being openly rebuked, "My feelings are hurt…I'm embarrassed…this is painful…," but Ezekiel 3:17–19 says:

> Son of man, I have made you a watchman to the house of Israel; therefore hear the word at My mouth and give them warning from Me. If I say to the wicked, You shall surely die, and you do not give him a warning or speak to warn the wicked to turn from his wicked way, to save his life, the same wicked man shall die in his iniquity, but his blood will I require at your hand. Yet if you warn the wicked and he turn not from his wickedness or from his wicked way, he shall die in his iniquity, but you have delivered yourself.

When we see the dealings of the Lord as it relates to rebuke in our generation, the work of the cross is plainly seen. Because of the work on the cross, grace and mercy are in operation. So when you look at the way that the Spirit of the Lord dealt with rebellion in the Old Testament, when they rebelled against leadership, they were instantly diseased and they died. Look at Achan when he stole temple elements. Achan and his whole family died.

Look at Ezekiel 9, when the children of Israel were in rebellion against God and began to worship Baal. The Spirit of the Lord commanded the man clothed in white linen to go into Jerusalem and put a mark upon the heads of those who sighed and groaned over the abominations that were being committed. But in verses 5 and 6 of this chapter, He said:

> And to the others He said in my hearing, Follow [the man with the ink bottle] through the city and smite; let not your eye spare, neither have any pity. Slay outright the elderly, the young man and the virgin, the infant

and the women. Begin at My sanctuary. So they began with the old men who were in front of the temple [who did not have the Lord's mark on their foreheads].

And we think now that someone correcting us is a big deal. The way I see it, it's better than dying without a chance to repent. Look at what the Lord prophesied to Zechariah that a mother and father would be required to do to a son who operated illegally in the Spirit:

> And if anyone again appears [falsely] as a prophet, then his father and his mother who bore him shall say to him, You shall not live, for you speak lies in the name of the Lord; and his father and his mother who bore him shall thrust him through when he prophesies. And in that day the [false] prophets shall each be ashamed of his vision when he prophesies, nor will he wear a hairy or rough garment to deceive, but he will [deny his identity and] say, I am no prophet. I am a tiller of the ground, for I have been made a bond servant from my youth. And one shall say to him, What are these wounds on your breast or between your hands? Then he will answer, Those with which I was wounded [when disciplined] in the house of my [loving] friends.
>
> —ZECHARIAH 13:3–6

Even then, the Lord declared that the individual who was being chastised and rebuked harshly would be taught to consider the person rebuking him as a friend. And you still think that your rebuke is harsh?

How Should We Respond to Correction?

People submit to godly leaders when they are being rebuked because someone with a pure heart and motives has confronted them. Literally, they have been confronted by righteousness, because this leader is submitted under God, saying what would be pleasing to Him. Now that we understand who is qualified to rebuke, let's look at the responsibility of the one receiving the rebuke:

> Obey your spiritual leaders and submit to them [continually recognizing their authority over you], for they are constantly keeping watch over your souls and guarding your spiritual welfare, as men who will have to render an account [of their trust]. [Do your part to] let them do this with gladness and not with sighing and groaning, for that would not be profitable to you [either].
>
> —HEBREWS 13:17

When I look at that scripture, the most powerful part of the scripture to me is when I am being told that one of my benefits of submission to authority and rebuke is that it gives my spiritual parents an opportunity to guard my warfare, to look at the warfare that I am encountering and monitor whether or not the enemy is cheating and throwing darts of oppression that are not allowed in this battle. They are making sure that I know my legal rights, as well as Satan knowing his legal boundaries.

I remember when I was under the tutelage of Pastor and Sister Nichols in Port Huron, Michigan, a time when I was going through a fiery trial and I went on a fast. About nine to ten days into the fast, I began to buckle emotionally under the stress of what I was encountering. Sister Nichols came to me and said very sternly, "You've got to fight." I began to crumble in tears and say, "I don't have the strength...I don't have the strength."

She looked at me and picked up by discernment that I was not eating. And she asked me, "Are you fasting?" I replied, "Yes." She asked me how many days I had been fasting. I said, "Nine." And as a mother in the Spirit, she immediately began to say to me, "This is a trial that you must battle in prayer. And in order for you to whip the demon that is trying to take you out, you need your physical strength." And she instructed me to come off of the fast. In doing so, I regained physical strength and mental clarity, and I was able to persevere through the trial—and came out with victory. She explained to me that sometimes in our zealousness, we can do spiritual things that are right at the wrong time. She was guarding my warfare. This is why Titus 2:9–13 teaches us:

> [Tell] bond servants to be submissive to their masters, to be pleasing and give satisfaction in every way. [Warn them] not to talk back or contradict, nor to steal by taking things of small value, but to prove themselves truly loyal and entirely reliable and faithful throughout, so that in everything they may be an ornament and do credit to the teaching [which is] from and about God our Savior. For the grace of God (His unmerited favor and blessing) has come forward (appeared) for the deliverance from sin and the eternal salvation for all mankind. It has trained us to reject and renounce all ungodliness (irreligion) and worldly (passionate) desires, to live discreet (temperate, self-controlled), upright, devout (spiritually whole) lives in this present world, awaiting and looking for the [fulfillment, the realization of our] blessed hope, even the glorious appearing of our great God and Savior Christ Jesus (the Messiah, the Anointed One)...

I believe the reason some people are not growing to the magnitude that God desires is because we have rejected the spirit of correction. This contributes to a lack of instruction in the house of God. Those who are supposed to receive instruction are resisting the message. And as I pointed out earlier, when we resist with our spirits, then in silence we begin to disagree with what is being preached.

If this goes uncorrected, cross breeding begins. Allow me to explain. Let's say that the Lord has mandated the pastor to lean hard on the message of servanthood and brokenness. However, at the same time someone outside of the ministry prophesies to you, "The Lord told me that He is going to raise you up." If you are not careful, you will become a victim of cross-breeding, because one is telling you to die to self and the other is telling you that God is going to raise you up.

Both prophets could be correct, but one of them could be out of the right timing. And if you are not grounded in truth, and if your spirit is not accustomed to correction and discipline, you will automatically begin to gravitate to the prophecy that makes you feel good—which, in turn, makes your spiritual parents appear to have missed God. Remember, many prophets who are not submitted themselves can see the height of where God desires to take you—but true spiritual parents understand the process by which you are to get there. They are called to prophesy the process.

It's like a mother telling her child before he or she leaves for school, "Don't take candy from anybody, and don't talk to strangers," but then the child gets to school and the teacher says, "On your way home if a person talks to you and offers you candy, take the candy and get to know the stranger." They are both leaders, but you as a follower must understand the difference between the one who is called to your life for a few hours, as opposed to the one who has been called to your life for a lifetime. When a person keeps giving you good prophecies, that person is giving you candy—nothing more, nothing less. The enemy is trying to win your favor and draw you out of your destiny. He starts by drawing you out of the favor of your leadership—those who have been called to bring your life into right standing with God.

This is why Paul exhorted Titus with this word of correction, "…nor to steal by taking things of small value *[not even paper clips or pencils from your job]*, but to prove themselves truly loyal and entirely reliable and faithful throughout, so that in everything *[not just some things, but I repeat, in everything]* they may be an ornament and do credit to the teaching [which is] from and about God our Savior" (Titus 2:10). Then Paul said in Titus 2:11–12:

> For the grace of God (His unmerited favor and blessing) has come forward (appeared) for the deliverance from sin and the eternal salvation for all mankind. It

has trained us to reject and renounce all ungodliness (irreligion) and worldly (passionate) desires, to live discreet (temperate, self-controlled), upright, devout (spiritually whole) lives in this present world.

The Benefit of Rebuke

In order for us to understand the benefits of rebuke, we must first come to realize the value that it brings. We must understand that spiritual rebuke, though it is painful, yet it is profitable. For 2 Timothy 3:16–17 says:

> Every Scripture is God-breathed (given by His inspiration) and profitable for instruction, for reproof and conviction of sin, for correction of error and discipline in obedience, [and] for training in righteousness (in holy living, in conformity to God's will in thought, purpose, and action), so that the man of God may be complete and proficient, well fitted and thoroughly equipped for every good work.

We must become submissive to the power of correction because it sends our spirit into training to learn how to recognize and renounce all ungodliness. Let me ask you this: how do you renounce ungodliness if you don't know what ungodliness is? For Ecclesiastes 8:5–7 says:

> Whoever observes the [king's] command will experience no harm, and a wise man's mind will know both when and what to do. For every purpose and matter has its [right] time and judgment, although the misery and wickedness of man lies heavily upon him [who rebels against the king]. For he does not know what is to be, for who can tell him how and when it will be?

God has worked it out so that we don't have to go around saying things like, "Well, I don't know if that's wrong or not, but I don't feel convicted about it, so it doesn't bother me." "It's all right; I can listen to that CD. It won't do anything to my spirit." You see, this is your opinion. That's why it is your spiritual father's job to rebuke and correct you, so that you can be made aware of what sin is—because in this last hour, everything seems to be gray. It's hard for people to understand what is holy and what isn't, what constitutes sin and what doesn't. Because there's so much "mixture" in the body of Christ, rebuke must come to bring clarity in our spirits.

> **THAT'S WHY WE MUST RECEIVE CORRECTION. OUR HEAVENLY FATHER HAS TO REBUKE US (THROUGH HIS WORD AND OUR LEADERS) TO EXPOSE UNGODLINESS AND TO KEEP SATAN'S DEVICES FROM BRINGING US HARM.**

We must be trained how to discern the right spirit. And the spirit of discernment can only be brought to maturity when rebuke is in operation. For when a person is rebuked because of a wrong spirit, that person becomes personally acquainted with that spirit. And I don't care if that spirit dresses up, dresses down, grows two heads and sixteen legs, you will still know that spirit...regardless of how it disguises itself. Oh, yes, there is power in rebuke.

Challenging Rebuke

Allow me, if you will, to show you the manifestations that are revealed in a person when he or she is trying to challenge rebuke. It is a very dangerous position to put yourself in, because once you begin to challenge rebuke, you join hands with rebellion. And when rebellion comes into operation, witchcraft is released, and when witchcraft is in full manifestation, the person becomes blinded by his own deeds, therefore launching them into full-fledged justification, denying what they have done and becoming blinded to the relationship that they once had with their heavenly Father. Let's go to Genesis 4:1–6.

> And Adam knew Eve as his wife, and she became pregnant and bore Cain; and she said, I have gotten and gained a man with the help of the Lord. And [next] she gave birth to his brother Abel. Now Abel

was a keeper of sheep, but Cain was a tiller of the ground. And in the course of time Cain brought to the Lord an offering of the fruit of the ground. And Abel brought of the firstborn of his flock and of the fat portions. And the Lord had respect and regard for Abel and for his offering. But for Cain and his offering He had no respect or regard. So Cain was exceedingly angry and indignant, and he looked sad and depressed. And the Lord said to Cain, Why are you angry? And why do you look sad and depressed and dejected?

Cain came before God and brought the fruit of the ground. Abel came and paid his tithes. The Father was pleased with Abel's offering, and Cain got upset—so God had to rebuke him. I can just hear the Lord saying to Cain, "What's wrong with you? What's the matter with your faith? Why are you looking like that? Why are you acting crazy like this?" Watch how God continued to correct him:

> If you do well, will you not be accepted? And if you do not do well, sin crouches at your door; its desire is for you, but you must master it.
>
> —Genesis 4:7

Allow me to break this down for you. God had to rebuke Cain about his actions so that he could learn to identify sin. God had to say, "If you don't do things the right way, with integrity, then your motive is incorrect—and that's called *sin*. But I love you enough to tell you the truth and to correct you." Listen to me. Because of this, your spiritual parent must be more concerned with keeping sin from crouching at the door of your life than he is with your feelings.

Anybody can make a mistake. But when that person rejects correction, that mistake becomes rebellion. I truly believe this is a problem throughout the body of Christ because, in our sin nature, we come from the lineage of Adam and Eve, God's first creation. They ate the forbidden fruit, were disciplined and cast out of the Garden of Eden, and then gave birth to Cain and Abel. Both sons were the firstborn of the new institution the Father called "family." They marked a new activity in the realm of the spirit—but error had passed down from their parents, and it multiplied with tragic results.

Sometimes our spirits can get into a position where we believe we are beyond correction. I see it happen all the time. It sounds like this: "Well, I speak in tongues, so you can't correct me. I know the Lord. I can discern the way myself." It's all about, *"I, I, I. What I can do now,"* instead of being about what God has already done!

God was trying to help Cain to understand by saying, "I'm not rebuking you to single you out—years from now, I want other servants to come through your loins. And their obedience has to come through your obedience."

Remember this: whatever God is correcting you about is beyond you. It is about your spiritual lineage—what's coming through you to the next generation. It is about what's going to happen because of the choice you make to either accept or reject correction.

God told Cain, "If you do well, will you not be accepted? And if you do not do well, sin crouches at your door; its desire is for you, but you must master it" (Gen. 4:7). But Cain rejected the word of the Lord.

When you reject correction, the first thing that happens is that the spirit of deception comes into play. You start doing things with the wrong motive. It happened this way with Cain. When Cain walked out of the presence of the Lord and into deception, he immediately asked his brother to go on a trip because he already intended to take his brother's life.

> And Cain said to his brother, Let us go out to the field.
> And when they were in the field, Cain rose up against
> Abel his brother and killed him.
>
> —Genesis 4:8

This reveals the second step: *murder.* I mean murder with your mouth—killing ideas in the church, killing people's spirits in the church, killing spiritual authority. This spirit will come in the church and refuse to praise God, killing and putting a weight on the anointing. Watch out! It won't stop there. If you allow it, this spirit will kill your marriage, your children's self-esteem, and whatever area you submit to its control.

When you reject God (in any way), your spirit automatically turns against Him. When you get a bad attitude when you are corrected, it's more than just a bad attitude or anger—your spirit has rejected the Lord. Then the spirit of deception starts perverting everything that comes from the pulpit. You no longer accept the Word the way it is delivered—you change it around in your mind so that it begins to fit where your emotions are sitting. For example, when your pastor says, "Lift your hands," you say, "God can move in my spirit without my hands being lifted." You begin to lose sight of the importance of being led. You want God to lead you by *your* spirit, not by His Spirit.

This is a vitally important point. Any time you are being instructed in the ways of God and you refuse this instruction, you open your spirit to every diabolical act of the devil. You become vulnerable to his strategies. Then your spirit opens up to principalities under the devil's control, which begin to take control of your atmosphere, hemisphere, and stratosphere. Everything about you changes, and before you know it, you are sitting smack dab in the middle of the devil's camp.

When God confronted Cain about what he had done to Abel, Cain responded:

> I do not know. Am I my brother's keeper?
> —GENESIS 4:9

You can always tell when somebody hasn't received correction, because he or she will become disrespectful and cocky. Cain was talking to God! He had rejected the power of rebuke, and his sin multiplied. Then the spirit of deception perverted his way and turned him into a murderer. Cain was in a state of full-blown rebellion. And from there, witchcraft literally took him over, because the Bible says that rebellion is as the sin of witchcraft (1 Sam. 15:23).

Rebellion Is Witchcraft

Oh, yes! When you reject correction, the spirit of witchcraft will take over—and no one on earth has to cast a spell or put something in your food. You drop something down into your own spirit and you hex yourself.

When you are under a spirit of rebellion, it can tear your life apart—your finances, your children, and even your marriage. When you open yourself to a spirit of witchcraft, everything you touch will crumble. And nothing is hidden from God. All of your actions are weighed, especially when it involves the offenses toward His people. Let's look at Genesis 4:10:

> And [the Lord] said, What have you done? The voice of your brother's blood is crying to Me from the ground.

The Lord is asking, "What have you done? I hear the spirit of the persons that you've talked to the wrong way in the church crying out to me. They are offended; what have you done?" "The prayers of the person that you offended in the choir have come up before me...he's heavy laden and burdened; what have you done?" Everything you do comes up before Him, because He created everything. And He is especially sensitive to those that are His.

> THE SPIRIT OF REBELLION WILL PUT YOU IN THE HANDS OF EVERY KIND OF EVIL ACTIVITY IN THE SPIRIT REALM.

Whenever God's people are being abused or hindered from fulfilling the purpose for which He created them, the offense comes up before God. So any time His Word is not fulfilled according to His purpose, then His anger is kindled against the person who tried to hinder His will. And He asks, "What have you done?" Galatians 5:7–10 says:

> You were running the race nobly. Who has interfered in (hindered and stopped you from) your heeding and following the Truth? This [evil] persuasion is not from Him Who called you [Who invited you to free-

dom in Christ]. A little leaven (a slight inclination to error, or a few false teachers) leavens the whole lump [it perverts the whole conception of faith or misleads the whole church]. [For my part] I have confidence [toward you] in the Lord that you will take no contrary view of the matter but will come to think with me. But he who is unsettling you, whoever he is, will have to bear the penalty.

So what happens after witchcraft sets in? A curse. As a result of his sin, Cain lacked prosperity:

> And now you are cursed by reason of the earth, which has opened its mouth to receive your brother's [shed] blood from your hand. When you till the ground, it shall no longer yield to you its strength; you shall be a fugitive and a vagabond on the earth [in perpetual exile, a degraded outcast].
>
> —Genesis 4:11–12

All of this happened because Cain brought the wrong seed to God. Something that small caused a divine domino effect. Cain became a deceiver and a murderer, and he was cursed with poverty, all because he wouldn't accept correction about his offering.

Remember, it's the little foxes that destroy the vine. When God sends correction to you about something small, you had better find yourself saying, "Yes, Lord." Because when you reject Him, the curse of being driven away from God's presence altogether will take effect—and that means losing your spiritual inheritance. Cain said this was too hard to bear:

> Behold, You have driven me out this day from the face of the land, and from Your face I will be hidden; and I will be a fugitive and a vagabond and a wanderer on the earth, and whoever finds me will kill me.
>
> —Genesis 4:14

Cain felt the pain of his disobedience to God and cried out, "My punishment is greater than I can bear...whoever finds me will kill me" (Gen. 4:13–14). God responded by saying, "I'm not going to kill you." (See verse 15.) Some would say, "Oh, that's the mercy of God." But let's look a little closer. I believe God was saying, "I'm not going to let anyone kill you, but I'm not going to give you the easy way out either—you're going to walk out the penalty. You're going to feel the results of rebellion. And every time something falls apart, you're going to be reminded that you chose rebellion rather than correction."

God's children aren't supposed to be without direction. When you belong to the Lord, He is obligated to lead you wherever He wants you to go, according to Proverbs 3:6:

> In all of your ways know, recognize, and acknowledge
> Him, and He will direct and make straight and plain
> your paths.

Why would He throw you into a spirit of confusion? The journey we are on is leading us into the mysteries of God. The Father is saying, "If I can't get you to submit to the pastor, and I can't get you to submit to correction, then I can't take you any further. If you don't submit, I cannot reveal My mysteries to you because you will operate as a 'loose cannon.'" God's process is to correct, train, and bless you while you are on ground level, so when you come into divine purpose you can stand the test of time.

If you stay submitted to spiritual authority, you can rise to a level where you are walking in the blessings of God because you understand His principles. Therefore, you don't offend God, because you hear His voice and obey. Are you ready to experience the fullness of His divine presence? Then let Him try your spirit through submission. Embrace the power of rebuke.

The first two verses of Psalm 133 tell us the order of how our blessings come:

> Behold, how good and how pleasant it is for brethren
> to dwell together in unity! It is like the precious oint-

ment poured on the head, that ran down on the beard, even the beard of Aaron [the first high priest], that came down upon the collar and skirts of his garments [consecrating the whole body].

The order of God is for the body of Christ to function in unity—from the top down. This is how the fullness of His wisdom can be revealed. First Thessalonians 5:21 instructs us, "Test and prove all things [until you can recognize] what is good; [to that] hold fast." That's why we have qualifications for leadership, and that's why a novice (an immature, inexperienced person) cannot serve in the ministry and have the capacity to watch over a person's soul.

After Cain's rebellion, God saw fit to restore the spiritual relationship of the first family, and Eve gave birth again, to Seth. When Seth (the third son) was born to Adam and Eve in Genesis 4:25–26, he then birthed the fourth generation, filled with men who began to turn their hearts back to God. As a result, prayer was restored, hearts were healed, and relationships were mended. Things started coming back into divine balance. Oh, yes! There is power in rebuke.

CHAPTER 8

The Absence of Correction

When you look at what God has demonstrated in the Scriptures, it becomes clear that receiving your spiritual inheritance means that God is going to discipline and prepare you to achieve greatness. God will make sure that you don't outrun, mishandle, or abuse the spiritual greatness He has put within you.

When I was a little girl, my mother used to call me in from outside and make me sit down. I didn't know why she used to make me sit down, but on one occasion, about five minutes after I entered the house, somebody was hit by a baseball bat. On another occasion, ten minutes after she sat me down, somebody was run over by a car.

Now I understand that my mother could pick up in her spirit when a satanic force was about to hinder or try to destroy the call God had placed on my life. So she protected it.

If I had disobeyed my mother, or snuck off and done things without her knowing where I was—it could have cost my life. Proverbs 20:18 says: "Purposes and plans are established by counsel."

Purposes and Plans Are Established by Counsel

Whatever the Father has for me, He will reveal His plans and purposes through the process of counsel. Let me say it to you another way. God will never give you an assignment that doesn't require counsel. If you plan to do something by yourself, then you can do that without asking anybody any questions. But if you want to confirm whether or not what you are about to accomplish is from the Lord, then one of the first signs is this: you will need help with it.

If you are going to do something great for the Lord, then you are going to need His help and also the benefit of sound spiritual counsel. God said to me one day, "The problem in the church isn't that people are not aware of what I'm calling them to do. They are aware." You see, you can be aware that the Lord has an assignment for your life but not realize its significance. God is doing so many great things in the lives of people nowadays that believers are no longer doing "average" works; they are doing works of greatness—things that may never have happened before in the history of their family.

The Mantle Dictates the Rules

During the Bible days of the prophets, there were laws that applied when someone was birthed in the prophetic. First of all, the Word of God must create something in you to establish who you are in the kingdom of God. Then rules must be established according to the mantle that is going to come upon you.

This means you can't do what everybody else does or wear what everybody else wears. You can't go where everybody else goes, because the anointing that is coming on your life is not yours. It's a creative anointing that has already been proven. This makes it vital for you to follow the rules.

For example, the Holy Spirit gives you a divine prophecy that you are going to preach all over the world. For many of you who are reading this book, your mother isn't a preacher, your daddy isn't a preacher, and your grandfather wasn't a preacher. Your great-grandfather didn't even preach. As a matter of fact, there are no preachers in your family. That's a creative anointing. That's when you know, without a doubt, that you are receiving the Father's portion and not your family's portion.

However, this impartation will require you to "sit" under godly teaching and training, because your portion came by revelation—you didn't inherit it from flesh and blood. It was created in the prophetic realm for you.

This principle can be illustrated by taking a look at the life of Samson.

> And the Israelites again did what was evil in the sight of the Lord, and the Lord gave them into the hands of the Philistines for forty years. And there was a certain man of Zorah, of the tribe of the Danites, whose name was Manoah; and his wife was barren and had no children. And the Angel of the Lord appeared to the woman and said to her, Behold, you are barren and have no children, but you shall become pregnant and bear a son.
>
> —JUDGES 13:1–3

Samson's mother was barren when the angel of the Lord told her that she was going to bear a son. It was the Father's portion for her, but it came with conditions:

> Therefore beware and drink no wine or strong drink and eat nothing unclean. For behold, you shall become pregnant and bear a son. No razor shall come upon his head, for the child shall be a Nazirite to God from birth, and he shall begin to deliver Israel out of the hands of the Philistines.
>
> —JUDGES 13:4–5

Because the mantle was a creative anointing, the Lord established the rules to which Samson would need to submit in order to inherit the full portion of the destiny God had for him.

The Philistines were enemies of God and His people, Israel. So He raised up Samson to become one of the judges for the nation. The purpose of the anointing God placed upon Samson was to deal with Israel's enemy. Samson wasn't blessed with the spiritual inheritance simply because God liked his mother. There was a divine purpose for his strength.

God has a purpose for what He is raising you up to do, and He will accomplish that purpose. I want you to see something here. Samson was told that he wasn't to touch anything unclean. He was instructed not to cut his hair. He was a *Nazirite*, which means he was separated and set apart. Samson couldn't run around with just anybody.

But one day, Samson went to Timnah and saw a Philistine girl. He had an anointing to destroy the Philistines, but there was something in his flesh that lusted after what God had deemed to be the enemy. Samson returned to his parents and said, "I like that girl; get her for me."

> But his father and mother said to him, Is there not a woman among the daughters of your kinsmen or among all our people, that you must go to take a wife from the uncircumcised Philistines? And Samson said to his father, Get her for me, for she is all right in my eyes. His father and mother did not know that it was of the Lord, and that He sought an occasion for assailing the Philistines. At that time the Philistines had dominion over Israel.
>
> —JUDGES 14:3–4

You see, Samson had not gone far enough in understanding the weight of what he was appointed to do to trust his eyes with his future. Now, watch what happened in verses 5 and 6:

> Then Samson and his father and mother went down to Timnah and came to the vineyards of Timnah. And behold, a young lion roared against him. And the Spirit of the Lord came mightily upon him, and he tore the lion as he would have torn a kid, and he had nothing in his hand; *but he did not tell his father or mother what he had done.*
>
> —EMPHASIS ADDED

As I read these verses, God kept bringing to my attention the fact that Samson didn't tell his parents about killing the lion. The Lord spoke something to me, whispering in my spirit this: "Had Samson told his mother and father that he had killed a lion, it might have given them an opportunity to say, 'Don't misuse the strength that God has given you. It's not for your own purposes.'"

Follow closely what happens next. Verse 5 told us that a young lion attacked Samson on his way to Timnah. After killing the lion, he continued on his way to Timnah where he had a conversation with the Philistine woman he wanted to take as his wife. Then he began the journey home, and in passing the carcass of the lion, he found a swarm of bees and honey.

Remember, Samson wasn't supposed to touch or eat anything unclean—but he desired it, so he ate the honey, anyway. Right then and there, Samson was headed for trouble.

His parents had raised him not to touch anything unclean or to cut his hair. Samson knew he was a Nazirite; therefore, he was to remain separated. But when he came into knowledge and recognized the power of God on his life, he started making the wrong decisions. People were telling him how strong he was. He could break the jaw of a lion by himself. I can just hear him thinking, *Now I can eat anything I want, and I can go where I want to go.*

Believers do the same thing today. We get a little knowledge of our portion and think, *I don't have to go to church. I don't have to be there every service. I don't have to come on time. I don't have to do what they tell me to do because I'm mature. That's for the others who are still babies.*

Wrong! Remember, your anointing may be mature, but it takes wisdom to properly execute that power.

Age of Accountability

After Samson ate the honey, his parents stopped challenging him. He scooped honey out of that which was unclean, and not only did he eat it, but also he gave some to his parents. Samson defiled them! You see, when you are a parent in the spirit, if you do not stay on guard in the spirit, your own child can defile you.

Notice the way Samson talked to his parents: "Get her for me." One translation reads, "Now get her for me" (NIV). Samson saw that woman and began to take advantage of the fact that he had power to control and manipulate his parents. But his soon-to-be wife would slip from his grasp. Fear was driving her to figure out his secret. Verses 12–20 tell the rest of the story. Samson gave a riddle, and she exposed what it meant. Afterward the Spirit of the Lord came upon Samson, and he killed thirty men of that city and took their clothes for spoil. Here again, he began using the power of God for his own purpose and for revenge.

Do you know why the Spirit of the Lord came upon Samson every time the Philistines did something to him? Because they were God's enemies. However, it didn't mean that Samson was killing with the right motive or in the right spirit.

You see, God can use you even when you are wrong, because He is sovereign. If a work needs to be done, He will use you in spite of your weaknesses. But be careful…you could be working for the kingdom while on your way to hell. God will use you against His enemy, Satan, for His Word's sake. Every time the enemy shows his head and you get the victory doesn't mean that you are right; it means that God is honoring His Word that when the enemy comes in like a flood, the Spirit of the Lord will lift up a standard against him. Samson had that anointing of strength because the Philistines were God's enemies.

> JUST BECAUSE YOU HAVE THE POWER OF GOD ON YOUR LIFE DOES NOT MEAN THAT YOU ARE TOTALLY SUBMITTED TO THE WILL OF GOD.

Samson had taken those first steps out from under the covering of spiritual authority. Then things continued to get worse for him. In anger, he killed thirty men and took their clothes. Then he became angry at his wife, and he left her to return back to live with his parents.

Samson's parents should have told him, "Go back and get your wife." Instead, he lived with his parents for four months. When the time for harvest came, he became full of lust and wanted sex with his wife. So he went back to Timnah with a gift for her and demanded to sleep with his wife (Judg. 15:1–2).

But her father replied, "I thought you didn't want my daughter, so I gave her away."

What did Samson do? He went and caught three hundred foxes, twisted their tails together, lit them with fire, and then sent them into the enemy's camp, scorching the harvest (vv. 4–5). At this point, Samson had great power, but he was out of control. He had an anointing—he had received a portion from God—but there was an absence of correction and discipline. Nobody was there to chastise him and channel that anointing.

A Proven Leader

Samson was called and prepared to be a leader, but the qualifications were not evident in his life. He had power, but he also had a bad temper. He had an anointing, but he lacked self-control. Samson wasn't disciplined or temperate. He wasn't longsuffering—he was just strong. And he justified his actions. Let's go to verse 3 of chapter 15:

> And Samson said of them, This time shall I be blame-
> less as regards the Philistines, though I do them evil.

In other words, he was saying, "I'm not to blame for what I'm about to do." People who are trying to operate in an anointing without correction will always justify their wrongdoings. They will blame it on "what God has said" and what He told them to do. They will justify their own sin by exposing the acts of the other person. They will blame what they did on everybody else.

There are many people in the body of Christ today who have moved out of God's direct call because they are going by what their own spirits told them to do. "Well, that's what I felt led to do," they will say, just as Samson did. By that time, Samson was in a position where everybody in the country knew that he was strong. Everyone knew he was raised up to be a judge. People knew he had the strength of God in his life, and nobody dared to correct him. What a dangerous place to be.

Rebuke is absolutely necessary for people who carry strength. Samson justified to himself that he was only paying the enemy back for what they had done to him. But that revealed a flaw—because a true anointing doesn't retaliate. An anointing that is under the correction and submission of authority never responds by using it to get back at anybody. Scripture tells us that after he retaliated against the Philistines, the enemy sought him out, and he picked up the jawbone of a donkey and killed a thousand men (Judg. 15:9–17).

Here was a judge of Israel, a man separated unto God from birth and raised up in strength and power. But because he had no one speaking truth into his life through the operation of rebuke, his actions grew progressively worse. In the sixteenth chapter of Judges, he traveled to Gaza and slept with a prostitute. And guess what? He was still God's anointed even though he was sleeping with a prostitute. He still had strength. He was still powerful. But he did not have anybody who was bold enough to say, "You can't do that; you're a Nazirite. Do you remember what God told you? You don't have any business sleeping with a prostitute. You're set apart; you're God's anointed." He lacked character.

By that time, everybody was interested in his gifts and talents. Everybody was impressed with how anointed he was. Hear me. That is why you have to pull back when people start giving you compliments, "Oh, you're anointed…God's going to use you." I personally don't want to hear that, because when I get through being used, I want to be saved! When I get through preaching, I don't want to be shipwrecked.

The Bible says a good name is rather to be desired than riches (Prov. 22:1). Samson desired a Philistine, and he fell deeper and deeper into defilement. It happened because there was an absence of correction in his life. When you refuse to accept correction and to submit your life under the proper authority, the devil confronts you with a demon that has been designed to match your strength.

The demon who came against Samson to draw him into sin became stronger as he became more powerful. When the baby demon couldn't stop Samson, when the carcass couldn't stop him, when the Philistine girl couldn't stop him, and when the prostitute couldn't stop him—the devil said, "I've got somebody for you…come on over here. You don't want to hear correction, so come on. You don't want to hear the counsel of someone who could straighten out your life. Oh, yeah, you've got victory in the gift and the call, but not in character, so come on over here, because I've got something that's going to match you in strength." That's when Samson got "set up" with Delilah.

Samson was a mighty man of God, but his flesh got out of control. That's what drove him to the Philistine girl. Samson never said, "I've prayed about it, and God showed me that this girl is going to minister to my life. She's going to help me fulfill my goal to become a judge over all Israel." No! He said, "Get her for me…I like her." From the beginning, he didn't submit to the leading of God through his parents, who were his earthly authorities.

A Father's Anointing Covers Your Vision

Samson became a mighty man with an anointing, but he did not have a covering anointing to guide his life. Are you getting this? There was a spiritual inheritance laid up for him by God—yet on every level, when he avoided correction, his sin multiplied. Finally Samson fell in love with Delilah, and a lying spirit jumped to the surface. When you reject correction, all kinds of spirits jump you!

> And Delilah said to Samson, Tell me, I pray you, wherein your great strength lies, and with what you might be bound to subdue you. And Samson said to her, If they bind me with seven fresh, strong guts-trings, still moist, then shall I be weak and be like any other man. Then the Philistine lords brought to her seven fresh, strong bowstrings, still moist, and she bound him with them. Now she had men lying in wait in an inner room. And she said to him, The Philistines are upon you, Samson! And he broke the

bowstrings as a string of tow breaks when it touches the fire. So the secret of his strength was not known.

—JUDGES 16:6–9

Samson broke free the first time, but when you keep messing with the devil, being anointed but not submitted, the devil is going to find your strength. He will discover what makes you tick. He will find a way to bring you down to the ground. And when you hit, you are going to hit hard. Samson lied to Delilah three times and broke free. But finally, he was trapped by his sin. For the Word says that a man is drawn away by his own lust, and when lust is conceived and full grown, it brings death. (See James 1:14–15.)

And she said to him, How can you say, I love you, when your heart is not with me? You have mocked me these three times and have not told me in what your great strength lies. And when she pressed him day after day with her words and urged him, he was vexed to death. Then he told her all his mind and said to her, A razor has never come upon my head, for I have been a Nazirite to God from my birth. If I am shaved, then my strength will go from me, and I shall become weak and be like any other man.... And she made Samson sleep upon her knees, and she called a man and caused him to shave off the seven braids of his head. Then she began to torment [Samson], and his strength went from him. She said, The Philistines are upon you, Samson! And he awoke out of his sleep and said, I will go out as I have time after time and shake myself free. For Samson did not know that the Lord had departed from him.

—JUDGES 16:15–20

This is a powerful revelation. Samson jumped up as he always did, thinking, *I've got power*—but he didn't have it. People do the same thing today—they jump up and preach even though they don't have the anointing anymore. People sing all the right notes in praise, but they aren't anointed as they used to be. What's worse, there are people saying, "Amen," to preachers based upon the anointing they used to recognize in those preachers. They shout and dance from the residue of what they used to have.

That's the problem with gifts and talents, and it's the trick of the enemy. If you have received a portion from God, yet you continue to avoid correction, the devil is going to take you out. He will let you keep sinning and keep "feeling the anointing" so you believe you still have it. But one day you are going to "shake," and the presence of the Lord will be gone.

The saddest thing about what happened to Samson is that he lost his eyesight. He lost spiritual discernment. Slowly but surely, he lost his ability to seek God in every situation. Therefore, he couldn't discern the enemy's devices, and he ended up being taken by a servant. Samson was supposed to be great in the kingdom; he ended up being led around by someone who did not know God or understand his call. You don't have any business being led around by someone who doesn't have a call of God on his or her life in the same way that you are called. But when you become unsubmitted and mess with the devil, you will begin to reject instruction and avoid correction. In doing so, you won't just lose your eyesight; you will lose your insight.

Near the end of his life, Samson cried out to God:

> O Lord God, [earnestly] remember me, I pray You, and strengthen me, I pray You, only this once, O God, and let me have one vengeance upon the Philistines for both my eyes.
>
> —JUDGES 16:28

The sad thing about this scripture is this: I believe Samson died with the enemy of the Lord because he still didn't get it. Even in his last cry, it was still about his vengeance, his eyes, his offense, and not about the purpose of God.

Eli's Disaster

Why is rebuke necessary? Let's take a look at Eli, the high priest in Israel when the word of the Lord was shut up in the land. (See 1 Samuel 1–3.) Eli knew his sons were sleeping with women in the temple, yet he would not correct them (1 Sam. 2:22–25). Because of this, the word of the Lord was shut up in the land. How could God speak to Eli about a nation when He couldn't even speak to him about his sons?

Three years later, as a result of prayer, Samuel was brought to the temple. That child, Samuel, didn't know anything. His mother dedicated him to the Lord and left him in his Father's house. One night in the temple, Samuel heard a voice calling his name (1 Sam. 3:1–10).

The fact that Samuel was dedicated to the temple means that he was also under a Nazirite's anointing—he was set apart. Anyone who has been set apart for the Master's use should be able to hear God speaking. Eli wasn't a good leader, but in spite of that fact, Samuel stayed there because that is where he had been placed. He maintained his position and stayed where God told him to stay. And that is a message all by itself.

This is a very powerful principle. If God told you to be where you are, then you can't leave unless God tells you to leave. Why? Because God is trying to birth a pair of ears in your spirit.

Remember, God still uses His anointed even when they become disobedient. If I were to turn into a prostitute today, I am still God's anointed. I would have to pay a penalty for walking in ungodliness, but God would never take back what He has spoken over my life. He may shut down my ability to use it in the magnitude that He had ordained, but I am still His anointed. That's why the Bible says, "Touch not Mine anointed, and do My prophets no harm" (1 Chron. 16:22). You must get this. Correcting leadership isn't your job; it is God's job. Your job as a son or daughter is to submit to the training.

Rebuke…godly correction…is part of God's preparation of His children for their spiritual inheritance. Rebuke comes your way because you are strong; it is a trick of the devil to make you reject correction. Why do you think the devil is pressing in on you like this? It is because he is trying to break your strength by sending you to weakness. Therefore, if your leader doesn't correct you, then the power and might of who you are in the Spirit would lead you into an illegal zone in the Spirit.

By this I mean that the devil will chase you into a realm for which you haven't been purified. You can operate there, but the battle is strong, and the devil will do everything he can to beat your brains out—because you haven't been purified to operate on that level. You can go to that level in the Spirit, but you can't fight on that level, because your spirit isn't pure enough to handle it. You have power and a gift, but not enough power in purification to throw the enemy down.

When you recognize that you're strong and your abilities begin to be evident to yourself and others, you had better get desperate to find an instructor. You had better cry out to God in prayer, "God, send me a teacher. Send me an instructor; send me someone who will channel this anointing on my life."

Without a spiritual parent, you will rise to a high level—but it won't be destiny. You will reach a mark, but you won't get all the way to the end. And you will have to settle for a substitute because you didn't have the maturity to be instructed. It takes a mature person to receive instruction. It requires you to recognize that the anointing you are carrying is bigger than the person you are.

> THE DEVICES OF SATAN COME TO BREAK YOUR STRENGTH. ALWAYS REMEMBER, REBUKE CHANNELS YOUR STRENGTH. SATAN BREAKS YOUR STRENGTH.

I am no exception. I could lose it all. It would only take one wrong turn, one wrong deal, one illegal counsel, one person telling me to step out and do something that God isn't telling me to do. That could cause me to have to go all the way around the mountain again, just like the children of Israel. Their journey to the Promised Land could have taken a few days—but it took them forty years, and the majority of the people who left Egypt didn't make it into the Promised Land. Remember, it was a three-day journey, but because they refused to hear God's leader, it took them forty years. My pastor always says it this way: "It is a sad thing to climb a high skyscraper, only to realize when you get to the top, you are on top of the wrong building."

It is for this reason that I was raised under firm instructors. From personal experience, I know why pastors, bishops, elders, and prophets must rebuke and correct. Remember Samson. He completed a job at the expense of prolonged mockery to the church. Think about Uzziah. He was raised up in his own strength and began to walk in realms that made him think more highly of himself than he should have. Saul couldn't find donkeys on his own, yet when he was elevated to a kingly position, he tried to put himself on the same level as Samuel, his spiritual father.

Why must our leaders rebuke? Because in the current-day absence of rebuke in the church, gifts and talents are running the church! Money and intellectualism are ruling the temple. God meant for the priests and consecrated ones to govern the house of God. But today it is conducted like a business. The church is no longer the temple of deliverance; it's just "big business." It's not the house of prayer where people come in and get set free. It's not where we cast out devils—it's a business, pure and simple.

The Sin of Achan

Why must our leaders rebuke? Look at the story of Achan, who stole the thing God had devoted to destruction and then lied about it. One man stopped the whole church! When Ai rose up in Joshua 7 and defeated the army of Israel, only a few people were able to chase three thousand Israelites away from their city gates. (See Joshua 7:1–5.)

Because of the lack of rebuke in the church today, the devil is able to run God's people around like a dog chasing its own tail and never catching it. There are more Christians today than ever, and still, we don't have authentic power over the devil. Why? Because there is sin in the camp. Our hearts are petrified because somebody is housing something in his or her spirit that is devoted to destruction. Somebody is hiding something from God. Someone is holding on to something that God wants to be put on the altar.

When Ai chased Israel off with only a handful of men, they only killed about thirty-six Israelites. (See Joshua 7:4–5.) The men of Ai didn't even kill enough people for Israel to be terrified! Now, if they had killed fifteen hundred men, it might have been different. I believe the people ran when thirty-six were killed because the Lord was no longer with them. Israel had the "numbers," but God wasn't there.

> Then Joshua rent his clothes and lay on the earth upon his face before the ark of the Lord until evening, he and the elders of Israel; and they put dust on their heads. Joshua said, Alas, O Lord God, why have You brought this people over the Jordan at all only to give us into the hands of the Amorites to destroy us? Would that we had been content to dwell beyond the Jordan! O Lord, what can I say, now that Israel has turned to flee before their enemies! For the Canaanites and all the inhabitants of the land will hear of it and will surround us and cut off our name from the earth. And what will You do for Your great name? Then the Lord said to Joshua, Get up! Why do you lie thus upon your face?
>
> —JOSHUA 7:6–10

There are some things you pray about and others that you step up to the plate on. God told Joshua, "This isn't the time to pray. This is the time to confront, rebuke, and instruct." Then He said, "Israel has sinned; *they* have transgressed My covenant..." (v. 11, emphasis added). God didn't indicate that it was one man who had transgressed His covenant—it was an entire nation. They were a company going to battle; therefore, in the eyes of God, "I" became "US" and the "ONE" became "WE" and "ALL."

> They have transgressed My covenant which I commanded them. They have taken some of the things devoted [for destruction]; they have stolen, and lied, and put them among their own baggage.
>
> —JOSHUA 7:11

Remember this. When you choose to fall into sexual sin, and then you go to church pretending and don't repent—you have just gotten not just *you*, but *us*, in trouble. When you play an instrument in the body of Christ, and your hands aren't clean and your heart isn't right, you are messing us up. Verse 12 indicates that because of one man's sin, "the Israelites could not stand before their enemies."

So why do we need correction? Why is there power in rebuke? We need correction because a whole nation failed when one person didn't learn how to stay in submission to God. A whole church could suffer if one person hides from correction.

> REBUKE RESTORES, DIRECTS, AND EMPOWERS.

Jonah caused a whole ship to reel and rock on a stormy sea because he was disobedient to God. When he was identified by lot and ultimately thrown overboard, it may have seemed harsh—but because those men heeded Jonah's voice and threw him into the sea, Jonah didn't die...he was brought into spiritual alignment. Though he ended up in the belly of a fish, he eventually repented, and God allowed him to redeem the time. He ended up in the right place, and the anointing came upon him, and he did a three-day journey in a day's time.

CHAPTER 9

The Spirit of Truth

*T*he reality is that God can give us a portion and bring His work to completion—but if we don't submit our lives to divine instruction, rebuke, and correction, we will end up shipwrecked in our faith.

> But as for you, continue to hold to the things that you have learned and of which you are convinced, knowing from whom you learned [them]. And how from your childhood you have had a knowledge of and been acquainted with the sacred Writings, which are able to instruct you and give you the understanding for salvation which comes through faith in Christ Jesus [through the leaning of the entire human personality on God in Christ Jesus in absolute trust and confidence in His power, wisdom, and goodness]. Every Scripture is God-breathed (given by His inspiration) and profitable for instruction, for reproof and conviction of sin, for correction of error and discipline in obedience, [and] for training in righteousness (in holy living, in conformity to God's will in thought, purpose, and action), so that the man of God may be complete and proficient, well fitted and thoroughly equipped for every good work.
>
> —2 TIMOTHY 3:14–17

It is not enough to have a great call on your life; it is not enough just to know there is a spiritual inheritance for you. Your call must be directed, confirmed, and proven by the word of Truth—that's how you know you belong to God.

Jesus said in John 10:25–27:

> The very works that I do by the power of My Father and in My Father's name bear witness concerning Me [they are My credentials and evidence in support of Me]. But you do not believe and trust and rely on Me because you do not belong to My fold [you are no sheep of Mine]. The sheep that are My own hear and are listening to My voice; and I know them, and they follow Me.

You have to know for sure that you got saved *for real*. My Bible tells me this: "Old things are passed away; behold, all things are become new" (2 Cor. 5:17, KJV). How can you be in the presence of almighty God, read His Word every day, and still desire to live in sin? The Holy Spirit (the Spirit of Truth), who lives inside of you, won't allow it—He will send conviction until you change. When Jesus washes your sins away, He gives you a new heart and then starts transforming your mind. And this should be determined before you ever attempt to seek out a calling.

Everyone who goes to church does not belong to the Father. Jude 4 says that demons that are clothed like believers have crept into the church. But when the Spirit of Truth shows up, He separates the wheat from the tares. People who don't belong to God cannot digest Truth. It is too much for them. They choke on it. Truth confronts the atmosphere—but if you belong to God, even though His Word may be cutting you to the core, your spirit will still say, "Ouch! God, this hurts! Nevertheless, *yes, Lord…I thank You.*"

The Book of Hebrews helps us to understand the importance of allowing the Truth to transform our lives through training, correction, and discipline:

> Therefore then, since we are surrounded by so great a cloud of witnesses [who have borne testimony to

the Truth], let us strip off and throw aside every en-
cumbrance (unnecessary weight) and that sin which
so readily (deftly and cleverly) clings to and entangles
us, and let us run with patient endurance and steady
and active persistence the appointed course of the race
that is set before us, looking away [from all that will
distract] to Jesus, Who is the Leader and the Source
of our faith [giving the first incentive for our belief]
and is also its Finisher [bringing it to maturity and
perfection]. He, for the joy [of obtaining the prize]
that was set before Him, endured the cross, despis-
ing and ignoring the shame, and is now seated at the
right hand of the throne of God....For the Lord corrects and disciplines everyone whom He loves, and He
punishes, even scourges, every son whom He accepts
and welcomes to His heart and cherishes. You must
submit to and endure [correction] for discipline; God
is dealing with you as with sons. For what son is there
whom his father does not [thus] train and correct and
discipline?

—HEBREWS 12:1–2, 6–7

For the time being no discipline brings joy, but
seems grievous and painful; but afterwards it yields
a peaceable fruit of righteousness to those who have
been trained by it [a harvest of fruit which consists
in righteousness—in conformity to God's will in
purpose, thought, and action, resulting in right living
and right standing with God]. So then, brace up and
reinvigorate and set right your slackened and weakened and drooping hands and strengthen your feeble
and palsied and tottering knees. And cut through and
make firm and plain and smooth, straight paths for
your feet [yes, make them safe and upright and happy

paths that go in the right direction], so that the lame and halting [limbs] may not be put out of joint, but rather may be cured.

—HEBREWS 12:11–13

In contrast we have the example of Judas, who walked with Jesus every day, hearing the Word and seeing miracles, but who was double-minded in all his ways. Even though he traveled with Jesus, I doubt that he spent much time in His presence—and that's when temptation gets the best of you. Judas was tired and dissatisfied, and he thought he saw something "bigger and better" on the horizon. He betrayed the Lord while trying to create a "portion" for himself, and then he died without receiving it. (See John 13:1–30; Matthew 27:3–5.)

> TOO MANY PEOPLE HAVE THEIR OWN IDEAS ABOUT WHAT THE FATHER SHOULD DO, BUT THEY ARE BLIND TO THEIR OWN SHORTCOMINGS.

Let me tell you something. If you can't handle the weight of the attack of the enemy, you will never be able to handle the weight of the anointing for anyone else—because the anointing is much heavier than anything the devil could even put on you.

While you are talking about getting to your next level in God, He's watching…closely. When you are going through a fiery trial, do you still come to church? Do you still praise Him, or do you just sit in the pew with your lips cocked to the side? If you are coming through some things in your finances, do you withhold your tithe? If your kids drove you crazy this week, did you let it affect your relationship with God? Are rivers of living water flowing out of your spirit?

I can just hear God saying, "How can I give you anything greater when you can't handle these light afflictions? What are you doing with what you already have?" The Bible says that persecutions will come because of the Word (Mark 4:17). So if you can't handle what you are going through now, don't look for God to give you more. Don't expect God to release a divine portion. He's not going to give you anything you can't handle.

When you are being prepared to walk into destiny, don't think you are just going to walk into it without any warfare. Stop panicking every time something doesn't go your way. Be a son. Be a daughter. Stay in the presence of your heavenly Father so you can stay submitted and please Him on earth. Learn the lesson by enduring the test.

Spiritual Racehorses

One day I saw a horse race while watching television. One horse was running really fast, so I said, "Oh, man, he's going to win." Another was about three to four horses behind. But he picked up speed when the jockey really started hitting him, and he ran straight past the rest of the horses and crossed the finish line. The horse that was once in the middle of the pack came forward and won the million-dollar prize. Everybody wants to win a race, especially when we see a reward.

But you must understand the essence of a winning horse. Not only was he trained, but also he was whipped to the finish line. He did not win by being "rubbed" there or "patted" to the Winner's Circle! He was driven to there, first by a trainer and then by a jockey. Scripture tells us that some *plant* and others *water*, but God gives the increase. (See 1 Corinthians 3:6–7.)

You have to decide who you are based on the Truth. Ask yourself, "Am I like a field horse or a racehorse?" Let's look at the process. From what I was told, horse trainers go to places like Australia and find wild horses—with strong muscles and teeth, beautiful structures, and shining coats—galloping through the hills. The horses are beautiful and free, but they lack purpose and direction.

The trainers track the horses, waiting until just the right time. Then they catch a horse off guard, put a noose around its neck, and, with great struggle, put it in a truck. The horse bucks and kicks all the way to the stables, sometimes damaging the vehicle. The trucks are made out of steel—because wild horses that are beautiful, powerful, and have great potential will always try to break out. And they will tear things up in the process.

Once back at the stables, the trainers put the horse in a stall. He is really bucking, so they tie him down by the jaw with the ropes close to the railing. (I have actually seen this done.) All night long, that horse kicks and howls. You wonder, *Why don't they let him out?* They can't. He has to be trained to stay in the stall—because during a race, he must stay there until the door is opened. He can't try to buck his way out. So the first thing the horse must learn is how to begin.

You see, trainers don't start by galloping the horse or giving him treats. They don't start by brushing his coat and telling him how beautiful he is. They start him in the position he is going to assume during a race. Do you see the revelation?

Then rebuke and correction begin. They tie a rope around the horse's neck, bring him out of the stall into a big, fenced area, and start walking. The whole time, he is bucking…does this sound familiar? Is the Lord leading you, but you are bucking Him, saying, "Why can't I go out and preach? Why can't I do this or that?" Just keep quiet and keep walking, because you are still wild. God is training you how to walk, and you are still galloping, rearing up, and complaining about what you are going through. "This rope is hurting my neck. You're trying to suppress me. You're trying to hold me back. You're choking me!" "Be quiet and keep walking," the Lord says. "I'm teaching you how to follow Me."

The hardest part comes when the trainer clamps a bit in the horse's mouth. The horse literally goes crazy, because he doesn't like anything controlling his mouth. The trainer, on the other hand, is trying to help the horse understand, "If you let me control your mouth, then when you are running a race, you can be weaved around anything that gets in the way. You can get past your struggle, past your opponent, and beyond anything that's trying to hold you captive. I can teach you how to win the prize."

The next step is to throw blankets on the horse's back before putting on a saddle. When the trainer throws the first blanket, the horse bucks because he doesn't want anything up there. Are you seeing this? You may be bucking against instruction, saying, "Oh, God has a great business for me. He has a great ministry for me." But you can't handle the weight of anything on your back. You can't even carry one blanket. That's one hour of prayer.

Let's take this further. Being faithful to God in your spiritual walk is your first blanket. Integrity in your relationships is your second, and so on. Once the blankets are in place, the horse can be saddled. Though the horse resists, he can never become a winner without submitting to this process—no matter how uncomfortable the process gets. The jockey must have a place to sit so that he can direct the horse to the finish line.

Listen to me. If you are going to reach destiny, if you are going to receive and activate your spiritual inheritance, you have to be willing to accept rebuke. When you are corrected, be humble and honest with yourself. You are not like a field horse. You are a thoroughbred from a royal family line. God is driving you to win.

> DON'T GET UPSET WHEN GOD USES SOMEBODY TO BRING CORRECTION IN YOUR LIFE.

Remember this. When a horse is running head-to-head with the pack, the jockey has to strike the horse with the rod. The jockey is saying, "I didn't train you to run with the pack. I trained you to be winner. You have something special inside of you. There's a fire in your belly...now, run!" So get your spirit right because God is training you. He sees greatness in you—He sees a winner.

Receiving the true portion of the Father is a process. We have to get clean, stop the falsehoods, get guile out of our mouths, and stop being deceitful and double-minded. When you learn to walk in the integrity of your spirit, that is when you are going to be able to see more, and that is when you will be able to receive and activate your spiritual inheritance. Jesus told Nathanael:

> Then He said to him, I assure you, most solemnly I tell
> you all, you shall see heaven opened, and the angels of
> God ascending and descending upon the Son of Man!
> —JOHN 1:51

Listen. You won't receive your spiritual inheritance just because you are having a high time in the Spirit. Your life isn't going to change just because you are shouting and dancing. No! God is calling for your participation, because for too long, the body of Christ has been sitting back saying, "Prophesy over me," and God is saying, "No! I've already done My part."

If you want to see heaven opened...if you want your divine portion...you don't need somebody to prophesy over you. When your life is full of integrity and you put your spirit in the posture to be trained, heaven will open.

So please understand me when I say that leadership can't be concerned about your feelings. Think about this: the clothes you are wearing right now have been cut according to a pattern. The Father created a pattern for you (from those who have gone before you). Now, He is making sure to cut you the right way so He can duplicate a pattern of righteousness in your children, friends, and others in your circle of influence. Again, it's not just about you. Do you want God to activate spiritual destiny in your life? Then submit to the training, preparation, and correction that prepare you for that destiny. Don't be satisfied with junk food, cookies, candy, and prophecies; only hunger *and thirst* for the presence of God in your life—learn to embrace the Spirit of Truth.

CHAPTER 10

The Making of a Son

A multimillionaire doesn't just give an inheritance to someone that multimilllionaire has just met. Inheritances are earned by way of DNA (that is, blood relationship), adoption, or close relationship. In order to receive an inheritance, you have to be born or adopted into a family and then live respectably within that family's guidelines.

There are many multimillionaire parents who birthed children who subsequently rebelled against their leadership. Thus, when the parents died, they left all of their inheritance to charities like animal foundations and breast cancer foundations, sometimes leaving the children with nothing. So just being born into a family and having the same DNA as your parents does not mean you will receive that inheritance.

When you have been born again and adopted into the Royal Family, you must embrace the truth. You now possess the DNA of your heavenly Father, and there will be some requirements for bearing His name. Hear this. In order to carry the name of Jesus and be associated with the kingdom of heaven, you must adopt a lifestyle of submission and obedience to your Father's will.

This requirement also applies to the spiritual leaders God has appointed to stand in His stead and speak on His behalf. A leader cannot speak on behalf of the Father and His Word if he or she has no relationship with Him. Without proper submission and obedience to God, a spiritual leader cannot hear the Lord—which means many simply hear their own intellect. When this happens, the people God has ordained to sit under their tutelage (as spiritual sons and daughters) aren't fed properly. Starving for true spiritual knowledge, these sons and daughters can become unruly in the spirit, because they are being pacified by intellectual stimulation when divine direction is needed.

God commanded Samuel to anoint David as king over Israel. It was an anointing for the future, the promise of a spiritual inheritance to kingship that would one day be his. Before David would become the king of Israel himself, he was placed in a position to serve King Saul, a man without an anointing to be a spiritual father. But David did not break rank—because he had already received his anointing from Samuel, who was his spiritual father. As we look back, Samuel had been raised in the temple under Eli, who was not a faithful priest or spiritual father to Samuel. Still, Samuel never broke rank, and thus the spiritual lineage of proper order and protocol was established.

Submission in the course of a relationship between a spiritual parent and a son or daughter is very powerful. Because we only want to embrace the good in our spiritual leaders, many people in the body of Christ are thrown for a loop when their leaders show unfaithfulness or weakness. We must learn to recognize that the bonds of spiritual relationship are strengthened by the process of walking through both good—*and bad*. That is the only way authentic relationships can be proven.

In every battle there must be an enemy, an opposition—a division. But to become authentic sons and daughters of the gospel, we must win the war against division. To be honored as spiritual children, our relationships must be tested and tried. The question we must all answer is this: when will I become mature enough to recognize that I am coming into sonship through a particular relationship?

A Man After God's Own Heart

In the life of King David, we have an example of a fully processed relationship. God said that David was a man after His own heart. Why?

Because he was a man of truth. David yielded himself completely to God, and when he messed up, he admitted his sins and got it right. Through every experience, David learned how to examine his own heart and submit himself to God. Whether it was a lion, bear, Goliath, or King Saul, David exemplified what being a son or daughter of the kingdom is all about. Let's look at this story closely.

David was a "ruddy" teenager when Samuel anointed Saul to be king over Israel. First Samuel 11:15 says, "All the people went to Gilgal and there they made Saul king before the Lord. And there they sacrificed peace offerings before the Lord, and there Saul and all the men of Israel rejoiced greatly." Earlier, in chapter 10, Samuel anointed Saul as king. Saul began operating in the anointing of Samuel immediately, just as though he was a schooled prophet. (See 1 Samuel 10:1, 10–11.) However, Saul did not examine his own heart; he had not made a full submission to God.

After Samuel anointed Saul, he did one more thing that bears significance in the process of becoming a spiritual son. He established the role of kingship within Israel and announced Saul's position to the people. The same day he anointed Saul (before Saul's actual coronation), Samuel said to all the people:

> Do you see him whom the Lord has chosen, that none like him is among all the people? And all the people shouted and said, Long live the king! Then Samuel told the people the manner of the kingdom [defining the position of the king in relation to God and to the people], and wrote it in a book and laid it up before the Lord. And Samuel sent all the people away, each one to his home.
>
> —1 SAMUEL 10:24–25

Spiritual authority and leadership must be defined. The role of a spiritual son or daughter in relationship with God and with his or her spiritual parent needs to be defined. Unless the body of Christ begins to understand this role, we will continue to hinder the move of the

Holy Spirit in the earth. We must begin to see leadership as people who are standing in the stead of God and learn to follow their spiritual direction.

That became a profound lesson for David, because shortly after King Saul grieved the heart of God through his disobedience, Samuel came to Bethlehem looking for David's natural father, Jesse. Now, let me explain the significance of David's appointment. Samuel had two natural sons who did not walk in his ways, and they served badly as judges over Israel. Therefore the people told Samuel they wanted a king (1 Sam. 8:4–7). In obedience to God, he anointed Saul as king.

But remember that Samuel had respected Eli's position. When King Saul rejected the Lord and Samuel's spiritual mentorship, Samuel remained obedient to God, wiped his tears, got up, and went to Bethlehem where he would anoint David as the next king of Israel. By the time Samuel reached David, something powerful had been released.

Samuel was a "spiritual father," so when he anointed David, an anointing of order from the heavenly Father was poured out upon David's life. (See 1 Samuel 16.) Once again, Samuel's obedience to God was absolute. Because of that anointing, proper spiritual protocol was poured out onto David. As a result, he too would never raise his hand against the Lord's anointed, no matter what King Saul ultimately would do to harm him.

> WE DO NOT WANT TO ACCEPT OUR PART OF THE RESPONSIBILITY OF THE RELATIONSHIP. WE ARE CALLED TO BE CHILDREN, JUST AS THEY ARE CALLED TO BE PARENTS. AND NEITHER PARTY HAS THE AUTHORITY TO RENOUNCE A DECISION IN THE FLESH THAT WAS MADE IN THE SPIRIT.

David not only received the anointing to become king, but he also received the supernatural ability to become a true son. But again, the problem was that Saul didn't know how to be a father. He was so busy enjoying how he became a king that he never bothered to inquire spiritually as to how he could remain a king in right standing with

God. Therefore, David had to walk through some kingdom lessons before his time would come to assume the throne. Do you see the principle? God is your Father in heaven. When He gives you a father in the earthly realm (your pastor), you must remain a son or daughter—even if your leader hasn't yet received the revelation that he or she is to be a father or mother.

Not long after Samuel anointed David, David was divinely placed in Saul's camp. David had won many victories for the king, but I believe that as a forerunner of Christ, he was prophetically made a son through the things he suffered (Heb. 5:8). First Samuel 18:10–11 says that an evil spirit from the Lord came upon Saul, and he threw a javelin at David in order to kill him.

Let me pause here. I believe that at times we enter into spiritual relationships with our leadership without knowing all of the details about what they have encountered in their own experiences with the Lord. We are not aware of the areas in their lives where they have disobeyed God and for which they may still be paying penalties. Every leader is going through his or her own process of becoming a son or daughter of God.

Our leaders have been called to lead, yet they are still going through their own personal relationships with God. Saul had disobeyed God, and because of his disobedience, he was suffering the penalty when David came into the camp. He was no longer enjoying the fellowship and power of his anointing from Samuel.

When David entered Saul's camp, David was walking in obedience to God, and as a result, his life demonstrated the power of his anointing. This distressed Saul, for it was a vivid reminder to him of the anointing he once had in his life.

Samuel was a prophet, so he wore a prayer shawl (a *tallit*). A prophet's shawl had four corners, each with five knots in the tassel that extended from it. These five knots represented the power and authority in the names of God. In 1 Samuel 15, Samuel confronted Saul with his disobedience and told him this: "Because you have rejected the word of the Lord, He also has rejected you from being king" (v. 23). Samuel further indicated that he would not return with Saul to the tabernacle and allow Saul to worship God. This greatly distressed Saul, and as Samuel turned to leave, Saul grabbed the hem of Samuel's mantle, tearing off a corner of it (v. 27).

The Bible translates the corner as the "hem" of the garment, which represented the authority of God. Recognizing the visual picture this act of disobedience would give to Saul, Samuel said to him, "The Lord has torn the kingdom of Israel from you this day and has given it to a neighbor of yours who is better than you" (v. 28).

Grasp the significance of this lesson. Once you (the person who is submitted under authority), by your disobedience, tear the authority of the person that is over you in the Lord, the same authority is automatically torn from you. This is a spiritual principle that you must never forget. It is one that Jesus did not forget when He endured every trial that He was required by the Father to walk through. If He had rejected that process, He would have been tearing God's authority from Him. This is why He said, "Not as I will, but Thy will be done." If His response to suffering had been anything else, then He would have thrown away His authority as the Son of God.

Remember, Jesus didn't say that He came to destroy the Law—He said that He came to fulfill it (Matt. 5:17). He couldn't *tear* His Father's authority—that would have sabotaged everything the Father had established from the beginning of time. After Jesus took His last breath on the cross and said, "It is finished," the Father brought to an end the old law and established the new by tearing the veil of the holy of holies from top to bottom. Jesus' assignment was to remain obedient. It was a perfect plan executed in perfect order.

In order for you to get power with God, you have to be able to see the vision of what *He* desires to take place—not the vision of a natural man. Let me explain. When Samuel laid his hands on David, Samuel knew that David would become the next king. The Spirit of the Lord came upon David "from that day forward" (1 Sam. 16:13), and he began to see the kingdom as God saw it. This is why he was able to take the victory every time he went out to battle. David was under the Lord's anointing to win the war for Israel! He saw his heavenly Father's vision in spite of what he was going through, and he stayed in his place.

The Prophetic Death Sentence

When Saul's daughter Michal fell in love with David, Saul recognized an opportunity to set David up to be killed. (See 1 Samuel 18.) He sent orders for David to bring him one hundred foreskins from the Philistine army as a prerequisite to marrying Michal. This was virtually impossible to do. Yet, because David had already received an anointing to walk into his next realm with God, he didn't bring back one hundred; he brought back two hundred (v. 27). Saul intended for David to be killed in the battle, but David came back victorious.

Because David was under proper spiritual alignment and had a contrite heart, God could place an anointing upon him to take down the spirit of the Philistines, which had worked through Delilah to snare Samson's strength. In reality, David's battle with the Philistines was not a natural one—and it wasn't the first time he had taken them down. (God birthed his ministry by helping him to take the head of Goliath.) When David came back to King Saul with a double portion of Philistine flesh, it confirmed that God was in the process of taking down a stronghold that existed before David's time.

If you remember, Samson's first marriage had been to a Philistine girl, and their marriage didn't work out. Ultimately he met Delilah—who matched his strength in the spirit realm because she was assigned to take him down. Because of this assignment, Delilah was completely taken over by the goddess of love and war that ruled the Philistines. And because Samson wasn't under proper spiritual alignment and didn't keep his heart in check, he fell under that spirit's power. Delilah laid an easy snare through deception—she became something she wasn't so that Samson would believe her and relinquish his authority. (Remember this point, because we will see this deceptive spirit in full bloom later.)

In the story of David's taking of a double portion of Philistine foreskins, King Saul had set the trap for David. But he did not realize that God was working something mighty through this situation. David came back with two hundred Philistine foreskins, won Saul's daughter in marriage, and dealt prophetically with the enemy's assignment against Israel—past, present, and future—all at the same time.

After Saul gave Michal to David in marriage, he became David's enemy continually. But the Bible says that David behaved himself wisely. (See 1 Samuel 18:27–30.) If you read the whole story of David and Saul, you will find that at least two or three times David is described as behaving and handling himself respectfully when Saul came against him.

On two different occasions, Saul threw a spear at David, and David escaped—yet he continued to behave himself. Regardless of what Saul did, David never got out of order. He learned how to remain under his anointing—because he understood his purpose. He also understood that he was called to minister to Saul. Whenever the evil spirit of the Lord would start overtaking Saul, David would start ministering (1 Sam. 16:15–23).

When we start seeing the enemy attack the men and women of God whose leadership we are under, we need to start ministering to them in the Spirit realm. This doesn't necessarily mean we will be able physically to go to them, because David couldn't go to Saul and say, "Let me tell you this from the Lord…" He used the gift that God had given him, and that gift ministered. David was anointed to play the harp, so he didn't try to prophesy to Saul (in words). Rather, he operated with Saul out of his specific anointing.

Some people are anointed to sing in the choir; others are anointed to play the keyboard or guitar. Some are anointed to usher or direct the choir. Still others are anointed to put together hospitality. When you see your spiritual leaders going through something, that's your opportunity to get in your anointing—because that is what ministers to them. Remember your "measure of faith"? It is part of how God makes you a son or daughter of the kingdom. Staying in your lane is important.

Let me take this further. When Saul began to pursue David, David disguised himself and ran into the city of Nob (1 Sam. 21). When he got to the tabernacle, Ahimelech asked him, "What are you, a mighty warrior, doing here by yourself?" (I'm paraphrasing.)

David said, "Well, I've come on a private mission that no one is supposed to know anything about." *Do you get this?* David was running for his life, yet he still wouldn't gossip and say, "Saul is out of his mind. He's raging and chasing me." No! He covered Saul and said, "I'm on a private mission, and nobody knows about it but King Saul and me."

> REMEMBER, WHAT YOU SOW AS A SERVANT, YOU WILL REAP AS A LEADER.

The wisdom of the Lord was speaking through David, and I will tell you why. There are things you will go through with your leadership that aren't for you to tell to anyone. Many times we miss the mark on this. We go around saying, "Let me tell you what he did..." "Let me tell you how she said it...she hurt me." No! You are on a private mission between you and your leadership, and you are not supposed to talk about it.

The next thing that happened was powerful. Let's go to 1 Samuel 21:8–9:

> David said to Ahimelech, Do you have at hand a sword or spear? The king's business required haste, and I brought neither my sword nor my weapons with me. The priest said, The sword of Goliath the Philistine, whom you slew in the Valley of Elah, see, it is here wrapped in a cloth behind the ephod; if you will take that, do so, for there is no other here. And David said, There is none like that; give it to me.

The only weapon they had in the tabernacle was the sword of the giant that David killed! Catch this! David could have Goliath's sword because he had fought and won that battle earlier! Goliath was a stronghold he had pulled down—a mighty giant that David got rid of. The reason many Christians can't walk in authority is this: we have no weapons, so we haven't ever brought down an enemy. You can only fight with what you have conquered. Yet when we submit to proper spiritual alignment and another enemy pursues us, we will be able to take up that same weapon and bring Satan's kingdom down.

Let me break this down for you. Have you fought and won the victory over lying? Then declare to the devil: "I don't lie anymore." Have you fought and won the victory over immorality? Then come against him, saying, "I don't fornicate anymore." Why? You can stand against the devil like this because, "Through the strength of the Lord, I killed that giant!"

Interceding for Your Spiritual Leaders

Saul continued pursuing David, but as he ran, he began to receive prophecies about his situation, prophecies saying things like, "Today, the Lord has delivered the kingdom into your hands..." But even in that, David never used those prophecies as permission to attack and kill his leader. Why? David loved Saul in spite of what he was going through. He never became so greedy for power that he was willing to sit on the throne at the expense of dethroning Saul. David knew he was the next king, but he also understood timing.

Do you want ministry so much that you would be willing to take that which belongs to another man before it has been properly given? God gives you ministry; you just don't take it.

One day, David and his men were in a place called En-gedi, resting in the darkness of a deep cave (1 Sam. 24). Saul came into that same cave, not knowing that David and his men were in the cave's "innermost recesses" (v. 3). David watched as Saul relieved himself, which represents a state of vulnerability or weakness because his private parts were exposed.

Let's look at this prophetically. David saw the waste, the filth that was coming out of Saul's body. I say "filth" because urine and bile are bacteria. They are the "trash" that gets purged from our bodies. David went up behind Saul and cut his robe. And when he came out of the cave, he yelled back at Saul, saying, "Saul, let me show you this. I have the corner of your robe." But look at what happened.

What you cut from your leader, you lose the right to use it:

And it came to pass afterward, that David's heart
smote him, because he had cut off Saul's skirt. And

he said unto his men, The LORD forbid that I should do this thing unto my master, the LORD's anointed, to stretch forth mine hand against him, seeing he is the anointed of the LORD. So David stayed his servants with these words, and suffered them not to rise against Saul. But Saul rose up out of the cave, and went on his way. David also arose afterward, and went out of the cave, and cried after Saul, saying, My lord the king. And when Saul looked behind him, David stooped with his face to the earth, and bowed himself.

And David said to Saul, Wherefore hearest thou men's words, saying, Behold, David seeketh thy hurt? Behold, this day thine eyes have seen how that the LORD had delivered thee to day into mine hand in the cave: and some bade me kill thee: but mine eye spared thee; and I said, I will not put forth mine hand against my lord; for he is the LORD's anointed. Moreover, my father, see, yea, see the skirt of thy robe in my hand: for in that I cut off the skirt of thy robe, and killed thee not, know thou and see that there is neither evil nor transgression in mine hand, and I have not sinned against thee; yet thou huntest my soul to take it. The LORD judge between me and thee, and the LORD avenge me of thee: but mine hand shall not be upon thee. As saith the proverb of the ancients, Wickedness proceedeth from the wicked: but mine hand shall not be upon thee.

—1 SAMUEL 24:5–13, KJV

I believe David became afraid of what he had done because order had fallen on him. David knew from what Saul had done with Samuel that you never usurp authority. He knew the danger in touching the anointed one. And when he came to himself, he immediately began to repent to Saul. Not only did he repent but he also became Saul's intercessor. He stood between his men and Saul, daring them to lay a hand on Saul. Do you see this?

David was being pursued by Saul, yet he made the decision to protect his leader. That takes maturity. This is why you see David getting into a prostrate position when he repented—he was demonstrating to Saul, "Yes, I cut the corner of your robe, but I repent, and not only do I repent, but also my position on the ground still speaks of my submission and my honor to you as my leader."

David was saying, "Saul, you're chasing me! You're doing me wrong! Yet, I'm not against you. I had an opportunity to kill you while you were wasting yourself. I saw your nakedness. I saw the filth coming out of your body. I could have taken your life then."

We need to learn from this. Whatever God allows you to see about your leadership, that is what takes you from being a baby saint and a "bench member" to an intercessor—because everybody in the church can't see it. When God starts allowing you to see certain things, it's because your leaders really need your prayers! They need the intercession of a mature believer. This is not as much the exposing of a leader as it may be the revealing and testing of your maturity.

In other words, there are things some believers have to see so that true intercession can go up to God. True intercession must go up, so that after our leaders have preached to others, they won't be disqualified.

Everybody isn't appointed to simply pray, "O God, bless the pastor. Continue to bless his finances. O Lord, touch his family..." Somebody has to say, "Father, You revealed this to me, and I'll take it to my grave. But God, let there be a mighty deliverance..." so that the inheritance that he or she must pass on is not aborted. The spiritual inheritance, the word that God has ordained for your leader to impart into your life, cannot be hindered by the flesh as long as you remain in your anointing. If you will stay in your calling, you will be demonstrating to God that you are ready to stand the test of real spiritual sonship, and you will become a real son or daughter.

Whether David realized it or not, by his actions, he was walking under the powerful anointing that Samuel had imparted unto him. The next time he ran into Saul, the king was sleeping. David took Saul's water pitcher and spear and went a safe distance away. I believe this is where you will see the most awesome lesson we will ever learn. Let's look at what happened:

> Then David went over to the other side, and stood on the top of an hill afar off; a great space being between them: And David cried to the people, and to Abner the son of Ner, saying, Answerest thou not, Abner? Then Abner answered and said, Who art thou that criest to the king? And David said to Abner, Art not thou a valiant man? and who is like to thee in Israel? wherefore then hast thou not kept thy lord the king? for there came one of the people in to destroy the king thy lord. This thing is not good that thou hast done. As the Lord liveth, ye are worthy to die, because ye have not kept your master, the LORD's anointed. And now see where the king's spear is, and the cruse of water that was at his bolster. And Saul knew David's voice, and said, Is this thy voice, my son David? And David said, It is my voice, my lord, O king.
> —1 SAMUEL 26:13–17, KJV

David told Saul's soldiers that they needed to die because they failed to protect Saul. They never should have let him get that close to Saul. It was as if he was saying, "What kind of watching are you doing?" David is revealing a supernatural love of a son for his father-in-the-making. Even though Saul was pursuing David to try to take his life, David was still concerned for Saul's life and his well-being.

This illustration spoke something into my spirit, a real truth that we need to heed. Just because our leaders may have a lot of people around them all the time does not mean they are spiritually protected. Why? Some people hang around a leader for association. Others stay close to their leaders to get the credit, because if any one of Saul's soldiers had been successful at capturing and killing David, he would have been considered "the man"! Those soldiers were more concerned with becoming "the man" in Saul's eyes than they were about protecting Saul's life.

The Making of a Son

It is important to remember in this illustration that David had been anointed as a son, but Saul had not yet received the anointing to be a spiritual father. But something still happened while David was running for his life. Let's go back and read 1 Samuel 26:17–19 (KJV):

> And Saul knew David's voice, and said, Is this thy voice, my son David? And David said, It is my voice, my lord, O king. And he said, Wherefore doth my lord thus pursue after his servant? for what have I done? or what evil is in mine hand? Now therefore, I pray thee, let my lord the king hear the words of his servant. If the LORD have stirred thee up against me, let him accept an offering: but if they be the children of men, cursed be they before the LORD; for they have driven me out this day from abiding in the inheritance of the LORD, saying, Go, serve other gods.

After this event, Saul declared that from that day forward, he would no longer chase David and try to harm him (v. 21). He blessed David as a son, and the era was ended—because David had passed the test. He was ready to abide in his spiritual inheritance and to be called "son."

God proved David so that whatever happened in the kingdom, David would always desire to do what was right in His eyes and not what was popular. Even when he made a mistake with Bathsheba, David still repented and returned to his Father—because he was a man after God's own heart. He endured the process of being made into a true spiritual son. Therefore, God could trust David with His kingdom...because He could trust him with His king.

God is saying today, "I can trust you with the kingdom if I can trust you with My king. I can trust you to cover My kingdom if I can trust you to cover My king." Are you ready to become a true son or daughter of the kingdom and receive your spiritual inheritance?

CHAPTER 11

The Seduction of Jezebel

n order to understand the process by which Jezebel is exposed and dismantled, we must understand the power of what having a lineage really means. Why? Because everything that God is dealing with you about individually isn't just about you. It's bigger than you are. It's bigger than me. The Father's portion is about generations. It's about relationships. This is why Christ came as a son from a Father into the womb of a mother. God is about *family*.

Why is this important? If you don't know where the root of a spirit comes from, you will be frustrated for the rest of your life fighting the symptoms. And I promise you that the body of Christ has been guilty of fighting Ahab and Jezebel, and not really getting to the root from which they came. In order for God to deliver the church from the attacks of Jezebel and Ahab, we must be able to establish them as symptoms—not the strong man.

The reason why Jezebel attacks and wins is because those who preach the gospel have not presented the full knowledge of where this spirit came from. This is why Hosea 4:6 says we are destroyed for a lack of knowledge. Yet this will not be our fate any more.

You might be asking yourself, "Why must we embrace a corporate call? Why must we embrace the church as the family of God?" It is because our adversary, the devil, has launched a counterattack—the spirit of Jezebel. Its goal is to achieve a much bigger purpose than just affecting one person. The spirit of Jezebel intends to frustrate the plans of our heavenly Father, to wreak havoc in the church, and to stop His purposes. Its deception is bigger than you can even imagine, but today, the truth about this spirit will be revealed.

The Lineage of Ahab

Although we are beginning this chapter with a very familiar name—Jezebel—and the story may be familiar to you, please don't allow the spirit of familiarity to cause you to miss this next layer of revelation. You see, in order to dismantle this spirit, you must first go to the root of the spirit. Let's just see how Jezebel came into existence so that we can determine if she has the power to stay.

King Ahab, Jezebel's husband, was the product of an evil lineage that started when God took the kingdom of Israel from Solomon (because he was worshiping other gods and living wickedly before the Lord). Because of his wickedness, the Father sent the prophet Ahijah to Jeroboam. In the natural, Jeroboam was not in the lineage of kings. However, like Saul, Jeroboam received a spiritual impartation directly from the Lord through the man of God. From Solomon's refusal to repent, God split the kingdom, and Jeroboam received ten of the twelve tribes of Israel. (See 1 Kings 11:28–40).

During his reign, Jeroboam had constant warfare with Rehoboam, Solomon's son. In fear of losing his kingdom, Jeroboam manipulated the people of God. He perverted God's prophetic plan by making golden calves in order to keep the people from leaving his kingdom to worship in Jerusalem. He also constructed "high places" and ordained the "lowest of the people" (who were not of the tribe of Levi) as priests unto God.

Making matters worse, he then ordained a counterfeit feast to duplicate the feast of the Lord that was held in Judah. This led the entire nation into idolatry (1 Kings 12:25–33). Later, he ordained himself a priest of the high places—and the Lord set Himself to cut off the house of Jeroboam from the face of the earth (1 Kings 13:33–34). Ultimately, God used Ahijah the prophet to confirm the curse upon Jeroboam. (See 1 Kings 14:7–16.)

Jeroboam was brought to the realization that when you have been given a mantle for which you have paid nothing, it is not yours to do with whatever you may desire. You cannot stretch it past its original assignment, nor can God allow it to rest on anything or anyone that is not clean or submitted. The Bible shows us how Jeroboam was judged. One day his son became ill, and rather than repent to the prophet and God for his behavior, Jeroboam told his wife to disguise herself and go to the prophet asking for prayer for their son to be healed. When Ahijah saw what they were trying to do, he not only pronounced a curse upon Jeroboam, but he also pronounced a curse on his whole lineage. When his wife returned home and her feet hit the doorstep, their son immediately died.

Do you see a pattern here? Jeroboam's story is a classic example and a warning as to how pride and greed can cause that which once was real and pure to become perverted. And as you will see, Jeroboam's counterfeit anointing went beyond his generations.

After eighteen years of walking in disobedience as a king of Israel, Jeroboam died. Then his son Nadab assumed the throne of Israel for two years—walking in his father's ways—until he was killed by one of his subjects, Baasha. Baasha reigned for twenty-four years and destroyed everyone in the house of Jeroboam, thus fulfilling the word of the Lord to Jeroboam. But the Bible says that he then walked in the way of Jeroboam (1 Kings 15:34). When Baasha died, his son Elah reigned in his stead for two years until he was killed by one of his subjects, Zimri. Zimri held the throne for seven days, until the people rose up against him and appointed another king—Ahab's father, Omri, captain of the host of Israel.

Upon becoming king, Omri went after Zimri—and when Zimri heard he was coming, he killed himself in a fire. Omri reigned for twelve years, but the Bible says he "did evil in the eyes of the Lord, even worse than all who were before him. He walked in all the ways of Jeroboam" (1 Kings 16:25–26). Because Omri was *Ahab's father*, Ahab became the seventh king after his death . . . and sin multiplied. During Ahab's twenty-two-year reign, "Ahab did more to provoke the Lord, the God of Israel, to anger than all the kings of Israel before him" (v. 33). Let's see why. Was it simply because he married Jezebel?

The spirit of Jezebel isn't just after you. It wants the spiritual inheritance that is to be given to those who are to come behind you in your spiritual lineage. Do you see this? Ahab came from a lineage of idolatry, which put him in a posture of weakness concerning the things of God. When you refuse to accept correction, which is the right way, you are drawn to perversion—the wrong way of doing things. You desire things that are outside of God's order. As a result, you are not willing to do things the right way before God or to receive things the right way. You would rather go around the corner and around the fence to get what you want than to come through the proper order of God.

> YOU WILL DISCOVER THAT WHEN YOU OPEN UP YOUR SPIRIT TO DISOBEDIENCE BY REFUSING INSTRUCTION AND AVOIDING CORRECTION, YOU BECOME PREY TO A FALSE ANOINTING.

Not only did Ahab begin to serve and worship Baal right after he married Jezebel, but he also did something else that really provoked the Lord to anger. Let's see what this was:

> And Ahab son of Omri did evil in the sight of the Lord above all before him. As if it had been a light thing for Ahab to walk in the sins of Jeroboam son of Nebat, he took for a wife Jezebel daughter of Ethbaal king of the Sidonians, and served Baal and worshiped him. He erected an altar for Baal in the house of Baal which he built in Samaria. And Ahab made an Asherah [idolatrous symbol of the goddess Asherah]. Ahab did more to provoke the Lord, the God of Israel, to anger than all the kings of Israel before him. In his days, Hiel the Bethelite built Jericho. He laid its foundations at the cost of the life of Abiram his firstborn, and set up its gates with the loss of his youngest son Segub, according to the word of the Lord which He spoke through Joshua son of Nun.
>
> —1 KINGS 16:30–34

For as long as I can remember, I was taught that the Lord was provoked to anger simply because Ahab married Jezebel. Let's consider this. Ahab came from an evil lineage. His spirit was already evil, so he was naturally attracted to an evil wife. God was not angry because the devil married the devil. If you will allow me, I will show you why.

The Lineage of Jezebel

Webster's dictionary defines the word *Jezebel* as "an impudent, shameless, morally unrestrained woman." *Impudent* means, "marked by contemptuous or cocky boldness or disregard for others." This vile spirit doesn't regard anybody. It is unteachable; it cannot be led—because it is sure it already knows the way.

What I must make known, first and foremost, is that Jezebel is the prop—the frame—not the real enemy. Jezebel's father was the high priest of Ashtoreth. His name was *Ethbaal*, which meant "Baal's man." Historically speaking, if a man was a priest in the Old Testament, then his children were also raised in the priesthood and taught the same passion of worship toward the gods that they served. Now we can see why Jezebel was so evil. She was raised in evil, therefore giving her a passion to operate in perversion (meaning taking God's version and God's way and twisting them until they fulfilled her own evil desires).

Another thing that weighed heavily in my spirit was the spelling of her name, *J-e-z-e-b-e-l*. The last three letters of her name are not spelled exactly like *Baal*, but it has been made clear that Jezebel was birthed from an idolatrous lineage when Ahab married her. When studying in the *International Standard Bible Encyclopedia*, I found that the names *Baal* and *Bel* could be used interchangeably.[1]

Something stirred within me when I read these words in the Book of Revelation: "I gave her time to repent, but she has no desire to repent of her immorality" (Rev. 2:21). *If Jezebel was given an opportunity to repent, then she must not have been the chief spirit.* Why? Because the devil can't ever repent and be saved! He has already been cast down from heaven—so he does not have the opportunity to repent. Neither do any spirits that are subject to him.

This confirmed to me that there is a ruling spirit that controls Jezebel. For years, the church has pointed the finger and declared, "It's Jezebel...it's the Jezebel spirit." We've lived under the illusion that Jezebel is controlling our churches, when in fact, Jezebel is the deception. *She's not the real thing.* She's the decoy that the devil has been using to shift our focus and to deceive us.

As a result, we have identified a "figure head" in the spirit realm and have been fighting the wrong battle. The real culprit behind Jezebel has been hidden for centuries. Let's go back and see why.

The Origin of Baal

First Kings 16:33 says:

> And Ahab made an Asherah....Ahab did more to provoke the Lord than all the kings of Israel that were before him.

This verse reveals what really provoked the Lord. It wasn't simply the fact that Ahab married Jezebel, because he was already evil. What provoked the Lord is that he erected a statue (an idolatrous image) called an *Asherah*. You may be wondering, *What is an Asherah?* Well, first, let's see how many times this term is mentioned in the Word.

> Also Maacah his mother he removed from being queen mother, because she had an image made for [the goddess] Asherah. Asa destroyed her image, burning it by the brook Kidron.
>
> —1 Kings 15:13

> He *[Hezekiah's son]* made a graven image of [the goddess] Asherah and set it in the house, of which the Lord said to David and to Solomon his son, In this house and in Jerusalem, which I have chosen out of all the tribes of Israel, will I put My Name [and the pledge of My presence] forever.
>
> —2 Kings 21:7

> And the king *[Josiah]* commanded Hilkiah the high
> priest and the priests of the second rank and the keep-
> ers of the threshold to bring out of the temple of the
> Lord all the vessels made for Baal, for [the goddess]
> Asherah, and for all the hosts of the heavens; and
> he burned them outside Jerusalem in the fields of
> the Kidron, and carried their ashes to Bethel [where
> Israel's idolatry began].
>
> —2 KINGS 23:4

Hear me! The church is not fighting against a mere woman! We must pull down the *stronghold*...the "proud and lofty thing" that controls her.

Let's start by understanding that Baal's evil legacy came into being through a natural son's disobedience. Do you remember the story of Ham, the youngest son of Noah, from Genesis 9? Ham uncovered his father's nakedness and was cursed. (See Genesis 9:20–26.) When looking at the lineage of Ham, you will see that ancient pagans knew his oldest son, Cush, as *Bel,* the Confounder. He was known as the *god of confusion* because he founded Babylon. Do you notice that the name that Cush was known by, *B-e-l,* has the same spelling as the end of the name, Jeze-*b-e-l*? Every time you see the words *Bel* or *Baal,* it is a suggestion that there is confusion in the midst.

Cush's son Nimrod is described in Genesis 10:8 as "the first to be a mighty man on earth."[2] He was the first man to war against his neighbors. What I want to make clear is that before Nimrod there was no existence of war. He was the first to establish what we call war today. On this same page, the *Chumash* states, "Nimrod ensnared men with his words and incited them *to rebel* against God." Do you see the word *rebel*? This is why rebellion is as the sin of witchcraft (1 Sam. 15:23). Because it contains *b-e-l,* it is guaranteed to put your life in a world of confusion—and God is not the author of confusion.

Nimrod's first conquest was Babel, one of the greatest cities of the ancient world. In its conception, the people decided to build a tower that would reach into the heavens. But when God realized that the motive for building this structure was to move toward Him *without* having a relationship with Him, He gave everybody a different language and scattered them over the face of the whole earth (Gen. 11:9). Why did this upset God? Because they had declared, "Come…let us make a *name for ourselves*"—not a name for God (Gen. 11:4). Does that sound familiar?

Now, let's move on. Then something very deep happened. Nimrod married his mother, Semiramis, and they became known in Egypt as Isis and Osiris. The pagans worshiped both the mother and the son as gods—which introduced the worship of Baal and his female counterpart, Ashtoreth. In the book *Jezebel vs. Elijah: The Great End Time Clash* by Dr. Bree Keyton (which is a book I highly recommend that you read), Dr. Keyton informs us that "…the worship of Baal and Ashtoreth was the religion of self-worship, self will…"[3] (This is the reason why, when we don't yield our will to the Lord and are *self-willed*, whether we know it or not, we are practicing Baal worship.)

Dr. Keyton continues her description of the worship of Ashtoreth: "…lewd, indulgent, reckless behavior, acted out in sodomy, sex orgies and perversion. Priestesses were actually temple prostitutes. Sodomites were made male temple prostitutes. They had extravagant orgies when worshiping their gods….Enormous quantities of images of Ashtoreth were found with exaggerated sex organs, designed to foster sensual feelings."[4]

This was the birthing of perversion, the further establishment of self-will when man stopped seeking after the will of God and started seeking his own.

Baal and Ashtoreth

Before I get into writing about this revelation, I remember when my editor, Paula Bryant, and I were working on my author review copy of the manuscript that I had received back from the publisher. While in this particular section, we were both feeling that there was something very deep about Jezebel that the body of Christ was missing. At the same time, whenever I talked about, studied about, or began to do research on Jezebel, I would become sick and distracted, and all kinds of manifestations of other distractions would occur. One night I asked Paula to continue reading for me, because I just couldn't. A little while later she called me back and said, "Prophetess, you won't believe what I've found."

We continued digging deeper in the Bible, the *Chumash*, the *International Bible Encyclopedia*, and other sources, and we began to find very disturbing things about Jezebel. We came to the realization that Jezebel was not the primary spirit—*she was the form that was being used by a much greater force.* When we first found it, it sobered me, because I had not heard this before. I vividly remember being a little shaken and a bit put back, as I thought, *O my God, should I release this? This is really deep.*

As we continued working on my author review of this chapter, a few days later I received a phone call. We had sent for the replica of the ark of the covenant, and it was being shipped to New Greater Bethel to be placed in the sanctuary where I conduct 5 a.m. prayer. I was on pins and needles about this ark, because every time it had to travel, there had been strange testimonies about odd things happening during shipment. Understandably, I was a bit on edge as I was waiting for the ark to arrive.

Right in the middle of our study and my additional writing, I got a phone call saying that the ark of the covenant had arrived. So I put on my clothes and rushed to the church, then went in the sanctuary and watched as they unboxed the ark. While in the sanctuary, a young woman walked over to the president of the women's department in New Greater Bethel and said, "I need to speak to Prophetess Bynum. I need to give her something."

The president asked the young woman what it was and then said, "Go ahead and give it to her."

When she walked over to me, she said, "Prophetess Bynum, six months ago I went to a bookstore, and this book was in a basket of books that were for sale." It was called *Jezebel vs. Elijah,* and she had purchased it for around five dollars. Then she continued, "I just felt led to pick it up. I've had this book for six months. I went straight to the chapter about Ashtaroth…" My eyes bugged open. And she told me, "When you got through preaching on Sunday about the spirit of Ashtaroth, God led me to give you this book. He told me that it would confirm some things to you."

Everything that was in this book, God had given us through our studies! Dr. Keyton had discovered the same things that we had, and that was my confirmation that as a prophet I was on the right track. God gave me a strong witness that I was to release this information to the body of Christ. As you read, I believe that you will agree.

As recorded in 1 Kings 16:30–34, temples of Baal and Ashtoreth were built together. This encouraged the Israelites to worship these false gods among the "groves" of trees that were cultivated in the temple. An *Asherah* was comprised of sacred poles (i.e., images of the goddess) that were placed in the grove near Baal's altar.[5] God revealed to me that these poles or trees being grown in the ground of the temple were intended to deny and denounce the root that would come out of Jesse, which was Jesus Christ.

They were established not only to shake, but also to denounce our position in Christ. Psalm 1:3 says that we shall be "like a tree firmly planted [and tended] by the streams of water, ready to bring forth its fruit in its season; its leaf also shall not fade or wither; and everything he does shall prosper [and come to maturity]."

The poles that were placed in groves in the temple also represented the interference of the flow of the Spirit. I can see why God was provoked to anger.

Let's look further at Baal, *The International Bible Encyclopedia* gives this description:

> As the Sun-god, Baal was worshiped under two aspects, beneficent [gracious and giving] and destructive.…The forms under which Baal was worshiped were necessarily as numerous as the communities which worshiped him. Each locality [location] had its own Baal or divine "Lord" who frequently took his name from the city or place to which he belonged

[this is very important and very vital, because whatever was worshiped in that local area, or in that city, was a direct act of disobedience to the will of God; it was an act that was the opposite of what God required]....All these various forms of the Sun-god were collectively known as... "Baals."[6]

This is the reason we must never get overconfident when we are being blessed even though we know that we are not living according to the Word of God. This spirit is designed to bless you in order to throw you out of focus concerning your life of purification, thereby being able to destroy you.

For example, if homosexuality were the dominant demonic activity in a city, then that city would be known for this characteristic. In other words, whatever the people "lobby" for in a particular city, state, or *local church* is what is actually being worshiped—not God. Anything that exalts itself against the knowledge, the will, or the way of God has become the object of worship in that place. The ruling spirit is what is being worshiped, no matter what you try to cloak it under.

True worship is not simply singing and dancing in the church. Dancing and singing are manifestations of that to which a person has submitted his or her lifestyle. For me, they are demonstrations of the lifestyle that I have submitted myself to—they speak of my complete surrender unto God. In other words, when I come to church to worship, I am demonstrating my walk to others by the worship to God. Through our song and dance, we are demonstrating that all week long we have surrendered our lifestyles to the God that we worship. We are able to bow down in church because we have already surrendered and bowed down everything in our lives to the God we worship. We come to church to demonstrate what our lifestyle has been all week. But we can see demonstrations of submitted lifestyles in gay rights, women's rights, or antiwar demonstrations. These demonstrations also show that people have submitted themselves to a cause that has become the focus of their lives.

Therefore, whenever anything else is on the throne of our hearts, or any other lifestyle is exalted (other than what God has stated to be correct in His Word), it becomes perversion. That "thing" becomes the worship of that individual, church, or region. That is why there were many Baals; there were many things that were taken into a perverted state from what God intended them to be.

For example, God intended for Israel to nurture the firstborn, allowing them to carry on the priesthood for their families and generations. So Baal's way was to take the firstborn and walk them "through the fire" by killing them. This whole idolatrous ceremony of walking the firstborn "through the fire" was a perverted state. It was part of their worship.

Every time we, as believers, disobey God by choosing another way (rather than God's way), then that thing becomes the Baal of our life. Whatever has exalted itself above what God has required of us—and whatever we deem to be the first and foremost thing that we focus our attention and interest on (which is not the will of God for our lives or our churches)—that becomes *the Baalim*.

All of the worship practices during these Old Testament times were filled with perversion. For example, God is supposed to be worshiped, not the sun. But Baal worshipers chose to worship the sun itself, which, as the creation of God, was beneath Him. Anything you choose to make your god that was already created to be beneath the living God has become a Baal in your life—just as there were Baals in every city and region. Everybody had them.

Believers today look into Old Testament history and think, *O my God, what a shame. O my God, that's awful.* But let me bear witness, my brother or my sister . . . it is still awful today, because it's still in our lives. It's still a shame, because it's still going on right now. Anything that God says, "Put down . . . don't touch . . . ," anything that God says *no* to and we say *yes* to, becomes our god. We are no different from the people who worshiped Baal. According to 1 Corinthians 6:19, we are temples of the Holy Spirit. Yet when we allow something to become a god in our lives, we have done exactly what they did in the Old

Testament. We have now erected another tree in our temples! There is no longer a free flow of God's Spirit in our temples because we are no longer temples of the Holy Spirit.

How did we become temples of the Holy Spirit? What was the process? Jesus Christ died on the tree to curse the power of the control of the *tree*. Jesus had to conquer the tree—the cross. He had to bring that perversion down for the sake of the Baals, to let them know that the power to overcome a person's life, or to bring a person to death, or to bring an individual to a state of idolatry and keep him there no longer existed. Jesus was able to say to the tree, "I have conquered you. You have lost your victory; you've lost your stronghold." And that's why I'm able to say, "O death, where is thy sting? O grave, where is thy victory?" (1 Cor. 15:55, KJV).

When God talks about our being planted "as a tree" by the rivers of living water, He is saying that we have been planted as the kind of trees that flourish. We are not trees that are held in bondage, not trees that walk children through the fire, not trees that cannot move or speak. *We are trees that bring forth life.* They blossom in due season and shall not wither; whatsoever these trees do shall prosper because of what Christ did on the tree. In this, Baal loses the victory again.

The *International Standard Bible Encyclopedia* concluded the section on Baal by saying this: "The Baals...took their place by the side of the female Ashtaroth and Ashtrim [the collective female form of the goddess of love and war, Ashtaroth (the *corporate* form of Ashtoreth)]."[7]

What does Ashtaroth have to do with Ahab making an Asherah? Let's go deeper. You see, Asherah was the goddess of fertility (love) and the wife of *Asir*, which was a war-god who became the national god of Assyria. Now get this, reader. I also read that Asir had a feminine part to him, which was Ishtar (Ashtoreth) of Ninevah, whose worship had spread throughout Syria and Canaan. The "supreme goddess of Canaan" and female counterpart of Baal, however, was Ashtaroth.

What does all of this mean? Let me give you the breakdown. Asherah and Ashtoreth were the singular forms; Asherim and Ashtaroth were the collective forms, just as Baal is the singular form and the Baalim (or Baals) are the collective forms. Now, let's review to make sure you understand. Asherah was the single form of the fertility goddess that was worshiped in certain localities; Asherim was the collective form of the same deity. This same principle was true of Ashtoreth (singular) and Ashtaroth (corporate), and the same is true for Baal and the Baalim (or Baals). Each took on a different name and form according to the weaknesses of the people in each location to look *common*. Therefore, each had different manifestations in each locality (i.e., location). Their names reflected the areas in which they were being worshiped.[8]

In order to be recognized as Ashtaroth, this spirit will transform itself into a form such as a snake, pig, cow, man, or woman. Then the worship would become snake worship, pig worship, cow worship, and, if it is a human being, it would be called *Jezebel*. Each of these manifestations is just the manifestation of the real stronghold, which is Ashtaroth. This is another reason why it is hard to spot this spirit—because its main objective is to look common, to look like us or like something with which we are familiar. This is why many have embraced this spirit unaware, thinking that it is just something common, when it is something deadly.

Although Ashtaroth had made the decision to take on a feminine form, she retained a memory of her primitive character and was the only goddess regarded on an equal footing with the male divinities. This means that this spirit is male *and* female, and it has the ability to change its sex depending on what the job requires.

A Natural Example

Now that we know that this spirit had many manifestations, let's look at a perfect example. One of Ashtaroth's manifestations is *Atar-gatis*, which is symbolized by the torso of a woman with the tail of a fish. Early one morning, the Lord revealed something very surprising. I was watching a television special about Hawaii. The program hostess was showing all of the islands where she had visited. Then she came to an aquarium. At some point during this segment, she began to talk about a certain group of fish, *Wrasse,* and described how in this species of fish, several females cohabited with one male. The male was bigger and stronger than all of the females, so it was his job to defend them against predators.

However, when the male dies, something interesting happens. The largest, most aggressive female literally undergoes a sex change and becomes a male! (You can tell this by an almost immediate change of color. The rest of the process takes a couple of weeks.) In another species, called *Anthias*, the male doesn't have to die. Instead, if he isn't aggressive enough, the most dominant female will begin to change its sex into a male. In some cases this happens overnight.[9]

Like this fish, when Ashtaroth (through the manifestation of ancient Atar-gatis, the woman with the tail of a fish) senses weakness in any authority figure, she automatically starts to assume authority. That explains why Jezebel was able to step in and say, "I'll do it. I'll take control." When Ahab demonstrated a desire that was not the way and the will of God, he provoked the spirit of Jezebel into operation.

Let me explain. There are two things that provoke the spirit of Jezebel to come into existence:

1. When leadership has an evil desire or a spirit of perversion in their hearts
2. When a leader takes on the mantle that was given to him by God and then begins to change the assignment and go in a direction that is not the intended direction for his ministry or his life

This happens when he begins to reach for ministry, which is considered to be a good thing, but it becomes a part of ministry that was not mandated for *his* ministry. For example, you may see that another ministry has a soup kitchen that seems to be growing and bringing in an increase in membership to another church. But God has called you to a prison ministry. But, desiring an increase in your own church, you switch your focus and say, "I want a soup kitchen on the same corner." However, that particular mantle or assignment was not what God mandated for you. That is when Jezebel steps up and says, "Oh, do you want a soup kitchen? I'll get that for you—by any means necessary." It does not matter who gets hurt or spiritually killed; this spirit is on an assignment to get you what you want—not what God has for you.

We must recognize that Jezebel did not *take authority*; she was *provoked into authority*. She only brought into manifestation what Ahab desired himself but didn't have the guts to do. She will operate in the same manner today when a believer desires something that is not pleasing to the Lord or a part of that individual mandate from God. When we have ought against each other or have things in our spirits that we desire to do to get back at someone else, or even desire to appear to be greater than we are, the Jezebel spirit can make entrance into our lives. There will be one who operates under a Jezebel spirit who will say, "Oh, do you want a ministry like that? I'll put together a press package for you that makes you look like you have a ministry like that." But beware, because that person is not designing a mantle for you—that person is designing destruction for you.

Would you like another example? There could be someone you know who tells you, "Oh, so she doesn't like you, she has something against you? I'll tell her off for you." You may stand back and watch that person read the other person the "riot act," claiming your own innocence in it. But the other person did it on *your* behalf, doing what you didn't have the guts to do yourself. Therefore, the Lord will bring judgment against both of you. The death of your ministry and the death of your destiny will become the penalty for embracing the spirit of Jezebel.

This is why Jezebel wasn't afraid to threaten Elijah's life after his victory over the prophets of Baal in 1 Kings 19. She was operating in the spirit realm (not the flesh form of Jezebel). The flesh form was a female. However, as believers we know that all actions that are made manifest through the flesh are merely the actions of a spirit, whether good or evil. The spirit of Jezebel is rooted in Ashtaroth, and the root of Ashtaroth is *androgynous*, which means this spirit is both male and female. Reader, this is an operation from another kingdom, so if you are not in the Spirit you will miss this revelation in the flesh.

Jezebel Enters Through Relinquished Authority

We see this same principle illustrated in the revelation from 1 Kings 16:30–34, when Jezebel was released into her full, false anointing after Ahab relinquished his authority. I have to repeat this: through the abdicating of his own authority, Ahab allowed the spirit of Jezebel to be loosed! She did not take or usurp his authority. *He gave it to her.* This spiritual principle cannot be ignored. There must be an agreement, a oneness, at some time or another between Jezebel and leadership before Jezebel can be activated. If this agreement has not been made and this spirit begins to operate independently, then it can be cast out by rebuking it…because it is operating illegally.

But if there is an agreement between Jezebel and leadership, whether it came through sexual favors or by spiritually illegal desires of the leadership, all parties involved will have to get into place spiritually before the prophetic word of God can break the spell of Jezebel off the leadership—thereby freeing them and the church.

Jezebel cannot rule where she hasn't been given authority. But she will assume authority through anyone—male or female, Jew or Gentile, minister or lay person—who gives her that place. In this way her actions are legal, and she knows that she cannot be denounced, dethroned, or rebuked because she did not take over—she was given the power. Think about this. *Her power is the power we gave up!* How does a believer give her that place? By not functioning in the spiritual authority you have already been given through your assignment. By being passive in the things of God—*disobedient.*

Remember that Jezebel doesn't just take over; she assumes legal authority in the absence of the real authority. For example, let's say that God told you to sing, and you said, "I don't feel like singing." At that moment Jezebel would say to Ashtaroth, "I'll sing." Because singers are needed, Jezebel joins the choir. Listen. Jezebel takes the position of every person in the church that is walking in disobedience.

Jezebel could not penetrate Christ's authority because Christ submitted every act to the obedience of the Father. Do you remember the word *idle*? Believers take that word lightly, but to be *idle* means to give a form of worship or duty to another god. When we are idle, doing something that we have not been called to do—doing church work or other things in the church, yet those particular works and things were not divinely assigned to us, it is like the instruments of the temple are being used out of place. For example, perhaps we are ushering when we should be over the children's ministry. Or we are in children's ministry when we should be heading up the women's Bible study. Or we are in the choir when we are supposed to be heading up the intercessory team.

The same would be true if the high priest went into the temple and took the table of shewbread out to the outer court. Then he brought the brazen laver into the inner court, took away the altar of incense, and set the brazen laver where the altar of incense was supposed to be—and then put the altar of incense in the outer court. Though all are holy instruments that God requires to be in the temple, when they are out of place it interferes with proper entrance to the throne room. As a result, proper vision is not available from the throne room. The fact that these items are out of place is a critical issue—it's idolatry. It's doing the things of God in another way than God has mandated.

It's like saying, "I'm going to take the things that are of God and do them in another way. I'll make them flow another way besides the way God wants it to flow." When all of our ways are not submitted to God, and He has not ordained all of our actions, then we are prime suspects for the spirit of Jezebel to enter in—because the spirit of Jezebel is always seeking for a way that Ashtaroth can be worshiped. Ashtaroth is always seeking for a people who will worship a god they would never obey.

She'll say, "Oh!" while people are singing in the choir who don't belong there. Because they are singing in disobedience, they are like sounding brass and tinkling cymbals. This spirit will say, "I think I'll go sing, too. Since the prerequisite in this church is not purification and obedience, then I can slide right in here unnoticed." When people who are functioning illegally cast out devils in the name of the Lord, He will say to them, "I never even knew you."

In all of this, it looks like God is still getting the glory. That's why people persistently do these illegal works! But really, God is not getting the glory. It is a "form" of godliness that denies His power because it's done another way.

If the placement of the temple instruments, as well as the construction of the temple, were not important to God and not necessary, we would not see measurements for the temple mentioned at all in the Scriptures. But God made sure to measure His temple, as we see in Exodus 25–27, 2 Chronicles 3, and Ezekiel 40–42. Each time it was measured, the Spirit of the Lord (His glory) came into that house when it was completed. (Even in the twenty-first chapter of Revelation, New Jerusalem is measured after it descends from heaven. From beginning to end, God was determined that we would get the construction of His temple right.) In like manner, people in the Old Testament were not only told exactly how to make an item—they were also told exactly where it should be placed. Proper order, placement, and function are vital in the eyes of the Lord.

Let's see yet another manifestation of this deceptive spirit. In other locations where Ashtaroth was worshiped, the dove was her sacred symbol. What does this have to do with the body of Christ?

When John was baptizing Jesus in the third chapter of the Book of Luke, the text tells us that the Spirit of the Lord came down upon Him in the form of a dove (v. 22). When the spirit of the dove descended, those present at the Jordan River (and ultimately the nation of Israel) must have come to recognize the Spirit of the Lord in that form. In a subtle ploy, the enemy had already adapted the dove as the symbol of Ashtaroth (Jezebel's chief goddess). This is the reason why the church has had such difficulty identifying her, because she cloaks herself in the form of the dove, looking and acting like the Holy Spirit.

People who are influenced by Ashtaroth can be very dishonest and manipulative. This chief spirit is a liar, just like her father, Satan. Therefore, it will lie, cheat, steal, and manipulate—but the minute you identify and confront it, this spirit starts to act spiritual, prophesying and speaking in tongues. *It takes on the image of the dove.* This deceptive spirit copycats the anointing to pervert what the word of the Lord has established, and ultimately it tries to hide.

Ashtaroth will change herself into any image of worship because that's what she is really after. The Philistines worshiped her as the goddess of war because their stronghold was a warring spirit. In other words, Ashtaroth (the goddess of love and war) works like a chameleon to capitalize on our flesh. And if we are not spiritual, then the same spirit that is destined to *make war* against us will *love* on us, only to get us deep enough into its clutches to then turn around and launch a war against us because it has learned our weaknesses. Only what we are weak in can hurt us. The only way that we, as believers, can be ensnared is through spirituality that was not birthed through purification and submission to God.

> CHURCH, WE MUST LEARN TO GO BEYOND JEZEBEL TO IDENTIFY AND BIND THE SPIRIT OF ASHTAROTH. BECAUSE WHATEVER WE "LOVE" THAT IS NOT GOD CAN OPEN THE DOOR TO HER DEMONIC MANIFESTATIONS.

Now, bear with me for a little more history. After the rise of solar theology, Baal (the sun god) and Ashtaroth (the moon goddess) changed manifestations again. The majority of the Babylonian gods were resolved into forms of the sun god, and their wives became part of solar Ishtar, otherwise known as the "daughter of sin." In other words, the spirit of Baal collected all of his Baalims, meaning his different forms and manifestations into one form of the sun god—Baal. And the spirit of Ashtaroth collected all of her female Asherims and manifestations of Ashtoreths into the form of the moon goddess.

The Lord showed me that the "daughter of sin" is a perversion of the "daughters of Zion," who can only be birthed by the Holy Spirit according to the counsel and purpose of God. This is another reason why Jezebel can appear to have accurate prophecy. Since Baal is the sun god and Ashtaroth is the goddess of the moon, those who follow them must consult the stars instead of hearing from God. This is called *astrology*. If you have ever read your horoscope, and it was right on target, don't make the mistake of thinking that God has anything to do with it.

So why was God angry with Ahab? Because when Ahab brought Baal and Ashtaroth together by building an altar and an Asherah, he reunited two spirits that had the ability to conceive and multiply a generation of decadence and sin. Just look at Jezebel's daughter, Athaliah (which we will see further in this chapter). No wonder the Father was provoked to anger! Ahab helped to consummate an evil union between Baal (the false "divine lord") and the "daughter of sin," which thrust Israel into one of the darkest periods of its history. The Bible is clear: the evil lineage of this idolatrous spirit multiplies, whether it manifests through a man or a woman.

Athaliah was more wicked than Jezebel. She was married to Jehoram, who had a heart after God and was raised in the order of the priesthood. He reigned as king of Judah for eight years, until she ultimately became the only woman to reign as queen.

Athaliah was raised in the house of evil, a part of generations that had worshiped Baal. She became so bloodthirsty for power (which is one of the manifestations of Ashtaroth) that she ordered for all of her grandchildren to be killed so that she could possess the throne. Though she sat on the throne as queen, she was there illegally. Does that ring a bell to you?

Jezebel trained her daughter by her own actions. She demonstrated how to get what she wanted illegally, and how to get what she wanted by murdering somebody else in order to receive what they had. Does that sound familiar in the body of Christ? When people are under the spirit of Ashtaroth and Jezebel, they will use their mouths to murder the credibility of other people just to get what they have. Athaliah thought that she had killed all of her grandchildren in order to possess the throne, but one by the name of Joash was hidden from her. When the people saw all the devastation that was being done under the leadership of Athaliah, they brought her grandson Joash out of hiding. (At the time he was only eight years old.)

They placed Joash on the throne. When all of the people saw him, they recognized that the lineage of Jehoram and Athaliah was still alive, and that Joash was next in line to take the throne. So they declared him king, even though he was yet a child. When Athaliah ran into the temple and saw what was being done, she screamed out, "Treason! Treason!," just as her mother had hollered to Jehu, "Traitor! Traitor!" when she was confronted.

The people of God knew that death was her end, but they did not want her blood shed in the temple, so they had her picked up and thrown out in the street in front of a moving army. She was trampled to death just as her mother had been. So, when she took after her mother's spirit, she also inherited her mother's demise.

Ashtaroth functions like a chameleon in the spirit realm to hide its true identity. Ashtaroth will change sex, color, attitudes, and manifestations—all depending on *who* is releasing this spirit and *where* it is being released. Please understand, for the sake of clarity, that Ashtaroth comes under the cloak of a male/female spirit, yet it manifests as a female divinity. Ashtaroth rarely adopts the same appearance twice, so our obedience must be absolute. We cannot give place to the devil (Eph. 4:27).

Please remember that Jezebel has been universally acknowledged as female, but the acknowledgment of her female origin is only female physically—*this spirit is not just a woman!* Because her spiritual origins are both male and female, she can work through a man just as easily as she can through a woman. Yes, there are men who have a Jezebel/Ashtaroth spirit. These characteristics of Jezebel do not just appear in women. These characteristics can be seen in the cord that runs through the Old Testament.

We cannot be passive about the things of God! Let me say this. If we know the Word of God and fail to do what we know, we can become a prey to this spirit. If we forget our God-given authority in Christ, Jezebel can take over. She will assume a place of authority and begin giving birth to her wicked fruits in our lives, just as she did when she gave birth to Athaliah.

Jezebel has gone wild in the kingdom. We have been foolish enough to diminish her in our thinking to being one sister in the church, daubed in makeup, who is after the pastor. We try to diminish her actions to a single offense. We have been foolish enough to think that she is just one person who is sowing disunity. As you have read, Jezebel is a lot bigger than that. Up to this point, the church hasn't even scratched the surface of who she is and from where she gets her power. She is not just after the local church. She is after the corporate anointing, the End-Time plan of God.

God must remain the voice of authority in your spirit, because the minute you take Him off the throne of your heart—detouring from what He emphatically told you to do, you will go right into the hands of Ashtaroth. In turn, Ashtaroth will use her female "form" Jezebel to get you everything that you think you desire—but you won't get it God's way. The end result will be that your vision, your dreams, and everything that God has ordained for your life will be thrown down to the ground. It will be devoured by the devil.

This is real. We must not be ignorant or passive about this deceptive spirit. We must walk boldly into our spiritual inheritance!

The Mantle of Elijah

Jezebel did come down, but the fall of Jezebel was not an isolated event; *it was a process.* In order for you to understand this process, I must take you back and show you how Jehu had the power to bring her down.

Do you remember the story about the prophet Elijah from 1 Kings 18:17–40? God sent Elijah into a direct confrontation with four hundred fifty prophets of Baal that served King Ahab and Jezebel—and he won the battle. In this story, these prophets built an altar to Baal, cried out to him from morning until noon, and Baal didn't answer. Elijah built an altar according to the pattern of the Lord, and God answered by fire—completely consuming the sacrifice. After witnessing this awesome display of the power of God, the children of Israel slew every prophet that had once served Baal.

When Jezebel heard what had happened, she did something that still reveals when she's in operation today. First Kings 19:2 says, "Then Jezebel sent a messenger to Elijah, saying, So let the gods do to me, and more also, if I make not your life as the life of one of them by this time tomorrow." Jezebel wanted to kill the prophet—the tangible voice and demonstration of the Spirit of God. Elijah was intimidated and ran away (v. 3). Ultimately, he ended up on Horeb, the mountain of God (v. 8). During his time alone with the Lord, the Father spoke to him, saying:

> Go, return on your way to the Wilderness of Damascus; and when you arrive, anoint Hazael to be king over Syria. And anoint Jehu son of Nimshi to be king over Israel, and anoint Elisha son of Shaphat of Abel-meholah to be prophet in your place. And him who escapes from the sword of Hazael Jehu shall slay, and him who escapes the sword of Jehu Elisha shall slay.
> —1 KINGS 19:15–17

This is where God doubled His ammunition against the enemy. When Elijah obeyed the word of the Lord by locating Elisha and casting his mantle on him (in 1 Kings 19:19–21), a new day was birthed in the Spirit. The Lord gave Elijah a spiritual son who would complete his assignment against Ahab and Jezebel and walk in his true spiritual inheritance.

Elijah's Prophetic Word

Because we introduced the lineage of Ahab and Jezebel first in this chapter, I would also like to show you the acts that led to their demise. Let's see what happened. When it was time for King Ahab's wicked dynasty with his wife, Jezebel, to end, Ahab was the first to die. (Do you see how the spirit of Ashtaroth works? It will make available to you the spirit of Jezebel to assist you in your illegal desires and wants, but as a result of these actions, you and your dreams will be the first to die.) Ahab's death came as the result of his wicked attempt to steal the property—and spiritual inheritance—of Naboth, who owned a vineyard coveted by the king.

> Now Naboth the Jezreelite had a vineyard in Jezreel, close beside the palace of Ahab king of Samaria; and after these things, Ahab said to Naboth, Give me your vineyard, that I may have it for a garden of herbs, because it is near my house. I will give you a better vineyard for it or, if you prefer, I will give you its worth in money. Naboth said to Ahab, The Lord forbid that I should give the inheritance of my fathers to you. And Ahab [already depressed by the Lord's message to him] came into his house more resentful and sullen because of what Naboth the Jezreelite had said to him.... And he lay down on his bed, turned away his face, and would eat no food.
>
> —1 KINGS 21:1–4

When Jezebel talked to her husband, he told her what had happened. This released her to operate under the covering of his false anointing. She told him:

> Do you not govern Israel? Arise, eat food, and let your heart be happy. I will give you the vineyard of Naboth the Jezreelite.
>
> —1 KINGS 21:7

She devised a plan, wrote letters in her husband's name, and executed the order to have Naboth killed. When she returned and told Ahab that Naboth was dead, "he arose to go down to the vineyard of Naboth the Jezreelite to take possession of it" (v. 16). God didn't waste any time either. Let's continue from the next verse:

> Then the word of the Lord came to Elijah the Tishbite, saying, Arise, go down to meet Ahab king of Israel in Samaria. He is in the vineyard of Naboth.... Say

to him, Thus says the Lord: Have you killed and also taken possession? Thus says the Lord: In the place where dogs licked the blood of Naboth shall dogs lick your blood, even yours. And Ahab said to Elijah, Have you found me, O my enemy?

And he answered, *I have found you*, because you have sold yourself to do evil in the sight of the Lord. See [says the Lord], I will bring evil on you and utterly sweep away and cut off from Ahab every male, bond and free, and will make your household like that of Jeroboam son of Nebat and like the household of Baasha son of Ahijah, for the provocation with which you have provoked Me to anger and made Israel to sin. Also the Lord said of Jezebel: The dogs shall eat Jezebel by the wall of Jezreel. Any belonging to Ahab who dies in the city the dogs shall eat, and any who dies in the field the birds of the air shall eat. For there was no one who sold himself to do evil in the sight of the Lord as Ahab did, incited by his wife Jezebel.

—1 Kings 21:17–25, emphasis added

In the next chapter of 1 Kings, though Ahab had repented in sackcloth and ashes, he rejected the word of the Lord through Micaiah. (See 1 Kings 22.) His death sentence was carried out when he went to battle against Syria with Jehoshaphat, king of Judah.

The king of Syria had commanded the thirty-two captains of his chariots, Fight neither with small nor great, but only with [Ahab] king of Israel.…a certain man drew a bow at a venture and smote [Ahab] the king of Israel between the joints of the armor. So he said to the driver of his chariot, Turn around and carry me out of the army, for I am wounded. The battle increased that day, and [Ahab] the king was propped up in his chariot facing the Syrians, and at nightfall

he died. And the blood of his wound flowed onto the
floor of the chariot.

—1 KINGS 22:31–35

Ahab died facing his enemies. When the battle ended, they carried his body to Samaria and buried him. But I want you to see this:
they washed the blood out of Ahab's chariot "by the pool of Samaria,
where harlots bathed, and the dogs licked up his blood, as the Lord
had predicted" (v. 38). Ahab despised correction and lost a generation.
Now, it was Jezebel's turn—because the word of the Lord to destroy her
would come to pass. God had marked their demise. His servants were
destined to find them out and take them down.

Jehu's Divine Assignment

Jezebel became angry after she heard what Elijah had caused to be done
to her prophets. And she sent a message to him indicating that what he
had done to her prophets, she would do to him. I believe that because
Elijah had just operated powerfully in the Spirit, he found himself both
spiritually and emotionally in a state of weakness, to the point that
when Jezebel's word came, he became afraid and ran to hide himself
in a cave.

In the midst of hiding in the cave, Elijah had a visitation from the
Lord. Scripture says that he sought the Lord and waited on an answer
from Him. The voice of the Lord came in the twelfth verse:

> And after the earthquake a fire, but the Lord was not
> in the fire; and after the fire [a sound of gentle still-
> ness and] a still, small voice. When Elijah heard the
> voice, he wrapped his face in his mantle and went out
> and stood in the entrance of the cave. And behold,
> there came a voice to him and said, What are you do-
> ing here, Elijah?
>
> —1 KINGS 19:12–13

Elijah began to answer the Lord, saying to Him (and I paraphrase),
"I stood for Your name's sake, and the Israelites have forsaken Your

covenant and have thrown down all Your altars and they've slain Your prophets with the sword." And he said, "I am the only one that is left and I'm jealous for Your presence" (v. 14). In other words, Elijah was saying, "My heart's desire is to see You exalted and to see Your throne being exalted, and to see You back in Your place in the life of Israel."

The Lord saw that Elijah was desperately seeking to do His will and that he wanted to make sure that the will of the Lord was done. So verses 15–16 say:

> And the Lord said to him, Go, return on your way to
> the Wilderness of Damascus; and when you arrive,
> anoint [first] Hazael to be king over Syria. And anoint
> Jehu son of Nimshi to be king over Israel, and anoint
> Elisha son of Shaphat of Abel-meholah to be prophet
> in your place.

This next part is very important. Elijah left there and found Elisha who was plowing with twelve yoke of oxen. When you look at this process, though God had told Elijah to anoint Hazael and Jehu to be kings, He instructed him *to anoint Elisha to take his place.* So when Elijah went into the field and found Elisha, he didn't just anoint him with a regular anointing; he used the same mantle that he had covered his face with while he was talking face-to-face with God in the entrance of the cave. Elijah tossed *that* mantle on Elisha!

I believe the reason why he had to toss that particular mantle on Elisha was because he knew that in order for Elisha to walk in his stead and in his place as a prophet, he would have his own face-to-face encounter with God.

Eleven chapters later, this story picks up in 2 Kings 9:1–7. This indicates that just because God places an anointing upon you, and just because it's been prophesied to you that the mantle you are going to walk in is yours, it doesn't mean that you're going to go out tomorrow and become what you're destined to be. That day Jehu was anointed to be king, but he didn't run out that day and begin to operate in the prophetic. Eleven chapters later in 2 Kings 9:1–2, we read:

> And Elisha the prophet called one of the sons of the prophets and said to him, Gird up your loins, take this flask of oil in your hand, and go to Ramoth-gilead. When you arrive, look there for Jehu son of Jehoshaphat son of Nimshi...

In other words, Elijah anointed Jehu to be king, but it wasn't until eleven chapters later, when Elisha had come into purpose, that he was able to anoint that same young man with an anointing from the prophetic. And notice that Elisha didn't send a layman to carry this mantle and flask of oil; he sent a prophet. Verses 2 and 3 continue:

> When you arrive, look there for Jehu son of Jehoshaphat son of Nimshi; and go in and have him arise from among his brethren and lead him to an inner chamber. Then take the cruse of oil and pour it on his head and say, Thus says the Lord: I have anointed you king over Israel. Then open the door and flee; do not tarry.

So the young prophet was carrying a prophetic flask of oil for Jehu that was originally from the prophet Elisha. When he arrived at Ramoth-gilead, the scripture says:

> And when he came, the captains of the army were sitting outside; and he said, I have a message for you, O captain. Jehu said, To which of us? And he said, To you, O captain. And Jehu arose, and they went into the house. And the prophet poured the oil on Jehu's head and said to him, Thus says the Lord, the God of Israel: I have anointed you king over the people of the Lord, even over Israel. You shall strike down the house of Ahab your master, that I may avenge the blood of My servants the prophets and of all the servants of the Lord [who have died] at the hands of Jezebel.
>
> —2 KINGS 9:5–7

Jehu had received his natural assignment to be king from the prophet Elijah. But when it was time for him to come into his spiritual assignment to take down the house of Ahab and to avenge the servants of the Lord who had died by the hands of Jezebel, Elisha (who had the double-portion mantle) sent the flask of oil from the anointing that was upon his life and poured that upon Jehu's life. He was now also getting ready to walk into a double assignment as both king and prophet to bring down the house of Ahab—and at long last, to bring down Jezebel. The Lord said in the eighth verse:

> For the whole house of Ahab shall perish, and I will
> cut off from Ahab every male, bond or free, in Israel.

And so here, we see Elisha passing this mantle down. Jehu didn't get to walk as a captain of an army to do this assignment. When Elisha sent him the double-portion oil of the anointing, Jehu would now have authority in two realms: in the earth realm as a captain and in the spirit realm as a prophet. This is the same mantle that God desires for believers to have today: a twofold anointing in the earth realm as men and women of God, yet in the spirit realm, as prophets of God to be able to bring down every spirit of Ahab and every spirit of Jezebel that we see operating in the church. With that mantle in place, we are in full authority to completely bring that kingdom down.

This portion of Scripture also shows us why the spirit of Jezebel hates order. Jehu wasn't anointed because he had fasted, prayed, and went on a consecration with some friends. He was anointed because God was executing His plan. *He was in his place;* he was in obedience to the prophet. The orders were being fulfilled! God had already given Elijah the mantle to bring down the prophets of Baal. Through Elijah, He had granted a double-portion anointing unto Elisha—and then Elisha sent a prophetic word to Jehu (the son of Jehoshaphat, a righteous king from David's lineage).

God's divine order would finally take down the wicked queen Jezebel and cut off the false anointing that had passed down the line through her husband, Ahab. Yes, spiritual alignment will always get her in the end—because it is a corporate anointing.

We Must Become a Company Coming

In the ninth chapter of 2 Kings, Jehu puts into action the Lord's plan to destroy Jezebel.

> So Jehu son of Jehoshaphat, the son of Nimshi, conspired against Joram [to dethrone and slay him]....So Jehu rode in a chariot and went to Jezreel, for Joram lay there....A watchman on the tower in Jezreel spied the company of Jehu as he came, and said, I see a company. And Joram said, Send a horseman to meet them and have him ask, Do you come in peace?
> —2 KINGS 9:14–17

How is the church going to destroy Jezebel? How are we going to dismantle that spirit? We have to become "a company coming." We must be seen in the realm of the spirit as one force. In other words, when we are in spiritual warfare with this spirit, one person can't say, "I really sense God wants us to go on a twenty-one day fast," while another is saying, "We need to pray more about it." Yet another person may be saying, "Why does it have to be twenty-one days? Why can't it be five days?" There is no order in that. Divine order must flow through the channel of the leadership as well as the congregation.

There are several ways a Jezebel spirit is exposed:

1. She will only serve "high." She will only work where she can completely take over.
2. She will protect her interest by connecting with a familiar spirit.

As we learned earlier, there is a time when we must respond as spiritual racehorses, stepping up into destiny under the leadership of our spiritual fathers. But in a horse race, only one can win the prize. When it is time for us to become "a company coming," we must respond like warhorses—charging toward the enemy as one. That is how the church leaders in the Book of Acts ministered unto the Lord in order to receive His direction. They stopped talking, started seeking, and kept obeying. And they did it in unity. That gave no place to the devil. They become one in the Spirit; that is a recipe that wins.

> **SUBMITTING TO ONE ANOTHER IN OBEDIENCE IS THE KEY TO DETHRONING THE SPIRIT OF JEZEBEL.**

As the people of God, we have to come against Jezebel as a company. We cannot be divided—because when we stand as one and all say the same thing, Jezebel cannot find a corner to whisper in. When she looks to the left, we'll be saying, "Holy." When she looks to the right, we'll be crying, "Holy." When she looks in the choir loft, we'll be singing, "Holy" and living holy. And when she looks at the praise team, the cry will still be, "Holy." The spirit of Jezebel will not be able to find a place of activation, because all will be submitted to God and in their divine places "doing" their divine assignments.

When King Joram saw the company of Jehu approaching, he sent one horseman out to meet the approaching army.

> So one on horseback went to meet him and said, Thus says the king: Is it peace? And Jehu said, What have you to do with peace? Rein in behind me. And the watchman reported, The messenger came to them, but he does not return.
>
> —2 KINGS 9:18

Joram sent a horseman out to meet Jehu (who represented the prophetic word of God), and Jehu didn't give him the answer he was looking for. When the enemy comes to engage you about your church or to get you to talk about the man of God, don't give him the time of day. Like the horseman who was instructed to fall in behind Jehu, a gossiping devil will have to get behind you. The enemy will get in your dust. But be aware that the devil is not going to stop trying after just one attempt. He is going to send his little imps again.

> Then Joram sent out a second man on horseback, who
> came to them and said, Thus says the king: Is it peace?
> Jehu replied, What have you to do with peace? Ride
> behind me. And the watchman reported, He came
> to them, but does not return; also the driving is like
> the driving of Jehu son of Nimshi, for he drives furi-
> ously. Joram said, Make ready. When his chariot was
> made ready, Joram king of Israel and Ahaziah king of
> Judah went out, each in his chariot. Thus they went
> out to meet Jehu and met him in the field of Naboth
> the Jezreelite.
>
> —2 Kings 9:19–21

Understand the order of the Lord. By allowing the enemy's messengers to approach you, He is really smoking out the king. For example,
when seven people are gossiping about something in the church, one
of them is the ringleader. So when you put each of the enemy's imps
behind you, the strongman will be exposed.

Notice that Jehu rode against Jezebel in a chariot. And when Joram
was approaching, he was also in a chariot. What does this mean? You
can tell when the enemy is coming against you, because he will try
to match you in power. But when Joram attempted to create a false
alliance with Jehu, King Jehu could not be deterred from carrying out
the plan of God:

> When Joram saw Jehu, he said, Is it peace, Jehu? And
> he answered, How can peace exist as long as the for-
> nications of your mother Jezebel and her witchcrafts
> are so many?
>
> —2 Kings 9:22

Do not allow the spirit of Jezebel to create a false alliance with your
spirit. One of the most conniving ways is to find a place of familiarity
with the individual that is sent against her. Remember, it can be a he
or a she. That person will begin to go from prophesying great things
to you to complimenting you from head to toe—doing anything that will

take the heat out of the battle against that spirit's tactics.

When you are tempted to align yourself with this spirit, make the same declaration as King Jehu made. Declare: "As long as I can still see traits in me that fornicate against God…as long as I don't mind watching certain types of movies…as long as I can date a man when I know he isn't saved…if I can continue entertaining gossip…then I know that there will never be any peace."

The body of Christ has to get beyond correcting symptoms. If you are to move into destiny, you must capture the strongman within; you must deal with the sin that is manifesting the symptom. When symptoms keep cropping up, it indicates that you haven't captured the strongman. For this same reason, Jehu couldn't stop with merely defeating Joram; he had to go all the way. He had to keep pursuing his enemies until he got Jezebel—the source.

> Then Joram reined about and fled, and he said to Ahaziah, Treachery, Ahaziah! But Jehu drew his bow with his full strength and shot Joram between his shoulders; and the arrow went out through his heart, and he sank down in his chariot. Then said Jehu to Bidkar his captain, Take [Joram] up and cast him in the plot of Naboth the Jezreelite's field.
> —2 KINGS 9:23–25

Jehu kept pursuing the enemy. He chased Ahaziah (Joram's brother), and the company killed him in his chariot.

> As surely as I saw yesterday the blood of Naboth and the blood of his sons, says the Lord, I will repay you on this plot of ground, says the Lord. Now therefore, take and cast Joram into the plot of ground [of Naboth], as the word of the Lord said. When Ahaziah king of Judah saw this, he fled by the way of the garden house. Jehu followed him and said, Smite him also in the chariot. And they did so at the ascent to Gur, which is by Ibleam. And [Ahaziah] fled to Megiddo and died

there. His servants took him in a chariot to Jerusalem, and buried him in his sepulcher with his fathers in the City of David. In the eleventh year of Joram son of Ahab, Ahaziah's reign over Judah began.

—2 KINGS 9:26–29

When leadership is functioning in divine order, we will chase the spirit of Jezebel and the evil spirits in partnership with the devil down until their power is destroyed. Jehu got rid of the imps, killed both of the kings, and went after Jezebel.

Jezebel Tries to Change Her Image

Jezebel knows the mighty warriors in the Spirit. She knows the choir that is going to sing until demons run out of the church. She knows the psalmist who is going to play the instruments until every principality is cast out of the atmosphere. She knows the intercessors who are going to drive the enemy out of the church. And she knows the man of God who is going to take a people to another level in God—stirring them to rise up like mighty giants in the Spirit.

Something interesting happened when Jehu arrived at Jezreel. Let's read 2 Kings 9:30:

Now when Jehu came to Jezreel, Jezebel heard of it, and she painted her eyes and beautified her head and looked out of [an upper] window.

God revealed to me that when it's time for Jezebel to die, the chameleon spirit (from Ashtaroth) always tries to take on another image. She suddenly starts acting sweet and kind: "Oh, I love you." "God bless you." And if that doesn't work, then she'll begin to revert to her spiritual knowledge of the moon and the stars, given to her through the spirit of Baal (the sun god) and the spirit of Ashtaroth (the moon goddess) and begin to prophesy in divination. Remember, one of the abilities of the moon goddess is to read the stars, which is why some of these evil prophecies are so on point. The enemy is familiar with the stars.

Though this deceptive spirit can prophesy through the divination of the stars, it cannot prophesy your process to purification. And who wants a gift with no God in it?

Nevertheless, God will say, "I still see you, Jezebel. You're the same demon, even though you painted your eyes and beautified yourself." Listen to me. You are not just dealing with a woman who puts on makeup and beautifies herself. The spirit and the manifestation of Jezebel are not just the seductive appearance of a woman. This is a seducing spirit. It is a spirit that seduces any believer who is carnal, who is unconsecrated and weak in the faith—and there are other images that it can transform into.

Of all the materials that I reviewed, I found that Dr. Keyton gives a very clear description of the characteristics of Jezebel. If you were to read pages 142–146 of her book, you would find a detailed list, from which I would like to name just a few of the manifestations of Ashtaroth through the form of Jezebel.[10]

- *Jezebel is a liar, a backstabber, and a usurper; she answers with evasion, deftly switching the truth and the facts.* She does not repent, even with the truth right in her face. She always has an excuse for her behavior, no matter how outrageous it may be. Jezebel targets worship leaders, pastors, elders, other people in authority, and their spouses. Jezebel prefers refined qualities, but she will use anyone. She hates civility, repentance, and true holiness. She causes pastors to become controlling and unyielding, and she is not accountable to others.
- *Jezebel can work through men who are flirtatious with women and vice versa.* She also gives prophetic words, dreams, and visions. She talks about them constantly and doesn't measure them against the sure word of prophecy, the

Bible. Jezebel maneuvers into leadership positions in order to control. She is a tyrant, a whore, and she lets nothing stand in the way of what she desires. Jezebel changes or bends the rules to suit her own ends. She believes that she is above the law. Jezebel is fiercely independent. She pretends to desire to protect and love others, while using information of weakness against them. Jezebel turns her followers into eunuchs and zombies; she drains the life out of her victims. Others that may fight against her, she divides in order to conquer. She keeps people at one another's throats through her lies and deception. She keeps parties in a conflict apart so that strife will continue and she can manipulate the results—because Scripture says where envy and strife is, there is every evil work.

- *Jezebel destroys evidence that proves the innocence of her victims.* She questions the integrity of others in order to discredit them. Jezebel sees herself as lofty, much higher than the sheep. She calls herself a *prophetess* (or a *prophet*). Jezebel is proud. She is a master of camouflage, a wolf in sheep's clothing. Jezebel is a man-hater and has contempt for the weak. There are always inconsistencies in Jezebel's story. She seeks recognition and is an obsessive chatterer, moody and brooding. Jezebel has no humility. Jezebel brags for hours on how long she intercedes. She also attacks true prophets with devastating false words. A Jezebel will fool you. And the Jezebels who fool you the longest are the most ruthless and dangerous.

- *Jezebel's personal life is messed up, yet it may be carefully hidden.* She seems genuine, but is spiritually off…there is a mixture in her spirit. Jezebel also controls money. She uses other's names to gain control of her own agenda; she is relentless and savage in her relationships and business dealings. Jezebel is sarcastic and derogatory. She is anxious and hyper; she has no peace, no joy. She is frustrated and upset and tries to hide it. Jezebel is always full of plans, plans, plans…always on the go…she always looks like she's busy for the Lord.

- *Jezebel is fast talking and nervous, and she covers up her true motivations.* She will attack immediately when threatened, creating lies and counter-accusations. Jezebel uses seduction to manipulate. There is no peace around Jezebel. She breeds a spirit of confusion, division, and strife. She pretends to be a worshiper and an intercessor, and she aligns herself with true prophets to give credence to her own agenda. Her agenda is to kill and discredit the true prophets of God, to destroy families, to promote homosexuality and pornography, and to bring the spirit of slumber, complacency, and apathy upon the body of Christ.

- *Jezebel causes fear, timidity, stress, strife, and intimidation.* She also causes physical weakness, discouragement, guilt, feelings of helplessness, and insatiable sexual desires, all the while bringing threats, frustrations, and moral failure. She manipulates through money or exerting financial control, domination, fierce independence, slander, and lies. She is vengeful and always has carefully orchestrated plans, making others totally aware that in her domination she will not live with anyone that she cannot dominate. The spirit of Jezebel submits to no one.

And you think that Jezebel is just makeup? Let's see how the prophetic spirit of Jehu confronted Jezebel. Yes, this spirit must be confronted.

> Jehu lifted up his face to the window and said, Who is on my side? Who? And two or three eunuchs looked out at him. And he said, Throw her down! So they threw her down, and some of her blood splattered on the wall and on the horses, and he drove over her.
>
> —2 KINGS 9:32–33

Now hear me on this. A eunuch is physically sterile, so he can't reproduce. Eunuchs were men who had given up their right as one who produces to serve Jezebel. May I point out that if you have ever seen this spirit in full operation, it is as if the persons that are under this spell are drugged, almost like you want to slap them and say, "Snap out of it."

In order for the eunuchs to remain committed to her, Jezebel had them castrated (meaning their sexual gender was removed), indicating that, "You only work for me, but you get nothing from me." This also means that in one's service to Jezebel, there will never be any pleasure. This is why you can find people working in the body of Christ who are angry and frustrated. They do not enjoy what they have been called to do—because when a person is functioning under this spirit, he or she is almost acting as a spiritual eunuch, working in the temple but producing nothing!

However, the flip side of this is that because the eunuchs worked in the temple and had no emotional or sexual soul ties to Jezebel, they were potential free agents—meaning they were in the position to be set free. So when Jehu arrived under the prophetic anointing and declared, "Who is on the Lord's side?" I believe that the sound of the power of God in his voice (under the double-portion anointing and mantle of both Elijah and Elisha) broke those eunuchs out of a zombie state, and they reacted to the will of God.

Now, that's true prophecy. They didn't go on a fast. They didn't go into a consecration. They didn't become prayer partners—they heard a clarion sound from the voice of a prophet who was walking with pure motives, and they were able to come against the spirit that controlled them for many years. When the eunuchs heard the word of the Lord coming out of the mouth of the anointed one, the aligned one, the consecrated one, the one who came with urim and thummim in his breast—the power of Satan was broken off of their minds. The zombie spirit was broken, and out of obedience to the voice of God coming out of the mouth of this prophet, they threw Jezebel out of the window. The dogs licked her bones, just as the word of the Lord had declared.

Jezebel Must Fall

Many believers have been too busy fighting over seats and titles in the church, ignoring the call to be servants and trying to get in the pastor's favor. Many have taken on the spirit of Jezebel unaware. This foul spirit must be exposed. The Holy Spirit is calling the body to "grow up." We must come to maturity so that we can be part of a mighty company that carries out the vision God has given to our spiritual parents.

In order to reach spiritual maturity, we must cry out to God and say, "God, my heart isn't right before You. Help me get to the place in You where I'm walking, talking, and living right." Take inventory of your motives. Does this sound like you? *I have to get my ministry off the ground. If I can meet this person, he can introduce me to that person, who can give me a loan to do this or that work for the Lord.* You will never defeat the spirit of Jezebel from your life or from the body of Christ with ungodly motives. It must be the Lord who is building the house. It must be the Lord who is leading you to step into destiny.

Your personal vision must support the vision of the man and woman of God. God is building His church, and no matter what kind of portion He has given us—it is to build His kingdom. The church isn't about seats or activities or personalities. It's not about *you*; it's not about *me*—it's much bigger than any one person. The Father's portion is about souls.

A New Day, a New Anointing

Jezebel cannot stay in power because the church is moving forward into our divine destiny. Know in the Spirit that as Jezebel rises up and battles against the church, the mantle of Elijah is also rising in power. As this awesome anointing flows in our churches, we must rise to the call, knowing that it is our time in the Father's prophetic plan. Jesus is coming soon, so God is getting His house in order. The "portion" He has set aside for you is being united with others to fulfill His purpose.

In a church that has been raised up to kill Jezebel, people want only the anointing of God. God is bringing people into the body of Christ who will say to their spiritual leaders, "Birth me into destiny...I'm here to serve. Even if you don't give me a dime, teach me how to be a servant." These people will be compelled in their spirits to say to their leaders, "How can I be of help? Where do you need me to work?"

Find time in your schedule to help to build the house of God. Receive your spiritual inheritance from the Father, and activate it. It's our time, and everybody's gifts and abilities are needed. When you get under the flow of an orderly anointing, God will bless your life more than you could ask or think.

If you have opened the door through disobedience and let Jezebel in, rebuking the devil isn't going to change a thing! But when you yield your life to God, He will throw the authority of Jezebel down. It is a life of obedience that throws her down—not talk. Jezebel's influence comes straight from the pit of hell, from Satan himself. But remember that Jesus destroyed the works of the devil. He has already stripped the devil of his power. Jesus is the real authority.

CHAPTER 12

Babylon's Fall

*J*ezebel may be wreaking havoc in the kingdom, but a day of reckoning is coming. Jezebel (Ashtaroth) has a thirst for power. Enough is never enough. This ancient enemy will continue trying to recapture and abuse the *most sacred* things in the church. But if we, God's people, will walk in our true inheritance, Jezebel cannot usurp our God-given authority! Jesus has already freed us from the curse of this deceptive spirit. As we walk in covenant authority (by submitting to the order of the Lord), He will restore the kingdom through us according to the biblical pattern.

In the end, Babylon is going to fall—God Himself will judge her. We can get a glimpse of that coming judgment by looking in Revelation 17:

> And [the angel] bore me away [rapt] in the Spirit into a desert (wilderness), and I saw a woman seated on a scarlet beast that was all covered with blasphemous titles (names), and he had seven heads and ten horns. The woman was robed in purple and scarlet and bedecked with gold, precious stones, and pearls, [and she was] holding in her hand a golden cup full of the accursed offenses and the filth of her lewdness and vice. And on her forehead there was inscribed a name

> of mystery [with a secret symbolic meaning]: Babylon
> the great, the mother of prostitutes (idolatresses) and of
> the filth and atrocities and abominations of the earth. I
> also saw that the woman was drunk, [drunk] with the
> blood of the saints (God's people) and the blood of the
> martyrs [who witnessed] for Jesus. And when I saw her,
> I was utterly amazed and wondered greatly.
> —REVELATION 17:3–6

Remember, Ashtaroth was birthed out of Babylonia…and
Babylon rides on the strength of the beast. The beast gives Babylon entrance to the kingdoms of the earth. Again, this parallels the entrance
of Ashtaroth into the kingdom of Israel when Ahab married Jezebel
and submitted to the gods of her fathers (1 Kings 16:30–33). Through
Ahab's marriage to Jezebel and through their wicked lineage, Ashtaroth
gained entrance into the kingdom! Now, we see her in the realm of the
spirit—all dressed up as an "angel of light," intoxicated by wreaking
havoc in the church. Let's keep reading.

> And [the angel further] said to me, The waters that
> you observed, where the harlot is seated, are races
> and multitudes and nations and dialects (languages).
> And the ten horns that you saw, they and the beast
> will [be the very ones to] hate the harlot (the idola-
> trous woman); they will make her cheerless (bereaved,
> desolate), and they will strip her and eat up her flesh
> and utterly consume her with fire.…And he shouted
> with a mighty voice, She is fallen! Mighty Babylon is
> fallen! She has become a resort and dwelling place for
> demons, a dungeon haunted by every loathsome spirit,
> an abode for every filthy and detestable bird.
> —REVELATION 17:15–16, 18:2

When Babylon goes down, every demon spirit will live there. This
really hit me. So many Christians have been running around binding
demons, but in reality we are just dealing with the symptoms! Each

demon has a specific manifestation (lust, pride, and so on)—but from these verses in Revelation we learn that Ashtaroth (symbolized by her birthplace, Babylon) is at the core of each manifestation. This passage tells us that in the end all demons are going back "home" to her. Babylon is their dwelling place. Babylon gets her power from the beast, and demons are released from Babylon.

Revelation 17:5 says that Babylon's name is a "mystery." She rides on the back of the "red beast" in full view for the world to see. *Babylon is a false bride with a false inheritance.* Not only does she control merchandising over all the earth, she will even control the "ten horns," causing them to give their power over to the beast. (See Revelation 17 and 18.) Think about this: Jesus has a bride through whom He moves in the earth. The devil tries to copycat this as well, flaunting his false bride with her stolen inheritance.

> HEAR ME! BELIEVERS ARE CHASING DEMON SPIRITS AND BINDING "SYMPTOMS," BUT OUR REAL ENEMY IS BABYLON— THEIR DEMONIC STRONGHOLD.

Still, Babylon is operating on borrowed time:

For her iniquities (her crimes and transgressions) are piled up as high as heaven, and God has remembered her wickedness and [her] crimes [and calls them up for settlement]. Repay to her what she herself has paid [to others] and double [her doom] in accordance with what she has done. Mix a double portion for her in the cup she mixed [for others]. To the degree that she glorified herself and reveled in her wantonness [living deliciously and luxuriously], to that measure impose on her torment and anguish and tears and mourning. Since in her heart she boasts, I am not a widow; as a queen [on a throne] I sit, and I shall never see suffering or experience sorrow—so shall her plagues (afflictions, calamities) come thick upon her in a single day,

pestilence and anguish and sorrow and famine; and
she shall be utterly consumed (burned up with fire),
for mighty is the Lord God Who judges her.

—REVELATION 18:5–8

God is mighty. Babylon's evil ministry is going to come back on
her, multiplied. When Jezebel died, dogs ate her flesh. By the time Jehu
sent men to get her body, all that remained were her skull, palms, and
feet (2 Kings 9:34–35). *Even this confirmed her counterfeit anointing!*
When Moses anointed Aaron as high priest, the first thing he did was
pour oil over his head (Lev. 8:12). Then he slaughtered a bull and two
rams. He placed the blood of the second ram, which was for the inau-
guration, on the right ear, right thumb, and right big toe of Aaron and
his sons—head...hand...foot (vv. 23–24).

On every level, this spirit has tried to copycat the order of the
Lord. But in the end, just like the beast on which she rides, Babylon
will be consumed with fire. In the realm of the spirit, there is a powerful correlation to that final destruction of Babylon:

Rejoice (celebrate) over her, O heaven! O saints
(people of God) and apostles and prophets, because
God has executed vengeance for you upon her! Then
a single powerful angel took up a boulder like a great
millstone and flung it into the sea, crying, With such
violence shall Babylon the great city be hurled down
to destruction and shall never again be found. *And the
sound of harpists and minstrels and flute players and
trumpeters shall never again be heard in you, and no
skilled artisan of any craft shall ever again be found in
you, and the sound of the millstone shall never again be
heard in you. And never again shall the light of a lamp
shine in you, and the voice of bridegroom and bride
shall never be heard in you again;* for your business-
men were the great and prominent men of the earth,
and by your magic spells and poisonous charm all

nations were led astray (seduced and deluded). And in her was found the blood of prophets and of saints, and of all those who have been slain (slaughtered) on earth.

—REVELATION 18:20–24, EMPHASIS ADDED

Do you see the significance of this? Everything counterfeit in the church is going to die—even the false voice of the "bridegroom and bride." Everything this deceptive spirit gained when the people of God willingly gave up their place of authority is going to be stripped away from her for good.

After Babylon falls, the saints rise in splendor and majesty! This is why the "false bride" Babylon controls the "merchandising" of all the fine things of the earth: purple, scarlet, linens, and every type of costly good. The counterfeit bride, the female companion of the beast, Babylon puts her merchandise on parade, showboating against the church. This is also why her thirst for wealth, power, and influence is never satisfied. It doesn't rightfully belong to her—*it is not her inheritance!* Now...look what happens after Babylon falls.

And again they shouted, Hallelujah (praise the Lord)! The smoke of her [burning] shall continue to ascend forever and ever (through the eternities of the eternities). Then the twenty-four elders [of the heavenly Sanhedrin] and the four living creatures fell prostrate and worshiped [paying divine honors to] God, Who sits on the throne, saying, Amen! Hallelujah (praise the Lord)! Then from the throne there came a voice, saying, Praise our God, all you servants of His, you who reverence Him, both small and great! After that I heard what sounded like the shout of a vast throng, like the boom of many pounding waves, and like the roar of terrific and mighty peals of thunder, exclaiming, Hallelujah (praise the Lord)! For now the Lord our God the Omnipotent (the All-Ruler) reigns! Let us rejoice and shout for joy [exulting and triumphant]! Let us celebrate and ascribe to Him glory and honor, for the marriage of the Lamb [at last] has come, and His bride has prepared herself. She has been permitted to dress in fine (radiant) linen, dazzling and white—for the fine linen is (signifies, represents) the righteousness (the upright, just, and godly living, deeds, and conduct, and right standing with God) of the saints (God's holy people).

—REVELATION 19:3–8

These verses tell us that the true inheritance is righteousness, our Father's character. It is "dazzling and white." Babylon will never have any part of it, so she wars against the church by parading the things she loves.

Babylon is glorified in prosperity. Therefore, saints must be careful, because prosperity is readily given through her false anointing. That's why it is critical in this hour to stay in spiritual alignment. We must be certain our prosperity is of the Lord. Hear me. *We can't judge by blessings.* Babylon controls the marketing (merchandising)—which isn't spiritual prosperity. True prosperity—our spiritual inheritance—comes by the favor of the Lord, which includes financial rewards. And when the Lord blesses His sons and daughters, there is no sorrow added with it. (See Proverbs 10:22.)

Those who are under Babylon's spell are arrogant and cocky about their prosperity. This is a sign of their bondage under Babylon. You will be able to see ugly things in their spirits—because they are under the false spiritual alignment of Baal and Ashtaroth. Babylon must come down, because too many of God's people are being deceived by the teachings of false prophets who only desire to build their own kingdoms. They know how to get money from the world, but they don't have the wealth of the Spirit. The fruit of the Spirit will be evident in the lives of those who stay under godly alignment, along with the blessings of God (Gal. 5:22–23).

Just as Hagar despised Sarah, Jezebel (as manifested through Ashtaroth and Babylon) despises the church. Sarah's son received the full inheritance of his godly lineage. Hagar's son didn't—*and what can match the fury of a jealous woman?* As it was in the natural, so it is now in the spiritual realm. Just look at Israel. The children of Sarah and Hagar are still fighting today, and the conflict is intensifying. As the people of God, we know where this is headed—and we know who will be victorious. It is time to rise up and take what rightfully belongs to us! We must keep moving forward, clothed with the Lord Jesus Christ. No weapon formed against us shall prosper.

It is time to rise up and take what rightfully belongs to us:

> For the Lord God is a Sun and Shield; the Lord bestows [present] grace and favor and [future] glory (honor, splendor, and heavenly bliss)! No good thing will He withhold from those who walk uprightly. O Lord of hosts, blessed (happy, fortunate, to be envied) is the man who trusts in You [leaning and believing on You, committing all and confidently looking to You, and that without fear or misgiving]! Lord, You have [at last] been favorable and have dealt graciously with Your land [of Canaan]; You have brought back [from Babylon] the captives of Jacob. You have forgiven and taken away the iniquity of Your people, You have covered all their sin. Selah [pause, and calmly realize what that means]!
>
> —PSALM 84:11–85:2

CHAPTER 13

The Real Authority

When Jesus was about to meet the woman at the well of Samaria, He said to His disciples that it was necessary for Him to go through Samaria (John 4:4). Why was it necessary? All of Israel knew that Samaria was a cursed land.

Let's take a closer look at this story to grasp the spiritual principle:

> And he [Jesus] must needs go through Samaria. Then cometh he to a city of Samaria, which is called Sychar, near to the parcel of ground that Jacob gave to his son Joseph. Now Jacob's well was there. Jesus therefore, being wearied with his journey, sat thus on the well: and it was about the sixth hour. There cometh a woman of Samaria to draw water: Jesus saith unto her, Give me to drink. (For his disciples were gone away unto the city to buy meat.) Then saith the woman of Samaria unto him, How is it that thou, being a Jew, askest drink of me, which am a woman of Samaria? for the Jews have no dealings with the Samaritans. Jesus answered and said unto her, If thou knewest the gift of God, and who it is that saith to thee, Give me to drink; thou wouldest have asked of him, and he would have given thee living water. The woman saith unto him, Sir, thou hast nothing to draw with, and the well

is deep: from whence then hast thou that living water? Art thou greater than our father Jacob, which gave us the well, and drank thereof himself, and his children, and his cattle? Jesus answered and said unto her, Whosoever drinketh of this water shall thirst again: But whosoever drinketh of the water that I shall give him shall never thirst; but the water that I shall give him shall be in him a well of water springing up into everlasting life. The woman saith unto him, Sir, give me this water, that I thirst not, neither come hither to draw. Jesus saith unto her, Go, call thy husband, and come hither. The woman answered and said, I have no husband. Jesus said unto her, Thou hast well said, I have no husband: For thou hast had five husbands; and he whom thou now hast is not thy husband: in that saidst thou truly.

—JOHN 4:4–18, KJV

That day at the well, Jesus immediately began to address her relationship. He quoted, "You have had five husbands, and the one you are with now is not yours." She was about to have an encounter with the Seventh Man.

Let's first look at the history of Samaria. Seven wicked kings ruled in Jeroboam's dynasty after God split Solomon's kingdom in 1 Kings 11 (see verses 29–39): Jeroboam, Nadab, Baasha, Elah, Zimri, Omri, and then Ahab. All were part of an evil, natural legacy, so none were true "fathers" of Israel. Death and destruction came to each one as the spirit of Jeroboam moved down the line—that would give us seven evil kings. When Jesus encountered the woman at Samaria, He canceled the wicked lineage (through the seven wicked kings) over the Samaritan woman's life and "perfected" God's prophetic plan.

One would ask: "Why would Jesus go from talking about water to worship?"

First, He asked for something to drink, and the woman replied, "You have nothing to draw with." Yet when we look in the spirit of the revelation of this story, we will see that Jesus represented the Living Water, and that she also did not have anything to "draw with." So she immediately recognized by His speech that He was a prophet. And since the worship of Ashtaroth and Baal was dominant in Samaria through the leadership of Ahab and Jezebel, it had been foretold that worship would be restored.

This was an opportunity for Jesus to inform her that because worship was such a common thing in paganism, true worship to God could only be done in spirit and in truth. In other words, worship was not a song. Worship was not a city...but worship was to become a way of life. In order to be a worshiper, everything in a person's life that was displeasing to the Lord had to be submitted to His lordship. When this impartation was made, the woman instantly became a true worshiper. She dropped her pots and evangelized the city.

It is no coincidence that she left her water pot and went directly to the men of Samaria with the word of the Lord in her mouth (John 4:28). Not only did these men come to believe in Jesus, but also many more believed and were delivered (vv. 39–42).

Isn't it just like God to send His Son to reverse the curse in that place, where Satan once had dominion? Remember, *it was necessary* for Jesus to go to Samaria, just as it was necessary for Him to do everything else the Father required in order to fulfill all righteousness. Once and for all, Jesus dealt with the spirit of Jezebel—through a woman who dared to be obedient, He canceled an evil spiritual legacy over her life, the lives of the Samaritans, and the entire world all at one time! She was a woman who came under real authority; then Jesus released her to go and minister!

As I was reviewing this passage, God said, "Right now, there is a transfer of power in the kingdom. I'm not calling for the religious or the sophisticated; I'm not calling for title or position. I'm calling for true worshipers." Why? Because those who worship the Father must worship Him in spirit and in truth (John 4:23). It is time to get honest...get real...and get back to the altar. True sons and daughters of the gospel must enter into spiritual travail and intercession to bring forth what God is releasing in the earth. It is time to take back what the devil has stolen from the church. When Zion travails, she shall bring forth! (See Micah 4:8–13.)

Do you see why you have to restore Jesus to His rightful place of authority? Do you understand why you must obey whatever He tells you to do? When you are obedient to the Lord, you don't have to worry about rebuking the devil. And you won't have to fight with Jezebel. James 4:7 says, "Submit yourselves therefore to God. Resist the devil [refuse him], and he will flee from you" (KJV). Submit and resist. When you yield to the Lord, the authority of God will cast Satan out! (In the next chapter, we are going to go even deeper into this through Zechariah 3 and Isaiah 11—our spiritual inheritance!)

God's people have been destroyed through the lack of knowledge. But now that we know Jezebel's roots, we can no longer let her live. Now, you should understand why simply quoting scriptures, going to church, or singing in the choir isn't going to break the power of the devil! *You must become a yielded vessel to what you read, sing, and preach.* Submitted…like Jesus…like that woman at the well. Believe me, Satan is petrified of your obedience—because when the Lord releases you, his evil kingdom will fall.

God Maintains His Power

God foreknew that the powers of darkness would fight to keep His eternal plan from coming to pass. But since He is the real authority, no power in heaven, on earth, or under the earth can resist Him. Let's look at Psalm 14:2–3:

> The Lord looked down from heaven upon the children of men to see if there were any who understood, dealt wisely, and sought after God, inquiring for and of Him and requiring Him [of vital necessity]. They are all gone aside, they have all together become filthy; there is none that does good or right, no, not one.

God looked out over the world He had created and was grieved at what He saw. He was grieved because man had eaten of the tree of good and evil. He was grieved that He had tried so many different ways to introduce His law and ways to the people, and every time they failed. He had given so many earthly demonstrations, like when He met with Moses through the fiery bush and when He opened up the Red Sea for the children of Israel to escape from their enemies. (See Exodus 3:1–4; 14:21–22.)

At other times, God sent discipline and correction, like when He opened up the earth and swallowed the families of Korah, Dathan, and Abiram for walking in rebellion—or when He struck Moses' sister with leprosy when she came against him. (See Numbers 16:19–32; 26:9–10; 12:4–15.) Later, God struck King Uzziah with leprosy on his forehead when he had become too strong for his own good. (See 2 Chronicles 26:18–21.) Then when you look at the might of Samson, you can see God projecting His power from heaven into the earth realm, trying to help His children understand that His laws and ways must be followed. (See Judges 13–15.)

When God brought the Israelites out of slavery in Egypt, He had to speak by feeding them quail and manna, leading them with a cloud by day and a pillar of fire by night. (See Exodus 16:12–15; 13:21–22.) Joshua and Caleb were the only ones of their generation to reach their destiny, because they were able to recognize and embrace their Father's vision. From the beginning of mankind, God has been saying, "You must follow Me. You must follow My ways. You must do things My way. There is no other way to reach destiny. You don't know this way."

Let's read Isaiah 53:

> Surely He has borne our griefs (sicknesses, weaknesses, and distresses) and carried our sorrows and pains [of punishment], yet we [ignorantly] considered Him stricken, smitten, and afflicted by God [as if with leprosy]. But He was wounded for our transgressions, He was bruised for our guilt and iniquities; the chastisement [needful to obtain] peace and well-being for us was upon Him, and with the stripes [that wounded] Him we are healed and made whole.... Yet it was the

will of the Lord to bruise Him; He has put Him to grief and made Him sick. When You and He make His life an offering for sin [and He has risen from the dead, in time to come], He shall see His [spiritual] offspring. He shall prolong His days, and the will and pleasure of the Lord shall prosper in His hand. He shall see [the fruit] of the travail of His soul and be satisfied; by His knowledge of Himself [which He possesses and imparts to others] shall My [uncompromisingly] righteous One, My Servant, justify many and make many righteous (upright and in right standing with God), for He shall bear their iniquities and their guilt [with the consequences, says the Lord].

—Isaiah 53:4–5, 10–11

Like I said before, when our heavenly Father foresaw mankind's need for a Redeemer, Jesus said, "Father, here I am…send Me." He willingly gave up the glory of heaven to come and give us an eternal inheritance. Did you see the promises in this scripture that ensure your victory over the enemy every time? It states, "…the will and pleasure of the Lord shall prosper in His hand." Because Jesus was uncompromisingly righteous, you can live upright and in right standing with God. *That's real authority!* That's what Jesus suffered, died, and rose again to give to you and me.

> WHEN YOU ARE IN CHRIST, JEZEBEL— OR ANY OTHER DEMON SPIRIT— DOES NOT STAND A CHANCE.

The grief our heavenly Father experienced can be transformed into divine pleasure through the obedience of Christ.

Jesus, Our Ultimate Example

Jesus became the ultimate example of sonship because He went through the process. He started out with the Father in heavenly places and was sent out from the Father to earth. He was sent; He didn't just go. Jesus was sent out from heaven to fulfill the vision and will of the Father in the natural realm. That's why it didn't matter how hard it was for Him to pay the price for our sins. Because He was sent, Jesus could say, "Nevertheless..." He was on a mission.

On that day at the well of Samaria (when Jesus was talking to the Samaritan woman), His disciples came and said, "Master, have you eaten?"

With all grace and truth, Jesus told them, "My meat is to do the will of the Father." He knew that eating natural food was necessary for the physical realm but recognized that at this place in His life, He had to eat the will of the Father in order to finish His course: agonizing in the Garden of Gethsemane, being marched from judgment hall to judgment hall before He was crucified. Jesus knew He would be persecuted beyond anything we could ever imagine.

He endured being beaten with a cat-o'-nine-tails, being spat upon, and having a crown of thorns pressed upon His head before carrying a cross up to a place where they would drive nails through His hands and feet. Yet our Lord said, "Nevertheless..."

During the early parts of His ministry, Jesus walked in the glorified state of being recognized as the Son of God because of the miracles He performed. In the end, He would be recognized as the Son of God who would never deny His birthright—who would never deny His Father in heaven no matter how much He was brutalized. It was His hour for true sonship to be proven by way of what He was willing to suffer. Jesus gave all to get the divine will of the Father done.

This comes into play today, and sadly, this is how Jezebel gets acknowledged into power. Everybody wants to stand in the pulpit and preach, lay hands on the sick, cast out devils, and get the accolades of the public. But when it is time for sonship to be proven, will you deny Christ? Will you throw in the towel? When everything you know is being tested and tried, and you feel as if your whole world is falling apart, will you still stand and say, "Nevertheless, I will do my Father's will. Not my will, Lord, but Thy will be done"?

This reminds me of earlier years when I was called to the assignment of corporate prayer. When the Lord first revealed to me that I was to start a 5 a.m. prayer meeting on Tuesday mornings, I was willing, in spite of being afraid to do what He was calling me to do. During the early stages of those prayer meetings, everything was not as accommodating as I would have loved for it to be. I remember pulling up one morning and discovering that the deacon had forgotten to turn on the heat. When we got in the sanctuary, it was so cold that I came very close to dismissing the group and telling them that prayer would be over after ten minutes.

As I brooded through this prayer session, the Spirit of the Lord grabbed hold of me and began to ask, "Where is your 'nevertheless' spirit?" He informed me that many times I would come into that building and everything would not be to my liking, but that my spirit must remain in the posture of "nevertheless" if I wanted to be blessed. After that service, it didn't matter how many showed up or whether the heat or air conditioning was on or off—I was determined that my "meat" was to do the will of the Father.

Through this, I learned the principle that serving God was not based on conditions. It was to be found in the place and the posture that the Father had called me to—and that was the posture of "nevertheless."

When Jesus completed the divine process as the Son of God, He said, "All authority (all power of rule) in heaven and on earth has been given to Me" (Matt. 28:18). And it truly was. In the first chapter of Revelation, Jesus said, "Fear not; I am the first and the last: I am he that liveth, and was dead; and, behold, I am alive for evermore, Amen; and have the keys of hell and of death" (vv. 17–18, KJV).

All power was put in Jesus' hands because He "gave up all" by going through the process of the Father in proper order—He was born of a virgin, raised in Bethlehem, baptized by John in the Jordan River, tempted for forty days and nights…I could go on and on. So let me ask this question: If God is for you (and He is), who can be against you? If God is for you, can you embrace submission and obedience? Can you trust God to order your steps and give you counsel through a spiritual father on earth? Can you trust Him in everything, even though you can't see what may happen tomorrow?

When Jesus was baptized and the Spirit of the Lord descended upon Him like a dove, God said, "This is my beloved Son, in whom I am well pleased" (Matt. 3:17, KJV). This recognition from the Father was powerful. God spoke out that He was pleased. Yet, at that time, Jesus hadn't done anything but come to be baptized.

As insignificant as this may seem, it was a huge statement. Jesus could have announced Himself. He could have refused to let John baptize Him, but He started His ministry correctly by submitting to the one who was already in authority before He came. He allowed John to baptize Him that day, which affirmed John's relationship with the Father. By doing this, it confirmed to the heavenly Father that when He went forth to do His will, He was willing to set forth a pattern in the earth realm for spiritual authority by submitting to divine order. By this, the Spirit of the Father foreknew that His Anointed One would completely fulfill His calling and purpose, for Jesus had already said *yes* in His heart.

That is why I said earlier that a spiritual father sees who you are to become. When a leader recognizes the calling of God on someone's life, there is something about that person's presence that satisfies the leader's spiritual intuition. Why? He knows this son or daughter will go through a process in the physical realm, even if he or she has already committed to assisting with the vision. There will always be a process.

Sometimes when I meet people, I'll see a glory cloud resting on them. To me, this not only reveals a higher anointing upon them to do mighty works, but the fact that this same anointing will have to preserve them through the process. When I see a person willing to serve in a low place, it tells me that he or she has the potential to make it all the way to his or her destiny. It shows me that in spite of a great anointing, this person is also walking in great maturity concerning the things of the Lord. Why? An immature person only sees what he or she needs, not the needs of the kingdom.

Many times this individual will have to face the spirit of death and be confronted by demonic forces from the pit of hell. So the anointing that will sustain through trials must be as great as the anointing to perform the acts and miracles of God.

I can't say it enough. We must become yielded vessels unto God because the authority of God through the anointing defeats the enemy. So when battles come, we can stand in faith knowing that what Jesus did at Calvary will carry us into our destiny. Jesus is the real authority. If a simple woman at a well outside of Samaria can become one of the greatest evangelists in history, what can you become in Christ when you embrace real authority?

There are three ways by which you can recognize when you are coming into true sonship.

1. You will see the vision that God desires to take place in the earth.
2. You will see the vision that God has given to your leadership.
3. Your response to that will be, "Here I am, Lord, send me. Not for my own purpose, but to help fulfill Your vision and passion."

CHAPTER 14

Our True Inheritance

*T*rue riches can only be found in our Father's house, and Jesus showed us how to do it. He demonstrated the way to become real sons and daughters of the kingdom—*and it's not by seeking a physical portion*. To become a son or daughter of the kingdom, you must embrace your Father's Spirit and do what pleases Him. In chapter three of this book we took a look at the prodigal son (Luke 15:11–32). He thought the financial part of his inheritance was all his father had to offer. But after leaving his father's house and losing everything—he discovered that physical rewards soon perish.

The father was still wealthy and powerful, but the son lost the benefit of his good name...*because he failed to recognize its value*. Proverbs 22:1 says, "A good name is rather to be chosen than great riches, and loving favor rather than silver and gold." The prodigal son disrespected his father's name, and in doing so, he despised his godly lineage—so he lost his place of authority. He became poor, like any other man without an inheritance. And he ended up eating with pigs just to survive.

Listen, because this is significant. Jesus said, "Do not give that which is holy (the sacred thing) to the dogs, and do not throw your pearls before hogs, lest they trample upon them with their feet and turn and tear you in pieces" (Matt. 7:6). Your "pearls" are sacred. Let's see why. In Matthew 13:45–46, a pearl describes the kingdom. In

Revelation 21:21, the holy city of Jerusalem (that will come down from heaven) is described as having twelve gates, each made of a solid pearl. The "gates of Hades" cannot prevail against those heavenly gates because they are built on a revelation of who the Father really is.

The revelation of the Father—and of His Son, Jesus—was not always recognized by those who walked with Jesus during His time on earth, but Simon Peter understood it and stepped into his destiny as a result.

> Now when Jesus went into the region of Caesarea Philippi, He asked His disciples, Who do people say that the Son of Man is? And they answered, Some say John the Baptist; others say Elijah; and others Jeremiah or one of the prophets. He said to them, But who do you [yourselves] say that I am? Simon Peter replied, You are the Christ, the Son of the living God. Then Jesus answered him, Blessed (happy, fortunate, and to be envied) are you, Simon Bar-Jonah. For flesh and blood [men] have not revealed this to you, but My Father Who is in heaven. And I tell you, you are Peter [Greek, *Petros*—a large piece of rock], and on this rock [Greek, *petra*—a huge rock like Gibraltar] I will build My church, and the gates of Hades (the powers of the infernal region) shall not overpower it [or be strong to its detriment or hold out against it]. I will give you the keys of the kingdom of heaven; and whatever you bind (declare to be improper and unlawful) on earth must be what is already bound in heaven; and whatever you loose (declare lawful) on earth must be what is already loosed in heaven.
>
> —MATTHEW 16:13–19

Gates represent power. Jesus was saying that if you truly know your Father, you have the authority to do His works. So if you don't, what happens? The enemy is legally allowed to prevail.

The prodigal son relinquished his power to the enemy because he was tired of submitting in his father's house. How do I know this? Because when he left home, he went as far away as possible. Then he immediately started doing everything he thought he had been missing. This son was tired of living under his father's direction, doing what was right. He wanted to do his own thing.

When he walked away from his true inheritance, he now had money, but no wisdom and no guidance. Then the enemy trampled his good name in the dirt, and if God had allowed it, he would have gladly taken his life as well. He ended up serving the needs of pigs—the very animals that demons begged Jesus to send them into in Matthew 8:28–32! I don't know about you, but I wouldn't want to be feeding anything that a demon would call its "home."

Too many in the body of Christ have left their fathers' houses in an untimely manner and have added stress to the vision of the kingdom. Then they wonder why trouble comes and everything starts falling apart. Hear me. Bible principles don't change. If you open the "gate" of your life to the enemy, he will trample everything under his feet and then try to take you out.

Jesus said, "You are the salt of the earth, but if salt has lost its taste (its strength, its quality), how can its saltiness be restored? It is not good for anything any longer but to be thrown out and trodden underfoot by men" (Matt. 5:13). Salt not only enhances the natural flavor of food, but it is also a preservative. In other words, whatever you apply salt to doesn't decay or rot. Do you see the revelation? Your lineage protects you from the enemy and enables you to serve beyond your natural abilities—because that is what you inherit from your heavenly Father—His character. When you despise your true inheritance, the devil won't be your only problem. People will disregard you as well, just as they did the prodigal son.

To understand the great call that is on your life, you must be willing to be led. It is your key to power with God. Look at Luke 2:43–52:

> And when the Feast was ended, as they were returning,
> the boy Jesus remained behind in Jerusalem. Now His

parents did not know this, but, supposing Him to be in the caravan, they traveled on a day's journey; and [then] they sought Him [diligently, looking up and down for Him] among their kinsfolk and acquaintances....And when they [Joseph and Mary] saw Him, they were amazed; and His mother said to Him, Child, why have You treated us like this? Here Your father and I have been anxiously looking for You [distressed and tormented]. And He said to them, How is it that you had to look for Me? Did you not see and know that it is necessary [as a duty] for Me to be in My Father's house and [occupied] about My Father's business? But they did not comprehend what He was saying to them. And He went down with them and came to Nazareth and was [habitually] obedient to them....And Jesus increased in wisdom (in broad and full understanding) and in stature and years, and in favor with God and man.

Even as a child, Jesus knew that being in His Father's house and serving the Father's vision was His first priority. But His parents didn't comprehend what He was saying—and many Christians today are in the same place. We don't understand the importance of submitting to a vision and helping to bring it to pass. Jesus was "habitually obedient" to His heavenly and earthly authorities. Therefore, His Father's character grew within Him. He gained wisdom and stature, and He had favor with God and man.

> **OBEDIENCE TO GOD AND YOUR OBEDIENCE TO THE GOD IN YOUR SPIRITUAL PARENTS WILL FORM AN UNSTOPPABLE SYNERGY OF POWER.**

So tell me, what happens when you are habitually disobedient? You lose rank in both places—heaven and earth, as well as with God and man. Look at the prodigal son. He lost everything—spiritually and physically. But, thank God, when he finally went back to his father's house, he only wanted to be a servant. He was finally ready to serve his father's vision—not to just "go through the motions" because it was the thing to do.

What about you? Are you serving in the house of your spiritual father or living to serve your own needs? Do you go to church to worship God or to be seen and approved by other people? Your true inheritance is in your Father's house. It is the strength of your spiritual parents.

The Seven Eyes of God

While we have discussed at great length the power of submission, oneness, and sonship, let's see what the true inheritance really is. God isn't in the business of handing out one-time blessings; He is imparting *true riches*. What God is doing in His people is much bigger than one person, one church, or even one nation. He is doing a work that will impact generations. He is rebuilding His temple and restoring true worship through the perfect manifestation of His character and power. We have entered the prophetic season where the Spirit of God is declaring to the church, "Not by might, nor by power, but by My Spirit...says the Lord of hosts" (Zech. 4:6).

Now more than ever, proper spiritual alignment is critical. While submitting to God through your spiritual parents, let's find out what that divine inheritance is. Although we introduced this scripture in a previous chapter, let's see how it all relates in Zechariah 3:7–10:

> Thus says the Lord of hosts: If you will walk in My ways and keep My charge, then also you shall rule My house and have charge of My courts, and I will give you access [to My presence] and places to walk among these who stand here. Hear now, O Joshua the high priest, you and your colleagues who [usually] sit before you—for they are men who are a sign or omen [types of what is to come]—for behold, I will bring forth My servant the Branch. For behold, upon the stone which I have set before Joshua, upon that one stone are seven eyes or facets [the all-embracing providence of God

and the sevenfold radiations of the Spirit of God].
Behold, I will carve upon it its inscription, says the
Lord of hosts, and I will remove the iniquity and guilt
of this land in a single day. In that day, says the Lord
of hosts, you shall invite each man his neighbor under
his own vine and his own fig tree.

During Zechariah's ministry, the Israelites had just come out of
slavery in Babylon and returned to Jerusalem to rebuild the temple—so
God set the *seven eyes* before the high priest. Do you see His order?
He imparted His vision and the manifestations of His character to
leadership, because Israel had a great work to complete. It had to be
accomplished by His might and power.

This scripture clearly reveals they are "types of what is to come"—in
other words, what was happening in Zechariah's day would happen
again in the last days. He wanted to make sure that in the heat of the End-
Time battle, we would have a spiritual recipe that would never fail us. He
wanted us to fully understand that this one Branch/Stone would be the
key to us always getting the victory and forever keeping the victory.

What does the stone represent? Prophetically, it speaks of Jesus,
the head of the church. Isaiah 28:16 and Psalm 118:22–23 say:

Therefore thus says the Lord God, Behold, I am laying
in Zion for a foundation a Stone, a tested Stone, a precious Cornerstone of sure foundation; he who believes
(trusts in, relies on, and adheres to that Stone) will not
be ashamed or give way or hasten away [in sudden
panic]....The stone which the builders rejected has
become the chief cornerstone. This is from the Lord
and is His doing; it is marvelous in our eyes.

However, if we ignore or disobey the Stone, 1 Peter 2:8–9 says:

And, A Stone that will cause stumbling and a Rock
that will give [men] offense; they stumble because
they disobey and disbelieve [God's] Word, as those

[who reject Him] were destined (appointed) to do. But you are a chosen race, a royal priesthood, a dedicated nation, [God's] own purchased, special people, that you may set forth the wonderful deeds and display the virtues and perfections of Him Who called you out of darkness into His marvelous light.

When we read the revelation given to Zechariah concerning the seven eyes of God, we must first realize that seven is the perfect number of God. The seven eyes of the Father have been given to the Son—and His vision is perfect. Nothing is hidden from His eyes. This is how every part of the church will become spotless, white, and without blemish. *Hear me*: The "might" and "power" of the flesh will fail. Only that which is birthed by the Holy Spirit (the sevenfold radiations of God) will fulfill the plan of the Lord in this final hour. The day of "human wonders" is over. God is doing things His way.

The Seven Spirits of God

The *seven eyes* of God in Zechariah 3 are directly related to the *seven spirits* of God in Isaiah 11:1–3, for they fully describe the character attributes of our Father. These supernatural characteristics are being given to every son and daughter of the kingdom that will hear His voice and obey. It is your inheritance. It is what you gained because He died and rose again:

> And there shall come forth a Shoot out of the stock of Jesse [David's father], and a Branch out of his roots shall grow and bear fruit. And the Spirit of the Lord shall rest upon Him—the Spirit of wisdom and understanding, the Spirit of counsel and might, the Spirit of knowledge and of the reverential and obedient fear of the Lord—and shall make Him of quick understanding, and His delight shall be in the reverential and obedient fear of the Lord.

Let's review. The seven spirits are:

1. The Spirit of the Lord
2. The Spirit of wisdom
3. The Spirit of understanding
4. The Spirit of counsel
5. The Spirit of might
6. The Spirit of knowledge
7. The Spirit of the reverential and obedient fear of the Lord

These perfect attributes are available to us through the Holy Spirit. Let's briefly look at each one.

Number one, the *Spirit of the Lord,* is the reflection of the authority of God as "the existing One," Lord and Master of the earth.[1] In Luke 4:18, Jesus said, "The Spirit of the Lord [is] upon Me..." This was after He had been "habitually obedient" to the Father and His earthly parents and was baptized by John. Jesus did everything according to the Father's pattern to stay in spiritual alignment...*and then He declared spiritual authority.* He maintained divine authority through consistent obedience. As you submit to Christ's authority, you will walk in consistent authority over the enemy.

Number two, the *Spirit of wisdom,* speaks of "skill in war, wisdom in administration, shrewdness or prudence in religious affairs, and godly (ethical) wisdom."[2] As you obey the Spirit of the living God, He will give you wisdom in every area so that you can war effectively in this final hour.

Number three, the *Spirit of understanding,* adds perfected insight, natural and spiritual, to the wisdom of the Lord to help you walk securely without fear.[3] Through the fourth attribute, the *Spirit of counsel,* God will advise you. He will reveal and confirm the counsel of His will through the divine illumination of His Word, both written and spoken, as well as through dreams and visions, and the direction of your spiritual parents.[4] This is the process of Proverbs 3:5–6:

Lean on, trust in, and be confident in the Lord with all you heart and mind and do not rely on your own insight or understanding. In all your ways know, recognize, and acknowledge Him, and He will direct and make straight and plain your paths.

Through the fifth attribute, the *Spirit of might,* you will receive "strength, might, valour, bravery…mighty deeds (of God)."[5] That means that in this last hour, God will give you strength to be equal to any task that is before you. The works you will do for the Lord will not be according to your own might, power, reputation, or intellect. They will be accomplished supernaturally by the power of the Holy Spirit. As you trust in the Lord and lean not to your own understanding, no weapon that has been formed against you shall prosper.

The sixth attribute, the *Spirit of knowledge,* adds perception and practical skill to wisdom and understanding.[6] In the spiritual sense, perception gives you immediate recognition, insight, and discernment concerning what He wants you to do. You will not only understand His counsel, but also you will be able to walk it out according to the Word with both skill and anointing. This means God will sharpen both your perception and the skills to match so that you can finish what He has called you to do.

And finally, the seventh attribute, the *Spirit of the fear of the Lord,* is what keeps everything in check. Proverbs 1:7 says, "The reverent and worshipful fear of the Lord is the beginning and the principal and choice part of knowledge [its starting point and its essence]; but fools despise skillful and godly Wisdom, instruction, and discipline." The fear of the Lord is described as "fear, terror, fearing…awesome or terrifying thing (object causing fear)…fear (of God), respect, reverence, piety…revered."[7] This means that as a true son or daughter in this season, you will have great honor and respect not only for God, but also for the things of God and the people of God. As a result, every other gift and ability will flow in and through you like a mighty river.

Let's go to Psalm 34 to see what the fear of the Lord releases:

> Come, you children, listen to me; I will teach you to
> revere and worshipfully fear the Lord. What man is he

who desires life and longs for many days, that he may see good? Keep your tongue from evil and your lips from speaking deceit. Depart from evil and do good; seek, inquire for, and crave peace and pursue (go after) it! The eyes of the Lord are toward the [uncompromisingly] righteous and His ears are open to their cry.

—PSALM 34:11–15

The prodigal son, before leaving, did not get the character traits of his father, and up until now, the same thing has been happening in the church. Too many people have been trying to operate in the things of the Spirit without the authority, wisdom, understanding, counsel, might, knowledge, and fear of the Lord! They have gifts and talents, but no eyes. This is an attack of the enemy through the root of Jezebel (Ashtaroth)—because this spirit always aligns itself with believers who relinquish their God-given inheritance—their seven eyes.

We are in the final, supernatural season. We are even closer to the day that the perfect government of the Lord Jesus Christ will rule in the earth. That is why God is getting His house in order. That is why powers are being shaken. That is why the bride must be "spotless and without blemish." And this is also why the enemy's attack has stepped up.

Now, go with me to Revelation 5:1–6:

And I saw lying on the open hand of Him Who was seated on the throne a scroll (book) written within and on the back, closed and sealed with seven seals; and I saw a strong angel announcing in a loud voice, Who is worthy to open the scroll? And [who is entitled and deserves and is morally fit] to break its seals? And no one in heaven or on earth or under the earth [in the realm of the dead, Hades] was able to open the scroll or to take a [single] look at its contents. And I wept audibly and bitterly because no one was found fit to open the scroll or to inspect it. Then one of the elders [of the heavenly Sanhedrin] said to me, Stop weeping! See, the Lion of the tribe of Judah, the Root (Source) of David, has won (has overcome and conquered)! He can open the scroll and break its seven seals! And there between the throne and the four living creatures (ones, beings) and among the elders [of the heavenly Sanhedrin] I saw a Lamb standing, as though it had been slain, with seven horns and with seven eyes, which are the seven Spirits of God [the sevenfold Holy Spirit] Who have been sent [on duty far and wide] into all the earth.

The sevenfold manifestation of the Spirit has already been released in the earth. Therefore, the perfecting work of God in His saints has intensified in this spiritual season. We must come into proper spiritual alignment according to the biblical pattern. We are in the season of the supernatural—the day of trying to do the supernatural with natural strength is over.

The Seven Lamps of God

As the Lord was releasing this word to me, He led me to Zechariah 4:1–7, where we read about the seven lamps of God:

And the angel who talked with me came again and awakened me, like a man who is wakened out of his sleep. And said to me, What do you see? I said, I see, and behold, a lampstand all of gold, with its bowl [for oil] on the top of it and its seven lamps on it, and [there are] seven pipes to each of the seven lamps which are upon the top of it. And there are two olive trees by it, one upon the right side of the bowl and the other upon the left side of it [feeding it continuously with oil]. So I asked the angel who talked with me, What are these, my lord? Then the angel who talked with me answered me, Do you not know what these are? And I said, No, my lord. Then he said to me, This [addition of the bowl

to the candlestick, causing it to yield a ceaseless supply
of oil from the olive trees] is the word of the Lord to
Zerubbabel, saying, Not by might, nor by power, but by
My Spirit [of Whom the oil is a symbol], says the Lord
of hosts. For who are you, O great mountain [of human
obstacles]? Before Zerubbabel [who with Joshua had led
the return of the exiles from Babylon and was undertak-
ing the rebuilding of the temple, before him] you shall
become a plain [a mere molehill]! And he shall bring
forth the finishing gable stone [of the new temple] with
loud shoutings of the people, crying, Grace, grace to it!

The church is being restored by the supernatural flow of the anointing! Let's take a closer look. The lampstand with seven lamps is the same
golden lampstand (menorah) that was in the original tabernacle. But on
top of it was something that wasn't in the tabernacle—a bowl with an
olive tree on either side and seven pipes running from it down to each
lamp (candlestick). Oil was flowing continuously into the bowl from
each olive tree, which then flowed through the pipes to the lamps.

According to Adam Clarke's commentary, the bowl represents
Jesus Christ.[8] The oil symbolizes the ministry of the Holy Spirit flowing
down to the church. The lampstand represents the church. This final
move of God is a "flow down" anointing, which means that everybody
who is going to be anointed has to be in the proper place, or they will
miss the oil—this means people will be gifted but not possess a legiti-
mate yoke-breaking anointing.

As to the hidden meaning (the mystery) of the seven
stars which you saw on My right hand and the seven
lampstands of gold: the seven stars are the seven angels (messengers) of the seven assemblies (churches)
and the seven lampstands are the seven churches.
—REVELATION 1:20, EMPHASIS ADDED

A lampstand has one branch in the center (like a trunk) and six
branches attached to the center (which represents the number of

man). It was formed and beaten with pure gold…without wood or measurements. To me, this speaks that the lampstand can only hold the illumination of the Spirit of the Lord supernaturally. Human effort and earthly wisdom cannot operate in this realm. Praise be to God, it also means there are unlimited resources we receive from the *seven eyes* and *seven spirits* of God—if we stay in spiritual alignment.

Let me pause to bring this confirmation from Scripture, because it indicates the hour we are living in. Isaiah 10:17 says, "And the Light of Israel shall become a fire and His Holy One a flame, and it will burn and devour [the Assyrian's] thorns and briers in one day." In Hebrew history, Israel is the olive tree, and the lampstand symbolized that Israel would become a light to the world. Have you noticed? Every day, Israel is coming to the forefront—not just in current events, but more importantly, in the hearts of God's people. The illumination has already begun.

That's why God told Zerubbabel, "Not by might, nor by power, but by My Spirit…" The bowl is testifying to us that the work of the Lord will prevail in this season—not the wisdom or works of man. The oil of the anointing is flowing directly from the Father through Jesus Christ by the power of the Holy Spirit to strengthen *His church*. This is why Jesus had to die, so that we would be guaranteed that He would never move from His place…therefore making the oil of the anointing always accessible to us without measure. This is why the faith that was delivered to the Lord was without measure. (See John 3:34.)

Do you see why you must get in the place God has for you (in the church) and submit yourself to divine authority? This is a solemn word, and the consequences—good or bad—will be eternal.

So hear the Lord: Your power or ability as a son or daughter to submit to your spiritual parents is going to be possible only through the Holy Spirit. And if you are a spiritual parent, you will only be able to lead by the power of the Holy Ghost! The flesh will profit nothing. The arm of the flesh will fail in this hour. Your total ability to either follow or lead will be the result of spiritual union with our Father in heaven, because remember, we don't know this way.

Let me take this one step further. Under the Old Covenant, the high priest wore a breastplate that contained twelve stones—one for each tribe of Israel. Inside of the breastplate was a piece of parchment containing the ineffable name of God. Through this parchment, *Urim* (light) and *Thummim* (completeness) caused individual letters of the tribal names on the breastplate to light up. If read in the right order, he received the "complete and true answer" to the prayers for the nation of Israel.[9]

What does this mean today? I believe that through a "supernatural" release of *urim* and *thummim*, true sons and daughters will be able to see what God has placed in the "bosoms" of their spiritual parents. I also believe God will use these same spiritual elements to illuminate the hearts of leaders and give insight for those under their care. Human patterns and formulas will no longer work; only the pattern and the formula of the Holy Spirit will prosper.

As the Old Testament priests had no ability to lead in the flesh, so shall it be in this time. Unless God reveals something in your bosom (your most intimate place with God), you won't be able to recognize your spiritual children or release the greatness within them.

To continually tap into this supernatural oil, our lives will have to remain pure before the Lord. Otherwise, spiritual life will cease. Under the Old Covenant, if a priest tried to serve without consecrating first, he would die just trying to set foot into the holy place. Now the same thing is happening in the spiritual realm. Leaders who don't stay consecrated before the Lord will experience death in their ministries, and messages preached from their pulpits will have no life. Songs will be spiritually dead and the worship will sound like sounding brass and tinkling symbols, because it too is suffering from lost fellowship with the heavenly Father. Therefore, the fellowship leaders have with their children will be instantly broken.

Sadly to say, many who are in leadership positions do not possess the *urim* and *thummim* in the breastplate, which represents righteousness (Eph. 6:14). Where righteousness is in question, there can be no illumination, which is revelation. And if the Father cannot be revealed, then we are left having church in the dark.

The conditions of our society are so extreme that leaders can no longer lead by intellect. We have to be led by the Spirit. We must possess the *seven eyes* and *seven spirits* of God by way of the *seven lamps*. If you are a leader, you must submit to Jesus Christ through the ministry of the Holy Spirit, or life will not flow through you to others.

The two olive trees are also very prophetic. Many scholars believe the olive trees represent the kingly and priestly offices of Israel. This was fulfilled in Zechariah's day because Zerubbabel was a civil leader, and Joshua was the high priest. As "adopted" sons and daughters, we are kings and priests unto God in the supernatural realm. First Peter 2:9 tells us this, but let's also look at Revelation 1:5–6:

> To Him Who ever loves us and has once [for all] loosed and freed us from our sins by His own blood, *and formed us into a kingdom (a royal race), priests to His God and Father*—to Him be the glory and the power and the majesty and the dominion throughout the ages and forever and ever. Amen (so be it).
>
> —Emphasis added

Here is another meaning of the olive trees that I believe is significant, because it talks about events that take place during the tribulation period before Christ returns. Come with me to Revelation 11:

> And I will grant the power of prophecy to My two witnesses for 1,260 (42 months; three and one-half years), dressed in sackcloth. *These [witnesses] are the two olive trees and the two lampstands which stand before the Lord of the earth.* And if anyone attempts to injure them, fire pours from their mouth and consumes their enemies; if anyone should attempt to harm them, thus he is doomed to be slain. These [two witnesses] have power to shut up the sky, so that no rain may fall during the days of their prophesying (their prediction of events relating to Christ's kingdom and its speedy

triumph); and they also have power to turn the waters
into blood and to smite and scourge the earth with all
manner of plagues as often as they choose.

—REVELATION 11:3–6, EMPHASIS ADDED

These two witnesses were given supernatural authority in the heavenly and earthly realms to bind, loose, and speak the word of the Lord. Power is building in the body of Christ toward the day when these two witnesses will declare the word of the Lord according to the *seven eyes* and *seven spirits*. Not long after, the kingdoms of this earth will become the kingdom of our God and His Christ! (See Revelation 11:15.)

Is your spirit picking up where the body of Christ is in God's prophetic plan? I sincerely hope so—because only those who are in proper spiritual alignment according to the orderly flow of the anointing will be divinely used in this final hour. Those who aren't will miss the mark.

The oil of the anointing is breaking every yoke of bondage—and according to the *seven lamps,* it isn't ever going to stop. But hear me. The Spirit of the Lord will only break yokes for those who have submitted themselves according to His pattern. You must be a true son or daughter of the kingdom, not a spiritual *lone ranger* with a personal agenda. If you have removed yourself from God's covering through a divinely appointed spiritual father or mother, you have exposed yourself to the enemy.

Haggai 2:4–9 says:

> OUR TRUE
> INHERITANCE—
> THE SUPERNATURAL
> CHARACTER OF OUR
> FATHER THROUGH
> JESUS CHRIST AND
> THE MINISTRY OF
> THE HOLY SPIRIT—
> IS WAITING TO BE
> RESTORED TO US IN
> THE HOUSE OF OUR
> SPIRITUAL FATHER.

> Yet now be strong, alert, and courageous, O Zerubbabel,
> says the Lord; be strong, alert, and courageous, O
> Joshua son of Jehozadak, the high priest; and be
> strong, alert, and courageous, all you people of the

land, says the Lord, and work! For I am with you, says the Lord of hosts. According to the promise that I covenanted with you when you came out of Egypt, so My Spirit stands and abides in the midst of you; fear not. For thus says the Lord of hosts: Yet once more, in a little while, I will shake and make tremble the [starry] heavens, the earth, the sea, and the dry land; and I will shake all nations and the desire and the precious things of all nations shall come in, and I will fill this house with splendor, says the Lord of hosts. The silver is Mine and the gold is Mine, says the Lord of hosts. The latter glory of this house [with its successor, to which Jesus came] shall be greater than the former, says the Lord of hosts; and in this place will I give peace and prosperity, says the Lord of hosts.

Do you see God's promise? The *latter glory* of the church will be greater than the former! We are in the greatest supernatural season that has ever been known to man. But it's *by the Spirit*, not by human knowledge, wisdom, gifts, or talents. This means the days of spiritual showboating, politicking, name-dropping, and the like are screeching to a halt. Now more than ever, we should be rejoicing in the fact that we are sons and daughters of the gospel. Remember what Jesus said to His disciples in Luke 10:19–20:

Behold! I have given you authority and power to trample upon serpents and scorpions, and [physical and mental strength and ability] over all the power that the enemy [possesses]; and nothing shall in any way harm you. Nevertheless, do not rejoice at this, that the spirits are subject to you, but rejoice that your names are enrolled in heaven.

This reveals the mystery of the prodigal son. Today's church is so much like him—we have taken the physical portion of our inheritance and left our father's house to waste it on our own desires. Our *true inheritance*—the supernatural character of our Father through Jesus Christ and the ministry of the Holy Spirit—is waiting to be restored to us *in the house of our spiritual father.* This takes me back to the word of the Lord in Haggai 2:

> Speak to Zerubbabel [the representative of the Davidic monarchy and covenant and in direct line of the ancestry of Jesus Christ] governor of Judah, saying, I will shake the heavens and the earth; and I will [in the distant future] overthrow the throne of kingdoms and I will destroy the strength of the kingdoms of the [ungodly] nations, and I will overthrow the chariots and those who ride in them, and the horses and their riders shall go down, every one by the sword of his brother. In that day, says the Lord of hosts, will I take you, O Zerubbabel, My servant, the son of Shealtiel, says the Lord, and will make you [through the Messiah, your descendant] My signet ring; for I have chosen you [as the one with whom to renew My covenant to David's line], says the Lord of hosts.
>
> —HAGGAI 2:21–23

God is shaking things today just as He was in Zerubbabel's time. And He is calling every member of the body of Christ to sonship through the same royal line. God has chosen us; we are that prodigal son. By the power of the Holy Spirit, He has made His true sons and daughters to be a "signet ring" in this hour. This means we must reflect our heavenly Father's "image and likeness" to the world—His divine character. When people see God's people, they should see Jesus.

For this is the day of Malachi 4:6:

> And he shall turn and reconcile the hearts of the [estranged] fathers to the [ungodly] children, and the hearts of the [rebellious] children to [the piety of] their fathers [a reconciliation produced by repentance

of the ungodly], lest I come and smite the land with a curse and a ban of utter destruction.

The spirit of "fathers" is returning into the earth as leaders are turning to our heavenly Father. As this happens, the order and flow of the anointing is rising up and breaking every yoke of bondage. No weapon formed against God's church will prosper! God is restoring the true pattern of worship so His people will become a bride, *spotless and without blemish*, prepared for Christ's return.

CHAPTER 15

It's Time to Rebuild

*L*ike Israel in Zerubbabel's day, as we receive our true inheritance, we can continue the mighty work of rebuilding the church. This work of rebuilding can be better understood by looking at the example of Ezra, who was called by God to rebuild the temple in Jerusalem after the Babylonian captivity of the children of Israel. (See Ezra 1:1–4.)

As we begin to look at Ezra, it's important to note that Ezra wasn't the high priest—that was Joshua's role. But Ezra was of royal lineage. He was the first to be called a scribe of the Law of Moses, because he had studied it diligently—even during Israel's captivity in Babylon. God used Ezra mightily in the rebuilding. He had great favor with the dignitaries that ruled over Israel. Cyrus was one of those kings.

Under King Cyrus, Persia and its ally (Media) conquered the Babylonians nearly *seventy years* after Babylon had taken Israel into captivity. Babylon is where the goddess Ashtaroth came into being... *do you remember Jezebel?* I don't think it's a coincidence that God's people were set free by Cyrus, a Gentile king who had taken authority over Israel's ancient enemy! What makes this even more powerful is the fact that on the same night Belshazzar (Nebuchadnezzar's son) had a big "Babylonian" feast, bringing out the sacred vessels of Israel's temple to drink wine, God snatched the kingdom out of his hands. (See Daniel 5.)

Right in the middle of their party, God wrote Babylon's death sentence on the wall (Dan. 5:5). None of Belshazzar's astrologers or

267

soothsayers could interpret the message. *Then the queen mother came in and told him about Daniel...* who had served his father (vv. 10–13). Daniel interpreted the inscription, and that night Belshazzar was killed. The kingdom of Babylonia fell to the Medes and Persians.

That's when God stirred up Cyrus's spirit. In the first year of his reign (the same time Persia and Media conquered Babylon), Cyrus decreed for the Israelites to rebuild the temple in Jerusalem—nearly *seventy years* after they had been taken captive by Babylon. When sin multiplied and the enemy started abusing the holy vessels of God, judgment hit, and God took down Israel's enemy in one day! Church, hear me; wickedness is multiplying in the earth, but the glory of the church is rising by the might and power of the Lord. The enemy's days are numbered.

The church, under the prophetic anointing of Cyrus, is beginning to be rebuilt. Everything the enemy has stolen must be returned—because we have a great task to complete for our Father. As we submit to His leadership, we will possess our rightful inheritance by way of the *seven eyes, seven spirits,* and *seven lamps.* Three sets of seven... *perfection* and *completion!* The glory of the latter house will be greater than the former!

Even in Cyrus's day, Babylon came down and the leaders rose up. (See Ezra 1:3–7.) The leaders rose up because God stirred them up. Let me put it this way: when it was time to rebuild the temple, God started the process by the power of His Spirit, much as He is doing today. He worked through the "spiritual fathers" He had appointed in the earth. Do you see the pattern? The leaders had been in captivity for almost seventy years, but when it was time to build, they heard the voice of the Lord and got in position. We should shout, *Hallelujah!* God is restoring everything the church has lost—and remember, it happened for Israel in one day! God always supports what He authorizes. We can see the pattern for God's restoration in Ezra:

> When the seventh month came and the Israelites were in the towns, the people gathered together as one man to Jerusalem. Then stood up Jeshua [Joshua] son of Jozadak, and his brethren the priests, and Zerubbabel son of Shealtiel, and his brethren, and they built the

altar of the God of Israel to offer burnt offerings upon it, as it is written in the instructions of Moses the man of God. And they set the altar [in its place] upon its base, for fear was upon them because of the peoples of the countries; and they offered burnt offerings on it to the Lord morning and evening.

—EZRA 3:1–3

True worship was restored according to the pattern of the tabernacle that God had originally revealed to Moses. After true worship was restored, "the fear of the Lord" came upon the people—and that was the releasing of everything else.

In the second year of their coming to God's house at Jerusalem, in the second month, Zerubbabel son of Shealtiel and Jeshua [Joshua] son of Jozadak made a beginning, with the rest of their brethren—the priests and Levites and all who had come to Jerusalem out of the captivity. They appointed the Levites from twenty years old and upward to oversee the work of the Lord's house. Then Jeshua with his sons and his kinsmen, Kadmiel and his sons, sons of Judah, together took the oversight of the workmen in the house of God—the sons of Henadad, with their sons and Levite kinsmen. And when the builders laid the foundation of the temple of the Lord, the priests stood in their vestments with trumpets, and the Levite sons of Asaph with their cymbals, to praise the Lord, after the order of David king of Israel. They sang responsively, praising and giving thanks to the Lord, saying, For He is good, for His mercy and loving-kindness endure forever toward Israel. And all the people shouted with a great shout when they praised the Lord, because the foundation of the house of the Lord was laid!

—EZRA 3:8–11

The priestly service came into order at the same time the temple's foundation was being laid. This couldn't have been a coincidence—it was divine destiny! And that's when true praise went up to God—according to the order of King David, a "father" of Israel and a *true son* of the kingdom. This is why spiritual alignment must be reestablished. When we worship God according to His pattern, He builds the church—and the gates of hell cannot prevail against it.

No matter how much you jump, shout, or roll in the aisles at church, it doesn't mean that *true praise* is in your belly. True worship is built on the foundation of godly character and prayer. This flows from the Spirit of God to His people. And when it comes to building His church, God's pattern is to flow through anointed leadership, who imparts the blessings to sons and daughters through example.

> EVERYONE MUST SERVE ACCORDING TO THE MEASURE OF FAITH GOD HAS GIVEN THEM—AND THIS WILL RESTORE US TO GOD'S PATTERN.

As the *seven eyes* and *seven spirits* of God stir today's spiritual leaders, all kinds of things are going to start changing in God's house! There will be changes with ushers who should be prophets, choir members who should be nursery workers, and changes among those who were made elders out of the spirit of familiarity and not from the divine order of God. This relates to Jeroboam in the previous chapters, who anointed men of the lowest estate and without character to be priests, even anointing himself as one of the priests of the high places. (See 1 Kings 13:33.) A great shaking is taking place in the body of Christ, and this process is of the Lord! Everyone must serve according to the measure of faith God has given them—and this will restore us to God's pattern. The Spirit of the Lord is rebuilding His church!

When God is bringing His house into order, the devil always tries to sabotage God's plan. He did in the days of Ezra's rebuilding, and he will in this day. The fourth chapter of Ezra tells the story:

> Now when [the Samaritans] the adversaries of Judah
> and Benjamin heard that the exiles from the captivity

were building a temple to the Lord, the God of Israel, they came to Zerubbabel [now governor] and to the heads of the fathers' houses and said, Let us build with you, for we seek and worship your God as you do, and we have sacrificed to Him since the days of Esarhaddon king of Assyria, who brought us here. But Zerubbabel and Jeshua [Joshua] and the rest of the heads of fathers' houses of Israel said to them, You have nothing to do with us in building a house to our God; but we ourselves will together build to the Lord, the God of Israel, as King Cyrus, the king of Persia, has commanded us. Then [the Samaritans] the people of the land [continually] weakened the hands of the people of Judah and troubled and terrified them in building. And hired counselors against them to frustrate their purpose and plans all the days of Cyrus king of Persia, even until the reign of Darius [II] king of Persia.

—Ezra 4:1–5

The Samaritans—people from the same wicked place where Ahab and Jezebel had ruled over Israel, people who were still worshiping Baal and Ashtaroth—tried to get in to hinder God's work. Now remember that Israel had been delivered from Babylon, so what did the "chameleon" spirit try to do? It transformed…and came back through the Samaritans. The enemy will do anything to stop the work of God, including coming to you as an "angel of light." He can only succeed by coming where you are and making you give up what is rightfully yours. Israel's fathers saw right through it. They told the Samaritans, "You don't have anything to do with this…"

Then the warfare intensified. The enemy hired professional "counselors" and sent them into Israel to frustrate the work of God. This is the same thing the enemy tried through the lives of Samson and Delilah. Samson's first wife was a Philistine, but spiritually, she was weak. So the enemy stepped up the plan by stirring up the men to hire a professional, Delilah. She matched Samson's strength. Why?

Because she never desired a *relationship* with Samson—*she was after his anointing.*

When I read this part of the story, something came up in my spirit. This is why only true *sons* and *daughters* should do the work of the ministry, not those who are just hired help (with no relationship in the family). Too many men and women of God are frustrated because they have "hired" workers who don't possess the character of their spirit. Hear me. This can shut down the divine process of the *seven eyes* and the *seven spirits* in a church.

The seven eyes of God represent movement (to get us where we are supposed to go), and the seven spirits reflect inner character. They go hand in hand. As a leader imparts the sevenfold character of God in his people, they become partakers of the divine inheritance from the Lord. That's why if even one character area is out of whack, it affects a person's ability to receive the impartation and flow in harmony with the vision. So what can happen if a person isn't a son or daughter? How could such a person possibly receive the anointing that breaks the yoke of the enemy? I am not trying to condemn people who are just trying to make a living, but this is a serious matter. In God's kingdom, you cannot serve God and mammon (Luke 16:13).

> **LISTEN TO ME. THE CHURCH CANNOT BE HINDERED IF WE STAY IN SPIRITUAL ALIGNMENT!**

Eventually, Israel's enemies wore God's people down, and they stopped building. How could this have happened? Between verses 6 and 9 in the fourth chapter of Ezra, the enemy kept building a stronghold. In the end, more than eleven enemy nations joined together and wrote a letter of complaint against Israel to Artaxerxes (king of Persia during that time). When Ashtaroth perceives a threat in the spirit realm, the spirit of Jezebel will always rise up and try to match your strength. And *notice,* she wasn't operating through women.

Then the work on the house of God in Jerusalem stopped. It stopped until the second year of Darius [I] king of Persia. Now the prophets, Haggai and Zechariah son [grandson] of Iddo, prophesied to the Jews in Judah and Jerusalem in the name of the God of Israel, Whose [Spirit] was upon them. Then rose up Zerubbabel son of Shealtiel [heir to the throne of Judah] and Jeshua son of Jozadak and began to build the house of God in Jerusalem; and with them were the prophets of God [Haggai and Zechariah], helping them.

—EZRA 4:24–5:2

This makes a powerful point. The prophetic ministry always moves the church forward. So it is in our day. The church is being restored, but not without the prophetic. The Spirit of the Lord came upon the leaders and the prophets—and that's when the enemy couldn't make them stop! This time, when the enemies of Israel wrote a letter, let's see what happened:

This is a copy of the letter that Tattenai, governor on this side of the River, and Shethar-bozenai and his associates, the Apharsachites who were on this [west] side of the River, sent to Darius [I] the king. They wrote: To Darius the king: All peace. Be it known to the king that we went to the province of Judah, to the house of the great God. It is being built with huge stones, with timber laid in the walls; this work goes on with diligence and care and prospers in their hands. Then we asked those elders, Who authorized you to build this house and restore these walls? We asked their names also, that we might record the names of the men at their head and notify you. They replied, We are servants of the God of heaven and earth, rebuilding the house which was erected and finished many years ago by a great king of Israel.

—EZRA 5:6–11

Notice this: when the people of God dropped their titles and just announced servanthood, it spoke of who the Divine Builder really was.

Remember, when the prodigal son went back to his father, he only wanted to be a servant. Israel did the same. Those who were rebuilding God's temple refused to cast their pearls before swine. Did you know that a natural pearl is formed when sand gets inside of an oyster's shell and causes agitation? The result is priceless. When leaders truly become the servants of God, no weapon formed against the church can prosper—each "agitation" from the enemy only makes the "pearl" more valuable. That's why David said:

> He refreshes and restores my life (my self); He leads me in the paths of righteousness [uprightness and right standing with Him—not for my earning it, but] for His name's sake. Yes, though I walk through the [deep, sunless] valley of the shadow of death, I will fear or dread no evil, for You are with me; Your rod [to protect] and Your staff [to guide], they comfort me. You prepare a table before me in the presence of my enemies. You anoint my head with oil; my [brimming] cup runs over.
>
> —PSALM 23:3–5

As the church comes into spiritual alignment, the Lord will literally take what the enemy uses to harm God's people and use it for our benefit. This is exactly what happened in Ezra 6:1–12:

> Then King Darius [I] decreed, and a search was made in Babylonia in the house where the treasured records were stored. And at Ecbatana in the capital in the province of Media, a scroll was found on which this was recorded: In the first year of King Cyrus, [he] made a decree: Concerning the house of God in Jerusalem, let the house, the place where they offer sacrifices, be built, and let its foundations be strongly laid, its height and its breadth each 60 cubits, with three courses of great stones and one course of new timber. Let the cost be paid from the royal treasury. Also let

the gold and silver vessels of the house of God, which Nebuchadnezzar took from the temple in Jerusalem and brought to Babylon, be restored and brought back to the temple in Jerusalem, each put in its place in the house of God. *Now therefore, Tattenai, governor of the province [west of] the River, Shethar-bozenai, and your associates, the Apharsachites who are [west of] the River, keep far away from there. Leave the work on this house of God alone; let the governor and the elders of the Jews build this house of God on its site.* Moreover, I make a decree as to what you shall do for these elders of the Jews for the rebuilding of this house of God: the cost is to be paid in full to these men at once from the king's revenue, the tribute of the province [west of] the River, that they may not be hindered. And all they need, including young bulls, rams, and lambs for the burnt offerings to the God of heaven, and wheat, salt, wine, and oil, according to the word of the priests at Jerusalem, let it be given them each day without fail, that they may offer pleasing sacrifices to the God of heaven and pray for the life of the king and his sons. Also I make a decree that whoever shall change or infringe on this order, let a beam be pulled from his house and erected; then let him be fastened to it, and let his house be made a dunghill for this. May the God Who has caused His Name to dwell there overthrow all kings and peoples who put forth their hands to alter this or to destroy this house of God in Jerusalem. I Darius make a decree; let it be executed speedily and exactly.

—EMPHASIS ADDED

When a man's ways please the Lord, even his enemies will be at peace with him. (See Proverbs 16:7.) Not only did King Darius honor Cyrus's decree to strongly establish the foundations of the church, but also he decreed that everything Israel needed for the sacrifices would be provided... *daily without fail.* Prosperity hits your life when you become a servant. God makes provision for His vision.

Many people in the church are trying to fill their pocketbooks instead of building the house of God. Instead of building the kingdom, they are building their own bank accounts. Remember the prophetic warning: *If you hinder the move of God in the sanctuary, a beam will be snatched from your own house.* And it will come quickly. That is why so many people are under what seems to be an onslaught—something goes wrong in one area, and when they fix it, something else happens. The beam is being snatched.

So how do we really start to rebuild? We do it by each one of God's people taking the posture of a servant—from the pulpit to the back door. When we take on that posture, we are sending a message to Satan, saying, "This is not my church. I am a servant, and I work for God. I do not need to fight in this battle, because the battle is not mine, it is the Lord's."

The Seven Attributes of True Worship

Let's pause here, because I want you to understand in advance why I have chosen to move into this last section the way that I have. As you finish this book, I want you to see and experience the results of your divine process being complete through the seven sacrificial elements of true worship. That way, you will feel like you are beginning a new process in the Spirit and not ending one. This is a new day for you as you embrace true worship and take on your Father's character through the *seven eyes/seven spirits* and *seven lamps.*

Each of the seven sacrificial elements that Darius restored to Israel gives a powerful revelation of how the Father's character operates in His sons and daughters:

1. Young bulls
2. Rams
3. Lambs
4. Wheat
5. Salt

6. Wine
7. Oil

Like the *seven eyes* and *seven spirits* of God, they must all work together, or the structure of our worship won't be stable—it won't be able to support the weight of the bricks.

Myles Munroe said, "If a person doesn't understand the purpose of a thing, abuse is inevitable." For example, if you tried to use the spirit of might (one of the *seven spirits*) without possessing the other elements, structural damage would be unavoidable. This is why learned spiritual principles must be imparted through examples from leadership. The orderly flow of the anointing—from the *seven eyes* and *seven spirits* through the *seven lamps*—can't ever be broken. It flows continually from the Spirit of the Lord. That's why Psalm 127:1 says:

> Except the Lord builds the house, they labor in vain
> who build it; except the Lord keeps the city, the watch-
> man wakes but in vain.

Let's take a look at each of these elements through the eyes of the prophetic. In the Old Testament tabernacle, a *young bull* was sacrificed in the sin offering. *Young* means without blemish, a first fruit of your increase. This reveals that as a true son or daughter you always seek to give your best to God. Live in purity, and have a repentant heart. Sons and daughters are always willing to come to the altar.

Two *rams* were also part of the sacrifice: one as a burnt offering and sweet savor unto the Lord, and one for consecration. This means that as a son or daughter of the kingdom you willingly separate yourself to pray and make intercession for others. The burden of the Lord is upon your heart. Like a deer that searches for water, you are constantly drawn into His presence—and you always want more. The anointing on your life is obvious.

In the Old Testament, *two lambs* were sacrificed daily: one in the morning and one in the evening. That means you willingly take up the cross and follow the Lord—no matter what—morning, noon, or night.

As a son or daughter of the kingdom, you are meek, humble, and obedient. You don't gossip, backbite, murmur, or complain against the Lord. You follow Him wherever He leads you. Sons and daughters are children of great sacrifice.

Wheat, salt, wine, and oil were part of every sacrifice. Together, they generally speak of the goodness of the Lord, His mercy, as well as joy and refreshing. *Wheat* often speaks of provision and blessing. It also represents the harvest and the fat of the land. This means that even in sacrifice your spirit rejoices in the Lord, and you are fruitful in the things of God. As a true son or daughter in the kingdom, your life demonstrates that you are the *head* and *not the tail*. When people see you, they see Jesus. They see the goodness of the Lord.

Salt was rubbed onto the meat of every sacrifice, and Hebrews rubbed newborn babies with salt. During Bible times, salt symbolized loyalty and friendship. It also symbolized purification, because we see in 2 Kings 2:21–22 that the prophet Elisha healed the waters by casting in salt. So as a son or daughter of God, you are truly "the salt of the earth." Salt not only enhances flavor, but it also preserves everything it touches. This means you not only stand firm in covenant relationship (with God and others), but you are also effective for His kingdom. There is no "death" in your walk with the Lord, even when God deals with you about an area you need to surrender to Him. Your spirit is *salted*; therefore, the fires of purification preserve you. Your fruit "remains."

Both *wine* and *oil* go through a process of pressing. Not only was wine used in the sacrifices as a "drink offering," but also Jesus used wine to represent His blood. He also talked about "new wine" in Matthew 9:15–17, which means "pressed out juice." Joel 3:16–18 says:

> The Lord will thunder and roar from Zion and utter
> His voice from Jerusalem, and the heavens and the
> earth shall shake; but the Lord will be a refuge for
> His people and a stronghold to the children of Israel.
> So shall you know, understand, and realize that I am
> the Lord your God, dwelling in Zion, My holy moun-
> tain. Then shall Jerusalem be holy, and strangers and

foreigners [not born into the family of God] shall no more pass through it. And in that day, the mountains shall drip with fresh juice [of the grape] and the hills shall flow with milk; and all the brooks and riverbeds of Judah shall flow with water, and a fountain shall come forth from the house of the Lord and shall water the Valley of Shittim.

The mountains represent the "high places" in the Spirit and the glory of God. This means that *fresh wine* keeps pouring from your spirit as you obey the Lord. You have "hinds' feet" in the things of God, which means you are confident and secure operating in the supernatural realm (2 Sam. 22:34). As a son or daughter of the gospel, the process of "pressing" in your life has yielded the peaceable fruit of righteousness.

> YOU HAVE TO STAY IN SPIRITUAL ALIGNMENT TO RECEIVE THE INHERITANCE OF THE LORD.

The *oil* represents the anointing of the Holy Spirit. Holy anointing oil was used to anoint the tabernacle—all the tabernacle elements as well as Aaron and his sons. So as a son or daughter of God, the anointing is evident as you serve. The Holy Spirit not only prepares you for every task, but He also empowers you to fulfill it. You willingly tap into the "measure of faith" because you hear the voice of the Lord clearly and follow His leading. As a son or daughter of the kingdom, you truly understand that nothing is impossible with God. Your spirit rejoices in Him—because you don't operate in the flesh. You see and move in the Spirit.

These seven sacrificial elements are a powerful confirmation that you have received your true inheritance by way of the *seven eyes* and *seven spirits* of God, through the *seven lamps*. These things do not come by human strength. Only the Spirit of the Lord can perform it. These "sacrificial elements" are the fourth group of seven. *Four* speaks of the *supernatural manifestation* of God. Remember, all seven elements were given to Israel's leaders (the servants of God in Ezra 5:11) through a leader (King Darius).

The House of the Lord Will Be Completed

As leaders submit to God (the *seven eyes*), authority, understanding, wisdom, counsel, might, knowledge, and the fear of the Lord (the *seven spirits*) will build the church from the ground up. And as long as we stay under the flow of the Spirit by way of the *seven lamps*, God's people will not be hindered—the church will be restored! Look at how this happened for Israel in Ezra 6:14–17:

> And the elders of the Jews built and prospered through the prophesying of Haggai the prophet and Zechariah son of Iddo. They finished their building as commanded by the God of Israel and by decree of Cyrus and Darius and Artaxerxes king of Persia. And this house was finished on the third day of the month of Adar, in the sixth year of the reign of King Darius. And the Israelites—the priests, the Levites, and the rest of the returned exiles—celebrated the dedication of this house of God with joy. They offered at the dedication of this house of God 100 young bulls, 200 rams, 400 lambs, and, for a sin offering for all Israel, 12 he-goats, according to the number of Israel's tribes.

Israel offered up *seven hundred* sacrifices when they dedicated the new temple. They also offered *twelve* he-goats for a sin offering, the number that not only represents the twelve tribes of Israel but also symbolizes government. Every new day brings us closer to the perfect government of Jesus Christ in Isaiah 9:6–7:

> For to us a Child is born, to us a Son is given; and the government shall be upon His shoulder, and His name shall be called Wonderful Counselor, Mighty God, Everlasting Father [of Eternity], Prince of Peace. Of the increase of His government and of peace there shall be no end, upon the throne of David and over his kingdom, to establish it and to uphold it with justice and with righteousness from the [latter] time forth,

even forevermore. The zeal of the Lord of hosts will perform this.

That is why spiritual alignment is being restored to the church. That is why the seven lamps are overflowing with oil in this final hour. That is why things are shaking in the realm of the Spirit! The kingdoms of the earth must become the kingdoms of our God and His Christ. *We are in transition.* Hear me. Don't resist the workings of God, because He gave His "Son" so that He could show us how to become sons and daughters.

We see the completion of God's pattern for restoration in the sixth chapter of Ezra:

> And they set the priests in their divisions and the Levites in their courses for the service of God at Jerusalem, as it is written in the Book of Moses. The returned exiles kept the Passover on the fourteenth day of the first month. For the priests and the Levites had purified themselves together; all of them were clean. So they killed the Passover lamb for all the returned exiles, for their brother priests, and for themselves. It was eaten by the Israelites who had returned from exile and by all who had joined them and separated themselves from the pollutions of the peoples of the land to seek the Lord, the God of Israel. They kept the Feast of Unleavened Bread for seven days with joy, for the Lord had made them joyful and had turned the heart of the king of Assyria [referring to Darius king of Persia] to them, so that he strengthened their hands in the work of the house of God, the God of Israel.
>
> —EZRA 6:18–22

The priests purified themselves, *and then* the Israelites separated themselves to seek the Lord. The anointing flowed and true worship was birthed in God's people, evidenced because they received *an inheritance,* not just a physical portion. God will give great favor and will strengthen our hands to rebuild His church, but we must be obedient. Leaders must obey the voice of the Father, and sons and daughters must honor leadership. The hearts of the fathers must return to the children, and the hearts of the children must return to the fathers, or the blessings of God cannot be released in the earth.

This reminds me of the prophet Elijah. After he defeated the prophets of Baal (that had served under Jezebel), he ran from Jezebel and hid in a cave, where he cried out to God. Remember what the Lord told him:

> And the Lord said to him, Go, return on your way to the Wilderness of Damascus; and when you arrive, anoint Hazael to be king over Syria. And anoint Jehu son of Nimshi to be king over Israel, and anoint Elisha son of Shaphat of Abel-meholah to be prophet in your place. And him who escapes from the sword of Hazael Jehu shall slay, and him who escapes the sword of Jehu Elisha shall slay. Yet I will leave Myself 7,000 in Israel, all the knees that have not bowed to Baal and every mouth that has not kissed him.
>
> —1 KINGS 19:15–18

I can hear God saying, "Don't run…build My church." God will never be unfaithful to us; He is our heavenly Father. He won't forget our labors of love. Remember, when Elijah followed the pattern of the Lord and defeated the false prophets at Mount Carmel, a new day was birthed in the Spirit. That is why God told Elijah to anoint new leaders—and among them were Jehu and Elisha, the two men who would ultimately take Queen Jezebel down. More than this, the Lord revealed to Elijah there was a remnant of *seven thousand* in Israel who still worshiped Him in Spirit and in truth.

Don't miss this revelation. It is time for the church to stop running from the enemy. He is raging because he knows his time in the earth is short—but he has already been defeated! God always has a remnant of sons and daughters who won't bow their knees to the enemy. *Are you part of that remnant?* Then come out of the cave by the Spirit of the Lord and enter a new day! Return to spiritual alignment, and the Holy Spirit will bring down every enemy in your life.

Always remember your spiritual history and destiny. When God judged the serpent in Genesis 3:15, He said, "And I will put enmity between you and the woman, and between your offspring and her Offspring; He will bruise and tread your head underfoot, and you will lie in wait and bruise His heel." Then in the twelfth chapter of the Book of Revelation, a pregnant woman was in travail with a male Child who was the Deliverer of the nations. This is Jesus!

The dragon, who had seven heads, ten horns, and seven kingly crowns, stood against the woman, but she delivered the Child safely and then escaped to a place God had prepared for her. (See Revelation 12:1–6.) That is when the final victory came:

> Then war broke out in heaven; Michael and his angels went forth to battle with the dragon, and the dragon and his angels fought. But they were defeated, and there was no room found for them in heaven any longer. And the huge dragon was cast down and out—that age-old serpent, who is called the Devil and Satan, he who is the seducer (deceiver) of all humanity the world over; he was forced out and down to the earth, and his angels were flung out along with him. Then I heard a strong (loud) voice in heaven, saying, Now it has come—the salvation and the power and the kingdom (the dominion, the reign) of our God, and the power (the sovereignty, the authority) of His Christ (the Messiah); for the accuser of our brethren, he who keeps bringing before our God charges against them day and night, has been cast out!
>
> —Revelation 12:7–10

A dragon has been fighting against you and trying to steal your spiritual inheritance. And though he's been using every demonic weapon in his arsenal, this is your divine day of victory! Why? Because the weapons of your warfare are not carnal; they are mighty through God to the pulling down of strongholds (2 Cor. 10:4). The Spirit of the Lord has already won the victory! Your heavenly Father will protect and cover you as you surrender to Him in total obedience and do things His way.

Tell the devil, "You have been forced out and down! Your head is under my feet because Jesus has already stripped your power!" Salvation is already yours: for your family, friends, church, and ministry. You have the power to stand, endure, and keep the victory in God. You have the power to walk in righteousness and holiness. You can dance, shout to the Lord, cast out devils, and do everything that your heavenly Father has called, appointed, and anointed you to do through Jesus Christ in this hour.

No weapon that has been formed against you shall prosper! You are going to finish your course with joy!

A mighty inheritance is yours, and it is in your Father's house: *seven eyes/seven spirits, seven lamps*, and *seven sacrificial elements*—a supernatural portion that can't be shaken.

Letter to the Reader

*I*n this final hour, the hearts of the fathers are being restored to their children, and true sons and daughters of the gospel are being birthed according to Malachi 4:6. This process of restoration is the key to unlocking our spiritual inheritance. It is also why a strong attack has been launched by the enemy against proper spiritual alignment in the body of Christ and the local church.

Delivering this word wasn't easy. It has weighed heavily in my spirit, so I expect it will continue to do the same in yours…because possessing your spiritual inheritance is definitely a weighty matter. It is far more important than merely receiving material blessings; it is about returning to our heavenly Father's house and taking on the attributes of His character. In this prophetic season, it will be a sure defense against the enemy's devices.

If you are looking for your spiritual parents, let me give you a word of hope. Psalm 68:5 tells us that our God is "a father of the fatherless, and a judge of the widows" (KJV). Even if you don't have a spiritual father at this moment, God still cares for you. He is willing and able to cover and guide you to your spiritual home.

The apostle Paul, a powerful father in the faith, was once a spiritual orphan. (You can read about it in Acts 9.) Since he was responsible for persecuting and killing so many in the church, God's people didn't want to receive him. But Barnabas, *the son of consolation* (Acts 4:36), accepted him. He took Paul under his wing and interceded for Paul to the apostles. And when they received him into fellowship, the body of Christ was multiplied. (See Acts 9:26–31.)

When I looked up the word *consolation*, I found that it was related to the word *comforter*. Jesus said in John 14:16, "And I will pray the Father, and he shall give you another Comforter, that he may abide with you for ever" (KJV). What a powerful revelation! Barnabas became known as a son of the Holy Spirit because he restored people to right relationships and true spiritual alignment. He took immature, broken believers under his care and gave them a spiritual home. That definitely reveals the heart of our heavenly Father, because that is exactly what He sent Jesus to do.

Even when you look at David in 1 Samuel 22:2, you see that he took broken vagabonds and restored them—and they all became men of God with integrity and stature. He was able to do this because, even when he was being tested by Saul, he kept his heart in alignment with the anointing that the prophet Samuel had placed upon him. David understood and respected the true, authentic anointing. When Saul was acting out of character, David was still able to maintain a respect for the anointing. Therefore, by that anointing, he was able to stand over the lives of others and lead them to victory.

Now, listen closely. This is the time you must begin to follow the divine instructions of your heavenly Father as He prepares you to walk in obedience to your spiritual father. It is important that you keep your spirit purified, as David did, to hear His every instruction. God will send you a spiritual father and mother on earth for the areas in the natural where you need to be led. There is an old saying: When the student is ready, the teacher will show up.

If you are a pastor or leader, and you desire for your life to be in complete alignment with the will of God, then you must not refuse any instruction of the Holy Spirit. If you do, it will only birth the spirit of disobedience in your sons and daughters—you will literally see it manifest as you resist His direction. Remember that you cannot command obedience in the spirit realm until your own obedience has been fulfilled. (See 2 Corinthians 10:6.)

I want to share a prophetic word the Lord gave me for the body of Christ, which I delivered on TBN's *Praise the Lord* program. Let me preface it by telling you how God prepared me to receive this word. He reminded me that when Ahab disobeyed God and married Jezebel, he did more evil in the sight of the Lord than any king in Israel before him. Not only did he begin to worship Baal, but he also built a temple for Baal and an Asherah (a garden with idolatrous statues) for Baal's female counterpart, Ashtaroth. (See 1 Kings 16:30–33.) Ahab and Jezebel ruled in Samaria.

Then I was taken to the fourth chapter of John where Jesus went to Samaria and talked to the woman at the well outside of the city. We have learned in this book that Ahab was the seventh king after Jeroboam began to rule Israel. He was the seventh man who had disobeyed and served idol gods. When Jesus met the woman at the well, He said to her, "For you have had five husbands, and the man you are now living with is not your husband" (John 4:18). Jesus was the Seventh Man. His trip to Samaria wasn't about meeting a single woman at a well (representing the body of Christ); He was reversing what the enemy had done in Samaria. He was reversing the curse in the earth. When Jesus came to her as the Seventh Man, it made that union at the well perfect.

And the word of the Lord in prophecy came to me for you saying:

> This was My plan that I would go in and reverse whatever the devil has done. According to the Scripture, people of God, everything the enemy thought he was going to accomplish in 2004 has been destroyed by the Perfect Man.

Then He took me to Zechariah 1:17–20, which says:

> Cry yet again, saying, Thus says the Lord of hosts: My cities shall yet again overflow with prosperity, and the Lord shall yet comfort Zion and shall yet choose Jerusalem. Then I lifted up my eyes and saw, and behold, four horns [symbols of strength]. And I said to the angel who talked with me, What are these? And

> he answered me, These are the horns or powers which
> have scattered Judah, Israel, and Jerusalem. Then the
> Lord showed me four smiths or workmen [one for
> each enemy horn, to beat it down].

God revealed to me that the four horns represented 2004. Then He began to interpret the four powers that have scattered Judah (meaning praise), Israel (meaning His people), and Jerusalem (meaning the place that He has designated to turn everything around). He said:

> Understand this, and tell the people that the enemy
> has set whirlwinds. The enemy has come against the
> body of Christ and the prophetic voice of God. There
> are many who have sold out to God, and a greater
> anointing is sitting upon them than ever before. Yet
> the warfare has been unbelievable. The warfare has
> been to the point that many felt like they weren't going
> to make it.

But God said from Zechariah 2:13, "Be still, all flesh, before the Lord, for He is aroused and risen from His holy habitation." Even now, as I speak, the Spirit of the Lord has gotten up from His resting place. You don't have to fight, because the whirlwind is blowing. Keep your "flesh" still, because He has released the workmen in the Spirit, and they are beating back the winds; they are tearing down the horns the enemy has erected.

And the Holy Ghost prophesied and said to me, "Go again, My daughter, to the third chapter." Beginning with the seventh verse, He said:

> Thus says the Lord of hosts: If you will walk in my
> ways and keep My charge, then also you shall rule My
> house and have charge of My courts, and I will give
> you access [to My presence] and places to walk among
> these who stand here. Hear now, O Joshua the high
> priest, you and your colleagues who [usually] sit before

you—for they are men who are a sign or omen [types of what is to come]—for behold, I will bring forth My servant the Branch. For behold, upon the stone which I have set before Joshua, upon that one stone are seven eyes or facets [the all-embracing providence of God and the sevenfold radiations of the Spirit of God].

—ZECHARIAH 3:7–9

By cross-referencing that scripture, you will be taken to the seven spirits of God in Isaiah 11:1–2: "And there shall come forth a Shoot out of the stock of Jesse [David's father], and a Branch out of his roots shall grow and bear fruit. And the Spirit of the Lord shall be upon Him—the Spirit of wisdom and understanding, the Spirit of counsel and might, the Spirit of knowledge and of the reverential and obedient fear of the Lord."

And the Lord says, "Even now, I am releasing in the atmosphere the authority of the seven spirits of God." Then He took me back to Zechariah 3:9, and said, "After you receive this 'sevenfold radiation of God,' I will 'carve upon it its inscription, says the Lord of hosts, and I will remove the iniquity and guilt of this land in a single day.' There will be no more reason to travail, for I shall deliver your house in a single day. I shall deliver your mind in a single day. I shall deliver your spirit in a single day."

God has already done it. It is not anything that we have to wait on.

Then the Lord said, "How do you know when I'm about to move? How do you know when I'm about to come? When evil multiplies and has reached its full maturity." So I say under the inspiration of God that many have been going through things, and it looks as if the enemy is winning. It looks as if he has reached his full potential and is about to overtake your house. But I came to declare with everything that is in me that the devil is the liar he has always been, and he will never have the victory over anything God releases in the earth.

Because the Holy Ghost said, "I gave you My Word, and because you have My Word, My Word shall stand." You see, you are trying to believe God with your strength and emotions. But the Lord has said that if you feel weak in your body, you can know that God is in your spirit. He has anchored your soul, and you shall not be moved. And from the first chapter of Luke, the Lord said, "For with God nothing is ever impossible and no word from God shall be without power or impossible of fulfillment" (v. 37).

Right now, by the power of God, I decree it to be so—every lying spirit and every foul spirit will take its hands off God's people. I decree and declare now that no spirit shall alter or change the destiny of the Lord's people. I decree it to be so that no diabolical attack, no psychological attack—no attack from the enemy's bottomless pit—shall come and infiltrate the minds of the people. For I decree it to be so, across the nation, that victory shall be ours in Jesus' mighty name. Amen.

As I close this letter, I urge you to take every issue God has brought to the surface as you were reading this book to Him in prayer. Now you know the dangers of a corrupt spiritual lineage—and you know the blessings of a godly one. Decide today to be a son or daughter of the kingdom, obedient to the voice of your heavenly Father and submitted to those He has given to you as a spiritual covering here on earth. As your final assignment, please read Ezekiel 34:11–31 and 2 Corinthians 13:7.

There is always hope when you put your trust in Jesus. He is the real authority. No devil can stop Him from leading you into your divine destiny—*but you can.* He has given you the power to choose. I beseech you today by the mercies of God to present yourself to Jesus as a living sacrifice and choose to obey His Word.

Allow me to pray this prayer with you:

Dear heavenly Father, thank You for revealing the truth about my spiritual inheritance. Forgive me for the times that I have removed myself from Your covering by either disobeying Your Word or failing to acknowledge the counsel of my spiritual parents. I now know that in their counsel I will find true riches. Father, I acknowledge my sin; cleanse me from all unrighteousness, and help me to become a true son or daughter of the gospel in this final hour. Create in me a clean heart, and renew a right spirit within me. Thank You, Lord, that I can hear Your voice, obey the counsel of Your Word, and activate the full measure of faith You have placed in my spirit. From this day forward, I thank You for helping me to become a true servant in Your kingdom. Amen.

Make this your prayer daily. Remember the Word of the Lord, and your foundation in the Spirit will be strong. I'm standing before God with you.

SUBMITTED TO HIS WORD,
JUANITA BYNUM

NOTES

Chapter 5
Stepping Over Authority

1. James Strong, *Strong's Exhaustive Concordance of the Bible* (updated) (N.p.: Riverside World, 1996), s.v. *qashab*, 7181, "hearken."

Chapter 7
The Power of Rebuke

1. *Webster's American Family Dictionary*, Sol Steinmetz, editor in chief (New York: Random House, Inc., 1998), s.v. "rebuke."

Chapter 11
The Seduction of Jezebel

1. *International Standard Bible Encyclopedia*, electronic database (Seattle, WA: Biblesoft, 1996), s.v. *Bel.*
2. Rabbi Nosson Scherman, *The Chumash*, The Artscroll Series/Stone Edition (Brooklyn, NY: Mesorah Publications, Ltd., 1998, 2000), 47.
3. Dr. Bree M. Keyton, *Jezebel vs. Elijah: The Great End Time Clash* (Chula Vista, CA: Black Forest Press, 2001).
4. Ibid., 39, 35–36.
5. Strong, *Strong's Exhaustive Concordance of the Bible*, s.v. *asherah*, 842.
6. *International Standard Bible Encyclopedia*, s.v. *Baal.*
7. Ibid.
8. Ibid.
9. Information obtained from a telephone interview with Delbeek, Waikiki Aquarium, March 7, 2004.
10. This list is adapted from Keyton, *Jezebel vs. Elijah: The Great End Time Clash*, 142–146.

Notes

Chapter 14
Our True Inheritance

1. See Strong, *Strong's Exhaustive Concordance of the Bible*, s.v. *Yehovah*, 3068; and W. E. Vine, *Vine's Complete Expository Dictionary of Old and New Testament Words* (Nashville, TN: Thomas Nelson, 1992), s.v. 113.

2. Strong, *Strong's Exhaustive Concordance of the Bible*, s.v. *choknah*, 2451.

3. Ibid., s.v. *biynah*, 998.

4. Ibid., s.v. *'etsah*, 6098.

5. Ibid., s.v. *gebuwrah*, 1369.

6. Ibid., s.v. *da'ath*, 1847.

7. Ibid., s.v. *yir'ah*, 3374.

8. *Adam Clarke's Commentary*, from PC Bible, version 3, Electronic Database, copyright © 1996 by Biblesoft, s.v. "Zechariah 4:2."

9. Scherman, *The Chumash*, 470.

Best-selling author Juanita Bynum has a message for all ages!

$\mathcal{C}$hange
FROM THE INSIDE OUT!

God isn't done with you yet. He is changing, refining, molding, and making you into His image every day. Here are several books by Juanita Bynum to help you along the way.

IS YOUR HEART SICK?
Dig a little deeper and explore the heart/mind connection and see why this key to intimacy with God is so vital to a healthy, satisfying, and effective life!

Matters of the Heart
$13.99/0-88419-832-4 (Paperback)

PREPARE YOUR NEW HEART EACH DAY!
Begin each morning with God's Word, and discover how Juanita Bynum's insightful *Devotions for Women* can help your heart beat stronger for God wherever you go!

Matters of the Heart Devotions for Women
$14.99/1-59185-229-3 (Hardcover)

INHERIT GOD'S SPIRITUAL BLESSING FOR YOU!
Don't miss receiving your full spiritual inheritance! In *My Spiritual Inheritance*, Juanita Bynum minces no words in explaining the scriptural significance of you understanding the role spiritual authority plays in inheriting all God destines for you.

My Spiritual Inheritance
$19.99/1-59185-412-1 (Hardcover)

TRACK YOUR SPIRITUAL JOURNEY!
Record your experience as you realize your full potential in Christ! This companion resource to Juanita Bynum's faith-building book *My Spiritual Inheritance* will help you see your progress and even share it with others.

My Spiritual Inheritance Journal
$11.99/1-59185-634-5 (Casebound)

ACCESS YOUR HEAVENLY FATHER'S LEGACY!
You need your daily spiritual inheritance from God to reach your full potential in Christ! Based on Juanita Bynum's faith-building book *My Spiritual Inheritance*, this 100-day devotional is a helpful spiritual-growth resource for believers seeking more of God.

My Spiritual Inheritance Devotional
$14.99/1-59185-559-4 (Hardcover)

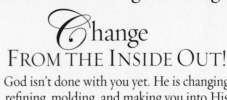

Charisma
HOUSE
A STRANG COMPANY

Call 800-599-5750 and order now.
Or visit ❧ www.charismahouse.com ❧ to save 25%.
MENTION OFFER # BP5C03

5417

Your Walk With God Can Be Even Deeper...

With *Charisma* magazine, you'll be informed and inspired by the features and stories about what the Holy Spirit is doing in the lives of believers today.

Each issue:
- Brings you exclusive world-wide reports to rejoice over
- Keeps you informed on the latest news from a Christian perspective
- Includes miracle-filled testimonies to build your faith
- Gives you access to relevant teaching and exhortation from the most respected Christian leaders of our day

Call 1-800-829-3346 for 3 FREE trial issues
Offer #A2CCHB

If you like what you see, then pay the invoice of $22.97 (**saving over 51% off the cover price**) and receive 9 more issues (12 in all). Otherwise, write "cancel" on the invoice, return it, and owe nothing.

Experience the Power of Spirit-Led Living

Charisma Offer #A2CCHB
P.O. Box 420234
Palm Coast, Florida 32142-0234
www.charismamag.com

1884A